MORE PRAISE FOR

GREEK FIRE, POISON ARROWS,
AND
SCORPION BOMBS

"Illuminating. . . . Excavates ancient attitudes toward biological and chemical arms that are startlingly relevant today. . . . Mayor is comprehensive about the history, ethics, and science of early biological and chemical weapons."

—JAY CURRIE, *Christian Science Monitor*

"A gift for any writer of historical fiction and any student of human history. A fascinating and horrifying read."

—DANA STABENOW, author of *A Cold Day for Murder: A Kate Shugak Investigation*

"Recounts in lively, sometimes darkly comic detail the diabolical stratagems devised by devious warriors."

—JOSEPH D'AGNESE, *Discover*

"This is the kind of book that should confound those who question whether the study of the ancient world has any 'relevance' for the present day. . . . Beautifully written."

—RICHARD STONEMAN, *Classical Review*

"Superbly researched."

—STUART FLEMING, *Expedition*

"Highly recommended."

—ZYGMUNT DEMBEK, *Naval War College Review*

"Mayor shows how the ancients' reactions to biological weapons prefigure contemporary attitudes. . . . [She] spices her astute commentary with diverse opinions about biological weapons."

—Booklist

"The book's many strengths include discussion of how animals, flammables, and poisons were employed on the battlefield. . . . Mayor does an excellent job of illuminating some fascinating and often overlooked methods, strategies, and events of ancient combat."

—Library Journal

ABOUT THE AUTHOR

ADRIENNE MAYOR is the author of *The Poison King: The Life and Legend of Mithradates, Rome's Deadliest Enemy,* which was a finalist for the National Book Award, *Gods and Robots: Myths, Machines, and Ancient Dreams of Technology,* and *The Amazons: Lives and Legends of Warrior Women across the Ancient World* (all Princeton). She is a research scholar in classics and the history of science at Stanford University.

GREEK FIRE, POISON ARROWS, AND SCORPION BOMBS

GREEK FIRE, POISON ARROWS, AND SCORPION BOMBS

UNCONVENTIONAL WARFARE IN THE ANCIENT WORLD

ADRIENNE MAYOR

PRINCETON UNIVERSITY PRESS

PRINCETON AND OXFORD

Published by Princeton University Press
41 William Street, Princeton, New Jersey 08540
99 Banbury Road, Oxford OX2 6JX

press.princeton.edu

Library of Congress Cataloging-in-Publication Data

Names: Mayor, Adrienne, 1946– author.
Title: Greek fire, poison arrows, and scorpion bombs : unconventional warfare in the ancient world / Adrienne Mayor.
Description: [Revised and updated edition] | Princeton : Princeton University Press, [2022] | Previous edition published by Overlook Press in 2003. | Includes bibliographical references and index.
Identifiers: LCCN 2021036196 (print) | LCCN 2021036197 (ebook) | ISBN 9780691217819 (hardback) | ISBN 9780691211084 (paperback) | ISBN 9780691211091 (ebook)
Subjects: LCSH: Biological weapons—History—To 1500. | Chemical weapons—History—To 1500. | Weapons, Ancient. | Military history, Ancient. | Military art and science—Rome.
Classification: LCC UG447.8 .M335 2022 (print) | LCC UG447.8 (ebook) | DDC 358/.38—dc23
LC record available at https://lccn.loc.gov/2021036196
LC ebook record available at https://lccn.loc.gov/2021036197

British Library Cataloging-in-Publication Data is available

Editorial: Rob Tempio and Chloe Coy
Production Editorial: Lauren Lepow
Text Design: Chris Ferrante
Cover Design: Chris Ferrante
Production: Erin Suydam
Publicity: Alyssa Sanford and Carmen Jimenez

This book has been composed in Adobe Text Pro and Octin

Printed on acid-free paper. ∞

Printed in the United States of America

10 9 8 7 6 5 4 3 2

FOR MICHELE AND MICHELLE

CONTENTS

PREFACE

I BEGAN THE REVISIONS and updating of this book while in lockdown in Palo Alto, California, during the worldwide coronavirus pandemic that began in early 2020. The massive mortality and the social, economic, and political upheavals around the globe rendered the subject even more sobering and timely than one would wish. For some, the rapid spread of the COVID-19 plague and the lack of preparation raised the disturbing realization that a devastating contagion could be used as a weapon. Indeed, rumors about the accidental leak of the coronavirus from two laboratories in Wuhan, China, where the outbreak originated, quickly developed into conspiracy theories, some based on assumptions of malicious intent.[1]

Such fears are not new, as the chapters of this book demonstrate. When plague struck Athens in 430 BC during the Peloponnesian War, for example, the Athenians' first impulse was to blame the Spartans. Fears of the deliberate transmission of plague arose in the Roman Empire, and in Europe during the Black Death. The havoc and mass deaths wrought by COVID-19 are sparking new, urgent concerns about bioweapons. The pandemic demonstrates the vulnerability of the world to new generations of biological threats. And the reality of genetic engineering biotechnologies combined with novel zoonotic contagions increases exponentially the potential impact of an attack.[2]

The first edition of *Greek Fire* was begun during another crisis, just after the destruction of the World Trade Center in New York by the terrorist group al-Qaeda, led by Osama bin Laden, on September 11, 2001. That momentous event was followed by a series of anthrax attacks by unknown perpetrators. Media coverage of the day typically depicted biochemical warfare as a uniquely modern phenomenon. But I knew that biological and chemical warfare had deep and ancient roots. I had been studying unconventional warfare in antiquity since the 1990s.[3]

Anxieties about bioterrorism, "weapons of mass destruction" (WMD) in the Middle East, and the unsolved anthrax attacks had everyone on edge. During preparations for President George W. Bush's invasion of Iraq in March 2003, it was assumed that Saddam Hussein would unleash germ and chemical weapons. Iraq had produced such armaments in the 1980s and '90s. In August 2003, US troops arrested Ali Hassan al-Majid, nicknamed "Chemical Ali," responsible for fatally gassing five thousand Kurds in 1988. The fear of WMD necessitated cumbersome protective gear and novel vaccinations with dangerous side effects for the American soldiers.[4]

Greek Fire, Poison Arrows, and Scorpion Bombs was originally published in October 2003, several months into the Iraq War. A macabre coincidence of a personal nature occurred three months later, when I underwent chemotherapy with a poison derived from yew trees, taxotere. From my research I knew that the tree was considered so deadly that Pliny the Elder had advised Romans to avoid even proximity to yews. Indeed, the ancient Romans poisoned arrows and spears with yew sap (chapter 2). I found it grimly amusing to share this fact with my medical team.

Meanwhile, the search for Saddam's dread WMD was proving unsuccessful. Amid these tensions, *Newsweek* joked darkly that finally "investigators have found evidence of biological weapons in Iraq . . . south of Mosul, in the ruins of a desert fortress at Hatra. And the weapons are . . . not what you think. They're clay pots once filled with scorpions and dropped on the heads of invaders by the citizens of Hatra at the turn of the third century AD. . . . Who knew Saddam Hussein had such a legacy to live up to?" *Newsweek* then revealed that their sham report was based on my description of Hatra's "scorpion bombs" in chapter 6 of *Greek Fire.*[5]

Since then, the idea of hurling scorpions in clay pots at enemies has captured the popular imagination and appears often in the media and other venues. Horribly enough, in 2014, it was reported that the Islamic extremist group ISIS terrorized Iraqi villages with their own version of the Hatra weapon, by launching canisters packed with live scorpions. The next year, ISIS spitefully damaged walls, temples, and statues at the ancient fortress of Hatra (see fig. 24).[6]

No physical evidence of scorpion bombs exists today around the ruins of Hatra, although one can find shards of clay pots in the sand. Is there any archaeological evidence for incidents of biological and chemical warfare in antiquity? Such weapons are by their nature ephemeral. It is difficult to monitor and prove the creation, stockpiling, and use of biological weapons today, let alone in antiquity. But some archaeological evidence for ancient biological and chemical weapons and tactics has been uncovered since the first edition of this book. For example, the intention to send carriers of disease into enemy territory is recorded on cuneiform tablets from Mesopotamia; Assyrian reliefs illustrate the use of naphtha firepots; ancient arrowheads tipped with crystallized venom in museum collections were found to be viable; and archaeologists have now discovered remnants of chemical fireballs hurled at Alexander the Great's army in Pakistan and medieval naphtha grenades in Egypt. Archaeological evidence analyzed by Simon James at the fortress of Dura-Europos, Syria, in 2009 suggested that Sasanian attackers deliberately created a deadly sulfur dioxide gas to suffocate Romans in a tunnel, in AD 256. The skeletons of twenty victims and residue of sulfur crystals and pitch burned in braziers seem to confirm the hypothesis. As chapter 7 notes, however, James's claims are disputed by other scholars who point out that those materials were used to make torches in the tunnels.[7]

Not long ago, Italian archaeologists excavating a Roman villa near Pompeii, destroyed in AD 79, discovered a large vat containing residue. Analysis of the residue, published in 2007, revealed a mixture of powerful medicinal plants, including opium poppy seeds, along with the flesh and bones of reptiles. According to the archaeologists, the vat may have been used to prepare a secret "universal antidote" believed to counteract all known poisons.[8] This sort of concoction, combining small doses of poisons and their antidotes, known as *Mithridatium*, had been invented by King Mithradates VI of Pontus (134–63 BC). As a master of experimental toxicology who used poisons against foes, Mithradates sought to immunize himself against all toxins. After his death, his recipe was "improved" by imperial Roman doctors. The original formula is lost, but the ingredients were said to include medicinal plants, opium, and chopped vipers, substances detected in the vat at Pompeii.[9]

In our own time, Mithradates's dream of immunity still motivates scientists. When this book first appeared at the height of widespread anxiety in 2003, I was invited to the international BioSecurity Summit in Washington, DC, and A&E's *Global View* interviewed me about the ancient origins of biochemical warfare; the other guests that day were *New York Times* reporter Judith Miller, a survivor of the 2001 anthrax attacks, and Serguei Popov, former top biological weapons researcher in the Soviet Union's massive Biopreparat program who defected to the United States in 1992. I spoke with the former bioweaponeer about his research at the National Center for Biodefense. After decades of developing extremely dangerous, genetically engineered superviruses intended as bioweapons for the Soviets, Serguei Popov now devotes his life to creating a modern *Mithridatium*, a "universal antidote" for our times. He and his colleagues hope to invent a vaccine to counter the most commonly weaponized pathogens. Biosecurity experts call a broad-spectrum vaccine the "holy grail" of shielding against bioattacks.[10]

The fear of biological and chemical weapons as the justification for war and defense planning makes answering historical puzzles about the practice of biological and chemical warfare in ancient cultures much more than a parlor game. We tend to think of such agents as monstrous inventions of modern technology, imagining that in antiquity warfare was always fair and honorable. But how realistic is our nostalgia for a time when biological or chemical strategies were unthinkable? This book demonstrates that there never was a time innocent of biological warfare. Biological and chemical weapons and strategies can be traced back to the beginning of human culture—and so can the practical issues and ethical concerns that surround them.

Working with virulent pathogens—whether to create bioweapons or to formulate biodefenses—entails the potential for "boomerang" effects and raises a Hydra's head of unintended consequences. The decision to use biological and/or chemical tactics in warfare is a double-edged sword. Blowback, friendly fire, collateral damage, and self-injury—these are recurring themes in attempts to use and to control poison weapons in antiquity and today. Even the entertaining and educational modern media events inspired by the historical incidents brought to attention in this book underscore the ever-present threat of self-injury when toxic armaments are handled. Take the scorpion bomb that quashed the Roman attack on Hatra, Iraq, in AD 198. As noted, this once-obscure weapon achieved popular notoriety after my description appeared in the first edition of *Greek Fire* in 2003. The concept appeals to museum curators designing major exhibits on poisons and venoms. When the Natural History Museum, London, developed their exhibit on venoms in 2017, the team consulted me about Mithradates's knowledge of viper venoms and the scorpion bombs used at Hatra. The American Museum of Natural History's *The Power of Poison* opened in New York in 2013 and continues to travel nationally and internationally. It was fun to see the Hatra vignette they had created: plastic scorpions crawling out of a shattered clay pot.

The editors of *National Geographic*'s poison issue, "Twelve Toxic Tales" (2005) were more audacious. They decided to make a real scorpion grenade and then X-ray it to show the live scorpions inside. As consultant for the venture, I sent the *National Geographic* team to my friend Dr. Cynthia Kosso, an archaeologist and potter, who created a replica of a terra-cotta pot similar to those excavated around Hatra. Next, the team obtained a number of deadly, live Iraqi deathstalker scorpions (*Leiurus quinquestriatus*) from an exotic pet shop in Rhode

Island. But then, in the studio, photographer Cary Wolinsky and his scorpion wranglers found themselves facing the same threat of "blowback" that the ancient defenders of Hatra had somehow overcome. How does one go about stuffing scorpions into a jar without getting stung? I told them that in survival boot camps, Indonesian soldiers taught US marines how to grab scorpions by the tail just below the stinger. I also mentioned that in antiquity there were several techniques for handling scorpions "safely"—none of them all that safe. Finally, the team hit on a method that was unavailable to the desert dwellers of Hatra. They chilled the scorpions in a refrigerator to slow them down, then carefully placed them in a clay jar and sealed it with burlap (see plate 5).[11]

As consultant for History Channel's "Ancient Weapons of Mass Destruction" (2006), I traveled to the TV studios in Burbank, California. I quickly realized that I had to convince the production crew that toxic armaments of twenty-five hundred years ago are still mighty dangerous today. The three young men running the show wanted to re-create the famous siege-breaking bioweapon used to poison the water supply of a Greek city in 590 BC (chapter 3). Showing me several pots of highly toxic hellebore plants purchased from a local nursery, they explained that they would film themselves crushing the hellebore, using a mortar and pestle. They were surprised that gloves and masks would be required, as the toxin can be absorbed through skin and has nasty physical effects. For the next scene, they wanted to reproduce the spectacular chemical incendiary weapon devised by the Spartans during their siege of Plataia (Plataea) in 429 BC, during the Peloponnesian War (chapter 7). With the cameras rolling, the crew planned to build a great bonfire of resinous pine logs in a public park and then dramatically toss great lumps of sulfur from a chemistry supply shop onto the flames. Alarmed, I pointed out that the resulting cloud of poisonous sulfur dioxide gas would be just as lethal today as it was in antiquity. Mandatory gas masks for film crew and entire neighborhood!

In 2012, I was contacted by a film production company making a documentary for National Geographic Channel's series *The Link*. They wanted to re-create the fearsome Byzantine naval weapon known as "Greek Fire," and requested advice on the "practicalities" for demonstrating the siphon and propelling apparatus to burn a replica ship. The materials are extremely volatile and perilous to manipulate (chapter 7). I strongly advised them to find a petroleum engineer familiar with the historical weapon, such as Zayn Bilkadi, or a knowledgeable Byzantine historian such as Professor John Haldon of Princeton, who had replicated the highly explosive weapon for a previous television show.

Keen interest in the origins and early practice of biological and chemical warfare keeps pace with today's advances in biochemical weapons and defenses against unconventional warfare. A lavishly illustrated article on my findings was published in *Military Officer*, and *Greek Fire* has been translated into Japanese, Chinese, Polish, Turkish, Greek, and Spanish. It is assigned for university courses and quoted in military, security, and public health manuals and in international arms control materials. I spoke about the history of bioweapons at Stanford Medical School's biosecurity course in 2013 and was interviewed by Russian REN TV private channel in 2016. This book has even been cited as evidence in court cases involving attack dogs and Agent Orange. Meanwhile, on the lighter side, *Greek Fire, Poison Arrows, and Scorpion Bombs* has become a favorite reference book among fantasy- and war-gamers and military history buffs around the world. Greek Fire–like weapons have appeared in films such as *Troy* (2004) and the TV series *Game of Thrones* (season 8, 2019). Several best-selling novelists have found inspiration in this compendium of insidious, ingenious bioweapons from classical antiquity. For example, the fictionalized historical characters in Margaret George's *Helen of Troy* (2006) discuss various fiendish poison tactics described here. Brad Thor's thriller *Blowback* (2005) imagines a secret bioterror weapon devised by Hannibal and rediscovered by modern terrorists (drawn from recipes in chapters 1 and 4). C. J. Sansom's medieval mystery *Dark Fire* (2005) turns on a lost formula for Greek Fire. Dana Stabenow drew on material in these chapters to inform scenes in her historical trilogy *Silk and Song*, about Marco Polo's granddaughter (2014–15), and *Death of an Eye*, about solving a murder in Cleopatra's court (2018).[12]

The evidence for biological and chemical warfare in antiquity gathered and analyzed for the first time in *Greek Fire* has also inspired encyclopedia editors to include entries and chapters on those topics for the first time. For Blackwell's *Encyclopedia of Ancient History* (2013), I was invited to write the entry "Greek Fire." My chapter "Animals in Warfare" appears in *The Oxford Handbook of Animals in Classical Thought and Life* (2014), and for *The Encyclopedia of the Roman Army* (Wiley, 2015), I contributed the entry "Roman Biological and Chemical Warfare." My chapters on the rumors that Alexander the Great died by poisoning; chemical and biological weapons and tactics in the ancient world; and Mithradates's universal antidote are included in *Toxicology in Antiquity*, 4th ed. (Elsevier, 2023).

The topic of unconventional warfare is both timeless and timely. While preparing this revised edition of *Greek Fire* in 2020–21, for example, I taught a class on biochemical weapons at the 92nd Street Y in New York City, and was interviewed on History Hit Podcast, History 'n' Games Podcast, Power Corrupts Podcast, ABC Radio Australia, and the BBC's Naked Scientist Podcast. The "Poisons and Pestilence" episodes on the history of biochemical warfare podcast by Brett Edwards (Institute for Policy Research, University of Bath) were based on this book.

※ ※ ※

It was exciting to undertake this revised and updated edition, with new maps and more than twenty new illustrations, ten in color. This edition presents new material on biological and chemical tactics in China, Japan, India, the Americas, Persia, Central Asia, and Islamic lands. I've also expanded the discussion of rules of war and qualms about unconventional weapons among ancient cultures. Since the original publication of this book, I've kept up with historians, scientists, archaeologists, and other scholars who study ancient and modern biological and chemical armaments. This edition includes new evidence that has come to light about toxic weapons of the past and updated information about modern military innovations. Here is a brief preview of some recent developments.

POISON PROJECTILES. According to ancient Greek legend, the warrior Odysseus was killed by a rare poison weapon—a spear tipped with a stingray spine (chapter 2). His manner of death is unique in Greek myth. In 2006, the famous environmentalist "Crocodile Hunter" Steve Irwin died by the same exotic poison. In a tragic accident, his heart was pierced by the venomous barb of a stingray.

Evidence for the use of poison projectiles by prehistoric cultures is now available in Philip Wexler's edited volume *Toxicology in Antiquity* (2019). The toxic weapons and tactics employed by indigenous peoples of the Americas are described by David E. Jones, *Poison Arrows: North American Indian Hunting and Warfare* (2007). Thanks to his study, we now know that the procedure for making the dread arrow poison of the nomad archers of the Scythian steppes—said to have been concocted by shamans by burying a bag of snake venom and putrefying organic toxins—was not unique but was also practiced in North America. In fact, remarkably similar techniques were widespread among indigenous cultures that depended on archery for hunting and warfare, thereby giving credence to the ancient Greek and Roman accounts of Scythian arrow poison.

In the fifth century BC, the Greek historian Herodotus mentioned small golden vessels attached to the belts of Scythian archers. In chapter 2, I suggested that they may have been vials to hold arrow poison. Notably, in 2009 an ancient Scythian grave (seventh century BC), containing rich golden treasures, quivers full of arrows, and other weapons, included a miniature, golden small-necked vial on a gold chain, purpose unknown. Could this be evidence for the little cups described by Herodotus? The archaeological report of 2009 does not say whether any residue was detected, but it might be worth testing to learn whether the vessel was decorative or contained some substance.[13]

For the first episode of the Smithsonian Channel's documentary series *Epic Warrior Women*—"Amazons" (2018), based on my book *The Amazons: Lives and Legends of Warrior Women across the Ancient World* (2014)—I was the consultant for Scythian costumes, equipment, and weapons. We devised scenes that dramatize two theories first presented in *Greek Fire* in 2003 (chapter 2). In one, the horsewoman archer shows her daughter how to dip arrowheads in a small vial of viper venom. In the next scene they paint their wooden arrow shafts with red and black designs that mimic snakeskin patterns, like those recovered from ancient Scythian graves (see plate 4).[14]

TOXIC WATERS, DEADLY VAPORS, the subject of chapter 3, led me to investigate the mysterious death of Alexander the Great in Babylon in 323 BC. Many of his followers and historians believed that the great commander was deliberately murdered, and some pointed to the toxic waters of the River Styx as the poison. Intrigued, I analyzed the ancient descriptions of his symptoms and demise and the lore surrounding the legendary river to understand why it was considered lethal in antiquity. I enlisted the help of a professional toxicologist, Antoinette Morris, and we investigated scientific possibilities of a real pathogen harbored by the Styx (Mavromati) River in the Peloponnese. Our findings and speculations were presented at the XII International Congress of Toxicology, Barcelona, Spain, 2010.[15]

WEAPONIZED PATHOGENS. New evidence was published in 2007 elaborating on the earliest documented case of biological warfare in the Near East, described in chapter 4. It appears that during the Anatolian War of 1320–1318 BC, the Hittites—even though militarily weaker than their enemies the Arzawans—won victory with a secret bioweapon. They drove rams and donkeys infected with deadly tularemia (known as the "Hittite plague") into Arzawan lands. The lethal plague was transmitted to humans via ticks and flies.[16]

It was a long-held belief that the spread of the Black Death in Europe originated when the Tatars, Mongols of the Golden Horde, used trebuchets to catapult corpses of their own infected comrades over the walls of Kaffa (Caffa), a fortress of Crimea on the Black Sea, in 1346. Chapter 4 now incorporates a revised theory of the probable transmission of the flea- and rat-borne plague to Europe via grain ships from Kaffa, as well as new studies that implicate human body parasites as the main vector.[17]

The concept of individuals deliberately spreading plague was first described by ancient Romans as *pestilentia manu facta*, man-made pestilence (chapter 4). During the coronavirus COVID-19 pandemic that began in 2020, US Homeland Security's intelligence briefing reported that a group of white supremacists discussed deliberately spreading the virus to spark civil or race war. Even more worrisome, artificially manufactured plagues and genetically engineered and even genetically targeted pathogens now loom as credible threats.[18]

INTOXICANTS, HYPNOTICS. Chapter 5 features the world's first military commander who was also adept in pharmacology. The general was a witch named Chrysame, who used drugs to cause temporary insanity in the enemy, in about 1000 BC. Mithradates stands out as a rare example of a general who was also an expert toxicologist; another is Kautilya, a military strategist who was also a scientist in India around the time of Alexander the Great. Modern scientific military research demands similar combinations of skills. It is interesting to learn that the general in charge of the Soviet DNA-hybrid bioweapons program was a trained molecular biologist. Today's terrorist groups also recruit chemists and biologists. Sophisticated principles of recombinant gene splicing are raising nightmarish possibilities. For example, a bioweapon of neurotransmitter endorphins piggybacking on bacteria could target the central nervous system, changing the enemy's perceptions and behavior, causing psychosis, insomnia, passivity, and confusion. In theory, enemies could one day create an aerosolized bioweapon of mass destruction by inserting, say, cobra venom into the DNA of an infectious virus.[19]

INSECTS AND ANIMALS AS WEAPONS. Venomous insects may have been some of the earliest zoological weapons in human history (chapter 6). Now, the full history and disturbing future of insects as military munitions is covered in Jeffrey A. Lockwood's *Six-Legged Soldiers: Using Insects as Weapons of War* (2009). The Pentagon's military research unit, DARPA, announced new advances in their vivisystems program of 2006, developing "rat-bots," "remote-control" primates, and "insect cyborgs" for use in warfare.[20]

The popular, historically accurate 3D video game *Rome: Total War* was first released in 2003. The game featured realistic war elephants. The following year, inspired by my description in chapter 6 of the best defense against war elephants known in antiquity, a new zoological weapon was introduced by the game's developers: pigs cruelly set on fire. One reviewer described the demonstration of the new feature on GameSpy.com: "I had waited 12 months for this! I was on the edge of my seat. The elephants came pounding down the hillside toward my legions. 'All right, let's send in the pigs!' the developers hollered. I was sweating with anticipation. At long last! Our superweapon unveiled! '*Cry Havoc and Let Slip the Pigs of War!*' I bellowed." But, he continued, "Here's the thing, the thing to remember about a flaming pig. *It doesn't go where you tell it to . . .* [the pigs] ran through my lines of troops, causing them to break formation. Men were running around, screaming, catching on fire, and howling with pain. The pigs went everywhere, everywhere except toward the elephants, who continued their charge unfazed, then rammed into our panicked troops like freight trains. How many strategy games offer THAT? *I must have this game.*"[21]

By 2012, "war pigs," first brought to popular attention by *Greek Fire* in 2003, had their own Wikipedia entry, and flaming pigs became an iconic unconventional weapon among ancient warfare–gaming aficionados. As vividly played out on modern war-gamers' screens, the lesson is that biological weapons are notoriously hard to control and aim; they tend to take on a diabolical life of their own, creating chaos in one's own forces and killing innocent bystanders. War-gamers can now purchase and paint their own miniature models of flaming war pigs for an ancient Roman Republican army unit manufactured by Xyston Miniatures, Scotland. And an Invicta animated documentary on YouTube (2020) illustrates this tactic, among others, to deflect war elephants in antiquity.[22]

CHEMICAL INCENDIARIES AND HEAT RAYS. Archimedes's notorious heat-ray weapon—a formation of polished bronze shields reflecting the sun's rays at enemy ships—was deployed against the Roman navy in 212 BC (chapter 7). This celebrated invention has fired the imagination of military scientists ever since. After this book's 2003 edition appeared, a professor at MIT took up the challenge in 2005. He and his students recreated Archimedes's mirror weapon and caused a wooden fishing boat to combust in San Francisco Bay, impressing the MythBusters, who filmed the feat for their TV show. In 2010, mechanical engineers at the University of Naples suggested another theory: that Archimedes's burning device might have involved steam-powered cannons that fired hollow clay balls filled with a chemical incendiary similar to Greek Fire.[23]

A controversial long-range microwave ray gun, mounted on a tank, was unveiled by DARPA in 2001 (chapter 7). Designed by Raytheon to sweep "menacing crowds" from a safe distance, the ray was supposed to cause excruciating pain without damage—as long as people could move out of the beam. The ray penetrates a victim's skin, heating it to 130°F, creating the agonizing sensation of being on fire. Amid criticism that the weapon was not really as harmless as claimed, the Active Denial System was withdrawn from public scrutiny. But in 2007, a new version of the heat-ray gun was announced with great fanfare again, and in 2010 the heat-ray weapon was sent to Afghanistan to be "tested" in the war zone. Ultimately, the military decided not to use the weapon in the war effort, amid controversies about ethics and injuries. Meanwhile, however, in 2010 the Los Angeles County Sheriff's Department eagerly installed a small-scale version of the weapon with the intention of using it on prisoners. By 2020, military engineers began designing solid-state lasers combined with mirrors to be mounted on naval destroyers.[24]

Attempts to replicate the devastating Byzantine incendiary naval weapon system known as Greek Fire are based on expert guesswork by chemical engineers. The most recent demonstration, by chemical weapons expert Stephen Bull, of the ammunition, storage, pumps, siphons, and nozzles to propel flaming naphtha to burn ships appears in the Smithsonian Channel documentary of 2020 *How Greek Fire Was Used to Target Enemy Ships*, in the *World of Weapons: War at Sea* series.[25]

RULES OF WAR. As the following chapters show, weapons that target human biological vulnerabilities are undiscriminating, capable of harming civilians as well as soldiers. Trying to control weapons based on deadly poisons, volatile chemicals, wind-borne smoke, unquenchable flames, virulent pathogens, venomous creatures, and unpredictable animals and materials has always posed dangers not just to the victims but to the perpetrators themselves. Practical and ethical issues were first broached in ancient Greek myth, and they show up again and again in real historical battles and military writings. The revised introduction considers new scholarship on Greek, Persian, Asian, and Muslim concepts of fair warfare and discusses evolving military and philosophical concepts of what is acceptable in war.

Blowback and the boomerang effects of resorting to unfair tactics and biological and chemical strategies have been understood since ancient times. Indeed, the ultimate boomerang effect is that using such vile weapons grants one's enemies a justification to use them too. Pragmatic military leaders eschew torture and mutilation of enemies based on the same rationale, to deny the enemy a justification for turning the tables and torturing one's own troops.

A related practical and ethical concern is how to dispose of indestructible biological and chemical weapons. The first chapter describes Heracles's solution, burying the lethally venomous head of the Hydra monster deep underground. That approach continues today but presents multiplying dilemmas. The emerging field of nuclear semiotics, discussed in the revised afterword, ponders how to devise warnings about dangerous biochemical weapons that will last for millennia. As we will see, no suggestion, however creative, inspires full confidence.[26]

In nearly all cultures, both ancient and modern, "biological and chemical weapons are seen as more repugnant than conventional weapons," remarked biochemical weapons expert Dr. Leonard Cole in the TV series *Avoiding Armageddon*. We should "nourish that sense of repugnance for out-of-bounds weapons," which should "have no place in civilized society." "Every weapon that we can develop a cultural antipathy for, so much the better." This, suggested Cole, could "create a model for how we might eventually minimize the use of all kinds of weapons" of war.[27]

The evidence from ancient myth and history shatters the notion that there ever was a time when biological and chemical warfare was unthinkable. But the evidence also shows that doubts about the use of such weapons arose as soon as the first archer dipped an arrowhead in poison. And that's a reason for hope, I think. To delve into the long history of humankind's ingenuity in weaponizing nature is a fascinating yet melancholy undertaking. Once released from the genie's bottle, the horrors of biological and chemical war technologies are loosed on the world. Yet one can also discover, embedded in ancient Greek myths, early warnings and attempts to restrain the dark sciences of war. While the impulse to weaponize deadly materials, animals, and animal products is among our deep legacies from the ancient past, so too is the recognition of the terrible dangers, physical and moral, that they pose. It is my hope that by learning more about the former, we will become more attentive to the latter.

HISTORICAL TIME LINE

1770 BC	Sumerian cuneiform tablets at Mari show understanding of contagion
1500–1200 BC	Hittite plague victims sent to enemy lands
1300–1100 BC	Later Bronze Age Greece
1300 BC	Destruction of Jericho by Israelites, about 1350
	Ten Plagues in Egypt, called down by Moses
1200 BC	Legendary Trojan War
	Philistine plague follows theft of Israelites' Ark of the Covenant
1000 BC	Solomon builds Temple at Jerusalem, plague spirits trapped in jars
	Chrysame's drugged bull strategy helps Greeks conquer Ionia
900 BC	Elijah's fire trick with naphtha, about 875
	Assyrian fire arrows and "grenades" depicted on stone reliefs
800 BC	Homer, about 750, describes Odysseus poisoning arrows and implies poison arrows in Trojan War
700 BC	Projectile weapons banned in Lelantine War, Greece

Sennacherib's Assyrian army struck by plague in Egypt/Jerusalem

Deuteronomy rules of war written

600 BC Kirrha, Greece, defeated by poison in water supply, about 590

Nebuchadnezzar sacks Jerusalem temple, releasing plague, 586

Baba Gurgur, eternal petroleum fire worshipped in Babylonia

Alyattes vs. Cimmerians, use of war dogs

Queen Tomyris of the Massagetae, army defeated with wine

Cyrus of Persia, d. 530

Cambyses of Persia, defeats Egypt with phalanx of sacred animals

500 BC Sun Tzu, *Art of War*, fire weapons

Scythian culture flourishes until about AD 300

Battle of Marathon, Greece, 490

Persian land invasion of Greece, 480

Herodotus, writing about 450

Peloponnesian War, 431–404

Plague of Athens, 430

Sparta vs. Plataia, 429, sulfur conflagration

Boeotians vs. Delium, 424, flamethrower

Thucydides, ca. 460–400

Sophocles, 496–406

Euripides, ca. 480–406

Ctesias, describes oil weapon of India

Thessalos, medical writer

Empedocles drains malarial swamps in Sicily

Sicilian disaster (Athens), 415–413

400 BC   Xenophon, ca. 430–354

Carthage invades Sicily, 409–396

Himilco and Maharbal poison enemy wine with mandrake

Clearchus, destroys army by forcing it to camp in swamps, 360

Alexander the Great, 356–323

Fireship at Tyre, Phoenicians vs. Alexander, 332

Porus's Indian war elephants defeated by Alexander, 326

King Chandragupta, Mauryan Empire, India, reign 321–298

Laws of Manu ban poison and fire arrows, India

Kautilya, *Arthashastra* advises poison and fire strategies, India

Chinese recipes for poison gas and toxic arrows

Battle of Harmatelia, India, poison arrows, 326

Aeneas the Tactician, about 350

Theophrastus, b. 371

Demetrius Poliorcetes vs. Rhodes, fire weapons, 304

300 BC Pyrrhus invades Italy with war elephants, 280

Antigonus Gonatus vs. Megara, elephants routed by pigs, 270

First Punic War, 264–241

Hamilcar Barca, ca. 275–228

Hannibal crosses Alps with war elephants, 218

Second Punic War, 218–201

Hasdrubal's head catapulted into Carthaginian camp, 207

Archimedes uses mirrors to burn Roman navy, Syracuse, 212

Sushruta Samhita, India, written sometime between 500 and 100

Berossus

Antiochus vs. Galatians, war elephants, 189

200 BC Hannibal catapults vipers, about 190

Third Punic War, 149–146

Aquillius poisons wells in Asia, 131–129

Varro, 116–27

100 BC Mithradates VI of Pontus, d. 63

Mithradatic Wars, 90–63

Cicero, d. 43

Sertorius vs. Characitani, Spain, choking dust, about 80

Virgil, b. 70

Strabo, b. 64

Lucullus's campaigns vs. Mithradates, 74–66

Pompey's army decimated by toxic honey, 65

Tigranocerta, flaming naphtha vs. Romans, 69–68

Samosata, burning mud vs. Romans, 69–68

Lucretius, ca. 99–55

Livy, b. ca. 64–59

Julius Caesar, b. 100

Diodorus of Sicily, ca. 90–30

AD 1   Ovid, d. 17

Arminius's revolt in Germany, 9

Germanicus, d. 19

Dioscorides, 40–90

Celsus, d. 50

Frontinus, 40–103

Pliny the Elder, d. 79

Tacitus, b. 56

Psylli, snake charmers of North Africa

Josephus, b. 38

Rufus of Ephesus

Lucan, b. 39

Seneca, d. 65

Domitian, b. 51

Silius Italicus, 28–103

Apollonius of Tyana, ca. 15–100

Titus destroys Temple in Jerusalem, 70

"Man-made plague," Rome, 90–91

Nitishastra, by Shukra (India)

AD 100   Plutarch, ca. 45–120

Marius, b. 157

Nicander, about 130

Florus, ca. 74–130

Pausanias, writing in about 150

Galen, 129–200

Appian, ca. 95–165

Polyaenus, writing about 160

Cassius Dio, b. 164

Commodus, b. 161

Apollodorus of Damascus, d. 130

Julius Africanus, b. ca. 160

Antonine Plague of 165–180, Temple of Apollo, Babylonia

Marcus Aurelius, d. 180

Lucius Verus, d. 169

"Man-made plague," Rome, 189

Testament of Solomon

Septimius Severus, 145–211

Hatra, scorpion bombs and naphtha vs. Romans, 198–99

AD 200   Aelian, d. 230

Chinese surgeon Hua T'o treats poison arrow wounds

Persians vs. Romans, Dura-Europos (Syria)

Plague of Cyprian, 249–262

Constantine, b. 272

AD 300   Quintus of Smyrna, about 350

Vegetius, about 390

Ammianus Marcellinus, about 350

AD 400   Nag Hammadi library

AD 500   Justinian vs. Chosroes of Persia, ca. 540

Byzantine naphtha "squirt guns"

AD 600   Quran written

Muhammad's siege of Ta'if, 630

Muhammad, d. 632

Kallinikos invents Greek Fire, 668

Greek Fire saves Constantinople 673

Ummayad Muslims besiege Mecca with naphtha, 683

AD 700   Greek Fire saves Constantinople, 718

AD 800   Baghdad destroyed by naphtha, 813

Naphtha troops in Islamic armies

Gunpowder invented in China, about 850

AD 900   Russians vs. Olga of Kiev, defeated by toxic honey

Chinese battle on Yangtze, naphtha disaster, 975

Firdawsi, Persian poet, describes Alexander as inventor of fire weapons

AD 1000   Poison Maiden lore, India

Mahmud of Ghazni catapults snakes at Sistan, Afghanistan

AD 1100   Second Lateran Council bans "Greek Fire"

Cairo destroyed by naphtha, 1167

AD 1200   Genghis Khan's conquest of China, using fire-carrying animals, 1211

Gunpowder known to Arabs and Europeans

AD 1300   Tatars said to catapult plague corpses at Kaffa, 1346

Tamerlane sacks Delhi, routing elephants with burning camels

MAP 1. Italy, Greece, and the Aegean. Map by Michele Angel.

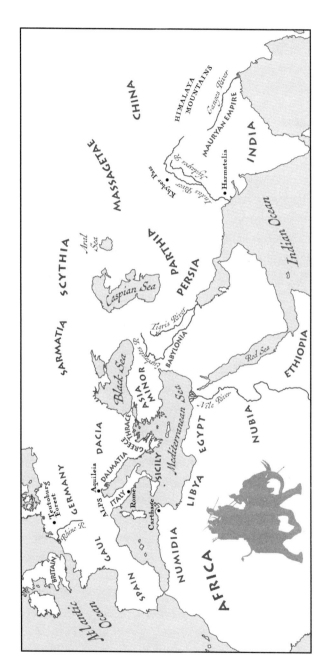

MAP 2. The Ancient World. Map by Michele Angel.

MAP 3. Asia Minor, Near East, Mesopotamia, and Parthia. Map by Michele Angel.

GREEK FIRE, POISON ARROWS, AND SCORPION BOMBS

WAR OUTSIDE THE RULES

In times of peace, individuals and states follow higher standards. . . . But war is a stern teacher.

—THUCYDIDES, *HISTORY OF THE PELOPONNESIAN WAR*

A PHALANX OF WARRIORS armed with swords and spears advances across an open plain to confront a force of similarly armed men. Following the rules of fair combat, the fighting is hand-to-hand and grimly predictable. After the battle, the dead are retrieved, and victory is clear and honorable.

This stark picture has been widely assumed to sum up the ancient experience of armed conflict. Images of a long-lost era of heroic combat by brave men wielding simple weapons continue to inspire us: the Trojan War of Homeric myth, the historic Battle of Marathon, the Spartans facing the Persians at Thermopylae, the outnumbered Athenian triremes defeating the Persian fleet at Salamis, the Romans resisting Hannibal. But behind these glorious vignettes lurks a darker military reality, and terrifying options that rendered the courage of warriors meaningless. This book chronicles how the genie of biochemical warfare first escaped.

Germ warfare? Chemical weapons? Most people assume these terrors are recent innovations. Surely the ability to turn pathogens, toxins, and chemicals into tools of war requires modern scientific understanding of epidemiology, biology, and chemistry, as well as advanced delivery systems. Besides, wasn't warfare in antiquity based on honor, valor, and skill? Outside of a few well poisonings, the odd plague victim catapulted over walls in the Middle Ages, and the fabled Byzantine recipe for Greek Fire, no one really waged deliberate biological or chemical warfare until the modern era. Or did they?

Ways of turning nature's armory into weapons of war were actually practiced—and documented—much earlier and more often in premodern eras than has been commonly realized. In their "History of Biological Warfare," for example, the microbiologists James Poupard and Linda Miller acknowledged that early civilizations used some crude forms of biological warfare, but they alluded to only two vague examples before the eighteenth century. "Historical documentation [of] the use of biological warfare has always been sparse," they wrote. "The murkiness of the historical record may discourage academic pursuit of the subject but does add a certain mystique to attempts to chronicle the history of biological warfare."[1]

Why has the ancient world remained uncharted territory in the history of chemical and biological warfare?

In the first place, many historians have assumed that biochemical weaponry required scientific knowledge not yet developed in antiquity. Second is the assumption that even if cultures of the past *knew* how to make war with toxins and combustibles, they generally refrained from such strategies out of respect for traditional rules of war. The third reason is the difficulty of systematically collecting widely scattered and little-known ancient accounts of biochemical weapons and their forerunners in the ancient world.

That evidence is gathered and analyzed for the first time in this book, and it far exceeds what we have been led to expect for prescientific societies. The evidence also reveals that despite some ancient literature expressing deep-seated aversion to the use of poison in war, toxic weapons were deployed by many ancient peoples. The sheer number of legendary narratives and historically verifiable incidents compels us to revise assumptions about the origins of biological and chemical warfare and its moral and technological constraints.

The ideas of poison and incendiary weapons were first described in ancient mythology, in stories about arrows dipped in serpent venom and toxic plants, water poisoned with drugs, and other tactics. The legendary Trojan War was won with poison arrows, and celebrated heroes of Greek myth—Heracles, Odysseus, and Achilles—deliberately treated their weapons with toxins.

But killing enemies by exploiting the lethal forces of nature was not just mythical fantasy. I've gathered accounts from more than fifty authors in the ancient world, along with modern archaeological finds, to provide evidence that biological and chemical weapons saw action in historical battles—in Europe and the Mediterranean, North Africa, Mesopotamia, Anatolia, the Asian steppes, India, and China. Among the historical victims and perpetrators of biochemical warfare were such prominent figures as Hannibal, Julius Caesar, and Alexander the Great.

This book is not exhaustive, but aims to reveal the depth and sweep of the evidence for biological and chemical warfare in antiquity. The time frame ranges over almost three thousand years, beginning with Near Eastern records of 1500 BC and archaic Greek myths first put in writing by Homer in about 750–650 BC. From the fifth century BC through the second century AD, Greek historians documented many examples of warfare waged by biological and chemical means, as did numerous Latin accounts, beginning with the foundation of Rome and continuing through the late Roman Empire of the sixth century AD. Meanwhile, in China and India, weapons of poison and combustible chemicals were described in military and medical treatises from about 500 BC onward. The story continues with the development of Greek Fire and other incendiaries described in Byzantine and Islamic sources of late antiquity, from the seventh through thirteenth centuries AD.

In each chapter, I present modern scientific discoveries and technological developments that help illuminate the ancient accounts and show how early unconventional weapons and strategies have evolved into many of today's biological and chemical armaments.

The range of human inventiveness in the early annals of biochemical warfare is staggering. But equally impressive is the way the ancient examples foreshadow, in substance or in principle, so many basic forms of biological and chemical weapons known today, even the most scientifically advanced armaments.

Pathogens and toxins unleashed on enemies? Since the invention of the atlatl and the bow, archers have created toxic projectiles with snake venoms, poison plants, and bacteriological substances. Other biological options included contaminating an enemy's water and food supplies, or forcing foes to camp in mosquito-infested marshes.

Anthrax, smallpox, plague, and other diseases as weapons? Deliberate attempts to spread contagion are recorded in cuneiform tablets and biblical traditions, and by Roman historians who decried "man-made pestilence." Vaccinations to protect against bioweapons? The ancients were the first to try to seek immunity against the toxic weapons of their day.

Today it is feared that a single "smallpox martyr" or other deliberately dispatched carriers of contagion could deliver a devastating biological attack. The practice of sending infected individuals into enemy territory was already operating more than three thousand years ago among the Hittites. Later, there were rumors of "Poison Maidens" sent to assassinate Alexander the Great and other military commanders.

What could be more modern than "ethnic" bioweapons? These agents, based on genetic engineering of DNA, would target certain racial groups. Yet the primitive intent of such weapons lies in the systematic slaughter of men and the rape of women, crude but effective blows against an enemy's reproduction. Practiced since earliest times, such strategies were documented in the breakup of former Yugoslavia in the early 1990s and other ethnic wars, most recently carried out in 2014–15 by the terrorist group IS/ISIL/ISIS (Islamic State of Iraq and the Levant/Islamic State of Iraq and Syria) and by Hindu fundamentalists against Muslims in India in 2019–20. And now, genetically engineered pathogens are emerging as a new and urgent biosecurity threat.[2]

Modern "wars on terrorism" have launched so-called nonlethal weapons, such as "calmative mists," to tranquilize, disorient, or knock out enemies, rendering them incapable of defending themselves. An early application of this principle, dating to about 1000 BC, was an ingenious drug plot by devised by Chrysame to help the king of Athens conquer Ionia (western Turkey).[3] Victories via intoxicants occurred in ancient military engagements in Gaul, North Africa, Asia Minor, and Mesopotamia. The biological "calmatives" of antiquity included toxic honey, drugged sacrificial bulls, barrels of alcohol, and mandrake-laced wine.[4]

What about stench warfare? Or acoustic weapons, such as the sonic attacks on US embassies beginning in 2016? These also have forerunners in ancient warfare. In recent years military scientists in the United States, Israel, China, and Russia have unveiled so-called psychologically toxic armaments designed by bioengineers to assault the senses with unbearable odors and intolerable sound waves, which can also inflict serious and lasting neurological damage. More than two millennia ago, armies in Asia and Europe employed noxious smells and blaring noises to disorient and overwhelm foes. (For ancient and modern stench and acoustic weapons, see chapter 6; microwave weapons, chapter 7.)

Rats wired to deliver explosives? Sea lions as sentinels or assassins? Bees enlisted to detect the presence of enemies and chemical agents? Even these modern biological operations have ancient antecedents. Live insects and animals have been drafted for war for thousands of years: wasps' nests were lobbed over walls, vipers were catapulted onto ships, and scorpion grenades were hurled at besiegers. A veritable menagerie of creatures—from mice and elephants to flaming pigs—became involuntary allies on the battlefields of antiquity. Generals even devised ways for animals to deliver combustibles and figured out how to exploit interspecies hostilities (chapter 6).

How about poison gas, flamethrowers, incendiary bombs? Propelling fire and creating toxic fumes have a venerable history too (chapters 3 and 7). Flaming arrows were only the beginning. The Assyrians tossed firebombs of oil, and during the Peloponnesian War, the Spartans created poison gas and flame-blowing machines to defeat fortified positions. Recipes for toxic smoke were secret weapons in ancient China and India, and asphyxiating gases suffocated many a tunneler in Roman-era sieges. Meanwhile, catapults shot firebolts fueled by sulfur. In the time of Alexander the Great, fireships laden with burning chemicals destroyed navies, and foot soldiers were incinerated by incendiary shrapnel in the form of red-hot sand. During the siege of Syracuse in 212 BC, mirrors were used to ignite ships, more than two thousand years before the development of high-tech laser and microwave guns.

Napalm? Invented in the 1940s, this petroleum weapon that flows like water and adheres like flaming honey wreaked devastation in Vietnam in the 1970s. So-called Greek Fire had similar properties and became the dreaded naval incendiary of the Byzantine era, until the formula was lost forever. But many centuries earlier, long *before* the invention of Greek Fire in AD 668, petroleum and other chemicals were combined to create harrowing weapons of unquenchable fire, used to immolate Roman soldiers in the Middle East.

░ ░ ░

What all these modern weapons and their ancient precursors have in common is the fact that they allow their creators to *weaponize nature*, according to the best understandings of the day. Not all of the ancient examples presented in the following chapters fit the strict definitions of biological or chemical weapons current today, of course, but they do represent the earliest evidence of the *intentions, principles, and practices* that evolved into modern biological and chemical warfare. The parallels between the prescientific methods of antiquity and the most up-to-the-minute armaments suggest the need to expand the definitions of biological and chemical weaponry beyond narrow categories.

Chemical warfare is defined as the military use of poisonous gases and incendiary materials, and includes blistering, blinding, and asphyxiating agents and mineral-based poisons. *Biological* weapons are viable, based on living organisms. The organisms include infectious bacteria, viruses, parasites, and spores, all of which can multiply in the body to intensify in effect, and can be contagious. The hostile use of plant toxins and venomous substances derived from animals, including reptiles, amphibians, marine creatures, and insects, constitutes another category of biological weapons. Living insects and animals turned to the service of war, and genetic strategies against adversaries, are additional types of weapons based on biology. The natural weapons arsenal also comprises disabling or harmful agents created through biology, chemistry, and physics to act on the body. These include pharmaceuticals, malodorants, light or sonic waves, microwaves, electric shocks, heat rays, and the like. Using scientific knowledge to create agents that give soldiers special powers or protection can also be considered part of the biochemical armory.[5]

In essence, biochemical warfare is the manipulation of the forces or elements of nature to insidiously attack or destroy an adversary's biological functions in ways that cannot be deflected or avoided. Biological agents and chemical incendiaries are "force multipliers"; they intensify levels of suffering and the scale of destruction of human life far beyond what would be expected in conventional warfare. In early antiquity, conventional weapons were sharp or blunt instruments of stone, wood, and metal: rocks, arrows, spears, swords. Over time, catapults and other siege machines came to be generally accepted as conventional, but poison weapons, despite their recurrent use, continued to arouse ethical concern and condemnation.[6]

Historical texts document specific episodes of biological and chemical warfare in datable conflicts, but myths and legendary events, ideas for creating biochemical weaponry, and recipes of evil effect also demonstrate the antiquity of the quest for ever more ingenious ways of turning nature to military use. The conscious *intentions* to communicate infectious disease, regardless of success, are valid criteria for analyzing biological warfare, according to the microbiologist and biowar historian Mark Wheelis. For example, the ancient practice of entreating the gods who were believed to control plagues to attack enemies demonstrates a clear *desire* to wage biological warfare. Accusations of the deliberate spread of epidemics also belong in this history, because, as Wheelis has noted, they "attest to the fact that biological attack" was imaginable and plausible.[7]

◢ ◢ ◢

After citing a few oft-repeated incidents of biochemical strategies in antiquity and the Middle Ages, typical histories of biological and chemical weaponry usually designate the gas warfare of World War I as the beginning point. Historians have assumed that biological and chemical weapons were exceedingly rare in antiquity because they were inhibited by societal or religious constraint and expressly forbidden in codes of war valuing reciprocal risk and honorable combat. Indeed, the existence of age-old "taboos" against the use of poisons in war, many historians argue, can serve as the moral backbone for creating sustainable, effective biochemical arms treaties today.

But as it turns out, war with poison and chemicals was not so rare in the ancient world and reactions to it were complex. An astounding panoply of toxic substances, venomous creatures, poison plants, animal and insect vectors, deleterious environments, virulent pathogens, infectious agents, noxious gases, and combustible chemicals were marshaled to defeat foes—and *panoply* is an apt term here, because it is the ancient Greek word for "all weapons." Many of these bioweapons and stratagems, some crude and others quite sophisticated, were considered fair, acceptable tactics of war, while others were reviled.

The ancient tension between notions of fair combat and actual practice reveals that moral questions about biochemical weapons are not a modern phenomenon, but have troubled humanity ever since the first war arrow was dipped in poison. Ethical revulsion for poison weapons did not arise in a vacuum but developed in reaction to real practices. Edward Neufeld, a scholar of ancient Mesopotamia, has suggested that the "deep aversion to this type of warfare" did not stem from humanitarian philosophies, but was a moral judgment that flowed directly from "feelings evoked by experience" with egregiously cruel and brutal weapons.[8]

Since antiquity it has been recognized that conventions of war are culturally and historically determined. In the first century BC, the geographer Strabo remarked, "Among all the customs of warfare and of usage of arms there neither is, nor has been, any single custom." The Greek historian Thucydides (fifth century BC) stressed that ideal standards of behavior in war were in constant conflict with expediency, ingenuity, and passion. In classical antiquity, a single day's battle between equally armed warriors was often decisive, and biological weapons may have been less of a temptation. Yet biological and chemical weapons were known from earliest times, and with the development of siege craft and long-drawn-out wars, unfair and secret weapons became ever more attractive. In sieges, civil wars, and rebellions, or in conflicts with exotic cultures, the whole population was considered the enemy, further lifting constraints on vicious weaponry and total-war tactics.[9]

"As fighting became more destructive," notes historian Peter Krentz, "a new, nostalgic ideology of war developed." Krentz was speaking of Greece after the savage Peloponnesian War (431–404 BC), but his words could also apply to modern historians who imagine that wars were somehow more humane and fairer in antiquity owing to "ancient taboos" or formal rules against toxic and incendiary weapons. As historian Josiah Ober remarks, however, "Any argument which assumes that a universal sense of fair play and decency was an innate part of early Greek military culture is easily falsified." The tension between the "fair fight" and "winning by whatever means necessary" was evident from the very beginning.[10]

In classical Greek combat—hand-to-hand fighting by hoplites (infantrymen armed with helmets, shields, and spears)—the mayhem of ordinary fighting with regular hacking and stabbing weapons was extreme (fig. 1). The Roman historian Sallust painted a vivid picture of the aftermath of a typical, decisive battle between Roman cavalry troops and Numidian and Moorish elephant and cavalry divisions in 106 BC. "The end of it was that the enemy were everywhere defeated.

FIG. 1. Heroic hoplite combat, face-to-face fighting between equally matched Greek warriors using conventional weapons of spear and shield. Attic black-figure neck amphora, 500–480 BC, 86.AE.78. Courtesy of the J. Paul Getty Museum Open Content Program.

The broad plain presented a ghastly spectacle of flight and pursuit, slaughter and capture. Horses and men were thrown down; many of the wounded, without the strength to escape or patience to lie still, struggled to get up only to collapse immediately. As far as the eye could reach, the battlefield was strewn with weapons, armor, and corpses, with patches of bloodstained earth showing between them."[11]

As dreadful as such carnage was, though, it was exactly what men and their commanders expected and prepared for. A well-armed and armored soldier trained for the fighting, steeled himself for the battle and the possibility of death, advanced into the fray, and fought the enemy face-to-face to the end. The glory and nobility of battle depended on the concept of "reciprocal risk."[12] Courage in the face of death and strong combat skills counted for something: a soldier could win or die honorably—and these were crucial values for ancient warrior cultures.

But clever ruses were also highly respected in warrior cultures. Odysseus, the archer-hero of Homer's *Odyssey* and *Iliad*, was a master of deception. A complex figure who practiced both acceptable and heinous ruses, Odysseus's most celebrated trick was the Trojan Horse. It was a tempting gift that the Trojans could have rejected. Odysseus played on their pride and greed, not their biological vulnerability; therefore the ploy seems fair. But Odysseus also poisoned his arrows, and Homer makes it clear that toxic projectiles were dishonorable. Archers were admired for their marksmanship, but they were never models of bravery, since they shot missiles from afar, avoiding direct confrontation.[13]

If long-distance weapons in themselves were regarded with ambivalence by classical Greeks and Romans, then treating long-distance projectiles with poison could elicit even more disapproval. Use of a poison arrow meant that even a poor marksman could inflict grievous suffering and death on the mightiest warrior, because even a slight nick sent lethal toxins into his bloodstream. In cultures that valued intelligent cunning as well as physical courage in battle situations, conflicting ideas arose over which weapons and strategies were acceptable and which were questionable. Were crafty methods—what some would call underhanded, cowardly ruses—ever justified? The traditional view held that underhanded tricks and treachery should be shameful to any true warrior. Like arrows and ambush, biochemical weapons also allowed one to surprise and destroy enemies from a position of safety, without risking battle. As the toxic equivalents of arrows and ambush, therefore, poison weapons could elicit criticism, yet they were certainly not always shunned. Drawing the line between creative resourcefulness and reprehensible tactics has always proved difficult in practice.[14]

▰ ▰ ▰

What do ancient rules of war have to say about insidious weapons? For the most part one must extrapolate ideas about biowar from military practices described in ancient accounts. Very little is known about Persian and Carthaginian rules of war, for example, and we must rely on Greek and Latin historians for descriptions of war among the Gauls/Celts, Africans, and Scythians of Central Asia. These peoples used poison projectiles, but they were also the victims of biological subterfuges by the Romans and Persians. Disapproval of the use of either poisons or chemicals can be found in ancient

Indian, Greek, Roman, Chinese, and Muslim traditions, but inconsistencies and contradictions cloud the issue of what was deemed acceptable in warfare.[15]

In ancient India, as in Greece, two kinds of warfare were recognized. There was righteous war carried out according to ethical principles with the approval of society, and there was crafty, ruthless war pursued in secret, without regard for moral standards. The tensions between these two approaches are embodied in two famous military codes of ancient India. The *Laws of Manu* are Hindu rules of conduct for Brahman rulers dating in oral form to about 500 BC, codified in Sanskrit in about AD 150. The *Laws* are commonly cited as the oldest prohibitions against biochemical warfare, because they forbade the use of arrows tipped with poison or fire. Reading further, though, one finds the *Laws* advising kings to "continually spoil the grass and water" of a besieged enemy.[16]

The *Arthashastra* represented the more unambiguously nefarious side of ancient Indian warfare. This military treatise, attributed to the Brahman adviser to King Chandragupta in the fourth century BC, is filled with instructions for waging war with secret weapons, and it urged kings to deploy poisons without qualms. The *Arthashastra*'s compilation of hundreds of recipes for toxic weapons and the unscrupulous tactics it describes foreshadow the sentiment attributed to the notorious Dr. Shiro Ishii, director of Japan's bioweapons program in World War II: if a weapon is important enough to be prohibited, it must be worth having in one's arsenal. Yet even the ruthless *Arthashastra* also advised kings to win over enemy hearts with their "own excellent qualities," and exhorted victors to spare the wounded and vanquished. Another example of dramatically opposite advice in the two Indian treatises applies to calmatives. The *Laws of Manu* forbade attacks on sleeping enemies, whereas the *Arthashastra* recommended intoxicants and soporifics, for the best time to attack is when foes are overcome by sleep.[17]

Contradictions can be found among rules of war and military manuals in China too. *The Art of War* by Sun Tzu (about 500 BC), for example, stressed *kueitao*, deceptive means, and advocated the use of fire as a terror weapon, and other Chinese treatises described myriad recipes for toxic smokes and poison incendiaries. Humanitarian codes of war of about 450–200 BC, however, forbade ruses of war, harming noncombatants, and causing unnecessary suffering.[18]

In the ancient Near East, the book of Deuteronomy (written between the seventh and fifth centuries BC) sets forth Yahweh's rules of war for the Israelites. The instructions include the famous law of retaliation "without pity," namely, "life for life, eye for eye, tooth for tooth, hand for hand." When God's chosen people besieged cities outside the promised land that "refused to become enslaved," the Jews were to kill all males and claim women and children as booty. Cities within Palestine were to be treated mercilessly, however: "You shall utterly destroy them, leaving nothing alive that breathes." Only orchards were to be spared. These rules were put into practice, for example, in the total destruction of Jericho in about 1350 BC. Biological weapons would not appear to be prohibited under these harsh "holy war" principles, and, notably, Exodus recounts some of the earliest intentions to carry out biological warfare, in the plagues called down on Egypt—although the motive in that case was resistance, not aggression.[19]

Some modern histories of biological and chemical warfare assert that the Quran (written in the seventh century AD) forbids the use of poison and fire as weapons of war. But the Quranic injunctions that might apply to biochemical strategies are vague: "Do not make mischief on the earth," "Show restraint," and "Do not transgress limits." These may have presupposed an unwritten "warrior code of honor known to its first hearers" now lost, suggests John Kelsay, a scholar of Islamic rules of war. There is literary evidence that pre-Islamic Persian and Arab Sasanians took pride in "purity" of warfare. In the ninth to twelfth centuries, a concept of youthful brotherhood, *futuwwa*, evolved from Persian and Arab traditions of honorable, noble, and proper conduct in battle into a code of honor or bond among warrior groups, which became known as "Islamic chivalry." *Futuwwa* ideals influenced European medieval notions of chivalry, such as courage, generosity, loyalty, fair combat, no night attacks, no attacks from the rear if the enemy is fleeing, no flammable weapons, and so on. In the seventh century, in a famous decree, Abu Bakr al-Siddiq (the first caliph after the death of his companion Muhammad in AD 632), gave his military commander a set of "rules for guidance on the battlefield: Do not commit treachery or deviate from the right path. You must not mutilate dead bodies; do not kill a woman, a child, or an aged man; do not cut down fruitful trees; do not destroy inhabited areas; do not slaughter any of the enemies' sheep, cows, or camels except for food; do not burn date palms, nor inundate them.... You are likely to pass by people who have devoted their lives to monastic services; leave them alone."[20]

Some rules have been inferred from later Islamic traditions, based on the deeds and sayings of Muhammad compiled after his death (in AD 632). In the opinion of modern Muslim scholar Hamza Yusuf, Muhammad "clearly prohibited killing noncombatants, women and children [and] poisoning wells, which I think can be applied to biological warfare." Muhammad also "prohibited using fire as a means to kill another being," because fire belonged to Allah. But the Quran prescribed punishment by fire for disbelievers: "For them are cut out garments of fire, boiling water shall be poured over their heads," and their skin and body "shall be melted." As many historians have pointed out, classical Islamic scholars differed over permissible weapons and tactics, depending on whether adversaries were Muslims or non-Muslims.[21]

Denying drinking water, even to enemies, was a grievous wrong in early Islamic belief. (In contrast, ancient Roman commanders had no qualms about achieving victories "by thirst.") In the civil wars after Muhammad's death, however, that rule was violated by the dominant Umayyad forces, who were censured for transgressions of Islamic ideals.[22]

Some classical Islamic jurists maintained that flooding, flamethrowers, and mangonels (to catapult burning naphtha; see chapter 7) were not to be used except for "dire necessity or self-defence." For some Muslim jurists, fire weapons were deemed especially brutal and therefore unacceptable. Yet fire weapons were used routinely by early Islamic armies, even against other Muslims. Muhammad lived at a time when petrochemical incendiaries were common in siege craft. During the siege of Mecca in AD 683, Muslim forces catapulted burning petroleum at the rival Muslim defenders. By AD 900, Islamic armies maintained special *naffatun* troops to wield devastating "liquid fire," which became a favorite weapon against the Crusaders. Perhaps because of bans on poisoning water or air, however, Muslims apparently refrained from adding toxins to their incendiaries, which were common in ancient Chinese and Indian recipes.[23]

No formal set of rules of war existed in Greece. The military historian Polybius (born 204 BC) stated that the "ancients" preferred open, hand-to-hand battle to deception and ruses, and followed a "convention among themselves" not to use "secret missiles or those discharged from a distance." But only two instances of sworn agreements prohibiting certain types of weapons are known in Greece. One, recounted by Strabo, was inscribed on a column in a temple in Euboea and recorded that in the Lelantine War (about 700 BC) the contending parties had agreed to ban projectile weapons. The other agreement directly applies to biological warfare. In the sixth century BC, after a Greek city, Kirrha, was destroyed by poison during an attack by an alliance of city-states, the alliance promised to refrain from such acts against fellow Greeks.[24]

A dozen informal rules of war were gleaned from ancient Greek literature by historian Josiah Ober. They concern declarations of war and truces; prohibit the killing of messengers, noncombatants, and captives; and express a distaste for projectile weapons. As Ober notes, these rules "were certainly not always honored in practice," and during the Peloponnesian War the "informal Greek rules of war broke down."[25]

The main sources for warfare practices are found in histories written in antiquity, but even then the writers rarely considered the rules of war unless some exceptional event occurred. It was only in describing unusual biological strategies that authors sometimes indicated the generally held standards of conduct in war. Herodotus, for example, the Greek historian writing in about 450 BC, described the moral outrage of Queen Tomyris of the Massagetae, when the Persians set out wine to drug her unsuspecting troops and then slaughtered them. There is no soldierly honor in your victory, she declared, only shame (chapter 5).

During the Peloponnesian War, which brought accusations of well poisoning and inventions of new chemical weapons, Thucydides wrote approvingly of one hoplite battle of 433 BC that was an increasingly rare instance in which "courage and sheer strength played a greater part than scientific methods." The brutality of the Peloponnesian War undermined the "general laws of humanity," despaired Thucydides. "Victory won by treachery" was now equated with "superior intelligence," and "most people are ready to call villainy cleverness." Profound disapproval suffuses his descriptions of atrocities against noncombatants.[26]

After the Peloponnesian War, Aeneas the Tactician wrote a manual on how to survive sieges. He advised defenders to poison water supplies, to throw burning materials onto attackers, and to choke them with noxious smoke. Significantly, all these biochemical tactics were intended for the *defense* of besieged cities. In antiquity, as today, biochemical weapons often seem more acceptable when used against aggressors.[27]

Roman notions of just war were articulated by the philosopher Cicero (106–43 BC), who believed that obeying rules of war and refraining from cruelty were what set men apart from beasts. But his laws concerned the legitimate grounds for going to war, rather than its conduct. Reactions to biological strategies are found in other Roman writers' remarks. The historian Florus, for example, castigated a Roman general for poisoning wells in Asia, and thereby sullying Roman honor; the poet Ovid deplored toxic arrows, and Silius Italicus declared that poisons brought "disgrace" to iron weapons. The historian Tacitus (AD 98) voiced grudging admiration for a German tribe who intensified "their savage instincts by trickery and clever" means, rather than opting for poison arrows like the Gauls and other groups. The Germans blackened their shields, dyed their bodies black, and "chose pitch dark nights for their battle," wrote Tacitus. "The appearance of such a ghoulish army inspires mortal panic, for no enemy can endure a sight so strange and hellish." This ancient example of creative psychological warfare was considered fair, whereas poisoning, Tacitus makes clear elsewhere, violated the old Roman tradition of open battle.[28]

In contrast, by the second century AD, the Roman strategist Polyaenus wrote a military treatise for emperors that openly advocated biochemical and devious stratagems for defeating "barbarians" without risking battle. As the empire was increasingly forced to desperately defend all its borders, the old ideals of forthright combat and leniency were replaced by policies of maximum force and treachery. The new policies were articulated by the Roman military strategist Vegetius, writing in AD 390: "It is preferable to subdue an enemy by famine, raids, and terror, than in battle where fortune tends to have more influence than bravery."[29]

Despite a general sense in antiquity that biological weapons were cruel and dishonorable, the evidence shows that they were employed in certain situations. So when might the rules of war be overridden?

Self-defense, mentioned earlier, was a time-honored rationale. Besieged cities resorted to all manner of resistance, including biochemical options, and desperate populations overcome by invaders turned to bioweapons as a last resort.

When one's forces were outnumbered or facing troops superior in courage, skill, or technology, biological and chemical strategies were a real advantage, as force multipliers. Indeed, the perils and loss of lives in a fair fight could be avoided altogether through the deployment of toxic weapons, an approach that appealed to Polyaenus and other Romans who admired the Greek mythic hero Odysseus as the model strategist.

When opponents are identified as "barbarians" or cultural outsiders, their alleged "uncivilized nature" has long served as an excuse for using unscrupulous weapons and inhumane tactics against them. Other situations, such as holy wars or quelling rebellions, also encouraged the indiscriminate use of bioweapons, targeting noncombatants as well as warriors. Some commanders used poison in frustration when losing a war, or to break a stalemate or a long-drawn-out siege. The threat of horrifying weapons might discourage would-be attackers or could be used by aggressors to bring about quick capitulation. Then there were those ruthless generals who had no compunctions about using any strategy or weapon at hand to win victory. And in many of the cultures encountered by the Greeks and Romans, poison arrows and ambush were the customary way of war.[30]

⚟ ⚟ ⚟

Although it is tempting to imagine an ancient era innocent of biochemical weaponry, in fact this Pandora's box of horrors was opened thousands of years ago. The history of making war with biological weapons begins in mythology, in ancient oral traditions that preserved records of actual events and ideas of the era before the invention of written histories. The evidence from ancient myth shatters the notion of a time when biowar was inconceivable; it also suggests that profound doubts about the propriety of such weapons arose along with their earliest usage.

After considering the mythic invention of poison weapons and their use in the legendary Trojan War in chapter 1, we turn to the actual practices of biological and chemical warfare in historical times. Ancient authors reveal exactly how arrow poisons were concocted from venoms and toxins, and who used them in the ancient world (chapter 2), and they describe the first documented cases of poisoning enemies' water supplies and maneuvering foes into deadly environments (chapter 3). Chapter 4 presents compelling evidence from Near Eastern, Greek and Latin, and Indian sources suggesting how plagues and other infectious diseases may have been deliberately spread. Toxic honey, tainted wine, and other attractive lures have long served as secret weapons, as chapter 5 reveals. Chapter 6 tells how venomous creatures and large and small animals have been drafted for war duty. Chemical incendiaries have a surprisingly ancient history too: chapter 7 begins with the earliest uses of poison gases and ancient versions of napalm before turning to the invention of Greek Fire in the seventh century AD.

The difficulty of controlling the forces unleashed when nature itself is turned into a weapon means that the annals of biochemical warfare are rife with risks of self-injury, friends fired upon in error, collateral damage, and unforeseen consequences, even for future generations, as noted in the afterword. Because unconventional weapons are intended to destabilize and play on the unexpected, such strategies by their very nature have cut an "erratic course" through history. It is only logical, therefore, that those who use biochemical weapons should reap a "whirlwind of unintended results."[31] The resort to secret weapons capable of mass destruction is a double-edged sword—a theme that first emerged in ancient myth and pervades the long history of biochemical weapons.

CHAPTER 1

HERACLES AND THE HYDRA

THE INVENTION OF BIOLOGICAL WEAPONS

The poison, heated by fire, coursed through his limbs. His
blood, saturated by the burning poison, hissed and boiled.
There was no end to his agony as flames attacked his heart
and the hidden pestilence melted his bones.

—DEATH OF HERACLES, OVID, *METAMORPHOSES*

IT WAS HERACLES, the greatest hero of Greek mythology, who
invented the first biological weapon described in classical literature. When Heracles dipped his arrows in serpent venom,
he opened up a world not only of toxic warfare, but also of
unanticipated consequences. In fact, the deepest roots of
the concept of biological weapons extend even further back
in time, before the Greek myths were first written down by
Homer in the eighth century BC. Poison and arrows were
deeply intertwined in the ancient Greek language itself. The
word for poison in ancient Greek, *toxicon*, derived from *toxon*,
bow. And in Latin, the word for poison, *toxica*, was said to

derive from *taxus*, yew, because the first poison arrows had been daubed with deadly yew-berry juice. In antiquity, then, a "toxic" substance meant "something for the bow and arrow."[1]

The great first-century AD Greek physician Dioscorides was one of the first to remark on the derivation of the word "toxic" from "arrow." But Dioscorides insisted that only "barbarian" foreigners—never the Greeks themselves—resorted to poison weapons. His assumption was widely expressed in antiquity and still holds sway today, as is evident in the declaration about poison arrows by Guido Majno, the medical historian whose specialty is war wounds in the ancient world: "This kind of treachery never occurs in the tales about Troy."[2]

Since antiquity, the Greek legends about great heroes and the Trojan War have been celebrated for their thrilling battles and heroic deaths in the realm of myth. To be sure, the typical weapons of Bronze Age warfare glorified in the myths—bow and arrow, javelin, spear, sword, and axe—unleashed enough gory mayhem and violent death on the battlefield to satisfy the most bloodthirsty audience. But most people today assume that the very idea of poisoning weapons was a barbaric practice abhorred by the ancient Greeks. Like the historian Majno, most take it for granted that heroes like Heracles and the warriors of the Trojan War must have engaged in the noblest forms of ancient combat, fighting fairly and face-to-face. They killed enemies but remained honorable in their behavior.

But not always. A deeper look uncovers compelling evidence of less noble, decidedly unheroic forms of warfare in these epic tales of classical culture. Mythical conflicts teem with treachery, and secretly poisoned arrows and spears were wielded by some of the greatest champions of classical mythology. This picture of morally unsettling ways of dispatching enemies is usually overshadowed by the larger-than-life figures and their exciting adventures. But once we begin to peer into the darker reaches of the mythic tapestry, scenes of nefarious trickery and ghastly suffering from poison weapons emerge from the shadows.

Upon closer inspection, two of the most famous Greek myths—the story of Heracles and the Hydra, and the Trojan War—turn out to have crucial information about the origins of biological weapons and ancient attitudes toward their use.

◢ ◢ ◢

Heracles (Hercules), the superhero of Greek myth, was renowned for his Twelve Labors. In his first labor, he slaughtered the fearsome Lion of Nemea. He then donned its skin and set out on his second task. His mission was to destroy an even more daunting monster, the Many-Headed Hydra. This gigantic, poisonous water-serpent lurked in the swamps of Lerna, terrorizing the people of southern Greece. The Hydra was said to have nine, ten, fifty, even a hundred heads—and, worse yet, the central head was immortal (fig. 2).

Heracles forced the Hydra to emerge from its lair by shooting fiery arrows coated with pitch—the sticky sap from pine trees.[3] The mighty hero then seized the giant snake with his bare hands, thinking he could strangle it as he had the Nemean Lion. Heracles was strong but no match for the Hydra. It coiled its huge body around his legs and poised its multiple heads to strike. Heracles began to smash the horrid snake heads with his club. When this proved futile, he drew his sword to chop them off.

The most diabolical thing about the Hydra was that it actually "thrived on its wounds," in the words of the Roman

FIG. 2. Heracles and the Hydra. Heracles (left) chops off the heads, while his companion (right) cauterizes the necks with torches. Attic red-figure volute krater, 480–470 BC, attributed to the Kleophrades Painter, 84.AE.974. Courtesy of the J. Paul Getty Museum Open Content Program.

poet Ovid. Each time Heracles cut off one head, two more instantly regenerated. Soon the monster was bristling with heads whose fangs dripped with venom. What to do? His ordinary weapons—hands, club, sword, arrows—were useless. So Heracles resorted to fire. Taking up a burning torch, he cauterized each bloody neck as he chopped off a head, to prevent it from sprouting new ones. But the middle head was immortal. This head Heracles hacked off and quickly buried alive in the ground. Then he placed a heavy rock over the spot. The ancient Greeks and Romans used to point out a colossal boulder on the road to Lerna, marking the place where Heracles had entombed the Hydra's living head.

Heracles was a hunter who took trophies. He had fashioned his signature hooded cape from the skin of the Nemean Lion. After slaying the Hydra, Heracles slashed open the body and

FIG. 3. Heracles killing the Hydra; Athena holds out a small vial to collect the venom for poisoning his arrows. Corinthian aryballos, about 590 BC, 92.AE.4. Courtesy of the J. Paul Getty Museum Open Content Program.

dipped his arrows in the potent venom of the monstrous serpent (fig. 3). Ever after, Heracles's oversized quiver carried a seemingly endless supply of arrows made superdeadly by Hydra venom.[4]

By steeping his arrows in the monster's venom, Heracles created the first biological weapon. The inspiration flowed naturally from his previous idea for magnifying the power of his arrows, by coating them in pine resin to create noxious fire and fumes (in essence, a chemical weapon). Heracles appropriated the Hydra's natural weapon of deadly venom to enhance his own weapons. Since myths often coalesced around a core of historical and scientific realities, the ancient story of the Hydra arrows suggests that projectile weapons tipped with combustible and toxic substances must have been known very early in Greek history.

Notably, the descriptions of poisoned wounds in the myths of Heracles—and the Trojan War—accurately depict the very real effects of snake venom and other known arrow toxins. In historical accounts of the ancient use of poison projectiles, archers concocted effective arrow poisons from a variety of pernicious ingredients, including viper venom. It is interesting that, according to the Greek historian Herodotus, Heracles was the cultural founder of the Scythians, real-life nomadic horse archers of the steppes who were feared for their snake-poison arrows.[5]

The mythical lore that grew up around Heracles's invention of snake-venom arrows reveals the complex attitudes of the ancient Greeks toward weapons that delivered hidden poisons. Deep misgivings were expressed in the earliest myths about warriors who destroyed their enemies with toxic weapons. Many mythological characters succumbed to Heracles's arrows. Almost as soon as they were created, however, the poison weapons set in motion a relentless train of tragedies for Heracles and the Greeks—not to mention the Greeks' enemies, the Trojans. With the very first deployment of his newly discovered biological weapons, Heracles proved powerless to avoid hurting his own friends and innocent bystanders.

The first victims included some of Heracles's oldest friends. On his way to another labor—killing the gigantic Erymanthian Boar—Heracles attended a party hosted by his Centaur friend, the half-man, half-horse Pholus. When Pholus opened a jug of wine, a gang of violent Centaurs invaded the party. Heracles leaped up to repel them, and in the ensuing clash many Centaurs were felled by Heracles's poison arrows as he pursued them over the landscape. The fleeing horde of horsemen took refuge in the cave of Chiron, a peaceful Centaur who had taught humankind the arts of medicine.

As the Centaurs cowered around Chiron, Heracles let fly a host of Hydra-venom arrows. By mischance, one struck Chiron in the knee. Heracles rushed to his old friend's side, deeply distressed. He drew the shaft out from Chiron's leg and quickly applied a special poultice, as Chiron directed. And here the mythographers explain just how terrible a wound from a venom-tipped arrow was: the pain was so horrendous that you would sell your eternal soul for a swift death. According to myth, Chiron was immortal, but the agony was so excruciating that he begged the gods to relieve him of immortality and allow him to die.

Chiron's plea was answered when the Titan Prometheus volunteered to take on Chiron's eternal life. The Centaur was released from endless pain, and expired. Prometheus was destined to regret his act, however. When he later stole fire from the gods and gave it to humankind, Prometheus's punishment was particularly horrifying because he could not die. As every Greek knew, every day for the rest of time, Zeus's eagle came to torture the immortal Prometheus.

While Heracles was tending the grievously wounded Chiron, his other Centaur friend, Pholus, became another unintended victim. Pholus removed an arrow from one of the Centaur corpses and wondered how such a little thing could have killed such strong creatures. As he curiously examined the arrow, it slipped from his hand and dropped on his leg (see plate 2). He was mortally wounded, and Heracles sorrowfully buried yet another victim of "collateral damage."

The danger of self-inflicted wounds or accidents with poison projectiles is always present, since even a mere scratch could be devastating. Legendary "friendly fire" incidents, like the tragic deaths of Chiron and Pholus, were favorite subjects of Greek and Roman painters and sculptors. Another innocent victim was Heracles's own son, Telephus. During the preparations for the Trojan War, the youth tripped on a vine and fell against a spear carried by Achilles, the great Greek warrior. The point struck Telephus's thigh, causing an incurable, festering wound. The unhealing wound implies that Achilles had smeared his spearpoint with some sort of poison. And as fate would have it, a poison arrow would bring about Achilles's own demise on the battlefield at Troy.[6]

In the most ironic twist of fate, Heracles himself ultimately succumbed to the Hydra venom that he had daubed on his own arrows. A wily Centaur named Nessus had abducted Heracles's wife, Deianeira. Enraged, Heracles shot Nessus in the back with a Hydra arrow that pierced his heart. As the Roman poet Ovid stressed in his version of the myth, it is not fair to shoot even a rogue in the back with a poison arrow. As in most mythic tales, treachery bred more treachery, and the venom multiplied in power, just like the Hydra's heads. The dying Centaur tricked Deianeira into collecting the toxic blood flowing from his wound. Advising her to keep it in an airtight container, away from heat and light, Nessus promised that if she smeared this substance on a tunic for Heracles someday, it would work as a love charm.

Years later, Deianeira, unaware of the potential for secondhand poisoning, secretly treated a beautiful tunic with
the Centaur's contaminated blood and gave it as a gift to her
husband. What happened next was the subject of a famous
tragedy, written about 430 BC, by the Athenian playwright
Sophocles. Heracles put on the tunic to make a special sacrifice. As he approached the fire, the heat activated the Hydra
poison. The envenomed tunic caused Heracles such fiery torture that he ran amok, bellowing like a wounded bull and
uprooting trees. In desperation, he plunged into a stream. But
the water only increased the poison's burning power, and that
stream ran scalding-hot forever after. Heracles struggled to
tear off the garment, but it adhered to his flesh and corroded
his skin like acid or some unnatural fire.

Unable to bear the pain of the burning poison, Heracles
shouted for his companions to light a large funeral pyre.
His arms-bearer and friend, the young archer Philoctetes,
was the only one courageous enough to obey. In gratitude,
Heracles bequeathed his special bow (originally a gift from
Apollo, the archer-god whose arrows brought plague) and
his quiver of Hydra arrows to his friend Philoctetes. Then
the mighty hero threw himself onto the flaming pyre and was
burned alive (see plate 1).[7]

Heracles's agony is a poetic representation of painful death
by viper venom, which was often compared to burning alive.
Indeed, fire motifs pervade the early mythology of biological
weapons. Flaming arrows and searing torches had destroyed
the Hydra, and now the Hydra venom was activated by heat
and took on the nature of unquenchable fire. The bite of a real
viper, called *dipsas* in antiquity, brought intolerable thirst and,
according to ancient writers, caused sensations of burning and

corrosion, making victims feel "on fire, as if they were lying on a funeral pyre."[8]

But the tragic consequences ignited by Heracles's invention of poison arrows did not end with the hero's death. When she learned the result of her unwitting use of a poison weapon, Deianeira hanged herself. And the quiver of deadly arrows went on to bring great misfortune to Philoctetes during the Trojan War.

* * *

"Mighty-walled Troy" of Greek epic was probably the Late Bronze Age city designated Troy VI in the series of ruined cities in northwest Turkey first excavated by Heinrich Schliemann in 1870–90. The ruins show that the citadel of Troy VI was destroyed by fire in about 1200 BC. The legendary Trojan War was most famously described by Homer in the *Iliad* in about 750–650 BC, but an extensive cycle of Trojan War stories circulated in Greek and Roman times, recounted by many other mythographers and playwrights, some of whose works now survive only as fragments.

Most classical scholars agree that the oral epics probably grew up around actual battles during the Bronze Age (1300–1100 BC), and that some residue of truth exists in the legends concerning the Trojan War, including many aspects of real warfare of that era. This cycle of myths and legends provides striking evidence of the two complex, parallel pictures of warfare in classical antiquity. There was the familiar, idealized Homeric version of clean, fair fighting, epitomized by heroes like Achilles in the *Iliad*, and there were other, more nefarious ways of overcoming foes, often attributed to barbarians, but admired in crafty Greek heroes like Odysseus.[9]

According to myth, Apollo's divine arrows inflicted deadly epidemics and fevers, especially during wartime. The *Iliad* opens with the god aiming his bow at the Greek army in the tenth year of their siege of Troy, cutting down King Agamemnon's troops with a devastating plague. (The gods took sides in Greek mythology: Apollo favored the Trojans while Athena helped the Greeks). In Homer's words, Apollo let fly his "black bolts of plague" on the soldiers for nine days. The god's first targets were the pack animals and dogs, then "one by one our men came down with it and died hard as the god's arrows raked the army." Funeral pyres burned night and day, and the Greeks' hopes of completing the siege of Troy were dashed.

This opening scene is a not-so-subtle reminder of the ancient etymological metaphor linking arrows and toxins. Several other passages in the *Iliad* hint strongly that poison weapons were wielded by warriors on the battlefield, although Homer never says this outright. When Menelaos was wounded by a Trojan arrow, for example, Machaon (son of the legendary god of healing, Asclepius) was summoned to suck out the "black blood." This treatment was the emergency remedy for snakebite and poison arrow wounds in real life. Elsewhere, Homer described "black blood" gushing from arrow wounds and referred to Philoctetes's "black wound from a deadly snake." Black blood signaled a poisoned wound to ancient battlefield doctors, and in fact snake venom does cause black, oozing wounds. In the *Iliad*, Machaon also applied a special balm prepared by the Centaur Chiron, recalling the treatment for the Centaur's own poison arrow wound.[10]

Only once did Homer explicitly describe a Greek hero actually searching out a poison for treating his arrows (not surprisingly, it was Odysseus, master of cunning tricks). But many

FIG. 4. Archer testing shaft and point of arrow; any archer who tipped his projectiles with poison had to avoid all contact with the sharp point. Carved chalcedony gem, 500 BC, signed by Epimenes. Fletcher Fund, 1931, Metropolitan Museum, New York.

other ancient mythographers make it clear that arrow poison was employed by both sides in the Trojan War (fig. 4).

The Trojan War began when the Greeks launched an expedition to avenge the abduction of the Spartan beauty, Helen, by the Trojan seducer, Paris. Heracles's old friend, the great archer Philoctetes, commanded seven of the twelve hundred Greek ships sailing to Troy. Homer specified that each of Philoctetes's ships was rowed by fifty expert bowmen. Did Philoctetes equip his archers with poison arrows from Heracles's quiver, which he was bringing to Troy? Homer does not say, but an ill-omened accident involving serpent venom did occur on the voyage.[11]

On the way to Troy, Philoctetes received a hideous "black wound" in the foot. According to some versions of the myth, he was accidentally struck by one of the poison arrows he had inherited from Heracles. In other versions, he was bitten by a poisonous *hydra*, a water-snake. Both versions underscore the perils of handling toxic substances used to create bioweapons. Philoctetes's accident was an inauspicious start for launching the war. The men found the stench of his festering wound intolerable and his howls of pain a very bad omen. The leader of the Greeks, Agamemnon, ordered his captain Odysseus to abandon Philoctetes on a tiny desert island called Chryse, near the island of Lemnos, and then sail on to Troy.

For a decade, while his companions besieged the Trojans, the abandoned warrior was marooned in unending pain and fever, as "a black flux of blood and matter" continued to ooze from his wound. Philoctetes, the most skilled archer after Odysseus, survived by shooting birds with Heracles's bow and poison arrows. The mythic description of Philoctetes's suppurating, never-healing wound and spreading necrosis is an accurate depiction of the aftermath of a snakebite.

In antiquity until about AD 150, Philoctetes's desert island, Chryse, was a popular landmark visited by Greek and Roman travelers. A small shrine there memorialized the warrior's ordeal with the poison arrows: the altar displayed Philoctetes's bow, his bronze armor, and a bronze water-snake. Philoctetes's tragic tale was widely known. He was celebrated as a god in Italy, where he was said to have settled at the end of his life. His tribulations were illustrated in numerous artworks and presented on the Athenian stage in plays by Sophocles, Aeschylus, and Euripides.

Ten years into the war with Troy, an oracle advised the Greeks that the Trojans could be defeated only by Heracles's original poison arrows. So Odysseus led an envoy of Greeks back to Chryse, the island where they had stranded Philoctetes so long before. The men were horrified to find the once-proud warrior living like an animal in a cave, whose floor was slick with the fetid pus draining from his wound. The emaciated archer, surrounded by feathers and bird bones, was still racked by pain from the arrow poison (fig. 5). The Greeks were filled with pity for their companion, yet they expressed no qualms about using the same nasty poison against the Trojans.

FIG. 5. On the way to Troy, Philoctetes was abandoned on a desert island after his accident with a Hydra-venom arrow. The despondent archer sits on a rock under a barren tree, with a bandaged foot and his quiver of poison arrows. Oil flask, 420 BC. 56.171.58, Fletcher Fund, 1956, Metropolitan Museum, New York.

The delegation tried to persuade the long-suffering Philoc- tetes to bring the arrows to Troy, but he refused, embittered by their cruel treatment of him. He even threatened to shoot them with the poison arrows. So Odysseus hatched a scheme to deceive Philoctetes in order to get the bow and quiver. But Achilles's son, an honorable youth named Neoptolemus, was outraged by Odysseus's lack of principles. He insisted that "vile tricks and treachery" should be shameful to a true warrior. The scene, as described by Sophocles, is fraught with the age-old tension between war by the rules and war by devious means.[12]

Finally, after the ghost of Heracles appeared and promised he would be cured, Philoctetes agreed to rejoin the Greeks. At Troy, Philoctetes's wound was treated by Machaon, the Greek army doctor. Out on the battlefield, Philoctetes became an avenging whirlwind with the Hydra arrows, destroying legions of Trojans. Then, in an archery duel with the Trojan bowman Paris, Philoctetes turned the tide of the war in favor of the Greeks.

Quintus of Smyrna, a poet of the fourth century AD, de- scribed the rain of deadly arrows in his epic *The Fall of Troy*, based on an earlier, now lost, Trojan War epic. He told how the mighty Greek warrior Achilles was brought down by an arrow deliberately aimed at his vulnerable heel. In myths of his birth, Thetis had held her infant son Achilles by the heel as she dipped him in the River Styx to make him impervious to iron weapons. His heel was his only vulnerable point. Normally, however, a wound in the heel would be superficial—only an arrow carrying poison could render such a wound fatal. In some versions of the myth, it was Apollo who shot Achilles from behind with one of his plague arrows. But others said that Apollo had guided Paris's arrow to the back of Achilles's foot.

As the arrow struck his heel, Achilles reeled with "sudden pangs of mortal sickness" and toppled "like a tower." Rolling his eyes and gnashing his teeth from the pain of the "envenomed wound," the dying Achilles expressed the traditional Greek warrior's visceral loathing of dishonorable death. Not only had he been struck by a weapon of hidden poison, but his cowardly adversary had struck from behind, just as Heracles had shot Nessus in the back. As the doomed champion sensed the toxins racing through his veins, bringing an unheroic, "piteous death," Achilles glared about murderously and shouted, "Who shot me with a stealthy-smiting shaft? Let him dare to meet me face to face! Only dastards lurk in hidden ambush. None dare meet me man to man. . . . Let him face me then!"

To avenge the shocking death of Achilles from a poisoned arrow in the heel, Philoctetes drew back his great bow and aimed a "merciless shaft" with its "terrible, death-hissing point" at Paris (the poet's words evoke the imagery of snakes). The first arrow grazed Paris's wrist, and the next one plunged into his side. "Torturing wounds" sent Paris into a "frenzy of pain, his liver seething as in flame." The Trojan doctors rushed onto the battlefield to apply salves and blood-sucking leeches to draw out the poison. But these means were useless against the "fierce venom which crawled through his innards with corrupting fangs." Parched with thirst, scarcely conscious, and writhing in pain, Paris desperately held onto the hope that a nymph he had once loved would bring special healing herbs. The nymph did arrive at last, but it was too late to save the Trojan warrior-lover, who finally perished in anguish.[13]

Despite the importance of the bow and arrow from the Bronze Age and onward in Greece, Homer and many other ancient writers tell us that archers were disdained because they shot safely from afar. Long-range projectiles implied an unwillingness to face the enemy at close range. And long-range projectiles daubed with poison seemed even more cowardly and villainous. Ambush from behind was another military practice that, like poisoning arrows, was usually attributed to barbarians. Traditional Greek—and Roman—warfare was supposed to be hand to hand, up close and personal, as ranks of similarly armed and armored soldiers engaged in face-to-face combat, or engaged in individual duels. Yet at the same time, clever, inventive deceptions were also admirable—as long as the tricks did not cross certain bounds. The line between acceptable and reprehensible ruses was difficult to pin down, but classical authors often indicate some generally accepted attitudes.[14]

Wounds in the back were never honorable, signaling cowardice or treachery on someone's part (the *Iliad*, the *Fall of Troy*, and other poems are filled with exhortations to face the enemy and avoid getting hit in the back or being taken by surprise).[15] Individual courage, working together as a group, physical strength, military prowess, and steadfastness were key—and poison weapons and ambush undermined every one of those values. The mythic episodes pose a timeless question, deeply disturbing to warriors of any era: What good are bravery, skill, and strength when your enemy attacks deviously with weapons made ever more deadly with poison?

After the carnage on the battlefield cut down the best of the Greek and Trojan champions, Odysseus devised the ingenious ruse of the Trojan Horse to gain entry to the citadel of Troy. The Greeks sacked the city. Then, after a series of adventures recounted in Homer's *Odyssey* and other epic poems and legends, the Greek victors returned home. After the destruction of Troy, a party of Trojan survivors led by their hero Aeneas set off for Italy to found Rome, described by the great Latin poet Virgil in his *Aeneid*. His epic poem, written during the reign of Augustus (first century BC), was intended to glorify Rome's legendary past and destiny. Virgil tells us that the Trojans brought their poison weapons with them to Italy. Here is Virgil's description of Aeneas's fellow warrior Amycus: "No man was more skilled at dipping darts and arming metal with poison."[16]

Meanwhile, what became of Heracles's quiver of Hydra-venom arrows after the Greek victory at Troy? According to legend, Philoctetes, like many of the other Trojan War veterans, restlessly wandered the Mediterranean after the war. After fighting various battles as a mercenary with his deadly bow and arrows, he finally settled in Italy. Before he died and was buried near Sybaris, in the toe of Italy, Philoctetes founded a Temple to Apollo at Krimissa. There, the old warrior dedicated his poison weapons to the god whose own divine arrows inflicted plague and pestilence from afar.[17]

▗ ▗ ▗

Ambivalence over the use of poison by Greek heroes stands out in a pair of passages in Homer's *Odyssey*, the epic poem recounting the postwar adventures of Odysseus. After ten years of wandering, Odysseus finally returned home to Ithaca to find his wife, Penelope, and his young son, Telemachus, besieged by a gang of swaggering suitors who had taken over his palace in his absence. The surly interlopers lay about drinking wine and idly speculating about how young Telemachus might try to roust them. Perhaps he'll travel to Ephyra, in Epirus, northwestern Greece, to obtain a poisonous plant that flourishes there, proposed one suitor. "He could drop the poison into our wine barrels and kill us all!"[18]

If Heracles was the mythic inventor of arrows poisoned with snake venom, Odysseus was the first mythic character to poison arrows with plant toxins. Homer tells us that Odysseus, the archer renowned for crafty tricks, once sailed to Ephyra on a quest for a deadly plant to smear on his bronze arrowheads. This explains the suitors' fears about Telemachus poisoning them.

Ephyra in Epirus, near the River Styx and the mouth of the Acheron River of Hades, was a fitting place to gather poisons, since it was famed in antiquity as one of the "gateways" to the realm of the dead. For one of his Labors, Heracles had descended by one of these entrances into the Underworld and dragged out Cerberus, the monstrous, three-headed hound of Hell. Foam from the beast's jaws had flecked the green grass and was transformed into the poisonous flowers of aconite (monkshood). Other plants with potent poisons—such as black hellebore and deadly nightshade—thrived here too, nourished by Underworld vapors so noxious that birds flying over the area dropped dead.

Odysseus had once come here to consult the pallid, embittered ghosts of the Underworld. Three centuries after Homer, in the fifth century BC, the ancient Greek historian Herodotus described a renowned *necromanteon*, an Oracle of the Dead, at Ephyra. Archaeologists have discovered the substantial ruins of an underground labyrinth, whose features match Homer's description of the Halls of Hades in the *Odyssey*. Scholars believe that local hallucinogenic plants were used in the ancient rites of the Oracle of the Dead at Ephyra.[19]

So Ephyra was a poisoners' paradise. But King Ilus, the ruler of the territory, being "a man of virtue," refused to supply Odysseus with the "man-killing" poison. Homer's wording makes it clear that the poison would be used for war, not hunting. Odysseus did finally succeed in obtaining some arrow toxin, from a friend on an island south of Ephyra. But the incident with King Ilus reveals the conflicted emotions about using toxic weapons. Creative trickery, ruses, and deception were respected by the ancient Greeks. Should they admire Odysseus's resourcefulness? Or should they agree with the honorable King Ilus that secret poisoning of foes was never virtuous? Perhaps the answer lies in what happened to those who resorted to poison weapons.

Given Odysseus's involvement with shrewd ruses and arrow poisons, it is no surprise that Odysseus himself was killed by a toxic spear, at the hands of his other son, Telegonus. Unknown to Odysseus, Telegonus had been born to Circe, with whom Odysseus had dallied on the long way home after the Trojan War. A sorceress-goddess who knew the powers of many mysterious *pharmaka* (drugs, chemicals, and poisons), Circe had enchanted Odysseus's men with a potion that turned them into swine. This was by no means the first time Circe used drugs to obtain a desired outcome. She had also once poisoned an entire river with "evil herbs, whose juices contained horrid powers," in order to destroy an enemy.

With a mother like Circe and a trickster father like Odysseus, it was not surprising that Telegonus would use a poison weapon. The youth had journeyed to Ithaca searching for his father. When he first encountered Odysseus, however, he mistook him for an enemy and ran him through with his lance. The spear was tipped with a barb of truly diabolical and ingenious design—the poisonous spine of a stingray.[20]

* * *

Awareness of the principle of biological weapons, so evident in the archaic Greek myths about Heracles, Philoctetes, Odysseus, and Apollo, obviously existed long before the first historical reports of the use of poisons in warfare. Myths are not historical evidence, of course, but myths can tell us what the ancients thought about themselves and what they thought was important, and the mythic stories helped to shape their thinking about the use of real biological and chemical weapons. One of the most remarkable features of these myths is the very early recognition of the ethical and practical questions that surround such methods. Again and again, the ancient myths drive home the idea that, once created, weapons based on poison seem to take on a life of their own, with tragic consequences that can extend over generations. Not only are biological weapons difficult to direct with precision, but they are almost impossible to destroy once created.

If the myth of Heracles and the Hydra was a poetic account of the real historical invention of envenomed arrows in the deep past, then Heracles was the perfect figure for the role. In his celebrated Labors and exploits, Heracles impulsively used his weapons to destroy all manner of monsters and enemies. Significantly, however, Heracles always managed to leave chaos in his wake. He was a paradoxical figure for the Greeks. An admired destroyer of monsters, Heracles also frequently brought destruction to those he hoped to protect.

The playwright Sophocles made it clear that when Heracles dipped his arrows in the Hydra venom, he was creating the possibility—even the inevitability—of his own death by the same agent. And his poison arrows certainly left a long trail of tragedy.[21]

The image of the "Many-Headed Hydra" has come to symbolize a multifaceted, thorny dilemma that generates new obstacles each time one difficulty is overcome or resolved. Indeed, the Hydra is a wonderfully apt symbol for the problems set in motion by biological weapons. The nightmarish image of infinitely replicating heads, the impossibility of ever completely destroying the monster, and the perils of unintended casualties: these are vivid details that capture the moral and practical dangers of creating and handling biochemical agents of destruction.

Like Heracles, Philoctetes was another complex, contradictory figure whose tragic story fascinated the Greeks. One of the many unintended victims of the Hydra arrows, Philoctetes survived to destroy multitudes of Trojans with the same arrows that had brought him so much suffering. Yet at the end of his life, Philoctetes decided to store the terrible bow and quiver safely in a temple of Apollo, instead of passing them on to another warrior. This conclusion to his legend suggests a mythic model for trying to contain the proliferating Hydra heads of biological warfare. The indestructible head of the Hydra monster still lurked somewhere under the earth, but at least the hellish Hydra-venom arrows could be retired from the battlefield, to be guarded by Apollo, who was also the god of healing.

The other heroes implicated in the use of bioweapons—Achilles, Paris, and Odysseus—were also ambivalent figures, fitting vehicles for provocative stories about challenging the ideals of fair combat. Homer's deep understanding of human nature allowed him to show how noble virtues vied with dishonorable impulses in these heroes' all-too-human characters. In the *Iliad*, Achilles was the brightest star among the Greek warriors, but he was also a savage berserker who committed reprehensible outrages against Hector and other Trojan foes. Paris, the playboy-warrior who started the Trojan War by taking up with Helen, was berated as a coward by his own brother, Hector, and by his lover, Helen. And the wily Odysseus was the quintessential trickster-warrior, always ready to stoop to devious weapons and ploys. All three of these heroes lived and died by poison weapons.

The mythic consequences of Heracles's invention convey a strong warning for those who contemplate the use of biological armaments. The fates of the ancient biowarriors fulfill an age-old folklore motif of poetic justice known as "the poisoner poisoned," in which each hero who employed poison weapons was himself harmed or destroyed by the toxic agents, either by accident or in retaliation. There are many modern military examples that demonstrate how "poisoner poisoned" effects, as well as "friendly fire" accidents, continue to threaten those involved in biochemical arms. In 1943, for instance, in the worst Allied seaport disaster since Pearl Harbor, thousands of American soldiers and Italian townspeople in Bari, Italy, were killed by exposure to poison gas when a US ship secretly carrying two thousand chemical bombs was shelled in the harbor by German aircraft. A more recent example is the cluster of health problems suffered by US troops who destroyed Iraq's biochemical munitions in the Gulf War of 1991. In 2003 it transpired that many of the biological agents used to create those weapons had come from the United States during the 1980s.[22]

Another telling feature of the mythology of biochemical warfare is the way the elements of poison, contagion, and fire are intertwined. The actions of deadly toxins and images of unquenchable fires are intermingled in several myths, foreshadowing the later historical accounts of military deployments of poisons and disease vectors, and prefiguring the invention of Greek Fire, as well as earlier petroleum-based weapons, generally considered to be among the most inhumane agents of war ever invented. Weapons based on poisons, contagion, and combustibles are, of course, the prototypes of modern biological weapons and chemical incendiaries. Amazingly, these elemental agents were already combined in the ancient imagination more than three thousand years before the invention of modern germ warfare, napalm, and nuclear conflagrations.[23]

Poison projectiles, created to inflict extreme suffering and bring ignominious death, were more feared than hand-to-hand combat with swords, spears, axes, and clubs. Poison arrows killed, but never cleanly. In the words of Quintus of Smyrna, they dealt "ghastly wounds that caused the mightiest man to lie faint and wasted with incurable pain." A simple scratch could result in a gruesome, putrefying wound that turned brave warriors like Philoctetes into pitiful, howling subhumans. Even the superhero Heracles was unmoored by the excruciating pain, uprooting trees and overturning altars, rampaging like a wild beast. "I was the bravest, the mightiest, of all time," he bellowed, tearing at the tunic soaked in Hydra-venom, "but now, a plague is upon me, which no amount of courage can withstand!" Images like these were grim indeed for a culture steeped in a warrior ethic, where bravery and physical might were valued above all and death in battle was expected to be violent, but at least swift and honorable.

In antiquity, as today, a blurry line separated acceptable ruses of war from reprehensible tactics and inhumane weapons. For example, Odysseus's subterfuge of the Trojan Horse seems admirably cunning, until we learn that the trick ushered in Greek atrocities against Trojan women and children. Other myths tell of poisoning rivers and wine to kill enemies, or giving lethal gifts that concealed poisons or combustible chemicals. But such weapons violated the guidelines of "fair" conflict and corrupted the meaning of courage and skill on the battlefield, for both victor and victim alike. In the face of hidden poisons and biochemical subterfuge, a warrior's valor was neutralized, and his physical strength and prowess were nullified. In the words of Ovid, subversive weapons of poison were feared and detested because they dealt a "double death." They could kill a man and extinguish his honor as well.[24]

The sheer number of great warriors felled by poison arrows and the numerous unintended casualties in the myths illuminate the powerful impact of the idea of warfare with bioweapons in antiquity. The payoff of such practices in actual conflicts could be substantial. Dipping one's arrowheads into something toxic or infectious would greatly magnify the damage inflicted, and it could be done at a safe distance. Poison projectiles gave confidence to unskilled archers or weak warriors. Even if one's aim was not very accurate (like Paris, who needed Apollo's guiding hand), a contaminated weapon would guarantee a high body count. It is easy to understand the appeal, and easy to imagine that people of the ancient world must have figured out how to create such arms very early in history.

The mythic messages about biotoxic weapons were important to the ancient Greeks and Romans, as shown by the many examples of artwork depicting Heracles killing the Hydra and decimating the Centaurs with poison arrows, Philoctetes's poison wound, the accidental wounding of Heracles's son Telephus by Achilles, and Heracles done in by his own toxic weapons and bequeathing his quiver to Philoctetes. Heracles dying in the poisoned tunic was painted by the famous Greek artist Aristeides in about 360 BC. Another painting on the Acropolis of Athens, admired by tourists as late as the second century AD, showed Odysseus trying to steal the bow and poison arrows from Philoctetes. Heracles's death, Telephus's wounding, and Philoctetes's anguish were also performed on the stage in tragedies by Euripides, Sophocles, and Aeschylus. And, as noted earlier, travelers used to point out the boulder that trapped the Hydra's immortal head under the earth, and honored Philoctetes, the inheritor of the first biological weapons, in at least three different shrines in Italy and the Aegean. Tourists in antiquity could even bathe in the hot spring of Thermopylae, where it was said that Heracles, driven mad by the tunic of burning venom, had plunged.

The legendary tales of Heracles and Philoctetes and other mythic figures were viewed by the ancient Greeks and Romans as reflections of actual historic episodes in their own very distant past. In popular memories, more recent historical events could also blur into legend, and ancient historians' accounts of real military campaigns sometimes echo mythological ones. But, as the following chapters show, detailed reports by numerous Greek, Roman, and other historians provide powerful evidence of how biological and chemical weapons were actually used in warfare.

CHAPTER 2

▰ ▰ ▰ ▰ ▰ ▰ ▰ ▰ ▰ ▰ ▰ ▰ ▰ ▰

ARROWS OF DOOM

To make wounds twice as deadly, these men dip
in viper's venom every arrow-tip.
—OVID, ON THE SCYTHIANS

It was their custom to throw javelins steeped in noxious
juices, thus disgracing the steel with poison.
—SILIUS ITALICUS, ON THE NUBIANS

"THERE IS NOTHING more dangerous than poisons and the bites
of noxious animals," wrote Galen, the great Roman physician
to gladiators and emperors. We can avoid most dangers by
fleeing or defending ourselves, Galen noted, but the toxins from
plants and venomous creatures are treacherous weapons because they strike without warning.[1] The ancients particularly
dreaded encounters with poisonous snakes, a problem that
plagued Alexander the Great and his army in India. Things
only got worse when the Greeks learned that Indian archers
tipped their arrows with snake venom. Alexander's soldiers
may well have recalled the scene in Homer's *Iliad* when the
Trojan archer Paris recoiled from face-to-face battle with the
Greeks. Homer compared Paris to "a man who stumbles upon
a viper in a mountain glen. He jumps aside, knees trembling,

FIG. 6. Roman soldier and horse startled by a snake. Bronze, early sixteenth century, Italian, 64.101.1419, Gift of Irwin Untermyer, 1964, Metropolitan Museum, New York.

face pallid, he backs and backs away." The scene neatly juxtaposes the ancient terror of snakebites with the fear of envenomed arrows (fig. 6).[2]

Facing battle required great courage. Knowing that one's enemies used deadly poisons on their weapons raised the horrors of war to exponential levels. From numerous Greek, Roman, and Indian texts, one learns exactly how virulent arrow poisons were concocted, who used them in the ancient world, and what sorts of countermeasures were attempted.

▰ ▰ ▰

Venomous animals enjoy "great confidence" in attacking, commented the natural historian Aelian, and they are hated by humans because they are blessed with such powerful weapons. Based on his own observations of nature in the third century AD, Aelian surmised that Heracles and other Greek heroes got the idea of using venom on their arrows from seeing wasps buzzing around the corpses of vipers. In antiquity, it was widely believed that stinging insects increased the potency of their stings by drawing venom from dead snakes, and, in turn, that snakes fortified their venom by devouring poisonous plants. A similar principle applied to harmful flowers, like aconite (monkshood), which drew their nutrients from entrances to the Underworld, with its unwholesome vapors. In the same fashion, a man could amplify the strength of his weapons by adding natural plant and animal toxins to them. In Aelian's words, "Heracles dipped his arrows in the venom of the Hydra, just as wasps dip and sharpen their sting."[3]

Today, many people think of biological and chemical weapons as inventions that depend on modern technology, toxicology, and epidemiology. Yet the idea of treating projectiles with noxious substances originated long ago in prescientific cultures, when observers noted that nature endowed certain plants with toxins to defend themselves, and certain creatures with venom to hunt prey and kill enemies. Observation and experiment led to some simple—as well as some surprisingly sophisticated—ways of borrowing natural poisons for projectile weapons.

A great variety of toxins—from wolfbane to snake venom—were weaponized as arrow poisons in antiquity. Snake venom may have been one of the first. In antiquity, the old myth of Heracles and the Hydra was thought to be a poetic exaggeration of the historical invention of arrows tipped with snake venom in the very deep past. Several authors, such as the historians Diodorus of Sicily (30 BC) and Pausanias (AD 150) and the poet Quintus of Smyrna (AD 350), assumed that Heracles's arrows were actually "besmeared with deadly venom of the fell water-snake" or an adder common in Greece. Pointing out that the ancient Greek word *hydra* meant water-snake, Pausanias suggested that perhaps an extra-large *hydra* specimen had inspired the myth of the Hydra monster.[4]

Ancient toxicology treatises from the Mediterranean and India described an impressive array of poisonous plants, minerals, marine creatures, insects, and snakes, along with scores of antidotes and remedies, some useful and others quite dubious. In about 130 BC, for example, the toxicology manual compiled by Nicander, a priest of Apollo at the Temple of Claros in Asia Minor, listed twenty vipers and cobras known in the Greco-Roman world. Descriptions by Nicander and other writers often provide enough details for modern herpetologists to identify the species. Moreover, the medical symptoms of snakebites and arrow wounds contaminated by venom are accurately described in the ancient accounts. First, necrosis appears around the wound, with dark blue or black oozing gore, followed by putrid sores, hemorrhages, swelling limbs, vomiting, wracking pain, and "freezing pain around the heart," culminating in convulsions, shock, and death. Only a very few lucky victims recovered from snake-venom bites or arrows, and sometimes the wounds festered for years, as described in the myth of Philoctetes (chapter 1).[5]

*/ */ */

An effective poison needs an effective delivery system, and the technology of the bow was perfectly suited to the task of killing with confidence from afar, whether the poison arrows were used for hunting or for combat. The first poison arrows were probably used for hunting, and later turned toward enemies in war. This progression, from hunting to war, is clear in the Greek mythology of poison arrows. Heracles's great quiver held some arrows for hunting animals and others for smiting foes. And indeed, the first victims of his Hydra-venom arrows were not humans, but a deer with golden horns, the Stymphalean Birds, and the half-man, half-horse Centaurs. Then, after Heracles's death, the arrows were inherited by Philoctetes, who intended to use them in the war against Troy. But their use on the battlefield was delayed until the tenth and final year of the war, while Philoctetes was marooned on the desert island. Philoctetes used the poison arrows to hunt birds for food for a decade before slaughtering any Trojans.[6]

According to the Roman medical writer Celsus, hunters in Gaul (Celtic people of western Europe) used serpent venom to bring down game, because it did not poison the meat (snake venom is safely digestible). Mirko Grmek, a scholar of the history of medicine, and the classicist A. J. Reinach have suggested that the Greeks and Romans thought of poison arrows as essentially weapons for hunting, and therefore disapproved of their use against fellow humans. Indeed, arrow poisons intended for hunting and those prepared for war differed in crucial ways.[7]

To be effective in hunting, the ideal toxin should be fast acting and lethal even if the wound was slight. Poisons that ruined meat should be avoided. But war arrows were very different. The most malignant toxins were selected, with the deliberate intention of inflicting a horrible death or an incapacitating, unhealing wound. Pure snake venom might be used on hunting arrows, for example, but for combat with foes the venom was contaminated with the most debilitating or disgusting ingredients for maximum physical and psychological impact. Killing cleanly and swiftly was *not* the point of poison military projectiles.

Surprising the enemy with biochemical weapons was one option, but there were also significant advantages if your enemies knew that archers were shooting arrows coated in virulent substances. The armies that used poison arrows in war seem to have calculated the terror impact on potential enemies. They made sure that their recipes for treating war arrows promised a gruesome death, and that these formulas were well publicized. Just as it is today, deterrence was an important factor in creating biological weapons.[8]

✦ ✦ ✦

Let's look first at the botanical options for arrow poisons. The ancients knew of at least two dozen dangerous plants that were used for medicinal purposes and could also be employed to create toxic weapons. As in modern pharmacology, the dosage drew the line between therapy and death. In very small amounts, many plant toxins are beneficial, while in larger amounts they are lethal—and some, like aconite, can kill even in tiny doses (see plate 3).

Some substances mentioned by Greek and Roman historians, such as *helenion* and *ninon*, smeared on arrows by the

Dacians and Dalmatians (ancient peoples of Romania, Hungary, and former Yugoslavia), have not been identified by modern scientists. But most of the arrow poisons named in the sources are well-known toxins. One of the most popular was hellebore, the all-purpose medicinal herb and the favorite prescription of doctors, including the father of medicine, Hippocrates. Two kinds of hellebore were identified by the ancients: black hellebore, the Christmas rose of the buttercup family (*Helleborus orientalis*), and white hellebore, a Liliacea (*Veratrum*). Interestingly, the plants are not related, but both are laden with dangerous chemicals so plentiful and diverse that it is surprising that anyone ever survived treatment. It was well known that hellebore killed horses and oxen, and people who collected hellebore sometimes fell ill or died. The plants were "not easy to gather, and very oppressive to the head," noted Pliny the Elder, the natural historian of the first century AD. In tiny doses, the roots caused sneezing or blisters, but in heavier doses they induced severe vomiting and diarrhea, muscle cramps, delirium, convulsions, asphyxia, and heart attack.

It was the immediate purgative effect that made hellebore a pet prescription for all manner of complaints. It's clear that some patients survived merely because the vomiting and diarrhea were so violent. As Pliny remarked, hellebore's reputation evoked such "great terror" that treatment required much courage—on the part of both doctor and patient. Indeed, wrote Pliny, "the various colors of the vomits are terrifying to see, and after that comes the worry of watching the stools!"[9]

Hellebore was obviously an excellent choice for arrow poison. Some ancient writers reported that hellebore was one of the "arrow drugs" used by the long-haired Gauls to hunt wild boars and other game. The hunters had to "run hastily" to cut away the flesh around the arrow before the poison sank in and the meat rotted, although the Gauls claimed that a small amount of hellebore tenderized the flesh of hares and deer. Today, traditional hunters in Tanzania, who use the plant poison *panjupe* on their arrows, also rush to pull out the arrow and discard the meat around the wound.[10]

The fact that the Gauls knew of at least two antidotes for hellebore poisoning suggests that they worried about self-inflicted injuries from hellebore arrows. The collection of hellebore and many other baneful plants in antiquity was surrounded by special rituals to avoid accidental poisoning, and the preparations of arrow drugs were time-consuming and delicate. To dig up hellebore, for example, one first prayed facing east, then incised a circle around the plant with a sword, all the while keeping an eye out for an eagle—to spot one spelled death for the herbalist.[11]

Another oft-mentioned arrow drug, brilliant blue flowering aconite or monkshood (sometimes called wolfbane), is one of the most dangerous plant poisons known to humankind. A minuscule amount brings tingling, giddiness, and a sensation of ants crawling over one's body; then it paralyzes the nervous system, with chills, drooling, and vomiting. Finally, the limbs go numb and death results. The excessive salivation may be the reason the poison was associated in Greek myth with a mad dog foaming at the jaws. Aconite may have been the arrow toxin sought by Odysseus in Ephyra, near the mouth of the Underworld (chapter 1). According to Pliny, a town on the Black Sea, Aconae, was held in "evil repute" because of its abundance of aconite plants. Notably, the name "aconite" derives from the ancient Greek word *akon*, for dart or javelin, which suggests that the tips were poisoned with the plant.[12]

Himalayan aconite (called *bish* or *bikh*) was so lethal that sheep had to be muzzled in its vicinity. This "mountain aconite" was used in ancient India for poisoning arrowheads, and aconite is still used in India by poachers who kill elephants for ivory. In the early 1800s, the Gurkhas of Nepal considered the plant "a great protection against enemy attacks," for they could destroy entire armies by poisoning wells with crushed aconite.[13]

Aconite is a widespread plant, commonly used as an arrow poison. Inuit and Aleut people ground and fermented aconite roots to treat their projectiles, as did the Ainu of northern Japan; aconite was also used to poison weapons in China from antiquity into the twentieth century. During the war between the Spanish and the Moors in 1483, the Arab archers wrapped bits of cotton or linen around their arrows and dipped them in distilled aconite juice. Five centuries later, during World War II, Nazi scientists extracted the chemical toxin aconitine from aconite plants, in order to manufacture poison bullets.[14]

According to Aelian, those who collected *hyoscyamus* or henbane—the sticky, gray-green, bad-smelling weed (*Hyoscyamus niger*) that contains the powerful narcotic poisons hyoscyamine and scopolamine—had to work without touching any part of the plant (all parts of henbane are in fact poisonous). One arcane method was to loosen the soil around the root with a dagger, then attach the stem to the leg of a trained bird. As the bird flew up, it uprooted the henbane. Pliny expounded on the dangers of henbane, which was sometimes used in tiny doses as an anesthetic. "In my opinion," he wrote, "it is a dangerous drug in any form," for it deranges the brain. Henbane poisoning can cause violent seizures, psychosis, and death. Henbane was another of the several arrow poisons said to be collected by the Gauls. Perhaps they used hellebore (with its meat-tenderizing effect) and fast-acting snake venom for game and reserved deadly henbane for their human foes.[15]

Preparing weapons from poisons evoked a lot of anxiety about self-inflicted wounds and "friendly fire" accidents in antiquity. The risks of handling biotoxins were (and still are) very real, as shown by complex preparation methods described by the ancient writers. One can gain further insights into ways the ancients may have avoided self-poisoning by looking at some special procedures for creating poison weapons.

In South America, many rainforest tribes use "poison arrow" frogs to treat arrows and blowgun darts. Batrachotoxins are found in certain frogs, beetles, even birds; there is no known antidote. The frogs secrete the extremely deadly chemical through their skin: one frog contains about two hundred micrograms of poison, and just two micrograms are instantly fatal to a human. The batrachotoxin of one poison dart frog can tip about fifty arrows. To avoid touching the powerful poison, most archers pin down a living frog with a stick and carefully wipe their arrows on the slimy skin. But a safer method invented by the Choco Indians in Colombia yields an even greater amount of concentrated poison. They roast a skewered frog on a stick over a fire, catching the dripping toxin in a bottle, into which they can safely dip their darts.

The Choco practice sheds some light on a puzzling passage in Pliny's natural history about the Psylli, a mysterious nomadic tribe of North Africa. The Psylli were snake charmers, and, as masters of myriad venoms from snakes to scorpions, they were said to be immune to all of them. After describing poisonous frogs and toads known in antiquity, Pliny says that he witnessed the Psylli placing toxic toads in heated pans. North Africa has nine species of toads that secrete bufotoxins. Modern scholars have wondered why the Psylli would have "irritated" the toxic amphibians in this way. Taking into account the Choco methods, however, a more logical explanation might be that Psylli were roasting the toads to obtain their poison, which was said to bring death more rapidly than the bite of an asp.[16]

The Spanish conquistadors were terrified of the poison darts of the indigenous peoples of South America. Despite the thick leathern cuirasses they wore to deflect the arrows, many early explorers died from weapons coated with deadly frog slime and the plant-based toxin curare, an alkaloid that causes fatal paralysis. A mere pinprick from a very tiny curare blowgun dart brings down a human or a large animal. In the Amazon rainforest, individuals carried as many as six hundred tiny curare darts in a quiver. There were horrifying reports that curare was used not only on projectiles, but in hand-to-hand combat too, for it was rumored that some warriors painted their fingernails with the toxin.

The art of preparing curare was extremely hazardous, yet a remarkable number of different combinations of curare arrow poison were invented. The naturalist-explorer Alexander von Humboldt was the first European to witness, in 1807, the mysteries of curare preparation by shamans in South America, a process that took many days and was fraught with danger. In North America, too, shamans were involved in preparing arrow poisons for many different tribes. In view of the secret powers of the Psylli and all the complicated ancient rituals for gathering poisons described around the Mediterranean, it seems likely that in antiquity, too, shamans or mystical herbalists were responsible for creating dangerous arrow poisons and their antidotes. In Gaul, for example, the Celtic wizard-priests called Druids may have prepared the poisons from henbane, hellebore, and snake venom. In Scythia, shamans known as the Agari were masters of snake venom both as a poison and as a healing agent.[17]

An expert in concocting poisons would have mixed the lethal dose of hemlock for the Athenian philosopher Socrates, who was condemned to die by drinking hemlock in 399 BC. Hemlock juice (*Conium maculatum*) killed by "congealing and chilling the blood," in the words of Aelian, but the effects are debated by modern philosophers and toxicologists. Did it really bring a pleasant death for Socrates, as famously described by his friend Plato? Or is death by hemlock excruciatingly painful, as others claim? Some believe that Socrates's "gentle" death draught was actually hemlock mixed with enough opium and wine to numb the violent effects. At any rate, pure hemlock sap on a projectile point would bring sure death, and some ancient writers stated that hemlock was one of the poisons used by the fearsome Scythian archers of the Black Sea area.[18]

Yew, the very poisonous tree known as *taxus* in Latin, has symbolized danger and death since antiquity, and was long used to poison arrows. The tall, dark, and dense tree, often planted in graveyards, has a "gloomy, terrifying appearance," observed Pliny. Yew was so lethal that "if creeping things go near it and touch it at all, they die." Pliny claimed that people who napped or picnicked beneath a yew tree had been known to perish. Yew berries contain a strong alkaloid poison, which brings sudden death by suppressing the heartbeat. Pliny also reported that in Spain, which had been brutally conquered by the Romans in the second century BC, souvenir canteens were carved from yew wood and sold to Roman tourists, many of whom died after drinking from the flasks.[19] Could this have been a sly biological sabotage by the Spanish against their hated oppressors?

Belladonna, the deadly nightshade, was known as *strychnos* to the Romans. Proof that *strychnos* was a very old weapon poison lies in its other name, *dorycnion*. The Latin word means "spear drug," and, as Pliny commented, "before battle, spear points were dipped in *dorycnion*, which grows everywhere." He also noted that *strychnos*-treated spears retained toxicity for at least thirty years. The poison causes dizziness, raving agitation, then coma and death. According to legend, ancient Gaelic berserkers took belladonna before battle as an "herb of courage."[20]

Yet another candidate for arrow poison was the sap of rhododendron, which flourishes throughout the Mediterranean, around the Black Sea, and in Asia. The showy pink and white flowers contain neurotoxins, and the nectar yields a poisonous honey, which was used as a biological weapon against the Romans in Asia Minor (see chapter 5).

⬛ ⬛ ⬛

Poisonous creatures, like the frogs of the Amazon, could also provide arrow drugs. In the Mediterranean, encounters with venomous jellyfish, sea urchins, and stingrays may have suggested the use of marine biotoxins as arrow poisons. The intense pain of a jellyfish sting is like a strong electric shock:

it can depress the central nervous system and bring cardiac arrest and death. Sea urchins have been mentioned as another possible source of arrow poison, since the spines deliver a sting similar to a jellyfish's, and life-threatening infections ensue if the wound is near tendons, nerves, or bone. Stingrays were also greatly feared, for, as Aelian wrote, "nothing could withstand the barb of the Stingray (*trygon*). It wounds and kills instantly and fishermen dread its weapon." Indeed, people had experimented with the stingray's weapon of self-defense. So deadly was the *trygon*, declared Aelian, that "if you stab the trunk of a large, healthy tree with the stingray spine, it withers as though scorched and all the leaves shrivel up and fall off."[21]

In the poetic justice of Greek myth, in which a poisoner is fated to die of poison, Odysseus succumbed to a wound from a spear tipped with the spine of a stingray. As mentioned in chapter 1, the blow was dealt by the son he never knew, Telegonus. The spear was forged for Telegonus by the blacksmith god of technology, Hephaestus, from a large ray killed by Phorkys, a Triton (merman) friend of Telegonus's mother, Circe. Hephaestus forged the ray's spine onto a shaft inlaid with adamantine and gold.[22] Several species of venomous stingrays inhabit Mediterranean waters; the most common is the stingray *Dasyatis marmorata* (*Trygon pastinaca*). The stiff, viciously serrated spine, up to fourteen inches long, is filled with extremely painful poison and makes a jagged, deep, and very bloody puncture. A stab in the chest or abdomen brings quick death. Without modern treatment, a wound anywhere would be likely to develop a fatal infection (fig. 7).

Classical commentators have considered the legend of Odysseus's strange death an example of overwrought myth-

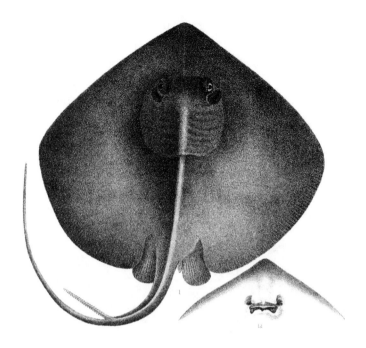

FIG. 7. Stingray, *Trygon pastinaca*, engraving, 1880–84.

making. As it turns out, the idea is not so far-fetched. Modern discoveries in Central and South America give credence to the Greek legend of death by a stingray spine affixed to a spear. In the 1920s, archaeologists were mystified by numerous sting-ray spines that they found among worked obsidian javelin points in ancient burial sites in Mexico and Latin America. The wooden shafts had long since rotted away, but it seems obvious that the sharp ray spines had served as ready-made arrowheads. Confirmation comes from Brazil where, as late as the 1960s, the Suya Indians manufactured arrows from sting-ray barbs, which they attached to wooden shafts.[23]

By far, the most feared toxic creatures in the ancient world were lurking snakes whose fangs dripping with poison brought sudden, agonizing death. Numerous species of poisonous snakes inhabit the Mediterranean region and Asia. The terror aroused by the idea of serpents was intensified when a soldier was the target of arrows steeped in their venom (fig. 8).

According to Greek and Roman writers, archers who "sharpened their arrows with serpent's poison" included the Gauls, Dacians, Dalmatians, Soanes of the Caucasus, Sarma-

FIG. 8. Battle between Greek hoplites and Scythian archers. The fallen Greek had decorated his shield with an image of a snake, perhaps to frighten enemies or to magically deflect snake-venom arrows. Red-figure kylix, 480 BC, Foundry Painter, 31-19-2, Gift of Arthur H. Lea, 1931, photo by Maria Daniels, courtesy of University of Pennsylvania Museum.

tians of Iran, Getae of Thrace, Slavs, Africans, Armenians, Parthians dwelling between the Indus and Euphrates, Scythians, and Indians. Poison projectiles of various sorts were known in ancient China too. Arrows tipped with aconite (monkshood) appeared in the *Pen Ts'ao*, the medicinal treatise attributed to the legendary father of Chinese medicine Shen Nung (probably a compilation of earlier oral traditions, about AD 200). Sun Tzu's *Art of War* mentions poison projectiles. Chinese texts of the second century AD describe the surgeon Hua T'o treating a general's poison arrow wound (with a game of chess and wine serving as the anesthetic). In the same era, the king of the Parthians was killed by a poison arrow in the arm, shot by the nomadic Tochari of the Chinese steppes. Chinese texts also describe a legendary poison called *Gu*; its formulators placed live scorpions, centipedes, and snakes in a vessel or sack and forced them to fight to the death with their poisons.[24]

In Ethiopia of the first century BC, according to the ancient geographer Strabo, a tribe called the Akatharti hunted elephants with arrows dipped "in the gall of serpents." ("Ethiopia" referred to East Africa north of the equator). Several African cultures of more recent times still use snake venom on weapons. Perhaps the Akatharti were the ancestors of the present-day Akamba (Kamba) people of Kenya in East Africa, elephant hunters renowned for their special arrow poison. According to the historian Silius Italicus, writing in about AD 80, Roman soldiers fighting in North Africa faced "twice harmful missiles, arrows imbued with serpent's poison." The Nasamonians of Libya were "skilled at disarming serpents of their fell poison," and the Nubians of upper Egypt and Sudan steeped their throwing javelins "in noxious juices, thus disgracing the steel with poison."[25]

Of all the groups who wielded envenomed arrows, however, the most inventive—and the most dreaded—were the Scythians of Eurasia and the steppes. In the fifth century BC, Herodotus thrilled and shocked the Greeks with his reports of these mounted archers who drank from the gilded skulls of their enemies. The nomad women rode to war too and were nicknamed "man-killers."

Warlike nomads whose vast territory stretched from the Black Sea east across the steppes to Mongolia, the Scythians dominated the region until about AD 300. They successfully repelled the Persian army led by King Darius I in the fifth century BC with their guerrilla raids and ambushes. Their consummate archery skills led the Athenians to hire Scythian bowman to fight alongside hoplite phalanxes in the fifth century. In 331 BC, Scythian horse archers defeated a contingent of the forces of Alexander the Great.

Scythian victories were due partly to their skill with the bow and their hit-and-run tactics, and partly to special weapon technologies. Indeed, they possessed the ultimate delivery system for pernicious biological agents: they had perfected a composite recurve bow whose power far exceeded other bows, allowing velocity and accuracy at great distances. Each Scythian warrior carried more than two hundred arrows into battle, and they were crack archers and expert biowarriors.

When Herodotus traveled around the Black Sea interviewing Scythians in about 450 BC, he discovered that the nomads revered the hero Heracles—the mythical inventor of biological weapons—as their founding father. Parts of the story the nomads told were misunderstood and omitted by Herodotus, who relied on a series of translators, but some intriguing details emerge. What survives of the lost mythology of the Scythians hints that it may have had some parallels to the Greek myth of Heracles and the Hydra-snake, and may have explained the origin of the Scythians' poison arrows. According to the Scythians, Heracles encountered a monstrous Viper-woman in Scythia and fathered three sons with her. He left his bow, arrows, and special belt to the youngest son, Scythes, the ancestor of the Scythians.

Heracles's belt had an unusual design. Hanging from the buckle or clasp was a little gold cup. And "to this day the Scythians wear belts with little gold cups attached," remarked Herodotus. Herodotus did not speculate on the vessel's function. Why would the archers' belt buckles be fitted with a little cup?

I think that the cryptic passage in Herodotus might be explained by the nomads' use of toxic arrows. It seems plausible that the small gold containers held the infamous *scythicon*—"Scythian toxin"—the substance the Scythians used for poisoning their arrows. Pure gold would be unaffected by contact with poison. Recalling the Choco method of gathering frog poison in a bottle for dipping, one can appreciate that it would be efficient and prudent for Scythian archers to dip their arrows into a vial of *scythicon* at the waist. It is interesting that in early vase paintings of Heracles killing the Hydra, the goddess Athena is shown holding out a vial with a narrow opening to catch the venom (see fig. 3).[26]

The Scythians also invented a special combination bowcase-quiver, called a *gorytus*. Artistic representations of these cases on vase paintings and gold artifacts—as well as actual quivers excavated from fifth-century BC Scythian tombs—show the ingenious design of the case. The *gorytus* hung from a belt and had two separate compartments: one

FIG. 9. Scythian archer with bow, drawing an arrow from *gorytus* quiver. Red-figure vase, about 520 BC, 1837.6–9.59. © The Trustees of the British Museum / Art Resource, NY.

held the bow, and the other was a pocket for arrows that could be tightly closed with a flap. This practice and the unique design of the quiver guaranteed that bows and arrows of various sizes and types were at hand for any hunting or battle situation, and the safety flap helped prevent contact with the razor-sharp, poisoned points (fig. 9).

As recently as the 1970s, the Akamba tribe of Kenya (mentioned earlier) carried their poison arrows in a similar combined bowcase-quiver of smoked leather, fitted with a cap to prevent scratches from the points. The Akamba followed further precautions to avoid the perils of handling poison arrows. Arrows for small game have very small, sharp retractable metal tips to carry the toxin; for large game, the poison was smeared on the long stem of the arrowhead. Until the last possible moment, the points were wrapped in soft antelope hide to keep the poison moist and to prevent accidental injury. Similar methods could have been used in antiquity.[27]

Going into battle, the Scythians may have stored precoated arrows in the special safety pocket of the *gorytus*. But when hunting or during a sniping ambush, an archer could dunk an arrow in *scythicon* in the cup or vial on his special belt just before shooting it. This practice would help avoid the kind of nightmarish accident that befell Philoctetes when he was carrying Heracles's quiver of arrows.

The most bloodcurdling ingredient of the *scythicon* was viper venom. Scythian territory is home to several poisonous snake species: the steppe viper *Vipera ursinii renardi*; the Caucasus viper *Vipera kasnakovi*; the Euroasian adder *Vipera berus*, and the long-nosed or sand viper *Vipera ammodytes transcaucasiana*. Simply dipping an arrow in one of these venoms would create a death-dealing projectile, since even dried snake venom retains its neurotoxic effect for a long time (herpetologists working with snake skeletons have suffered envenomation by accidentally puncturing themselves with the fangs of dried-out snake skulls). But the Scythians went much further in manufacturing their war arrows.

The complex recipe for *scythicon* can be reconstructed from statements attributed to Aristotle; from fragments of a lost work by the natural philosopher Theophrastus (fourth century BC); and from the formula given by Aelian. Since psychological terror is a chief aspect of biowar, the method for brewing the poison and its nauseating ingredients were probably gleefully recounted by the Scythian archers serving with the Athenian army in the fifth century BC.

First, the Scythians killed poisonous vipers just after they had given birth, perhaps because the snakes were sluggish then and easily caught. (Most vipers, also called adders, give birth to live young.) Then, the bodies were set aside to decompose. The next step required specialized knowledge, and because shamans were important figures in Scythian culture and the keepers of arcane knowledge, they probably oversaw the complicated preparation of the poison, which required additional ingredients.

One ingredient was taken from humans. "The Scythians," Aelian wrote, "even mix serum from the human body with the poison that they smear upon their arrows." According to Aristotle and Aelian, the Scythians knew a means of "agitating" the blood to separate the plasma, the "watery secretion that somehow floats on the surface of the blood." Theophrastus is cited as the source for this remarkable forerunner of the modern centrifuge, but unfortunately the full description of the technique is lost.[28]

The human blood serum was then mixed with dung, placed in leather bags, and buried in the ground until the mixture putrefied. Dung or human feces itself would be a simple but very effective biotoxin for poisoning weapons. Even without an understanding of modern germ theories, experience would have taught the dangers of dung-contaminated wounds. As the historian Plutarch remarked in the first century AD, "creeping things and vermin spring out of the corruption and rottenness of excrement." Excrement is loaded with bacteria that can cause morbid infections. The "punji sticks" deployed by the Viet Cong against US soldiers during the Vietnam War are a modern example of the use of feces on sharp weapons intended to inflict deep, septic wounds.[29]

In the third step, the Scythians mixed the dung and serum with the venom and matter from the decomposed vipers. The stench must have been overpowering. A comment by Strabo, who was a native of the Black Sea region, seems to confirm this. The Soanes, a Scythian tribe of the Caucasus Mountains near the Black Sea, "used remarkable poisons for the points of their missiles," he wrote. "Even people who are not wounded by the poison projectiles suffer from their terrible odor."[30]

The reek of poison arrows may have been an intentional feature. They were an ancient version of modern "stench weapons" designed by military chemists to be "psychologically toxic" to victims. Modern stench weapons are based on the finding that excrement and rotting corpses are the two universally intolerable odors for humans across cultures—and with good reason, because corpses and feces are sources of potentially lethal pathogens. The logic was evident in the prescientific era, when foul odors or miasmas were thought to actually cause disease. Feces, urine, and other foul-smelling and pathogen-laced substances were used in ancient warfare in China, Europe, and the Americas, as well. Today's modern military stench weapons are artificially concocted powerful malodorants. They are meant to be deployed as "nonlethal" crowd-control weapons, but their toxicity and violent delivery methods can cause injury and death.[31]

Scythian arrow poison was obviously *not* intended for hunting animals. The laborious process of contaminating putrid venomous snakes with blood and feces created a bacteriological weapon clearly meant *only* for human enemies, since no one would eat game tainted by such toxins. As Renate Rolle, an expert on the ancient Scythians, has stated, the result was "a pernicious poison" calculated to cause agonizing death or long-term damage, since "even slight wounds were likely to prove fatal."

Likely indeed: putrefied human blood and animal feces contain bacteria that cause tetanus and gangrene, while the rotting vipers would contribute further bacterial contaminants to wreak havoc in a puncture wound. (Unless it was collected separately, the venom itself would probably lose neurotoxicity if allowed to decompose in the snake.) Rolle consulted Steffen Berg, a forensic physician, who theorized that the poison delivered by a Scythian arrow would probably take effect within an hour. As the victim's blood cells disintegrated, shock would ensue. Even if the victim survived shock, gangrene would set in after a day or two. The gangrene would bring severe suppuration and black oozing of the wound, just as described in the ancient myths of envenomed wounds on the battlefield at Troy. A few days later, a tetanus infection would probably be fatal. Even if a victim miraculously survived all these onslaughts, he would be incapacitated for the rest of his life, like Philoctetes and Telephus in the Greek myths, by an ever-festering wound.[32]

And as if the horrific effects of the poison were not enough, literary and archaeological evidence reveals that Scythian arrow smiths added yet another feature to their airborne weapons: hooks or barbs. Deploring the odious Scythian missiles for their "promise of a double death," the Roman poet Ovid described how victims were "pitifully shot down by hooked arrows" with "poisonous juices clinging to the flying metal." Poison arrows with ingeniously designed breakaway barbs had decimated a Roman army facing mounted archers in Armenia in 68 BC, according to the historian Cassius Dio. The arrowheads had a loosely attached second point that broke off deep inside the wound when the shaft was pulled out.[33]

"In order to render the wound even nastier and the removal of the arrow more difficult," writes Rolle, thorns were affixed to the arrowheads, and others were barbed or hinged. Even a superficially lodged barbed arrow would be extremely tricky and painful to pull out. Projectiles "fitted with hooks and soaked in poison were particularly feared," notes Rolle. Such weapons modified to inflict more injury and pain than conventional arms aroused moral disapproval among Greeks and Romans, who conveniently ignored their own legacy of biological weapons. Interestingly, the ancient criticism of weapons specifically designed to intensify suffering foreshadows modern war protocols that prohibit projectiles that cause "superfluous injury or unnecessary suffering."[34]

The Scythians not only formulated their own extremely potent toxin and figured out how to increase damage by adding barbs to arrows shot from technologically advanced bows; they also invented ways of safely handling their hazardous ammunition with their quiver and belt designs. But their creativity did not stop there. In the 1940s, the Soviet archaeologist Sergei Rudenko was the first to excavate several tombs of Scythian warriors, from the permafrost of the Russian steppes. The graves, dating to the fifth century BC, were filled with equipment, weapons, and artifacts, many of which were accurately described more than two thousand years ago by Herodotus. Gold, wood, leather, wool and silk, metal, and even the mummified bodies of tattooed warriors, were unearthed from the frozen mud, which Rudenko thawed with boiling water.

Since Rudenko, many other archaeologists have excavated more tombs containing male and female Scythian warriors and a wealth of artifacts and weapons. Many bowcase-quivers and arrowheads carved from antler, horn, and bone, and cast in bronze, have come to light. Wooden artifacts are rare in most archaeological sites, but the Russian permafrost preserved quantities of wooden arrow shafts in excellent condition, with the vivid colors of paint still visible (see plate 4).

Many of the shafts (about thirty inches long) were painted solid red or black, while others had red and black wavy lines and zigzags. Rudenko illustrated numerous examples of these arrow shafts in his book, *The Frozen Tombs of Siberia*, but so far no scholars have commented on the curious decorations. Our knowledge that the Scythians treated their arrowheads with snake venom, however, leads to an intriguing idea. Were the striking designs on the shafts inspired by patterns on the skins of snakes? Most poisonous vipers have zigzag or diamond patterns. The Caucasian viper, for example, has a serrated black stripe along its red body, and *Vipera berus* has bold zigzags.[35]

The designs may have been intended to magically empower the envenomed arrows, or they could have been a psychological device aimed at demoralizing the enemy. By painting the shafts to resemble much-feared vipers and making arrows with barbs that replicated fangs dripping poison, the Scythians transformed their arrows into the equivalent of flying snakes. "Snake-arrows" zinging through the air certainly would strike fear into the hearts of victims. The effect would be especially harrowing when a warrior impaled by "a bitter-biting arrow" saw that its shaft carried the patterns of a deadly viper.

The painted markings might also have designated different arrow types for the archer. Quintus of Smyrna commented that Philoctetes carried two different sorts of poison arrows in his quiver, some for hunting and others for killing foes, and many cultures around the world use different types of toxic arrows for war and hunting. Perhaps a certain design was used for arrows coated with pure snake venom to be used for hunting game, while another design marked arrows tipped with the bacterially enhanced and labor-intensive *scythicon* to be used for battles. Solid red or black shafts may have been used for unpoisoned arrows, to serve for target practice and the many contests the nomads held to show off their skills.

Scythian archers' accuracy and range were phenomenal, even on horseback. Archaeologists have discovered skulls of their victims with arrowheads embedded right between the eyes. Pliny wrote that these nomads were so skilled that they used their arrows to dislodge valuable green turquoise nuggets in the rocks of "inaccessible icy crags" of the Caucasus Mountains. From an ancient inscription at Olbia on the Black Sea, we know that a Scythian archer named Anaxagoras won a prize for long-distance shooting. His arrow traveled 1,640 feet (500 meters), far exceeding the average range of an ancient Greek bow, estimated at 900 feet (250–300 meters).

Facing a horde of mounted Scythian warriors was a hair-raising experience. The battle would begin with a hail of hideously poisoned arrows blotting out the sun, as each Scythian archer shot about twenty shafts a minute.[36] And the soldiers, crouching behind their shields, had heard all about the dire effects of *scythicon*. In virulence and the ability to inspire terror in the ancient world, only the poison arrows of India could rival the Scythians' flying vipers.

* * *

India, marveled the ancient writers, was fabulously rich in drugs and deadly plants, and infested with noxious reptiles. Poison weapons could be made from a wealth of nefarious substances, from aconite to bug guts and cobra venom. In the fourth century BC, Alexander the Great's men faced many daunting and marvelous dangers as they marched through India—nearly impassable mountains, strange valleys whose vapors killed birds, weird poisonous plants, scorching heat and thirst, monsoons, deadly serpents of colossal size, and new and bizarre living weapons in the form of Indian war elephants—but the worst were the snake-venom arrows.

One of the most feared poisons of far eastern lands was obtained from the so-called Purple Snake of the "hottest regions" of Asia. According to Aelian, this snake was short, with a deep purple or maroon body and a head as white as milk or snow. It seemed "almost tame" and did not strike with fangs, reported Aelian, but if it "vomited" on a victim, the entire limb putrefied and death usually was quick, although some victims wasted away over several years, "dying little by little."

The Purple Snake has never been identified by modern herpetologists. When I contacted Aaron Bauer, who has studied reptiles in Asia, about Aelian's description, he was struck by two details, the remarkable white head and the habitat in the "hottest part of Asia." If Aelian's account came third- or fourthhand from Southeast Asia, suggested Bauer, the Purple

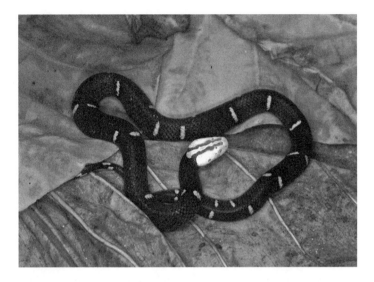

FIG. 10. The Purple Snake of India, as described by Aelian and Ctesias, had a distinctive white head. It may have been the poisonous *Azemiops feae*, discovered by scientists in the late 1800s. Courtesy of R. W. Murphy, Royal Ontario Museum.

Snake would refer to the rare, white-headed viper that was unknown to science until 1888. The *Azemiops feae* viper is the only venomous snake of tropical Asia with a distinctive white head. It is found in south-central China, Myanmar (Burma), and Vietnam (fig. 10). The short and stout body is dark blue-black with red marks and looks purplish, especially as the scales reflect light or if a preserved specimen is observed. Notably, herpetologists describe the *Azemiops* viper as "docile but dangerous," which comports with Aelian's remark that the snake seems "almost tame." This primitive viper has relatively short fangs, which it may or may not deploy, and small venom sacs, which could explain Aelian's report of no fangs and the disastrous result of "vomiting" on a victim. The venom of

Azemiops has not been fully analyzed, but the "long-term effects would be devastating with significant necrosis."

Collecting the toxin of the Purple Snake is difficult and dangerous, says Aelian. To extract the venom, one suspends the reptile alive and head down over a bronze pot to catch the dripping poison, which congeals and sets into a thick amber-colored gum. When the snake eventually dies, the first pot is replaced with another to catch the watery serum flowing from the carcass. After three days, this foul liquid jells into a deep black substance. The two poisons of the Purple Snake are kept separate, as they kill in different ways, both dreadful. The black poison causes a lingering, wasting death over years from spreading necrosis and suppurating wounds. The amber poison (the pure venom) causes violent convulsions, and then the victim's "brain dissolves and drips out his nostrils and he dies a most pitiable death."[37]

Feeling queasy? That reaction was exactly the intention of poison arrow makers in Scythia and India. Just dipping arrows in pure venom would be deadly enough, and, as noted, the venom's protein-based toxins were probably lost during rotting, although they might contribute contamination agents. But soaking war arrows in the most grotesque poisons and broadcasting the horrid recipes to potential enemies was an important psychological aspect of biological warfare. The very idea of facing archers supplied with *scythicon* or Purple Snake poison was a terrifying prospect.

When Alexander the Great and his army advanced over the Khyber Pass from Afghanistan into Punjab in 327–325 BC, India was an unknown land of fabled wonders. The Greek veterans brought back accurate information about the natural history of India, along with some tales that defied belief.

In a decisive battle on the Hydaspes River in northern India, Alexander's soldiers were astounded by the sight of the giant King Porus atop his huge elephant. This was the first time the Greeks had encountered war elephants in action, but Alexander's army managed to defeat Porus by hemming in the elephants and killing the mahouts (drivers) who controlled them (chapter 6).

After that victory, many cities and kingdoms capitulated to Alexander, but others still resisted. It was Alexander's dream to push eastward to the Ganges River and thence to the ocean, but his troops were exhausted by the long campaign so far from home and dispirited by rumors of invincible armies of a powerful kingdom that ruled northern India. Demoralized by the drenching monsoons and the strange deadly plants and terrible serpents of India, the Greeks mutinied and refused to advance.

Alexander conceded to his men's wishes. His army followed the Indus River south to the Indian Ocean, where his forces divided, half heading home by sea and the others trudging west through the waterless wilderness of Gedrosia (southern Pakistan and Iran) with their leader.

As they pressed south, Alexander's men met with many adventures and battles with exotic peoples. They encountered an herb that instantly killed their pack mules, and the soldiers suffered eye injuries from the blinding, squirting juice of prickly cucumbers. Men perished from thirst, tropical diseases, and eating unripe dates. And then there were the deadly cobras and vipers. "In the sand-hills," wrote Strabo, "snakes crept unnoticed and they killed every man they struck." Snakebites soon became such a menace that Alexander was obliged to hire Hindu physicians to accompany his army. Any soldier who was bitten was to report to the royal tent for emergency treatment by the Hindu healers.[38]

It was after conquering the Kingdom of Sambus that Alexander and his men arrived at the fortified city of Harmatelia, in 326 BC (probably Mansura, Pakistan). Here, the Greeks faced a "new and grave danger," wrote the historian Diodorus of Sicily. The Harmatelians were reported to be oddly confident of victory. When three thousand warriors rushed out of the city to meet Alexander's army, the Greeks discovered the source of their confidence.

The Harmatelians "had smeared their weapons with a drug of mortal effect." The historian Quintus Curtius says their swords were poisoned, and Strabo says their arrowheads, carved of wood and hardened in fire, were also steeped in poison. Diodorus elaborated further: he says the poison was derived from dead snakes, but by a different technique from that used for the Purple Snake. Like the Scythian adders, the snakes of Harmatelia were killed and left to rot in the sun. As the heat decomposed the flesh, the venom supposedly suffused the liquefying tissue. It is interesting that both the Scythians and the Indians used the entire bodies of vipers to make arrow poisons. A recent herpetological discovery suggests a good reason. Not only would the rotting flesh of any prey in the snake's stomach contain harmful bacteria, but researchers have learned that vipers retain surprisingly large amounts of feces in their bodies over many months. In a dead viper, the volume of rotting excrement would contribute further foul bacteria to the mixture.[39]

Diodorus's description is vivid. The wounded men went immediately numb, then suffered stabbing pains and wracking convulsions. Their skin became cold and livid, and they vomited up bile. The wound exuded black froth, and then purple-green gangrene spread rapidly and "brought a horrible death." Even a "mere scratch" brought the same gruesome death.

Because India is so famed for its cobras, modern scholars have simply assumed that the poison was cobra venom. I asked herpetologist Aaron Bauer for his expert opinion. Considering Alexander's route through India and the detailed symptoms recorded by Diodorus, Bauer concluded that the venom came from the deadly Russell's viper, *Vipera russelli russelli*, rather than from a cobra species. The symptoms suggest that pure snake venom was used on the arrows; in his description Diodorus apparently conflated other accounts of rotting viper poisons, or perhaps the story was circulated by the Harmatelians to discourage attackers. The Russell's viper venom causes numbness and vomiting, then severe pain and gangrene before death, just as described by Diodorus, whereas death from cobra venom is relatively painless, caused by respiratory paralysis.

Watching so many of his men, even those with only slight wounds, die one after another in agony, Alexander was deeply distressed. He was especially aggrieved by the suffering of his beloved general Ptolemy, who had been grazed on the shoulder by an envenomed arrow. According to Diodorus and Curtius, one night Alexander dreamed of a snake carrying a certain plant in its mouth (according to Strabo's version, a man showed him the plant). The next morning, Alexander found the herb and applied a poultice of it to Ptolemy's blackened wound. He also made an infusion of it to drink. With this therapy, Ptolemy recovered, as did a few other wounded men. Seeing that the Greeks had discovered the antidote to their arrows, the Harmatelians surrendered.

Strabo surmises that the fantastic story of Alexander's healing dream was fabricated after someone—probably one of the
Hindu doctors accompanying the Greek army—informed him
of an antidote for the snake-venom arrows. Indian physicians
were experienced in treating snakebites and wounds made
by snake-venom arrows. They would have immediately recognized by the symptoms what kind of venom Harmatelians
were using on their weapons.[40]

The use of poison arrows for war was common in India,
and yet, as in many other ancient cultures, the practice
aroused mixed reactions. Toxic weapons violated the traditional Hindu laws of conduct for Brahmans and high castes,
the *Laws of Manu*. The laws, recited over generations in oral
verses, date back to about 500 BC (some say even earlier), and
were therefore known at the time of Alexander. The *Laws of
Manu* proscribed the use of arrows that were "barbed, poisoned, or blazing with fire."

The *Laws of Manu*'s principles of correct and noble warfare for Brahmans were countered, however, by another
treatise from the time of Alexander's adventures in India, the
Arthashastra. This book on ruthless statecraft is attributed
to Kautilya, the Brahman military strategist for King Chandragupta, ruler of the Mauryan Kingdom who rose to power
in about 323–320 BC. The *Arthashastra* has been described
as "revolting" and "cynical" by the medical historian Guido
Majno, but political scientists and historians see it as a fascinating and valuable example of ancient realpolitik. Kautilya
advised King Chandragupta to use any means, with no moral
constraints, to attain his military goals, and enumerated an
astonishing number of methods to secretly poison enemies,
including several complex recipes for creating biochemical

weapons, based on venomous snakes and other noxious ingredients. The Harmatelians (identified as Brahmans by the ancient Greek historians) probably felt justified in using toxic measures similar to those recommended by Kautilya to defend themselves against such a formidable foreign invader as Alexander the Great.

How many of Kautilya's biochemical recipes were actually put into practice is unknowable, but the deterrent effect of the weird, loathsome ingredients may have been part of the book's impact. Indeed, Kautilya himself referred to the valuable propaganda impact of exhibiting the frightening effects of his poisons and potions to induce "terror among the enemy."[41]

In a startling revival of ancient biowarfare in modern India, Kautilya's *Arthashastra*, compiled some twenty-three hundred years ago, became the subject of intensive study by Hindu military experts and Pune University scientists in 2002. Funded by the Indian Defence Ministry, the scientists began researching Kautilya's ancient "secrets of effective stealth warfare" and biochemical armaments to use against India's enemies. According to reports by the BBC and other news agencies, the military scientists experimented with ancient recipes reputed to give armies special biological powers, such as a potion of fireflies and wild boar's eyes to endow soldiers with night vision. Special shoes smeared with the fat from roasted pregnant camels or the ashes of cremated children and bird sperm are supposed to allow soldiers to walk for hundreds of miles without fatigue. The scientists also studied Kautilya's formulas for powders from nefarious substances that were intended to cause madness, blindness, or death in one's adversaries.

The Indian military experiments might be dismissed as magical thinking. Yet the Hindu scientists are not alone in the search for unusual biochemical agents to give armies special biological powers. For example, in 2002 military scientists funded by the Defense Advanced Research Projects Agency (DARPA) of the US Defense Department initiated a search for special stimulants and agents based on "genes in mice and fruitflies" that would eliminate the need for sleep in American soldiers.[42]

▰ ▰ ▰

The possibilities for creating arrow poisons from natural toxins were myriad in the ancient world, and the search for antidotes and treatments for poison wounds kept pace. Remedies for envenomed wounds in Greek myths reflected the actual treatments used by battlefield doctors. For example, the festering wound suffered by Heracles's son Telephus, caused by a puncture from Achilles's poisoned spear, was cured with iron rust. Pliny described a famous painting that depicted Achilles using his sword to scrape rust from his spear into Telephus's wound (a relief sculpture of the same scene was found in the ruins of ancient Herculaneum: fig. 11). According to Pliny, scrapings of iron rust and bronze verdigris mixed with myrrh staunched oozing poisoned wounds. Archaeologists have discovered sets of rusty nails and old metal tools for this very purpose in Roman military surgeons' kits. The effect of rust on poison arrow wounds is unknown, but iron oxide does have healing properties and is used in modern medicine. Myrrh has antiseptic properties.[43]

The physician Rufus of Ephesus (first century AD) advised military doctors to ask deserters and prisoners of war about

FIG. 11. Telephus's poison wound treated with rust scraped from Achilles's spear. Marble relief, found at Herculaneum. Museo Archeologico Nazionale, Naples. © DeA Picture Library / Art Resource, NY.

their army's use of poisons, so that antidotes could be prepared. Purple spurge and the gum resin from giant fennel were supposed to be effective against envenomed arrows, according to Pliny, who also recommended a plant called "centaury" or "chironion" (*Centaurium*), after the Centaur Chiron. An astringent for drying up septic wounds, centaury's power to close torn flesh was "so strong that pieces of meat coalesce when boiled with it." Supplies of centaury have been discovered by archaeologists in the ruins of ancient Roman military hospitals in Britain.

Pliny claimed there was an antidote for every snake venom, except the asp (cobra). Aelian agreed that the victim of asp venom was "beyond help." Some antidotes, such as rue, myrrh, tannin, and curdled milk, were beneficial or at least harmless; others were dangerous, and still others seem downright silly, such as boiled frogs, dried weasel, and hippopotamus testicle.[44]

There were also notions of trying to develop resistance to snake and other venoms. It was well known that natives of lands with venomous creatures such as scorpions or snakes often had some immunity to the toxins, so that a scorpion sting simply itched or a snakebite merely stung. The resistance of some natives was said to be so powerful that their breath, saliva, or skin repelled vipers or cured their bites. The Psylli of North Africa were considered the outstanding example of this kind of resistance. According to the Romans, the Psylli were so habituated to snakebites that their own saliva was an effective antivenin. Antivenin is derived from antibodies to live snake venom, and the implication is that the Psylli achieved immunity by the same antiserum principle. Psylli saliva was eagerly sought by the Romans to counteract snakebites during their African campaigns.[45]

It was also a belief in antiquity that ingesting poisons in small amounts, along with the proper antidotes, could offer protection against the poisons, a concept related to the modern techniques of immunization. The idea is evident in the ancient Hindu *Laws of Manu*, which advised kings to mix antidotes to poisons in their food. King Mithradates VI of Pontus on the Black Sea (chapter 5) was the most famous practitioner of this systematic poison-resistance program in antiquity.[46]

Another remedy for snake poison was to try to remove the venom from the victim. Philoctetes's festering wound from the Hydra-venom arrow was cured when the poison was sucked out and a poultice applied. This was the standard remedy for both snakebite and poison arrow wounds, which were characterized by black gore instead of bright red blood. Warriors felled by toxic arrows were immediately tended by army doctors who either sucked the venom themselves or applied leeches, salves, or suction cups to draw out the poison.

Sucking out snake venom by mouth could be hazardous for the doctor, though. The death of a medicine man in Rome in about 88 BC demonstrates the peril. While exhibiting his snake-handling skills to fellow practitioners, he was bitten by one of his cobras. He managed to successfully suck out the poison himself but was unable to rinse out his mouth with water soon enough. Aelian recounts the horrible result: the venom "reduced his gums and mouth to putrescence" and spread through his body. Two days later he was dead. To avoid such an accident, Trojan doctors used leeches, while Indian doctors stuffed a wad of linen in their mouths as a filter.

The medical writer Celsus, writing about a hundred years after the Roman snake handler's death, recommended a cup to suction out the poison, but if none was available, the alternative was to send for someone adept at drawing out venom by mouth. The fabulous reputation of the Psylli, whose saliva was said to neutralize serpent venom, was probably a misunderstanding on the part of inexperienced observers who had watched a Psylli healer sucking out venom. According to Suetonius, the future emperor Augustus sent for Psylli snake charmers to suck venom from Cleopatra's fatal asp bite in 30 BC. The physician Celsus revealed that their skill actually came from "boldness confirmed by experience." He correctly pointed out that anyone "who follows the example of the Psylli and sucks out a wound will be safe," provided that "he has no sore place on his gums, palate, or mouth."[47]

Snake venom can be digested safely, as long as no internal abrasions allow it to enter the bloodstream. That fact was also understood by Lucan, a Roman historian in the first century AD. Lucan described, in page after page of lurid details, the "unspeakable horrors" of death by various snakebites and scorpion stings during Cato's arduous Civil War campaigns in the North African desert in the first century BC. The Psylli came to Cato's rescue. Just as the Hindu doctors skilled in treating snakebites aided Alexander the Great in India, the Psylli joined Cato's army to treat the constant stream of snakebite victims carried into their tents. Whereas the Hindu doctors recognized the species of venom on the Harmatelian arrows by the symptoms of the wound, Lucan claimed the Psylli could identify the species of snake by the taste of the venom. The Psylli apparently encouraged the notion of their special immunity to boost their monopoly on curing envenomed wounds, and soon after the Civil War some Psylli practitioners were in Rome plying their arcane toxicology skills. They were criticized by Pliny and Lucan for importing deadly poisons and venomous snakes and scorpions of many exotic lands into Italy for profit. Apparently the Psylli had become purveyors of poisons for nefarious plots.[48]

In ancient India, doctors were well versed in dealing with snakebites, but removing arrows, including those coated in venom, was a special skill of the *shalyahara* ("arrow-remover"). These surgeons had to decide whether to pull the shaft out or push it all the way through the body. Sometimes they used magnets to locate and help draw out iron arrowheads, and sometimes tree branches or horses were used to jerk a deeply embedded arrow out speedily, with the hope that it was not barbed. Barbed weapons "have always been the curse of battlefield surgery," remarks the historian of battle wounds and treatments Guido Majno. In the Mediterranean world, however, special instruments were designed to deal with barbed arrowheads, like those of the Scythian nomads. In about 400 BC, Diokles of Karystos invented a tool, called the "spoon of Diokles," to ease a hooked arrow out without further damage to the flesh.

But in spite of all the remedies, antidotes, panaceas, and drastic emergency treatments—and Alexander the Great's legendary dream—the grim sight of black blood trickling from an arrow wound was cause for despair. A terrible toxin was already coursing through the body, which almost always spelled doom. The survival rate of real-life warriors pierced by poison projectiles was slim, probably no better than the dismal rate of recovery in Greek myth, where only two victims, Telephus and Philoctetes, recovered, and then only after years of suffering. Even Chiron the Centaur died, despite treatment with a special healing plant, and antidotes were futile in the cases of Achilles, Paris, Odysseus, Heracles, and the many other mythic warriors felled by poison weapons. In the event of biologically contaminated wounds on real-life battlefields, the reaction among warriors was undoubtedly "gloom and frustration."[49]

Despite the perils of obtaining and handling the hazardous materials to make toxic weapons—and the moral disapproval that often clouded their use—the guaranteed casualty rate, the vast arsenal of natural toxins, and the lack of effective antidotes, plus the advantages of long-distance projectiles, made poison arrows the most popular bioweapon in antiquity. But a great many other natural agents were also manipulated to achieve military victories. The next two chapters look at delivery systems for poisons and contagion, capable of destroying enemies en masse. With the ancient myths as models, instead of picking off one's foes arrow by arrow like Heracles or Odysseus, one could copy the sorceress Circe and poison entire bodies of water—or even imitate the god Apollo and spread contagion.

POISON WATERS, DEADLY VAPORS

Aquillius finally brought the Asiatic war to a close by the
wicked expedient of poisoning the springs of certain cities.

—FLORUS, 120 BC

SUCCUMBING TO THIRST is a terrible way to die. The Greek
historian Thucydides described the horrific outcome of the
rout of the Athenians after they invaded Sicily in 413 BC,
their worst defeat in the Peloponnesian War. In their failed
siege of Syracuse, the Athenians had destroyed the pipes
conveying drinking water to the city, a common practice
in ancient warfare. But the tide shifted and the Syracusans
retaliated in kind. They chased the demoralized Athenian
forces overland, constantly denying them access to water.
When the parched army, already sickened by swamp fevers,
finally reached a river, chaos erupted as the mass of delirious soldiers trampled each other trying to reach the water.
The Syracusans stood on the cliffs above and slaughtered
the Athenians, who kept on drinking the muddy water, now
fouled with blood and gore, until the river was dammed up
with heaps of bodies.[1]

In the next century, in India, the Greek army of Alexander the Great was so wracked by thirst that the desperate soldiers would leap into wells armor and all. The historian Strabo wrote that the crazed men drowned trying to drink while submerged. Their bloated corpses floated to the surface, corrupting their only available source of water. In this case, the Greek army polluted their own water, but Indian strategists of that era knew many ways of poisoning water along enemy routes.[2]

Cutting off an enemy's water supply to force surrender was one method of attack, but thirst could be compounded by compelling foes to drink foul waters. Actually poisoning the water was a more subtle strategy, especially effective in siege craft. A related large-scale biological ploy was to take advantage of unhealthy terrain. The enemy could be maneuvered into malarial marshes or other environments where bad water or air ensured that illness would take a high toll.[3]

The earliest historically documented case of poisoning drinking water occurred in Greece during the First Sacred War. In about 590 BC, several Greek city-states created the Amphictionic League to protect the religious sanctuary of Delphi, the site of the famous Oracle of Apollo. In the First Sacred War, the League (led by Athens and Sicyon) attacked the strongly fortified city of Kirrha, which controlled the road from the Corinthian Gulf to Delphi. Kirrha had appropriated some of Apollo's sacred land and mistreated pilgrims to Delphi. According to the Athenian orator Aeschines (fourth century BC), the Amphictionic League consulted the Oracle of Apollo at Delphi about Kirrha's religious crimes.

The oracle responded that total war against the city was appropriate: Kirrha was to be completely destroyed and its territory laid waste. The League added a curse of their own, in the name of Apollo: the land should not produce crops, all the children should be monstrous, the livestock too should have unnatural offspring, and the entire "race should perish utterly."[4] The biological disaster described in the curse evokes an eerie "nuclear winter" scene. Then, taking into their own hands Apollo's divine powers of sending sickness, the League destroyed the city of Kirrha by means of a biological stratagem. The event received a remarkable degree of attention from ancient historians.

During the siege of Kirrha, someone "thought up a contrivance." Depending on whose account one reads, four different historical individuals were credited with variants of the plan. According to the military strategist Frontinus (writing in the first century AD), it was Kleisthenes of Sicyon, the commander of the siege, who "cut the water-pipes leading into the town. Then, when the townspeople were suffering from thirst, he turned on the water again, now poisoned with hellebore." The violent effects of the poison plant caused them to be "so weakened by diarrhea that Kleisthenes overcame them."

In the account of Polyaenus (second century AD), "the besiegers found a hidden pipe carrying a great flow of spring water" into the city. Polyaenus says it was General Eurylochos who advised the allies "to collect a great quantity of hellebore from Anticyra and mix it with the water." Anticyra was a port east of Kirrha, where hellebore grew in great profusion. The Kirrhans "became violently sick to their stomachs and all lay unable to move. The Amphictions took the city without opposition."[5]

Pausanias visited the site of Kirrha in about AD 150, more than seven hundred years after its destruction. "The plains around Kirrha are completely barren, and people there will not plant trees," he wrote, "because the land is still under a curse and trees will not grow there." Pausanias attributed the fateful plan to Solon, the great sage of Athens. In this account, Solon diverted the channel from the River Pleistos so that it no longer ran through Kirrha. But the Kirrhans held out, drawing water from wells and collecting rainwater. Solon then threw "a great quantity of hellebore roots into the Pleistos." When he determined that "the water was drugged enough, he sent it back through the city." "The parched Kirrhans glutted themselves on the contaminated water, and of course became extremely ill," wrote Pausanias. "The men defending the walls had to abandon their positions out of never-ending diarrhea." Helpless to respond to the attack, the people of Kirrha were annihilated as the League hoplites overran the city.[6]

The use of a treacherous ruse to breach a city's defenses, which then resulted in further atrocities inside the city, echoes what happened in the legendary Trojan War, in the aftermath of the Greeks' Trojan Horse trick. That subterfuge was followed by the rape of Trojan women and the massacre of children and old people by the Greek warriors.[7] In both myth and history, then, there is evidence that once an army has resorted to insidious strategies outside the traditional conventions of combat, further violations ensue, such as the mass killing of noncombatants. Unconventional strategies often result from frustration, and when devious or unscrupulous behavior appears to be the only way to victory, the door is then opened to atrocities.

The destruction of Kirrha in 590 BC features some other striking mythological coincidences. The town happens to be located near the place where the Centaur Nessus was said to have died of the Hydra-venom arrow shot by Heracles, just west of Delphi (chapter 1). According to ancient legend, the Centaur's rotting carcass poisoned the area's water, making it unhealthy to drink. In the mid-nineteenth century, H. N. Ulrichs of the Bavarian Academy of Sciences discovered a brackish spring near Kirrha that induces violent diarrhea. Possibly, the besiegers' knowledge of that naturally foul spring was the inspiration for their idea of poisoning the Kirrhans' water with the violent purgative hellebore.[8]

The fourth man credited with the plan to poison Kirrha was a doctor named Nebros, an *asclepiad*, or follower of the legendary healer Asclepius, son of Apollo. According to ancient medical sources, Nebros was an ancestor of the great physician Hippocrates, author of the Hippocratic Oath in the fifth century BC. The account, included in the Hippocratic corpus, is attributed to the medical writer Thessalos, reportedly a son of Hippocrates. Thessalos visited Athens in the late fifth century BC as an ambassador from Cos, the seat of Hippocratic medicine. He wrote that after a horse's hoof had broken open the secret pipe carrying Kirrha's water supply during the siege, Nebros helped the besiegers "by introducing into the aqueduct a drug that brought intestinal illness to the Kirrhans, allowing the allies to take the town."[9]

The reported involvement of a doctor in the destruction of the populace of Kirrha is startling. Are we to imagine that Nebros, in sending sickness to Kirrha, saw himself carrying out Apollo's wrath on the town? The god's oracle and the curse were used to justify total war. Trying to rationalize Nebros's participation in the town's destruction, Thessalos avoided naming the drug, although it was identified by all the other sources as hellebore. And Thessalos implied that its debilitating effects were only temporary.

But the implication that the drug's effects were only temporary was duplicitous in this case. Everyone—especially doctors—knew that hellebore was extremely dangerous and that the dosage in medical treatments was notoriously difficult to calibrate. Hellebore was known to kill large animals, and it was used as a deadly arrow poison. Doctors never prescribed hellebore for the old or weak, or for women or children. Clandestinely contaminating a city's drinking water with "a great quantity of hellebore" would sicken not just the guards and soldiers of Kirrha, but all the people inside the city walls, young and old. Taken by surprise and already suffering from thirst, they would have had no time to try to prepare antidotes. To deliberately harm noncombatants was proscribed by the ancient Greek notions of fair war, but during sieges of cities the entire population was considered the enemy.

The ancient attempt to justify use of a "temporary" toxin to soften resistance was echoed in a modern biochemical attack on noncombatants in Iraq, in 1920. After the fall of the Ottoman Empire in 1917, the British occupation of Iraq was resisted by the Kurds. According to Geoff Simons in his 1994 book *Iraq: from Sumer to Saddam*, in 1920 the colonial secretary Winston Churchill proposed a "scientific expedient" to quell the "turbulent tribes" of Kurdistan. He suggested using poison gas as a preliminary measure in bombing operations against the villages. Some British authorities protested that the villagers were defenseless and had no medical knowledge of antidotes. Discounting the protesters' "squeamishness about the use of gas . . . against uncivilised tribes," Churchill claimed that the chemical gas—which had only recently caused such devastation and moral revulsion in the First World War—would inflict "only discomfort or illness, but not death," and would be a good way to demoralize the enemy.[10]

In reality, however, the gas caused blindness, and killed children, the infirm, and the old. Like Kirrha, the Kurdish villages were easily wiped out after the poison was administered. And in keeping with the timeless tendency to further violate codes of war once a rule of fair war has been transgressed, several newly developed inhumane weapons were first tested in Kurdistan with devastating effects.

Mirko Grmek, the Croatian historian of science who devoted his career to medical ethics, has given some thought to the story of Kirrha. He points out that it would be in the interest of Thessalos, a practitioner of the healing arts and a son of Hippocrates, to try to exonerate Nebros, a fellow physician and an ancestor of Hippocrates, for devising a plan that so obviously violated the Hippocratic ideal that a doctor should do no harm.[11] The Hippocratic Oath was not formally written down until the fifth century BC, but earlier doctors in the tradition of Asclepius, like Nebros, were still supposed to heal, not injure. The poisoning of Kirrha is a classic example of using specialized natural knowledge to harm humans rather than to do them good. The incident makes one wonder: Was the unscrupulous role of his ancestor Nebros at Kirrha what moved Hippocrates to write the oath?

We can't know that, of course, but it is fascinating to find a doctor implicated in the first recorded incident of poisoning a civilian population in war. This is the earliest account of a medical professional helping to wage biological warfare, but it is certainly not the last. Nebros's actions have been repeated down through history, and around the globe. For example, an Italian physician was responsible for deploying contagion against French forces in 1495, and French doctors carried out similar acts during the Franco-Prussian War. An American surgeon was court-martialed for deliberately spreading yellow fever during the Civil War. Medical horrors on a vast scale were perpetrated by Nazi and Japanese doctors during World War II, and in South Africa revelations during the 1999 trial of Dr. Wouter Basson—the eminent cardiologist who founded the government biochemical program in the 1980s to create an arsenal of poisons to be used against antiapartheid activists—led to his sobriquet "Dr. Death." Doctors were involved in ghastly experiments with biological weapons in Iraq under Saddam Hussein in the 1980s and '90s, and the regrettable list goes on.[12]

▰ ▰ ▰

The oracle and the curse against Kirrha were used to justify the unusual ferocity of the First Sacred War in 590 BC. A few scholars have suggested that the destruction of Kirrha may have been a legendary event, but the fact that it is mentioned in a recorded speech by the Athenian orator Aeschines and so many other credible writers has convinced most historians that it really took place. As Grmek concluded, whether the defeat of Kirrha by hellebore was legend or fact, the story of the poisoned water—and the attention it received from historians of the age—reveals the deep ambivalence over using biological measures in antiquity. Even the fact that four different men were implicated implies that people were uneasy about assigning blame or taking credit for the act.

Was there a debate outside the walls of Kirrha among the League allies about the morality of using hellebore, just as some British authorities protested Churchill's plan to gas the Kurds in 1920? That we'll never know, but we do know that remorse about the method of the destruction of Kirrha was acted upon in the aftermath of the destruction. In an ancient forerunner to the 1924 Geneva Convention (in response to the bioterror of gassing in World War I), after the battle of Kirrha the defenders of the sacred site of Delphi agreed that poisoning water was unacceptable in a religious war, and among the allies of Delphi should they ever find themselves at war with one another. According to the Amphictionic League's new rule of war, articulated by the Athenian orator Aeschines, contaminating drinking water was to be forbidden in conflicts of a special, sacred, nature.[13]

As military historians note, rules against using biological weapons are nearly "as old as the weapons themselves," but their effect has always been fleeting and inconsistent. For example, the *Laws of Manu*, the code of conduct for high-caste Hindus dating to about 500 BC, is considered the earliest attempt to prohibit biological and chemical strategies in a culture where poisons and subterfuges were pervasive and widely accepted. As described in chapter 2, however, the Harmatelians of India attacked Alexander the Great's army with deadly snake-envenomed weapons, even though the *Laws* prohibited them. When one "fights foes in battle," stated the *Laws*, "let him not strike with concealed [or treacherous] weapons, nor with weapons that are barbed or poisoned or blazing with fire." The *Laws* also advised against "spoiling the enemy's water," and yet the military treatise of the same era, the *Arthashastra*, urged rulers to use a vast arsenal of biochemical weapons.[14]

Despite the good intention of the rule against tampering with water, drawn up after the First Sacred War, many incidents and rumors of poisoning besieged towns and enemy troops were recorded after Kirrha. Not all instances evoked criticism, however. Purely *defensive* biological tactics seemed justified. For example, in 478 BC the Athenians deliberately fouled their own cisterns as they abandoned their city to the Persian invaders led by King Xerxes I. They were following an accepted, age-old defensive practice—known as the "scorched earth" policy—of burning one's own crops and spoiling foodstuffs, water, and other resources in order to leave nothing of use to conquering armies.

The defensive principle legitimated biological strategies against aggressors. But the idea of an *aggressor* surreptitiously poisoning the water supplies of people trapped inside a city, as happened to Kirrha, was more troubling. Evidence that such practices were feared and suspected in antiquity appeared in *The History of the Peloponnesian War*, by the Athenian historian Thucydides. While the Athenians were trapped in their city by the Spartans in 430 BC, a devastating plague broke out in the harbor of Athens (chapter 4). Perhaps recalling the famous story of Kirrha, the Athenians immediately accused the Spartans of poisoning their wells (fig. 12).[15]

After the Peloponnesian War, the general known as Aeneas the Tactician drew on his own and others' wartime experiences to write (in about 350 BC) a siege-craft manual for military commanders. Aeneas recommended several biological tactics. One was to "make water undrinkable" by polluting rivers, lakes, springs, wells, and cisterns. In 1927, the British commentators on Aeneas were shocked and declared that "this horrible practice was against the spirit of Greek warfare."

FIG. 12. Women drawing water at a fountain house. During a siege, a city's water supply could be poisoned. Hydria, 510 BC, 1843,1103.17, Priam Painter. © The Trustees of the British Museum / Art Resource, NY.

But as the Kirrha episode showed, the expedient has appealed to ruthless war leaders from early antiquity onward. Examples can be found around the world, from ancient India and China to the New World. In North America, for example, more than a thousand French soldiers were felled by illness after Iroquois Indians deliberately polluted their drinking water with flayed animal skins in 1710. Tossing animal carcasses into wells was a standard practice during the American Civil War, and in countless conflicts before and since.[16]

Interfering with water by diverting rivers was another age-old environmental ploy in war. Frontinus, the Roman commander and author of *Stratagems*, had campaigned against the savage Silures of Wales, the Chatti of Germany, and "other troublesome people" at the fringes of the Roman Empire. His book, written in a popular style accessible to military leaders, presents numerous examples of clever and successful unconventional war strategies from Greek and Roman history, including the poisoning incident at Kirrha. Frontinus's interests in quelling bellicose tribes, and later his office as manager of aqueducts at Rome, were combined in a section of his book titled "On Diverting Streams and Contaminating Waters."

On diverting rivers, Frontinus wrote of Semiramis, the legendary queen of Assyria (seventh century BC), who boasted in an inscription that she had extended her borders with courageous and cunning conquests: "I compelled rivers to run where I wanted, and I wanted them to run where it was advantageous." According to Frontinus, Semiramis conquered Babylon with a brilliant water trick. The Euphrates River flowed through the city, dividing it in two. Semiramis, who undertook many waterworks projects during her reign, had her engineers divert the river, so that her army could march right into the city in the dry riverbed. Notably, the same feat was attributed by other authors to the mythical witch Medea and to two historical conquerors of Babylon, the Persian king Cyrus the Great and Alexander the Great. Another legendary queen, Nitocris or Nitocret, mentioned by Herodotus, weaponized a river to avenge her brother's murder by his subjects in Egypt. She devised a cunning plot and built a spacious and splendid underground chamber. She then invited his murderers to a lavish banquet in the chamber.

While they feasted, she let the river in upon them by a secret channel and drowned them.[17]

In 143 BC, the Roman commander Lucius Metellus, fighting in Spain, diverted a stream to literally flush out an enemy. The Spaniards had foolishly camped on an easily flooded plain alongside a stream. The Roman legionaries damned the stream and waited in ambush to slaughter the panicked men as they ran for high ground. Some years later, in 78–74 BC, Rome began a difficult campaign in a rugged region of Asia Minor called Isauria (in eastern Turkey). The Isaurians were fiercely independent mountaineers, labeled by the Romans as "brigands and bandits." Publius Servilius, leader of the campaign, finally reduced the fortified towns of Isauria by diverting the mountain streams where the Isaurians drew their water, "and he thus forced them to surrender in consequence of thirst." A couple of decades later, Julius Caesar, on his campaign in Gaul (now France), diverted the water of the city of Cadurci. Because the town was surrounded by a river and many springs, this took a lot of labor, digging extensive networks of underground channels. Then Caesar stationed his archers to cut down any Gauls who attempted to reach the river. The stratagem was successful: Cadurci surrendered in 51 BC.[18]

Polyaenus, a Macedonian lawyer from Bithynia, wrote a military treatise for the Roman co-emperors Lucius Verus and Marcus Aurelius in AD 161. In it he claimed that the mythic hero Heracles had changed the course of a river in Greece to destroy the Minyans because he was afraid to face such skilled cavalrymen in open battle. The story was intended to justify reliance on devious tricks, instead of risky face-to-face battles, for the co-emperors, who were facing a daunting war against the invincible Parthians of Persia (Iran). The Parthians, renowned for their armored cavalry and formidable horse archers, had just invaded the eastern empire and, in fact, were never defeated by the Romans.[19]

Cunning tricks like diverting rivers to gain access to a city or to cause floods are examples of creative unconventional warfare, not biological strategies based on special natural knowledge. Unless such ploys killed entire populations by drowning (as occurred in some Islamic attacks by flooding in the early Middle Ages), diverting rivers aroused little moral tension, because a well-prepared city or army should be able to anticipate or counter such tactics. But secretly poisoning the water or food supplies that the enemy must depend on was another matter—and such insidious practices often raised ethical questions in ancient societies. In the Punic Wars against Carthage in North Africa (264–146 BC), for example, the Romans were accused of polluting wells with carcasses of animals. But many Romans bristled at the idea of resorting to poisons of any sort in warfare, as not in keeping with traditional ideals of Roman courage and battle skills.[20]

Consider the disturbing reports that circulated in Rome after a revolt that was quelled in Asia in 129 BC. It was said that the consul Manius Aquillius had defeated the rebelling cities by pouring poison in their water supplies. Aquillius was a cold-blooded commander notorious for his harsh military discipline—whenever his lines were broken by the enemy, it was his habit to behead three men from each century (a unit of one hundred) whose position had been breached. The *History of All the Wars over 1,200 Years*, attributed to the Roman historian Florus in about AD 120, describes what happened in Asia.

The insurrection, led by Aristonicus of Pergamum, challenged Roman rule in the newly declared Province of Asia

Minor. The rebellion was especially threatening to the Romans because Aristonicus was mobilizing slaves and lower classes, and he was succeeding. Several important cities in Asia Minor had joined the revolt before the Romans arrived in 131 BC. Aristonicus was captured at last and executed in Rome, and Aquillius, wrote Florus, "finally brought the Asian war to a close." But his victory was a clouded one, because Aquillius had used "the wicked expedient of poisoning the springs to procure the surrender" of the rebel cities. Florus was clear about the immorality of such measures. "This, though it hastened his victory, brought shame upon it, for he had disgraced the Roman arms, which had hitherto been unsullied by the use of foul drugs." Aquillius's measures, thundered Florus, "violated the laws of heaven and the practice of our forefathers."[21]

Florus's ringing condemnation of "un-Roman warfare" would have appealed to many Romans. His patriotic nostalgia obscured earlier incidents of well and crop poisonings in the Romans' ruthless wars against Carthage, however, not to mention countless political assassinations by poison during the republic and empire. Tacitus, the moralistic historian of the reigns of Rome's first two emperors, Augustus and Tiberius, referred to similar nostalgic ideals of honor in his *Annals of Imperial Rome*. In AD 9, a rebellion in Germany led by the brilliant chieftain Arminius had resulted in the treacherous destruction of three Roman legions. The Germans had cleverly lured the legionaries into the marshy Teutoburg Forest (near Osnabruck) and slaughtered them as the men and horses foundered in the difficult terrain. A war-chief of the neighboring Chatti tribe wrote to the emperor Tiberius offering to poison Arminius.

Professing to be deeply offended by the offer, Tiberius replied to the Chatti chief: "Romans take vengeance on their enemies, not by underhanded tricks, but by open force of arms." By this "elevated sentiment," commented Tacitus, Tiberius compared himself to noble "generals of old" who had rejected a plan to poison the Greek invader Pyrrhus of Epirus when he was ravaging Italy in 280–275 BC. In that case, Pyrrhus's own doctor, Cinneas, secretly offered to poison Pyrrhus in exchange for money. "We Romans have no desire to make war by trickery," had been their reply to the would-be assassin, and they revealed the plot to Pyrrhus himself.[22]

Historians like Tacitus and Florus and their audiences greatly admired Virgil, the poet-propagandist commissioned by the emperor Augustus to write the epic saga of the glorious origins of Rome and the story of how the legendary forefathers of Rome, the Trojans, had colonized Italy after the Trojan War. The imperial historians chose to overlook a salient passage in Virgil's *Aeneid*, which stated that among Rome's founders there was an expert at poisoning arrows and spears.[23]

*   *   *

Besides poisoning a city's wells, one could take advantage of naturally unhealthy environments—or even create a contaminated environment to sicken and disable foes. Contaminating water and vegetation along the route of an enemy's march was a well-known stratagem in ancient India. Kautilya's *Arthashastra* suggested several poison mixtures for polluting the foodstuffs and drink of the enemy. In book 14, chapter 1, "Ways to Injure an Enemy," he described powders and ointments made from various plants, animals, insects, and minerals that caused blindness, disease, insanity, lingering death, or instantaneous death. Some of the ingredients were thought to have magical properties (crabs, goat hoof, snakeskin, cow urine, ivory, pea-cock feathers), but many others are truly poisonous. There was special smoke to destroy "all animal life as far as it is carried off by the wind," and certain compounds that would poison grass and water to kill livestock. One powerful mixture of toxic plants and minerals could contaminate a large reservoir "one hundred bows long": it killed all the fish and any creature who drank or even touched the water. One could even poison "mer-chandise," such as spices or cloth, and send it to the foe.[24]

Notably, Kautilya also provided remedies for these bio-logical weapons, in case of backfire that threatened one's own troops, or retaliation in kind by enemies. Other Indian writ-ers explained how to counter military poisons too. Accord-ing to an ancient medical treatise by Sushruta, the *Sushruta Samhita*, composed between the sixth and first centuries BC, deliberately polluted water could be detected and purified with mineral and plant antidotes and special rituals. Water that has been poisoned, wrote Sushruta, "becomes slimy, strong-smelling, frothy, and marked with dark lines on the surface. Frogs and fish die without apparent cause [and] birds and beasts on its shores roam about wildly in confusion from the effects of the poison." Countermeasures against biologi-cal contaminants entailed the use of practical agents such as charcoal, clay, and alcohol—which have natural filtering and purifying capabilities against toxins and bacteria—along with magical incantations. For example, Sushruta recommended purification of contaminated water with ashes, an effective form of charcoal filtering. For poisoned ground, stone slabs, and animal fodders, Sushruta listed antidotes such as sprin-kling with perfumes, wine, black clay, and the bile of brown cows, and beating drums smeared with "anti-poisonous compounds." At least, the alcohol in wine and the absorptive clay would have had disinfectant and filtering effects.[25]

⊿ ⊿ ⊿

Avoidance of diseases and unwholesome environments that endangered their men was a key concern for military leaders. Xenophon, the Greek mercenary commander who recorded his memoirs in the fourth century BC, advised leaders to vigilantly guard the health of their soldiers. "First of all, always camp in a healthy place." By this he meant camping where the air and waters were pure, avoiding swamps and other places where the water and atmosphere were insalubrious and caused illness.[26]

Some lakes, streams, and valleys were infected by "miasma," an exhalation or atmosphere known to be harmful to living things (*miasma* is the ancient Greek word for "pollution"). In some places the vapors and waters were said to be so deadly that animals died on the spot and birds flying overhead dropped out of the sky. A number of these locales, such as Ephyra in western Greece, were identified as entrances to the Underworld, where noxious plants thrived on the noxious fumes (chapter 1). The deadly River Styx in the Peloponnese, whose water was thought to have poisoned Alexander the Great, is another example. Modern science shows that some of these locales were in fact geologically active thermal sites, where fumeroles and hot springs emit bad-smelling sulfurous and other poisonous gases from the earth. In antiquity there was a strong association between foul odors and disease, based on experience and observation, and geologists have shown that methane and other fumes released from the earth can adversely affect humans and wildlife.[27]

A mythic explanation was also offered to account for the origin of a stinking marsh in the Peloponnese so baneful that the fish in it were toxic. It was rumored to be the place where a group of Centaurs, wounded by Heracles's poison arrows, had attempted to wash away the Hydra venom. A similar place of noxious exhalations, caused by the poison arrows that killed the Centaur Nessus, was known to exist near Kirrha, the town destroyed by poison (above). The ancient idea that the water, land, and atmosphere had been contaminated by poison weapons from the past finds a modern counterpart in the deadly environmental pollution caused by testing or dumping biochemical and nuclear weapons.[28]

Swamps and marshes in general were considered dangerous to the health, and with good reason: wetlands with stagnant water certainly were breeding places of mosquitoes carrying malaria, which was endemic in certain areas in antiquity. The exact causes of fevers that emanated from swamps were not understood, but the health benefit of draining marshes was already recognized as early as the fifth century BC, when the natural philosopher–doctor Empedocles alleviated the raging fevers (now known to be malaria) that beset the Sicilian town of Selinus. He devised a sophisticated hydraulic engineering plan to drain the swamps there. (Malaria was not fully eradicated from Italian marshlands until the 1950s.)[29]

Virgil, in his first-century BC work on farming, described a pestilence that killed cattle and wild animals, whose corpses then poisoned drinking water (fig. 13). Varro (116–27 BC), an erudite Roman scholar, anticipated modern epidemiology when he stated, "Precautions must be taken in the neighborhood of swamps," because they "breed certain minute creatures which

FIG. 13. Illustration of a pestilence described by Virgil's *Aeneid*: "The air was poisoned and a terrible, insidious sickness" destroyed humans and crops. *Morbetto: Plague in Phrygia*, Marcantonio Raimondi, 1515–16, engraving after Raphael.

cannot be seen by the eyes, but which float in the air and enter the body through the mouth and nose and cause serious diseases." Lucretius, a natural philosopher writing in about 50 BC, also offered a perceptive theory of invisible microbes. "In the earth there are atoms of every kind," and although "certain atoms are vital to us, there are countless others flying about that are capable of instilling disease and hasten death." When these harmful atoms accumulate in mists or in earth rotted by too much water, the "air grows pestiferous." These "hurtful particles enter the body [and] many noxious ones slip in through the nostrils" when we breathe; some enter through the skin; and many are ingested through the mouth. By inhaling polluted atmospheric particles from places like swamps, wrote Lucretius, "we can't help absorbing these foreign elements into our system."[30]

According to the historian Livy (first century BC) the pernicious effects of making camp in unhealthy lowlands also brought disease to the Gauls attacking Rome in about 386 BC. It was extremely hot that year, and the wind blew "choking clouds of ashes and dust" from the conflagrations set by the Gauls in the area. The infection raged throughout the Gauls' camp, and the exhausted survivors piled the corpses in heaps and burned them. Afterward the place came to be called the "Gallic Pyres."[31]

Livy and Silius Italicus described a terrible contagion in the Second Punic War, during the siege of Syracuse in the hot autumn of 212 BC. The disease affected both sides, the forty thousand Romans led by Marcellus and the Sicilian-Carthaginian force of more than fifty thousand led by Himilco. The pestilence arose from intolerable heat and the "deadly stench" of the stagnant marshes: first the dogs and wild animals died; then the soldiers perished by the thousands. Cadavers lay unburied, further polluting the air and water. The "dead wreaked havoc on the sick and the sick on the healthy," wrote Livy. But notably, Marcellus was able to move his troops to higher ground, and the Sicilians among the Carthaginians slipped away at the first sign of the disease. The Carthaginians perished to a man, including their general Himilco.[32]

Looking back to the Plague of Athens during the Peloponnesian War, Diodorus of Sicily surmised that the disease had been a result of floods the previous wet winter, which created marshes filled with "putrid, foul vapors which corrupted the air" and spoiled the crops. The Athenians, trapped in their crowded city by the Spartans that hot summer, he noted, were especially susceptible to disease. By the fourth century AD, it was a commonplace among generals that "an army must not use bad or marshy water." "Foul water is like poison and causes plagues," cautioned the Roman military strategist Vegetius. Moreover, if an army camps too long in one place, the air and water "become corrupt [and] unhealthy." Without frequent changes of camp, he wrote, "malignant disease arises."[33]

Xenophon's advice to always camp in a healthy place was based in part on his knowledge of what befell the Athenians on their ill-fated expedition against Sicily in 415–413 BC. The swamp fevers, mentioned earlier, that decimated the Greeks during the Sicilian disaster were described by Thucydides, Diodorus of Sicily, and Plutarch. These historians all agreed that the Athenians' crushing defeat in Sicily was attributable in part to fevers (now identified as malaria) contracted in the marshes where they made their summer bivouacs. Diodorus of Sicily pointed out that later, in 396 BC, the Carthaginians would bivouac in the same marshy hollow where the Athenians had camped and were annihilated by pestilence. The Carthaginians would be decimated again in 212 BC in the same campsites, as noted above.[34]

It is not clear whether the Athenians made the fatal mistake of camping in malarial swamps on their own, or whether the Sicilians "took particular measures to lead the Athenians into such noxious conditions." But, as Thucydides repeatedly demonstrated, the Sicilians were hyperaware of denying advantageous terrain to the Greeks, constantly depriving them of water and opportunities for foraging.[35] The local people were also very familiar with endemic pestilence of the region around Syracuse. It's plausible that the Athenian invaders succumbed to a biological subterfuge by the Sicilians.

Some modern military writers exclude maneuvering armies into "unsanitary" areas from their discussions of biological warfare, but as Grmek notes, in antiquity this was an effective strategy based on sound biological knowledge. Knowing the ill effects of local marshes and rank water, an astute commander would ask, How can I manipulate these naturally malignant miasmas against my enemies? Luring or driving an enemy into these virtual minefields of microbes could be decisive.[36]

The German tribes were masterful at maneuvering enemies into lethal landscapes. When the Romans were fighting the Teutons in 106 BC, the military writer Frontinus assumed that the Roman engineers "had heedlessly chosen a campsite" near the Germans' stronghold without realizing that the only water supply was the river flowing along the enemy palisades. Teuton archers would pick off anyone who attempted to drink. In this case, though, the site may have been selected by the commander, Marius, on purpose. Plutarch says that Marius intended to goad his men into attacking fiercely by the biological expedient of thirst. When his desperate soldiers complained, he pointed to the river between the camp and the Teuton fort. "There is your water," replied Marius, "but it must be bought with blood." The Romans begged to be given the order to storm the fort "before our blood dries up!"[37]

Recalling Germanicus Caesar's arduous campaigns in Germany in the first century AD, Pliny the Elder noted that noxious plants and beasts were not the only treacherous things in the countryside. Certain geographical areas and their waters were also "guilty of harm." The Germans consistently forced the Romans to fight and camp in unhealthy marshes and boggy woods (especially around modern Osnabruck), where the legionaries were easily ambushed and suffered extremely heavy losses. Tacitus described the emotions of Germanicus and his men when they came upon the jumbled masses of skeletons of horses and mutilated men, all that remained of the three Roman divisions that had been massacred six years earlier in the "sodden marshland and ditches" of the Teutoburg Forest by Arminius and his men. When the Romans finally managed to maneuver the Germans into fighting on level, dry ground, reported Tacitus, a spontaneous war cry rang out: "It's a fair fight! On fair ground!"

Pliny was intrigued by the experience of the veterans of Germanicus's campaign who had been forced to camp in the coastal wetlands of northern Germany, where there was only one place to draw drinking water. Drinking it caused disease, and even the survivors lost all their teeth and suffered severe degeneration of the joints. Ever optimistic about nature's balance, Pliny pointed out that a remedy for these maladies grew in the swampy area, a kind of aquatic weed called *britannica*, known to the locals. The German manipulation of the Roman legions into a place where they would be forced to drink the infected water without knowledge of the antidote was most likely a biological stratagem.[38]

A particularly villainous strategic use of insalubrious terrain occurred a century or so after the Greek defeat in Sicily. What makes this event especially reprehensible is that it was the commander *himself* who plotted the destruction of his own men. The story comes from Polyaenus, the strategist who compiled a treatise on how to protect armies and overcome enemies for the co-emperors at the beginning of the Parthian War.

Drawing on several historical accounts, Polyaenus told how Clearchus, a cruel tyrant (one of several tyrants who had studied with the philosopher Plato), took power in Heraclea, on the Black Sea, in 363 BC. He surrounded himself with mercenaries, and he ordered them to sneak out at night and rob, rape, and assault the citizens of Heraclea. When the citizens complained, the tyrant shrugged and compelled the people to build him a walled acropolis. After ensconcing himself in his new citadel, however, Clearchus "did not check the mercenaries, but granted himself the power to wrong everyone." Using trickery, the tyrant arrested Heraclea's democratic Council of 300, and then he devised a vicious scheme to get rid of the rest of the dissident citizens.

All local men between the ages of sixteen and sixty-five were drafted for a bogus campaign against the Thracian city of Astachus. It was the hottest part of the summer of 360 BC, and Astachus, in western Turkey, lies in an area surrounded by marshes. Pretending that he and his mercenaries "were going to bear the brunt of the siege," Clearchus occupied the high ground with shade trees, running water, and refreshing breezes. He commanded all the citizens to camp below in a hot, stifling swamp filled with stagnant water. To exhaust them, he ordered continual guard duty. Then he "stretched out the 'siege' all summer until the unhealthy marshiness of the camp killed his citizen troops." When all of the men had died, Clearchus returned to Heraclea with his mercenaries, claiming that a plague had wiped out the citizens.[39]

This story is shocking but certainly plausible. Any general of Clearchus's day knew that troops forced to endure such conditions would succumb to the diseases we now know to be malaria and dysentery. (Perhaps there is grim satisfaction in knowing that a few years later Clearchus himself was murdered.) The story of a tyrant who turned biological agents against his own people almost sounds too evil to be true, but there are too many modern examples to permit us to dismiss the tale as pure invention.

In a widely publicized attack in March 1988, for instance, Saddam Hussein responded to Iraqi Kurds' resistance by bombing villagers with poison gas. An estimated five thousand men, women, and children were killed. After the fall of apartheid in South Africa, trial testimonies before the Truth and Reconciliation Commission in the late 1990s revealed that the South African government planned to systematically poison citizens who protested apartheid in the 1980s and early '90s. The tale of Clearchus's premeditated elimination of his own citizens and soldiers by forcing them to endure a deadly environment also stirs disquieting memories of well-documented, clandestine US government experiments with nuclear, bacterial, and chemical agents on its own citizens and soldiers during the Cold War of the twentieth century.[40]

As Grmek has pointed out—and as demonstrated by the numerous ancient examples of the manipulation of poisons and disease-ridden atmospheres to sicken foes on a large scale—it would be a mistake to assume that the ancient preoccupation with "miasmas" or "vapors" as the source of illness presented any conceptual "obstacle to utilizing contagion for military ends."[41] In antiquity, long before the modern terminology of epidemiology was developed, experience and observation led to insights into how disease could be used as a blunt instrument of war. Could that instrument somehow be refined into a capacity to spread epidemics among entire populations?

CHAPTER 4

A CASKET OF PLAGUE IN THE TEMPLE OF BABYLON

The plague arose in Babylonia, when a pestilential vapor
escaped from a golden casket in the temple of Apollo.
—JULIUS CAPITOLINUS

ONE OF THE MOST oft-cited incidents in the annals of biological warfare was said to have occurred in 1346 in Crimea. In 1344, the Tatars (Mongols of the Golden Horde) laid siege to the city of Kaffa (Caffa), a Genoese fortress in Crimea on the Black Sea. In 1346, with their troops suffering from bubonic plague, the Tatars withdrew. An Italian contemporary, Gabriele de' Mussi, reported that as they departed, the Tatars catapulted the infected corpses of their own soldiers over the walls of Kaffa "in the hope that the intolerable stench would kill everyone inside."[1]

Some details of this macabre incident, often reported as the first-ever instance of biowarfare and long believed to have been the origin of the spread of flea-, lice-, and rat-borne bubonic plague from Central Asia to Europe, have been called into question. Historian Hannah Barker argues that the spread of the Black Death from the steppes to Europe did not originate in Kaffa. She proposes that the plague was chiefly transmitted by ships carrying Black Sea grain—and rats, fleas, and bacteria—from Kaffa to Venice, Genoa, and other European cities. Those ships were free to sail after the siege and embargoes were lifted. Barker concludes, "Plague's movement across the Black Sea was certainly not a matter of bioterrorism during the siege of Caffa."[2]

But did Tatars really catapult plague-ridden corpses into Kaffa, as reported by Mussi? Such an act would indicate intent to spread disease. The claim is unverifiable, although not implausible. The Tatars' siege machines at Kaffa included a dozen trebuchets. Barker notes that "corpses or severed heads were sometimes thrown into besieged cities," but she says this was done only for psychological, not biological, effects. But what Mussi's claim does show is that people of that time and place feared the deliberate *intent* to spread contagion by contact with plague victims. Significantly, Mussi noted that the people inside the walls quickly moved the corpses and disposed of them in the sea, presumably while trying to avoid contact. Mussi also mentions "stench" as the mode of transmission. Since antiquity, disease was commonly attributed to breathing noxious odors of rotting cadavers or malodorous miasmas. It was already known at the time of the siege of Kaffa that the Black Death could be spread through close contact, even speaking with and breathing near infected people. Long before scientific knowledge of pathogens and epidemiology, experience had taught that proximity to corpses in an epidemic would almost certainly lead to more deaths. Indeed, contact with bodily fluids, blood, open wounds, or excreta of infected cadavers can transmit bubonic plague, and inhalation of airborne *Yersinia pestis* microbes causes the more virulent respiratory form. Bodily fluids, fleas, and lice remaining on corpses or their clothing could have transmitted the Black Death at Kaffa. Some studies suggest that human ectoparasites—body lice, fleas, and ticks—were more responsible than rats for the spread of bubonic plague, although other studies contradict this.[3]

Apart from the biological outcome of the alleged act by the Tatars, the psychological impact would have been horrendous, and horror has always been one of the goals of biological warfare. Terrifying the enemy was the sole object of a catapulting incident in 207 BC, during the Second Punic War, when the Romans hurled the head of the Carthaginian general Hasdrubal into the camp of his brother, Hannibal. In this case, the act was intended to demoralize Hannibal, dashing his hopes of getting the reinforcements he needed to conquer Italy. Interestingly, Hannibal himself would later use catapults to fling venomous vipers at a different enemy in Asia Minor.[4]

So far, no clear reports of *catapulting* disease-bearing cadavers or clothing have come to light before the fourteenth century, but the purposeful spread of contagion among enemies by other means could have occurred much earlier than Kaffa. Although the exact mechanisms of infection remained mysterious, people of many ancient cultures recognized that "foul and deadly miasmas arose" from plague-stricken cadavers, and that cloth or other items that had touched a plague victim could spell death. That knowledge made possible the use of disease-ridden animals and people and their clothing as weapons of war.[5]

An incident reported by the historian Appian described how a besieging army was defeated by contagion from dead bodies. In 74 BC, King Mithradates VI of Pontus began a long siege of the city of Cyzicus on the Black Sea. The defenders of Cyzicus resisted with every strategy they could come up with, from breaking the invaders' siege machines with rope nooses to hurling burning pitch. As the siege wore on, Mithradates's troops began to suffer from hunger and sickness. Then, when "corpses that were thrown out unburied in the neighborhood brought on a plague," Mithradates gave up the siege and fled. Although it is not clear whether the defenders of Cyzicus deliberately spread pestilence by throwing out their dead, or whether the corpses belonged to the besiegers of the city, the account shows that the link between the corpses and the plague was well understood (fig. 14).[6]

Greek and Latin historians demonstrated perceptive insights about epidemics, noting that those who tended the sick fell ill, and that unburied or unburned corpses spread

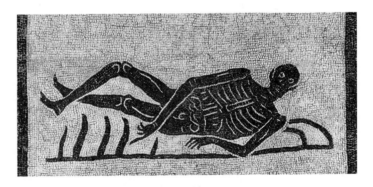

FIG. 14. It was realized early in human history that contact with corpses of victims of epidemics, or their possessions, could spread disease. Roman skeleton mosaic, first century BC, Via Appia, Italy.

disease (chapter 3). As the Roman historian Livy remarked in the first century BC, during epidemics "the dead proved fatal to the sick and the sick equally fatal to the healthy." Thucydides, in his history of the Peloponnesian War, described the great Plague of Athens, which arrived in Piraeus, Athens' port, in the summer of 430 BC. The virulent epidemic (possibly smallpox, typhus, measles, or bubonic plague, according to competing theories offered by modern medical historians) killed more than a quarter of the population, an estimated eighty thousand people. Thucydides, one of those who survived the plague, recognized the role of contact with the sick in transmitting the disease. Notably, the Athenians initially accused the Spartans of poisoning their wells.[7]

Some scholars have noted that the symptoms suffered by the mythic hero Heracles dying in the Hydra-poisoned tunic resemble those of a smallpox victim. In Sophocles's version of the myth, written in about 430 BC when the epidemic was raging in Athens, the playwright used medical terminology for pustules and plague to describe the burning torment of the tunic that killed Heracles. Sophocles's tragedy reflects the popular knowledge that not only poison but disease could be transferred by clothing. That idea was also expressed by Cedrenus, a historian who described the Plague of Cyprian (a pandemic that spread from Egypt to Scotland in about AD 250), when he remarked that the disease was transmitted not just by direct contact but also by clothing.[8]

Actually, the recognition that diseases could be transmitted by contact with the ill and their personal belongings goes back much earlier in recorded history, to ancient Sumer (in Syria). The evidence comes from several royal letters inscribed on cuneiform tablets in about 1170 BC, from the archives of

Mari, a Sumerian kingdom on the Euphrates in Mesopotamia. One of the royal letters forbade people from an infected town to travel to a healthy town, to avoid "infecting the whole country." Another letter described a woman whose cup, chair, bed, and physical presence were to be avoided because of the danger of contracting her disease, which was very contagious (*mustahhizu*, literally "keeps on catching or kindling").

The modern epidemiological term for articles like cups or clothing that harbor infectious pathogens is *fomites*. The principles of fomite contagion and quarantine were evidently understood thirty-eight hundred years ago. But ancient accounts of epidemics were often expressed in symbolic language or metaphors such as "angels of death smiting armies" or gods shooting "arrows of plague." Because of the metaphorical imagery, descriptions of epidemics in Near Eastern and biblical texts and Greek mythology have often been viewed by scholars as superstitious explanations, even though they may have been based on sound empirical knowledge, as shown in the Mari letters.[9]

As noted, historians have long considered the 1346 Kaffa incident, reported by Mussi, to be the first documented case of a deliberate attempt to spread contagion to achieve military victory. But much earlier incidents of transmitting disease for strategic purposes can be found in the ancient sources. Some of the evidence is legendary or inconclusive, like the Cyzicus event, but many other historical accounts record clear intentions to transmit disease to enemies in chillingly feasible ways.

The earliest clear examples of deliberate attempts to spread contagion appear in cuneiform tablets of the ancient Hittite civilization of Anatolia (1500–1200 BC). The tablets tell of driving animals and at least one woman infected with epidemics out of the city into enemy territory, accompanied by a prayer: "The country that accepts them shall take this evil plague." The intention is unmistakable, and the means would have been quite effective. Further evidence came to light in 2007. During the Anatolian war of 1320–1318 BC, the Hittites fought a militarily stronger enemy, the Arzawan confederation. But the Hittites secured victory by means of a secret bioweapon. They sent sheep and donkeys infected with deadly tularemia into Arzawan lands. The lethal "Hittite plague" was transmitted to humans via ticks and flies.[10]

▰ ▰ ▰

The ancient Hittites and Babylonians worshipped the archer-god Irra, who was said to shoot arrows of plague to afflict enemies in military contexts. In Greek mythology, it was the god Apollo who destroyed armies with his invisible plague arrows—and by sending infestations of rodents, which were widely recognized in antiquity as harbingers of pestilence (see chapter 6). These mythic beliefs reflect the fact that epidemics did frequently coincide with military invasions, owing to overcrowding and unsanitary conditions, stress, lack of food and pure water, infestations of rodents and other disease vectors, and exposure to new germ pools. When people of antiquity implored the gods to inflict pestilence on invaders, diseases that broke out among the enemy forces were seen as answered prayers. In an example from the fourth century BC, the people of Pachynus, Sicily, prayed to Apollo to strike the approaching Carthaginian fleet with pestilence. And, in fact, in 396 BC, a devastating epidemic did break out among the Carthaginians, causing them to abandon their plan to attack Sicily.[11]

It must not have been long before humans began to wonder whether, instead of relying on requests to the gods, they could also take matters into their own hands and sow contagion and biological calamities among their adversaries by practical means, as the Hittites did by sending infectious animals into enemy lands. Some modern commentators have speculated on whether the Ten Plagues that Moses called down on the Egyptians (in about 1300 BC), might represent the earliest incidents of using nature to gain strategic goals.

Was the first plague, the red waters of the Nile that killed fish and fouled the water for drinking, due to deliberate contamination by the Israelites? According to Exodus, the Pharaoh's "magicians" were able to produce a similar phenomenon, which would place them among the world's first biochemists. Indeed, techniques for poisoning fish, by dumping powdered roots of deadly plants mixed with toxic chemicals such as lime, were also practiced in early Roman times in the Mediterranean, according to Pliny the Elder. On the other hand, the blood-red, polluted water of the Nile might have been a natural phenomenon, such as a toxic algae bloom or an influx of red sediment.[12]

Seasonal occurrences account for the frogs and insects of the second, third, and fourth plagues; as well as for the hailstorm, locusts, and hot dust storm (*khamsin*) of the seventh, eighth, and ninth plagues in Egypt. But what about the diseases of the fifth and sixth plagues? In the fifth plague sent by Yahweh, the Egyptians' herds and flocks were killed; in the sixth, a rain of "ashes" caused black boils on beasts as well as humans. The progression from animals to humans strongly suggests pulmonary anthrax, with the boils caused by powdery black "ashes" describing the black sores of the cutaneous form of anthrax (the word comes from the ancient Greek for "coal"). The fact that the Israelites' cattle were spared could be attributed to their grazing in separate, poorer pastures.

A similar epidemic appeared in Homer's *Iliad*, set in about 1200 BC, when the Greeks were laying siege to Troy and were assailed by a plague sent by Apollo. Homer's details are realistic. The first to sicken from Apollo's "black arrows" were the pack animals and dogs, and then the men began to die. Outbreaks of anthrax are devastating to both livestock and humans. The "Black Bane" anthrax epidemic that swept Europe in the 1600s, for example, killed millions of animals and at least sixty thousand people. Like the smallpox virus and other infectious material, anthrax spores can remain viable for a very long time, and they could conceivably be manipulated by humans. On the other hand, natural cycles of anthrax have attacked periodically throughout history.[13]

Although neither the *Iliad* nor Exodus implicates humans in the anthrax-like plagues, the priests of Apollo and Yahweh took credit for summoning the epidemics. This definitely reveals both the *desire* and the *intention* to wage what we now call germ warfare, and it demonstrates that people *feared* that such things were possible. A series of fortuitous successes in calling down pestilence in the past may well have instilled the idea that humans themselves might inflict them. The Ten Plagues of Exodus were most likely a series of natural calamities that were advantageous for the Israelites. Inherent in the story, however, is the strong suggestion that plagues and biological disasters could be powerful weapons against enemies.[14]

The tenth plague, the sudden death of the Egyptians' firstborn children, has been called the "ultimate biological weapon." Although the Israelites' children were spared the final plague, again there is no hint of human agency in Exodus.

It is true that if one could systematically destroy the genetic material of an enemy people, however, that would indeed constitute a biological strategy with a devastating effect on the population. Blocking an enemy's genetic reproduction by killing entire populations, or, alternatively, by slaying all males and/or systematically raping the women, was an effective way of wiping out an enemy "root and branch" in antiquity.

The most notorious modern example of such biological strategies is the Nazis' attempt to eliminate all Jews and "Gypsies" (Roma) in World War II. But ethnic-cleansing murders and/or systematic rapes by soldiers have since occurred in former Yugoslavia, Burma, Rwanda, Syria, China, and India. More advanced genocidal methods are being developed. After the fall of apartheid in South Africa, the Truth and Reconciliation investigations (1998) revealed that government-sponsored doctors had researched "a race-specific bacterial weapon" and "ways to sterilize . . . the black population." As early as 2003, a US military report described a proposal for creating "nonlethal" weapons based on "genetic alteration." Unfortunately, the specter of "ultimate biological weapons" that target DNA and certain ethnic groups is now a real possibility, thanks to techniques for engineering genetic material.[15]

Ancient examples of attempts to interfere with genetic reproduction are numerous. Before the onset of the Ten Plagues in Egypt, for instance, the pharaoh had ordered midwives to kill all male offspring born to Hebrew women. Later, in the first century BC, King Herod's preemptive biological strike—his order to kill all Jewish boys under age two—was another example of the same strategy. In Greek myth, during the sack of Troy, the Greek warriors killed the infant son of Hector to make sure that none of the Trojan champion's bloodline would survive (the tragic scene was featured in many Greek vase paintings).[16]

Greek and Roman historians report wars in which the victors killed all the males of an enemy population and raped and abducted the women en masse. The legendary Rape of the Sabine Women by the founders of Rome is a famous example. In his survey of war tactics, Polyaenus referred to this legend when he noted that the Roman founders invited the Italian natives, the Sabini, to a festival and then abducted all the virgins. The Indian manual on devious ways of war, the *Arthashastra*, insinuated that there were secret ways of interfering with opponents' reproduction: "When an archer shoots an arrow he may miss his target, but intrigue can kill even the unborn."[17]

▰ ▰ ▰

The Latin expression *pestilentia manu facta*, "man-made pestilence," shows that intentionally transmitted contagion was a suspected biological weapon in Roman times. The term was coined by the philosopher Seneca, Nero's adviser in the first century AD, to refer to epidemics attributed to deliberate human activity. Livy and other Latin historians referred to the malicious transmission of plagues without giving specifics, but Cassius Dio, a Greek historian born about AD 164, reported on two man-made epidemics in detail.[18]

According to Cassius Dio, the plagues were begun by saboteurs acting in Rome and in the provinces, apparently to spread chaos and undermine unpopular emperors' authority. The first instance occurred before his time, in AD 90–91, during the reign of Domitian (himself suspected of poisoning his brother and predecessor Titus). The conspirators dipped needles in deleterious substances and secretly pricked many victims, who perished of a deadly illness. According to Cassius Dio, the plague-spreaders were caught and punished after informers spoke out.

A similar plot occurred in Cassius Dio's lifetime, during the reign of Commodus. Commodus had succeeded his father, the emperor Marcus Aurelius, who died in AD 180 during the plague that was brought back to Italy and Europe by Roman troops fighting in Babylonia (discussed below). While Commodus was emperor, in about AD 189, another plague wracked the empire, killing two thousand people a day in Rome. This pestilence was said to have been spread by saboteurs who "smeared deadly drugs on tiny needles [and] infected many people by means of these instruments."[19]

These accusations may or may not have been true, but they clearly reflect the belief in antiquity that human beings—not just the gods—could propagate disease at will. The method, sticking victims with infected needles, was certainly plausible, and rumors of such biological sabotage aroused panic in Rome. Indeed, the rumors were in themselves a form of bioterror that has proven effective through history. During the ravages of the Black Death in the Middle Ages, rumors that enemies were deliberately spreading the disease caused widespread hysteria. Fears fueled by rumors rose in the United States in the aftermath of the anthrax attacks of 2001 and amid continuing alarms over bioterrorist activities. During the coronavirus COVID-19 pandemic that began in 2020, conspiracies arose in the United States, China, Iran, and other nations, with accusations of intentional spread of the pathogen.[20]

In India, during the fourth century BC, the ruthless strategist Kautilya demonstrated a clear intention to transmit infectious diseases to enemies. In the *Arthashastra*, he gave a recipe for burning frog entrails and plant toxins whose smoke he claimed would infect adversaries with gonorrhea; the addition of human blood to the recipe was supposed to bring a wasting lung disease. Powdered leeches, bird and mongoose tongues, donkey milk, plus jimsonweed (a toxic plant related to deadly nightshade) and other poisons were intended to cause fevers, deafness, and various diseases. Four different recipes were said to spread leprosy: one called for special seeds kept for a week in the mouth of a white cobra or lizard, then mixed with cow dung and eggs of parrots and cuckoos. The ingredients of the concoctions may seem silly to modern readers, but keep in mind that one of Kautilya's stated purposes was to terrify his enemies with biological threats.[21]

As noted, the ancient idea of "manufactured pestilence" has taken on a new, sinister meaning in view of recent genetic engineering discoveries. Richard Preston, whose popular fiction and nonfiction chronicle what he termed "Dark Biology," speculated back in 2002 that scientists could easily create a virulent version of mild mousepox by adding a mammalian gene to the smallpox-like virus. In experiments with diseases that attack humans, scientists had proved that synthetic replicas of epidemic viruses could be created chemically in the laboratory from scratch, without live cells, simply through the replication of the published DNA sequence of a natural virus. One of the earliest experiments used a blueprint for poliovirus downloaded from the Internet and chemical material available by mail order.[22]

Some two thousand years after Seneca coined the phrase *pestilentia manu facta* to refer to pestilence manipulated and spread by humans, the potential for terrorists or rogue governments to fabricate man-made epidemics has become a scientific reality. Genetically engineered and synthetic pathogens as bioweapons are now achievable via CRISPR gene-editing technologies and Gain of Function (GOF) virology experiments.[23]

The Greek myth of Pandora, who opened the sealed jar and released plagues and pestilence upon humankind, is one of the earliest mythic expressions of the ancient notion of confining disease in a sealed container (fig. 15). The related idea

FIG. 15. The Greek myth of Pandora's Box is one of the earliest expressions of the idea that contagion could be "trapped" in a sealed container. Red-figure amphora, 460–450 BC, Niobid Painter, 48.2712, The Walters Art Museum, Baltimore, Creative Commons.

of sealing a virulent contagion in a container with the specific intention of inflicting plague on enemies who break open the seal is a very widespread folk motif—and one that has scientific and historical plausibility. Some of the traditional stories about such bioattacks may reflect wishful thinking or imaginative worst-case scenarios. But the potential for deliberately spreading epidemics like smallpox or bubonic plague was real, since infectious matter on fomites and aerosols (tiny airborne particles) can retain virulence over long periods of time.

The biblical story of the Philistines' problems with the Ark of the Covenant, recounted in 1 Samuel, is a provocative early example of disease sealed in a container. In the twelfth century BC, when the Philistines were at war with the Israelites, they feared that Yahweh would smite them with plagues as he had done to the Egyptians. Sure enough, when the Philistines captured the Ark of the Covenant from the Israelites and took the sacred wooden chest to their capital, an epidemic decimated the population (fig. 16). The disease was marked by swellings (buboes) in the groin (a classic sign of bubonic plague), and it was accompanied by rats in the land. The survivors sent the Ark away to a series of Philistine towns, and each was struck with the same epidemic. The Philistines attributed the plague to Yahweh, and they associated the disease with infestations of rodents (bubonic plague is carried by fleas and lice on rodents).

The coincidence of a plague breaking out upon the arrival of a special casket in each town raises interesting questions. It may simply have been that the Philistines who carried away the Ark brought the disease with them. But tales recur across history and geography of plagues begun when sealed containers from enemies were opened, and we know today that such a scenario is plausible. One cannot help but wonder: Could the

FIG. 16. Bubonic-type plague, and rats, afflicted each Philistine town visited by the Ark of the Covenant, the sacred wooden chest that the Israelites were forbidden to touch, twelfth century BC. *Plague of the Philistines at Ashdod*, engraving by G. Tolosano, after Poussin. Wellcome Collection, Creative Commons.

Ark have contained some object, such as cloth, that harbored aerosolized plague bacteria, or an insect vector that infected rodents and humans in Philistine territory? The Ark of the Covenant was recovered later and placed in Solomon's great temple in Jerusalem. Understanding of fomites or vectors was not necessary for people to learn through experience and observation. Notably, the Ark itself was never to be touched or opened by the Israelites themselves. It was always carried suspended by poles through rings, to avoid physical contact with the Ark. One Israelite who accidentally touched the Ark died instantly.[24]

Two other legendary narratives about the temple in Jerusalem suggest that material carrying plague could be hidden away, stored in a safe place against the possibility of a military invasion. Consider, for example, an ancient legend about sealing up "plague demons" and placing them in the temple at Jerusalem. The legend appears in the Testament of Solomon and other ancient texts of Hebrew, Gnostic, and Greek origins, dating to the first to fourth centuries AD, but based on earlier traditions. Solomon was a historical king who built the first temple in Jerusalem in the tenth century BC. According to legend, King Solomon summoned a crew of evil spirits of disease and disaster and forced them to help build the magnificent temple of Jerusalem.

Then Solomon imprisoned the demons inside copper vessels and sealed them with silver. Copper, mined in the Negev Desert in antiquity, is antimicrobial, resisting corrosion and inhibiting growth of bacteria and mold. Silver is also antibacterial. In the legend, Solomon placed these sealed vessels inside large jars or casks and buried them within the foundations of the temple.

The legend can be seen as evidence of the belief that evil spirits could be magically imprisoned in containers, like genies or djinns in bottles. But, as the Mari tablets from Sumer showed, people of the ancient Near East also understood at an early date that things such as cloth and cups could actually transmit fatal disease. That knowledge, and the Old Testament tale of the Ark accompanied by outbreaks of plague among the enemy, gives the legend about Solomon deeper significance.

Indeed, the biblical stories of the plagues sent by Yahweh against the Egyptians in the time of Moses and against the Philistines who stole the Ark had already planted the idea of contagion as a weapon, and Solomon's reserves of plague do seem to be intended as a defensive weapon. The Testament of Solomon contained a prediction that when the temple of Jerusalem would be destroyed by a king of the Chaldeans, the plague spirits would be released. And in fact, in 586 BC, Nebuchadnezzar (the cruel king of the Chaldeans, or Neo-Babylonians) sacked and burned Solomon's temple in Jerusalem. "In their plundering," writes a Greek chronicler, the invaders found the copper vessels and assumed that they contained treasure. The Babylonians broke open the seals and the pestilential demons flew out and "plagued men again."[25]

The ancient legend of Solomon imprisoning the evil spirits in the temple at Jerusalem is well known in Islamic lore. Some Muslim fundamentalists who practice "Islamic science"—a hybrid of modern scientific terminology and Islamic mysticism—identify invisible supernatural djinns as the sources of nuclear energy and of epidemics. They point to Solomon's ability to "harness energy from Djinns" as evidence that special "spirits" of atomic power and contagion such as anthrax could be manipulated by secret knowledge. In 1980s and '90s the leading Pakistani nuclear engineer, Bashiruddin Mahmood, spoke of and wrote about "communicating" with the invisible but powerful djinns or spirits that were long ago "harnessed by King Solomon." Since 2001, Mahmood has been detained in Pakistan after plans and diagrams for creating anthrax-spreading devices were found in his offices in Afghanistan.[26]

Solomon's temple was rebuilt in the fifth century BC. In 1945, a trove of early Christian writings buried in about AD 400 were discovered at Nag Hammadi in Egypt. One of the scrolls contains a different version of the Solomon legend. It dates to the first or second century AD. During the siege of Jerusalem by the future Roman emperor Titus in AD 70, the second temple was destroyed and, according to the scrolls, Roman soldiers discovered the ancient jars hidden by Solomon and broke them open looking for plunder. The plague demons, imprisoned in the foundations since the time of Solomon, escaped. Notably Suetonius, the Latin biographer of Titus, records that "Titus's reign was marked by a series of dreadful catastrophes," including "one of the worst outbreaks of plague ever known."[27]

Almost a century later, in the same geographical region, a remarkably similar scenario was played out when looting Roman soldiers destroyed a Greek temple in Babylon.

▰ ▰ ▰

The terrible plague of AD 165–80 swept out of Babylonia and raged across the Mideast and Mediterranean, reaching Rome and even Gaul and Germany. The great doctor Galen described the symptoms in vivid detail, leading medical historians to suggest that the disease may have been smallpox or measles. The devastating pandemic, known as the Antonine Plague or Plague of Galen, is estimated to have killed about seven to ten million people.[28]

Accusations reported in two fourth-century Latin accounts of the Parthian War in Babylonia, one in the *Historia Augusta: Lives of the Later Caesars* and the other in a history by Ammianus Marcellinus, suggest that this plague—or at least the ancient accounts of it—might belong in the annals of biological sabotage. The pandemic began during the Roman campaign against the Parthians in Mesopotamia, led by the co-emperors

FIG. 17. Marcus Aurelius and Lucius Verus, co-emperors during the Great Plague of AD 165–80; said to have begun when Verus's soldiers broke open a golden chest in the Temple of Apollo in Babylon, allowing the "spirits of plague" to escape. Marble busts, AD 160–170, 1861,1127.15 and 1805,0703.103, British Museum, photo by Carole Raddato, 2015.

Lucius Verus and Marcus Aurelius (fig. 17). The Parthians dominated Central Asia from the Indus River to the Euphrates, and constantly threatened Roman power.

"The pestilence is reported to have arisen in Babylonia, when a *spiritus pestilens*, a pestilential vapor, escaped from a golden casket in the temple of Apollo," wrote Verus's biographer, "Julius Capitolinus" (one of the pseudonyms used by the anonymous authors of the *Lives of the Later Caesars*). A Roman soldier had "cut open the casket and from thence [the plague] filled the Parthians' land and then the world," extending all the way from Persia to the Rhine.

Lucius Verus was accused, by the Syrians and others, of deliberately spreading the plague. But the plague was not really Verus's fault, claimed Capitolinus, who said that the blame really lay with Verus's ambitious general, Avidius Cassius. In AD 164, the bloodthirsty Cassius had stormed Seleucia, a Greek city on the Tigris River in the district of Babylonia (the Parthians had used the city as their summer quarters). Cassius's army committed atrocities and laid waste to Seleucia, one of the last bastions of Hellenic culture, despite the fact that the Seleucians had welcomed the Romans. Cassius thereby violated a generally accepted convention of war that interdicted attacking a friendly city or breaking a truce. It was Cassius's soldiers who plundered the Greek temple and released the contagion, according to Capitolinus and Ammianus Marcellinus.[29]

The idea that plundering a temple or sacred object or site would be punished by plague was a very old one. The capture of the Ark of the Covenant by the Philistines followed by outbreaks of plague is one of the earliest examples. Another example was mentioned in chapter 3, when the Carthaginian army was struck by plague in 396 BC at Syracuse. That plague began after the Carthaginian soldiers pillaged the Greek temple of Demeter and Kore. Appian told how plague ravaged the Gauls after their attempt to loot Apollo's Oracle at Delphi in 105 BC, and the pestilence spread among the Getae and Illyrians as the Gauls fled. Capitolinus's account also conveyed the strong implication that Cassius and his men had offended Apollo, the god who scourged invading armies with plagues. According to inscriptions discovered by archaeologists, the oracle at the Temple of Apollo at Claros (on the coast of Turkey) issued many dire warnings during the pandemic, attributing the plague to the anger of the god and advising cities to erect statues of Long-Haired Apollo wielding his bow to ward off the contagion released by the Roman looters. The link between temples and plague appears again in AD 540, when the Byzantine emperor Justinian ordered the destruction of the Temple of Isis at Philae, Egypt. The next year bubonic plague—the Plague of Justinian—swept out of Egypt and engulfed the Roman Empire, spreading to Constantinople and Persia, as well as Italy, Spain, Gaul, and Britain.[30]

But how might a casket in a temple come to harbor the plague in the first place? Stories implying that biological weapons were stored in temples raise a flurry of questions. Why would biologically dangerous materials ever be stored in temples?

In the Greco-Roman world, temples often served as museums of revered relics, and all sorts of weapons with mythic and historical significance were treasures commonly displayed in temples. Indeed, Heracles's original bioweapons—the Hydra-poisoned arrows—were said to have been stored in a temple in Italy, by the archer Philoctetes who dedicated them to Apollo, the god whose arrows carried pestilence (chapter 1).

But surely items of deadly biological potential were not merely retained for posterity. Evidence from antiquity relates that priests of the temples of Apollo were very knowledgeable about poisons and studied their effects. For example, the celebrated toxicologist Nicander was a priest of Apollo at the Temple of Claros in the second century BC—the same temple that issued oracles about the plague of AD 165. Nicander compiled an encyclopedia on venomous snakes, plants, and insects. Apollo was also the patron of doctors, and it was said that the doctor Nebros had used his knowledge of poison to help destroy the town of Kirrha, which had offended Apollo (chapter 3). With these clues in mind, one is tempted to ask whether some temples may have functioned as ancient laboratories for experiments with poisons and antidotes, with diseases and even primitive vaccines.

In fact, some Greek temples were repositories of real disease vectors. Apollo was the guardian of rodents (in antiquity, no distinctions were drawn among mice, rats, and voles). Rodent swarms were a presage of epidemics—and all sorts of rodents can be vectors of bubonic plague, typhus, and other diseases. At least one temple of Apollo—at Hamaxitus near ancient Troy—actually housed a horde of sacred white mice or rats around the altar, which were fed at public expense.[31]

Another intriguing example of disease vectors associated with temples involves Athena, the Greek goddess of war. Her temple at Rhocca, Crete, was notorious for its rabid dogs, and Athena of Rhocca was invoked to cure human victims of rabies. Aelian described a complicated experiment by an old shaman-like character that took place in the vicinity of Rhocca, in which he administered marine biotoxins—from the stomach acid of seahorses—to counteract rabies in a group of boys bitten by mad dogs. It is now known that seahorses contain cathepsin B, an anti-inflammatory enzyme. But, as Aelian acknowledged elsewhere, the bite of a mad dog was always fatal. Notably, in his section on various venoms and arrow poisons, Aelian included a reference to rabid dogs. The saliva of a mad dog could even imbue a piece of cloth bitten by the dog, noted Aelian, causing secondhand, fatal rabies to anyone who came in intimate contact with it. This ominous remark insinuates that mad dog "venom" could have weapon potential, although no evidence survives that the idea of using rabid dog "venom" on arrows was pursued in ancient Greece or Rome.[32]

There are, however, two bioweapon recipes in the *Artha-shastra* of the fourth century BC that appear to be evidence of such an attempt in India. One describes how to make a poison arrow with a mixture of toxins and "the blood of a musk rat." Anyone pierced with this arrow will be compelled to bite ten companions, who will in turn bite others, wrote Kautilya. The other weapon, concocted from red alum, plant toxins, and the blood of a goat and a man, induces "biting madness." These symptoms of biting mania sound suspiciously like rabies. About a thousand years later, Leonardo da Vinci envisioned a bomb made from mad dog saliva, tarantula venom, toxic toads, sulfur, arsenic, and burned feathers (which create sulfur dioxide; see chapter 7). In 1650, the possibility of weaponizing rabies in projectiles also occurred to an artillery general in Poland. He referred to catapulting "hollow spheres with the slobber from rabid dogs [to] cause epidemics."

Going back to the original line of thinking, about temples as places where toxins or pathogens and antidotes were sometimes stored, and taking the idea a step further, a question arises: Were some priests in temples of Apollo or Athena the keepers of lethal biological material that could be weaponized in times of crisis? One can imagine that a garment or other item contaminated with, say, dried scabs and other smallpox matter, could have been sealed away from heat, light, and air in a golden casket in the temple of Apollo in Babylon, until a time of need (fig. 18). Such items could maintain "weapons-grade" virulence for many years.[33]

Besides the literary evidence that temples might serve as emergency arsenals of disease vectors and fomites, there is historical and archaeological evidence that usable weapons were stored in temples in antiquity. For example, a cache of catapult bolts from the 370s BC was discovered in the Parthenon, the great temple of Athena on the Acropolis in Athens. These were placed in the temple a generation after the invention in Syracuse of the crossbow-style catapult, a terrifying weapon that took warfare to a higher level of destruction. Other temples in Greece, Anatolia, and Bactria held stores of weapons in antiquity. For example, in preparation for the

FIG. 18. Woman placing cloth in chest. If the material had belonged to a victim of an epidemic such as smallpox, it could retain virulence for many years. Terra-cotta pinax from Locri, IG 8332. Courtesy of Museo Archeologico Nazionale, Calabria.

great battle at Chaeronea in 338 BC, Greek temples contributed their weapons to the defense.[34]

Sacred sites and weapons have been linked in later times too. During the Crusades, for example, when the new chemical incendiary weapon based on naphtha, Greek Fire, inspired terror, Arabic sources reported that great stocks of volatile naphtha were stored in Byzantine churches. Earlier, in the fourth century AD, it was rumored that the "Devil" had smuggled naphtha, used as an incendiary weapon, into the church of Saint Nicholas in Myra (on the coast of Turkey).[35]

In classical antiquity, the placement of catapult bolts in Athena's temple suggests that the technologically advanced ballistic armaments were watched over by the goddess of war. Likewise, it seems that the most virulent biological ammunition was guarded by the god of plagues, Apollo.

▰ ▰ ▰

It is notable how often plague gods like Apollo were "invoked in defensive military contexts [to] bring plague against an invading or besieging army," remarks Christopher Faraone, a scholar of ancient religion. Like other commentators, he saw the story of the casket of plague in Apollo's temple in Babylonia as simply another "curious historical anecdote," further proof that Apollo was worshipped as the source of epidemics, which often coincided with invasions by armies.

But the story is much more complex, with significant implications for the history of attitudes toward justifiable biological warfare. There are many ancient accounts of people calling on gods who control plague to help them *resist* an invading enemy or oppressor, which seems to suggest that using biological weapons was acceptable in situations of defense but less permissible as a "first strike." In Exodus, for example, the Israelites called on Yahweh to send plagues against their Egyptian captors. In Homer's *Iliad*, the priest of Apollo called down the god's plague arrows on the invading Greek army after they destroyed the priest's city, Chryse, and captured his daughter. Even the biowarrior-hero Heracles, who was regularly invoked for help by Greek armies, could offer aid only in defensive situations. For example, when the Syracusans sacrificed to Heracles to ask for assistance during the Athenians' invasion of Sicily, Heracles could only promise to help "provided they did not seek battle, but remained on the defensive."[36]

The principle of summoning plague for self-defense may be related to the reality that invaders are "immunologically naive" and therefore more vulnerable to endemic diseases in foreign lands than the local population. Epidemics often strike invading forces more severely than indigenous populations. But another factor appears to be a strong intuition from earliest times that poisoning and spreading contagion could be justified when it was reserved for desperate emergencies. This principle allowed the practice of polluting water in advance of an invading army or booby-trapping an abandoned outpost. The same defensive principle appears in the modern Biological Weapons Convention (1972, with 183 nations ratifying by 2021), which prohibits offensive weapons but allows "defensive" research to continue.

Various military leaders have hesitated to approve biochemical weapons for aggressive purposes. For example, Louis XIV rewarded an Italian chemist for inventing a bacteriological weapon, but on the condition that the man would never reveal the formula; in a similar account, Louis V had declined an offer of the "lost" formula for Greek Fire. Even Hitler, a fan of Greco-Roman culture, reportedly forbade offensive biological weapons research in 1939, although his scientists continued to develop nerve gases and other biochemical agents. Of course, there have been and still are countless systematic violations of bans against offensive uses of weaponized contagion. Many modern nations simply label bioweapons research and production as "defensive security," even though nothing precludes the use of the weapons in a first strike. Military scientists and virologists use a circular logic argument, that biological (and chemical) weapons must first be invented so that countermeasures can be prepared, and this justifies their secret production. The salient point in the ancient accounts, though, is the surprising antiquity of the attitude that there is something heinous about *attacking* with contagion, but as a weapon of resistance, self-defense, or retaliation, it is acceptable as a last resort.[37]

The Syrians and others accused the Romans of intentionally spreading the plague and taking it back to Rome. But the Romans themselves were the main victims of the epidemic. It is not impossible that the Romans encountered a biological time bomb, a kind of booby-trapped Pandora's box, set against the invader, activated despite the dangers of friendly fire (their enemies, the Parthians, were also affected). If so, the chest in the temple would resemble mechanical devices against looters in ancient graves in Egypt and Scythia, and were a precursor of booby-trapped treasure chests in the late Middle Ages that were rigged with primitive explosives. In this case, trying to direct contagion only at the Roman enemy, without incurring collateral damage, must have been seen as a drastic last resort.[38]

Imagine the scene at the Temple of Long-Haired Apollo, god of plague, in Babylon. Lucius Verus's generals are laying waste to Babylonia, and Cassius has utterly destroyed the friendly Greek city of Seleucia. Roman soldiers burst into the sacred temple, looking for loot before setting it afire. They spy the golden casket, and the priests of Apollo allow the biologically devastating "accident" to happen, knowing that at least the Roman army will contract the plague and spread it across their provinces all the way back to Italy. Soldiers far from home and living in crowded conditions were, as Christopher Faraone notes, "excellent targets for a variety of new bacteria and viruses for which they had no immunity."[39]

Some of the local populace may have been immune to the pestilence stored in their temple, but the dangers of keeping plague as a secret weapon inside one's own city would be considerable. Just as those who handled poison arrows and toxic substances suffered friendly fire accidents, handling contagion always involves the chance of self-contamination.

Indeed, the backlash problems associated with handling contagion as a weapon persist in modern times. A prime example of the "poisoners poisoned" effect occurred in 1941, during Japanese attacks with infectious agents against eleven cities in China. The Japanese troops themselves are reported to have suffered thousands of biological casualties trying to spread contagion in the city of Changteh alone. In grim irony, Dr. Shiro Ishii, the director of the bioattacks, became a victim of his obsession with germ warfare: he suffered from chronic dysentery. During the offensive bioweapons research program in the United States in 1943–69, there were reports of more than forty inadvertent "occupational infections," and since the 1950s military experiments with germ warfare agents have been linked to several outbreaks of disease in civilian populations. After smallpox was eradicated in the 1970s, routine vaccinations were halted and laboratories around the world supposedly destroyed their stores of the virus, except for two authorized sites, one in the United States and the other in the Soviet Union. But in 2002, evidence emerged that Russia continued to create staggering amounts of the virus, and that vials of new smallpox strains (rumored to be resistant to vaccines) lurk in lab freezers across the globe. The perilous situation is chronicled in Richard Preston's 2002 book *The Demon in the Freezer*, a striking title that calls to mind the ancient plague demons trapped in stoppered vessels in temples.[40]

Ancient recognition of the danger of trying to weaponize plague is evident in traditional Greek prayers urging Apollo to set aside his bow and quiver of plague arrows during peacetime.

And an ancient Hittite prayer bluntly requested their own plague-bringing god to "shoot the enemy, but when you come home, unstring your bow and cover your quiver."[41]

▰ ▰ ▰

The biological sabotage that I have suggested may have been planned by the priests at the temples at Babylon and Jerusalem took advantage of the invading enemies' greed and lust for loot. The contagion was delivered in the form of something attractive. Indeed, the next chapter shows how military commanders could take advantage of adversaries' desires, vices, or overindulgence. But before we turn to toxic sweets and tainted wine as weapons, let's consider a unique subterfuge that concealed doom in an alluring gift.

In India, where all manner of toxic substances could be had, poisoning was a favored method of political assassination in myth and history. One of the most ingenious methods described in Sanskrit literature was to send an irresistible gift in the form of a so-called Poison Maiden (*Visha Kanya*). In the *Katha Sarit Sagara*, a collection of Indian lore compiled by the poet Somadeva (about AD 1050), King Brahmadatta "sent poison damsels as dancing-girls among the enemy's host." In an ancient twist on the modern idea of "sleepers"—undetected, lurking assassins or terrorists who await orders to kill—Poison Maidens were carefully "prepared" and dispatched as secret weapons. A touch, a kiss, or sexual intercourse with one of these ravishing but deadly damsels brought sure death.

The idea that certain individuals were personally poisonous, capable of killing with their mere touch or breath, is a folk motif of great antiquity. According to popular belief, bodily toxicity could be achieved by a lifelong regimen of ingesting poisons and venoms, the same regimen followed by historical paranoid kings, such as Mithradates VI of Pontus, to become resistant to poisons. Nathaniel Hawthorne's 1844 short story about a poison maiden, "Rappaccini's Daughter," and the medieval tales of the "Poison Sultan" Mahmud Shah (1500) are two examples of the theme in Western and Indian-Persian literature, respectively. The tales reflect folk knowledge of the possibility of gaining immunity to toxic plants and venoms (exemplified by the Psylli, the snake charmers of North Africa), but they also appear to be early attempts to explain how contagion is mysteriously passed from person to person.[42]

According to ancient Indian and Arabic legends, King Chandragupta and Alexander the Great were intended victims of Poison Maidens. King Chandragupta's Mauryan Empire became the most powerful dominion in India after Alexander's death in 323 BC. Chandragupta's minister Kautilya, author of the *Arthashastra*, the book of Machiavellian statecraft, saved the king from numerous assassination attempts. In the seventh century AD, the historian Visakhadatta described how a plot to send a Poison Maiden to the king's bedchamber was thwarted by Kautilya, who cleverly rerouted the girl to one of the king's enemies instead.

A similar intrigue was said to have been hatched to kill Alexander the Great, according to a body of ancient and medieval legends. The earliest version of the conspiracy to send a Poison Maiden to the Macedonian conqueror appeared in about AD 1050 in a Latin book, based on an earlier Arabic translation of a lost Greek manuscript. In that story, the king of India sent Alexander many precious gifts, among them a "beautiful maiden whom they had fed on poison until she had the nature of a venomous snake." Smitten by her beauty, Alexander "could scarcely contain himself and rushed to embrace her." Her touch or bite, even her perspiration, it was said, would have killed Alexander—had not his trusted adviser, the philosopher Aristotle, foiled the plot and prevented him from making contact with the "messenger of death."[43]

The story of Alexander is clearly legendary (for one thing, Aristotle never visited India). But the concept of a Poison Maiden could contain a germ of truth. Comparing the beautiful girls to snakes plays on the idea that snake charmers gained immunity by ingesting small doses of venom, and as folklorist Norman Penzer points out, there was a popular notion in antiquity that their bite might be as venomous as that of the snakes they handled. Penzer also investigated the possibility that the "poison" transmitted by intimate contact with deadly maidens was really venereal disease or other fatal infectious illnesses transmitted by personal contact, such as smallpox. This is the most probable source of the Poison Maiden tales—they were human disease carriers, weaponized to infect foes.[44]

The strategy of sending disease-ridden but alluring women to foes appeared again in later military history too—for example, during the Naples Campaign of 1494. The Spanish not only poisoned French wine with contaminated blood, but, according to the medical writer Gabriele Falloppia, they also "intentionally chased beautiful, infectious prostitutes into the French army camp."[45] Although the biological strategies are nearly three thousand years apart, this Spanish "poison prostitute" plot also has parallels to the ancient Hittite ritual of driving a plague-infected woman into enemy territory. Offering something tempting but lethal to a foe is an age-old path to victory via biological agents.

CHAPTER 5

SWEET SABOTAGE

Men by their unbridled appetites are the victims
of plots against their food and drink.
—AELIAN, *ON ANIMALS*

He'll come with a deadly poison,
pour it in our wine, and kill us all.
—HOMER, *ODYSSEY*

XENOPHON WAS PLEASED with the campsite he had selected in
the territory bordering Colchis, in Pontus along the southeastern shore of the Black Sea (northeast Turkey). The land
was fertile and well-watered. It was 401 BC, and the great general was leading ten thousand Greek mercenaries on the long
march home from Babylon, north through Mesopotamia, Armenia, and Anatolia. The hoplites had fought with distinction
in the attempted coup d'état by the Persian rebel Cyrus the
Younger against the grand army of his brother, Artaxerxes II,
king of Persia. But when Cyrus was killed by Artaxerxes's men
in the battle of Cunaxa (near modern Baghdad), the cause was
lost. The Persians had invited the Greek generals to negotiate.
At the supposedly friendly banquet, however, all the generals
were assassinated, and the Greek army was left stranded in a

precarious situation with no leaders and thousands of miles from home.[1]

Xenophon emerged from the ranks as their new leader. The murder of the Greek generals and his knowledge of Persian history made Xenophon exquisitely aware of treachery, but even he was unprepared for what happened in Pontus.

Xenophon always followed his own advice to military leaders, "Above all, camp in a healthy place." His men had battled hostile inhabitants and plundered towns for supplies all along the march from Babylon. Here it seemed safe for the ten thousand homesick soldiers to rest and dream of soon reaching Greece. The villages were well-stocked with food. "There was nothing remarkable about the place," wrote Xenophon in his memoir of the expedition, "except for extraordinary numbers of swarming bees." And there was even the special treat of wild honey for the taking. The men soon discovered the beehives and raided them for the sweet.

After feasting on the honey, however, the soldiers "succumbed to a strange affliction," and began to act like intoxicated madmen. Soon they were staggering about and collapsing by the thousands. Xenophon reported that his troops were sprawled over the ground like victims of a terrible rout. As though under a spell, the men were totally incapacitated. Some even died. A "great despondency prevailed," wrote Xenophon. The next day, the survivors began to recover their senses but were unable to stand until three or four days later. Still feeling weak, the army broke camp and continued west. The vulnerability of his men to an ambush in enemy territory while they were unconscious greatly troubled Xenophon.

Unknown to Xenophon, the culprit in this situation was naturally toxic honey, produced by bees that collected nectar from poisonous rhododendron blossoms. The powerful neu-rotoxins of the flowers have no effect on the bees. The inhab-itants of the Black Sea region knew all about the beautiful but baneful rhododendron plant. Its sap could be used as an arrow poison, and in very tiny doses the honey was a *pharmakon*, taken as a tonic or mild intoxicant. Today in northern Turkey and the Caucasus region, the honey is known as *deli bal* ("mad honey"). A small spoonful in a glass of milk is considered a traditional pick-me-up, and a dollop in alcoholic beverages gives an extra kick. In the eighteenth century, *deli bal* (*miel fou* to Europeans) was a major export from the Crimea, and tons of toxic honey were shipped to Europe to be added to drinks sold in taverns.

Strangers unfamiliar with the delicious honey made from poison flowers are liable to overdose, like Xenophon's sol-diers who eagerly devoured the honeycombs. I interviewed an American anthropology student who barely survived a bout with toxic honey in Nepal where great rhododendron forests thrive. His hosts, nomadic yak herders, had warned him about the dangers of wild honey and told him how to distinguish toxic from safe honey. One method is to hold a handful: a tingling sensation indicates toxicity. But the student observed that the herders purposely gathered the toxic honey. Assuming that it was a hallucinogenic drug, he sought out a beehive in the rhododendron forest, identified the toxic honey, and ate an ounce or so. The high began pleasantly enough, he recalled, but soon turned ferocious. Tingling and numbness progressed to vertigo and severe vomiting and diarrhea. His speech be-came garbled and the psychedelic visual effects were frighten-ing, with whirling colored lights and tunnel vision. Delirious, he was able to reach the village just before muscle paralysis caused complete collapse. The villagers nursed him back from near death. A few days later, following the same course of recovery experienced by Xenophon's men, the student was still weak, but able to stand. Later, he learned that the herders fed tiny doses to their yaks as a spring tonic. They told him that the amount he had ingested was enough to kill a huge Tibetan mastiff.

By Roman times, the "mad" honey of the Black Sea area was well-known to natural historians. Pliny the Elder mused on the paradox that the "sweetest, finest, most health-promoting food" could be so randomly lethal. Noting that nature had already armed bees with venomous stings, Pliny surmised that the bees deliberately borrowed the toxins from poisonous plants to create an additional weapon, one intended to protect their honeycombs from human greed.[2]

Xenophon's close call was due to accidental poisoning, but it was only a matter of time before someone figured out how to use the honey as a biological weapon. As John Ambrose, a historian of insects in warfare, commented, the ancients "were clever enough to realize that the honey . . . could have a military usage not unlike that of poison gas today."[3] Honey was just one of many attractive lures that could serve as a secret biological weapon to disable or kill enemies in antiquity. And fears of biotoxins inspired the search for antidotes and immunities, which were themselves sometimes based on poisons.

◢ ◢ ◢

Four centuries after Xenophon's experience, in about 65 BC, a Roman army marched through the same region. They too feasted on the delicious honey of Pontus, this time with fatal consequences. The commander of the army was Pompey the Great, during the long campaigns to conquer Rome's most dangerous enemy in the first century BC, the brilliant King Mithradates VI of Pontus. Mithradates's colossal army—feared for its hellish war chariots with rotating scythes attached to the wheels—had swept across Asia Minor, and had slaughtered tens of thousands of Romans. Pompey's predecessor, Licinius Lucullus, had failed to finish the war against the elusive Mithradates in an arduous campaign of 74–66 BC. Pompey's legions finally defeated Mithradates's grand army in 65 BC, but the wily king slipped away over the Caucasus Mountains to Crimea and began to plan an audacious land invasion of Italy.

Mithradates was a ruler with a phobia of assassination by poison, and with good reason: he had murdered his own mother, his brother, his four sons, and many others, and poison was a favorite weapon in his milieu. A team of Scythian shaman-doctors, the Agari, accompanied Mithradates at all times (chapter 2). Even the king's sleep was said to be protected by unusual guardians: a bull, a horse, and a stag. These animals alerted him with a three-alarm cacophony—bellowing, whinnying, and roaring—whenever someone approached the royal chamber.[4]

Early in his life, Mithradates had devised a remarkable personal poison survival plan. His program was based on the practice of ingesting a minute amount of a toxin or contagion, just enough to confer immunity when the body encounters the toxin again (the principle of hormesis and of modern vaccines). The king swallowed smidgens of poisons and antidotes every day. Extremely erudite, Mithradates studied texts in many languages. Indian medicine was much admired and disseminated as far as Rome by his day. The king may have known that in ancient India fears of assassination by poisoning were addressed in the *Laws of Manu*, the Hindu sacred code of conduct dating to about 500 BC. Perhaps the idea for his special regimen was influenced by the verse that instructed, "Let the king mix all his food with medicines that are antidotes against poisons."[5]

Searching for a perfect theriac, a universal antidote to all poisons, Mithradates also tested various *pharmaka* on prisoners, friends, and himself. Eventually he created an elaborate compound of more than fifty ingredients, including antidotes and tiny amounts of toxins, combining these into a single drug for his own protection. His special theriac became known as *Mithridatium*. Over the years after his death, the formula was improved on by various Roman toxicologists, including the personal physician to the emperor Nero (in about 60 AD), who added ten more ingredients, including chopped viper flesh and opium. The imperial physician Galen prepared daily doses of this new, improved *Mithridatium* for three emperors who feared biological attack, including Marcus Aurelius.[6]

Complex concoctions thought to have pan-antidotal powers were also created in ancient India. The Indian medical writers Charaka and Sushruta (about 400 BC) mention two universal antidotes to poisons, one called *Mahagandhahasti*, with sixty ingredients, and another with eighty-five. *Mithridatium* was exported over the Spice Route to China. Vials of *Mithridatium* continued to be very popular in Europe in the Middle Ages and Renaissance—and they were still dispensed by French and German apothecaries up to the late nineteenth century.[7]

Commanders who used poison weapons themselves were especially sensitive to the need for antidotes or immunities.

In his Indian military manual, the *Arthashastra*, Kautilya included a chapter on preparations to be administered to an army (and its animals) "before the commencement of battles and the assailing of forts," to protect them against the enemies' biological weapons and the potential backfire of their own biochemicals. The ingredients included known poisons, such as aconite, along with numerous plant, animal, and mineral substances of varying medicinal effects, such as jackal blood, mongoose and crocodile bile, gold, turmeric, and charcoal (these last three are genuinely effective agents in modern medicine). In a modern echo of Kautilya's plans, in 2002, as the United States threatened invasion of Iraq (ancient Babylonia) to destroy its stores of bioweapons, Saddam Hussein reportedly attempted to obtain antidotes for nerve gases in vast quantities, in an effort to protect his army from their own weapons.[8]

Mithradates's and Kautilya's efforts to ensure immunity to poison weapons are mirrored in other crude—and sophisticated—methods today. For example, Indonesian military training includes drinking the blood of venomous snakes and undergoing snakebites to boost soldiers' immunity to venom and poison arrows. In the United States during the anthrax and bioterror fears of 2001, the apocalyptic survivalist company Tetrahedron sold "Essential Oils for Biological Warfare Preparedness," claiming that they could protect against anthrax and bubonic plague.[9]

A complex example of the unanticipated results of attempting to defend against one's own biological tactics occurred in World War II in Europe. The Germans had polluted a large reservoir with sewage, which caused outbreaks of highly contagious typhus. To protect themselves, the Nazis relied on testing the blood of local people to avoid going into areas rife with typhus. In Poland, however, the Nazis' defense was turned against them. Local doctors secretly injected the Poles with a vaccine that gave false-positive readings for typhus in the Nazis' blood tests, leading the Germans to stay away from the region.[10]

Just as making poison arrows or bottling plague could threaten accidental self-contamination, ancient and modern methods of seeking immunity to poison weapons can also have deleterious boomerang effects. At the beginning of the Gulf War of 1991, the US military vaccinated and medicated American soldiers to protect them from biochemical weapons that were expected to be unleashed in Iraq. In the years after the war, however, the veterans have been afflicted by clusters of serious health problems, referred to as Gulf War syndrome, attributed in part to the drugs that were intended to protect them.[11]

In antiquity, Emperor Marcus Aurelius feared assassination by poison and/or plague. (Some accused him of poisoning his co-emperor Lucius Verus, who died in AD 169.) To protect himself, Marcus Aurelius ingested a dose of Galen's opium-fortified *Mithridatium* every day. The emperor become an opium addict and died in AD 180 during the great plague brought back to Rome from Babylon by his own army, commanded by Verus (chapter 4).[12]

Even King Mithradates's search for immunity to poisons did not save him in the end. Having escaped from Pompey, the king was hiding out in his Crimean kingdom planning an invasion of Italy, when his son led a revolt. Cornered in his castle tower, Mithradates was forced to commit suicide in 63 BC. He took poison, which he always kept at hand. The

Romans liked to claim that his attempt to die peacefully was ironically thwarted by his lifelong regimen of toxins and antidotes. But a more logical explanation is that the suicide poison was ineffective because he shared the single dose stored in his dagger hilt with his two daughters who were trapped in the tower with him. They died, but not enough poison remained for Mithradates, who had to order his bodyguard to kill him with a sword.

Meanwhile, Pompey seized the king's headquarters and royal possessions, including an extensive library of toxicology treatises in numerous languages (Mithradates knew nearly two dozen tongues). Pompey also recovered a treasure trove of Mithradates's handwritten notes on his experiments with poisons and antidotes. Recognizing their value, Pompey sent the books and notes to Rome with orders that they be translated into Latin.

Pliny, writing a century later, consulted Mithradates's personal toxicology library and cited several antidotes written out in Greek in the king's own hand. In his biotoxins gardens and laboratory, Mithradates's experimental agents included arsenic; the blood of Pontic ducks who lived on poisonous plants; a pink flower he called *mithridatia*; and *polemonia*, "the plant of a thousand powers." Pliny was deeply impressed by the "untiring research into every possible experiment in compelling poisons to be useful remedies."[13]

As king of Pontus and scholar of toxicology, Mithradates was well aware of the deadly properties of the rhododendron honey of his kingdom. He would have kept some in his royal stores of *pharmaka*, and he may have included it in his *Mithridatium*. He was certainly familiar with the arrow poisons concocted by his allies the Soanes and Scythians. And he knew all about Xenophon's experience with the poisonous honey in his kingdom of Pontus (described earlier). In that instance, Xenophon's army survived because they had not been attacked while they lay helpless. With his knowledge of the effects of local rhododendron honey, Mithradates had a great advantage over Pompey and his Roman army, who were unaware of the danger as they pursued Mithradates into Pontus in about 65 BC.

Mithradates's allies in the region near Colchis, the Heptakometes, were described by Strabo as dwellers in tree forts, living on "the flesh of wild animals and nuts." The tribe was feared for attacking wayfarers, suddenly leaping down on them like leopards from their tree houses. The Heptakometes may have received specific orders from Mithradates on how to ambush the Roman army. What we do know is that they gathered up great numbers of wild honeycombs dripping with toxic honey and placed them all along Pompey's route. The Roman soldiers stopped to enjoy the honey and immediately lost their senses. Reeling and babbling, the men collapsed with vomiting and diarrhea, and lay on the ground unable to move. The Heptakometes easily wiped out about a thousand of Pompey's soldiers.

Raw honey and its fermented product, mead, were the only natural sweets in antiquity, as irresistible as candy. The Heptakometes simply used a natural resource of their landscape, wild honey that happened to be a deadly intoxicant, as a biological agent to incapacitate the Romans so they could be easily slaughtered. The same advantage could be gained with fermented honey, set out as alluring bait to entrap enemies. Later in the Black Sea region, for example, the Russian foes of Olga of Kiev fell for a ruse in AD 946, when they accepted several tons of fermented honey from Olga's allies. Was the mead fortified with *deli bal*? That is not known, but all five thousand Russians were massacred as they lay in a stupor. Several centuries later, in 1489, in the same area, the Russian army slaughtered some ten thousand Tatar soldiers after they had gulped down great casks of mead purposely left by the Russians in their abandoned camp.[14]

*   *

Aelian noted that soldiers on campaign were especially vulnerable to plots involving food and drink. The simplest biological ploy other than denying enemy soldiers drinking water was to take advantage of their hunger or overindulgence in eating and drinking. As Pliny lamented, "Most of man's trouble is caused by the belly.... it is chiefly through his food that a man dies." Aeneas had advised commanders in the fourth century BC to wait until the enemy grows reckless and begins "looting to satisfy their greed." They will "fill themselves with food and drink and, once drunk [will] become careless ... and impaired in performance." Writing in the same era in India, Kautilya told how to administer poisons "in the diet and other physical enjoyments" of the enemy.[15]

Hannibal the Carthaginian relied on this tactic during his invasion of Italy in the third century BC. Noticing the lack of firewood in the district and aware of the dietary habits of the Roman army, he devised a cunning plan. He knew that the Roman soldiers were used to eating cereals rather than meat. So Hannibal abandoned his camp, leaving a herd of cattle behind, and waited in ambush until the Romans eagerly took possession of the cows as booty. They slaughtered the cows, but when they could find no wood for cooking fires, they stuffed themselves with the "raw and indigestible" beef. Unused to such heavy, uncooked fare, the soldiers became severely bilious and lethargic from their steak tartare feast. Returning in the night when the indisposed Romans were "off their guard and gorged with raw meat," wrote the military tactician Frontinus, the Carthaginians "inflicted great losses upon them."

In his first victory in northern Italy in December 218 BC, Hannibal had used another simple ploy based on biological vulnerability. Drawing up his forces at first light, he tricked the Romans into fighting in the freezing snow before they had eaten breakfast. Hungry and numb with cold, they were easily annihilated by the well-fed Carthaginian troops. Some decades later, Tiberius Gracchus, the Roman commander battling the Celtiberians in Spain in 178 BC, also used hunger as a weapon. He learned through spies that the enemy was suffering from a lack of provisions. Like Hannibal, he abandoned his camp, leaving behind "an elaborate supply of all kinds of foods." After the Celtiberians "had gorged themselves to repletion with the food they found," says Frontinus, "Gracchus brought back his army and suddenly crushed them."[16]

If setting out tempting food worked to trick enemies, plying them with inebriating liquor was even more effective. Barrels of alcohol could be left for them to find, or they could be sent gifts of wine (fig. 19). Many Greek myths tell how semihuman creatures, Centaurs, Satyrs, and Tritons, were captured or killed after being lured with wine. This simple biosubterfuge also figured in historical military engagements, especially those fought against "barbarians" (non-Greco-Romans) who were thought to be especially susceptible to liquor.

FIG. 19. Jugs of wine could be sent to enemies or left in an abandoned camp. Foes who fell into a drunken stupor were easily wiped out. Detail, Apulian bowl, 375 BC, 14.130.13, Rogers Fund, 1914, Metropolitan Museum, New York.

A historical example occurred in North Africa. The ruthless emperor Domitian (AD 81–96), vexed by the revolt by the Nasamonian nomads of Numidia, declared, "I forbid the Nasamonians to exist!" When Flaccus, Domitian's governor in Numidia, learned that the tribe had discovered barrels of wine and were lying helplessly unconscious, he sent troops to "attack and annihilate them, even destroying all the non-combatants."[17]

Polyaenus, who compiled the "stratagems of war" handbook for Marcus Aurelius and Lucius Verus, offered advice on how to defeat barbarians in Asia in the second century AD. He began his book with an "archaeology" of mythical examples of successful trickery, assuring the emperors that courage and strength in battle were all well and good, but the wisest generals should know how to achieve victory *without* risk, in other words, by cunning arts and subterfuges. When the god Dionysus marched against India, declared Polyaenus, he concealed his spears in ivy and distracted the enemies with wine, then attacked while they partied under the influence.

Polyaenus also shrewdly twisted the ancient myth of Heracles and the Centaurs. Although the myth says Heracles was forced to fight the Centaurs when an unruly mob of them crashed a party to get wine, Polyaenus claimed that Heracles had planned to wipe out the entire Centaur race all along and lured them to their death by poison arrows by setting out jugs of wine.

Turning to real-life battles, Polyaenus cited the Celts as an example. Like all barbarians, he wrote, the Celtic race was "by nature immoderately fond of wine." He reminded his imperial readers that during treaty negotiations with them, the Romans had sent many gifts, including "a large amount of wine as if to friends." After the Celts "consumed a great deal of the wine and lay drunk," wrote Polyaenus, "the Romans attacked and cut them all to pieces."

It is notable that in the historical accounts of using wine in warfare, the victims were identified as barbarians, considered inferior to the civilized cultures of the Greeks, the Romans, and the Carthaginians. (Similar justifications were expressed in British decisions to use chemical poisons against "ignorant and uncivilized" peoples in Asia and Africa in the early twentieth century.) The Greek and Roman tacticians who recounted the stories consistently stressed the barbarians' inordinate passion for alcohol, as though to justify a biological treachery that would not be employed against more cultured, noble enemies. For example, Polyaenus advised the emperors on how to defeat Asians by turning their "propensity" for trickery and terrorism, and their love of intoxicants, against them.[18]

Polyaenus, it seems, was rather enamored of the method of defeating enemies with intoxicants. He also described how Tomyris, queen of the Massagetae, was said to have lured the Persian king Cyrus the Great to an ignominious death in 530 BC. But Polyaenus, writing nearly seven hundred years after the event, garbled the story. In his version, Tomyris pretended to flee in fear from the Persians, leaving casks of wine in her camp. The Persians consumed the wine all night long, celebrating as if they had won a victory. When they lay sleeping off their wine and wantonness, Tomyris attacked the Persians, who were scarcely able to move, and killed them all, including the king.[19]

In fact, Cyrus did die during the conflict with Tomyris, but according to the Greek historian Herodotus, it was Cyrus who had tricked the milk-drinking nomads with strong wine. Herodotus's version was based on information he gained from personal interviews with Scythians about a hundred years after the event, and seems more plausible than Polyaenus's version.

Tomyris's Massagetae were nomadic Saka-Scythian mounted archers living east of the Caspian Sea. These formidable warriors were unfamiliar with wine—their favored intoxicants were hashish and fermented mare's milk. When Cyrus began a war to annex their territory to his empire, his advisers recommended a clever stratagem. Since the Massagetae "have no experience with luxuries [and] know nothing of the pleasures of life," they could be easily liquidated if the Persians set out a tempting banquet for them, complete with "strong wine in liberal quantities."

Herodotus stressed the moral aspect of the story, that Cyrus used biological treachery because his men lacked the skill and bravery necessary for a fair fight. The Greek historian Strabo, who also discussed the event, made the important point that Cyrus was in retreat after losing a battle with the nomads and therefore had to resort to underhanded trickery.

Cyrus ordered a fancy banquet to be set out under the Persian tents and withdrew, leaving behind a contingent of his most feeble, expendable soldiers. Tomyris's army arrived and quickly killed the weak men whom Cyrus had sacrificed to the ruse. Congratulating themselves, the nomads then took their seats at the splendid feast laid out for them and drank so much wine that they fell into a stupor. Cyrus returned and slew the drunken Massagetae. He also captured Tomyris's son, but the youth killed himself as soon as he sobered up the next morning.

Enraged by the bloodshed achieved through such base biosabotage, Tomyris sent a message to Cyrus equating wine with poison. "Glutton that you are for blood, you have no cause to be proud of this day's work, which has no hint of soldierly courage. Your weapon was red wine, which you Persians are wont to drink until you are so mad that shameful words float on the fumes. This is the poison you treacherously used to destroy my men and my son." Leave my country now, she demanded, "or I swear by the Sun to give you more blood than you can drink." Cyrus ignored the message.

The battle that ensued was one of the most violent ever recorded, wrote Herodotus. According to his informants, the two sides exchanged volleys of arrows until there were no more, and then there was a long period of vicious hand-to-hand fighting with spears and daggers. By the end of the day, the greater part of the Persian army lay destroyed where it had stood. Tomyris sent her men to search the heaps of dead

FIG. 20. Queen Tomyris of the Massagetae taking revenge on King Cyrus of Persia for poisoning her army with wine. *Head of Cyrus Brought to Queen Tomyris*, Gaspard Duchange, 1713, engraving after Rubens, Elisha Whittelsey Fund, 1951, 51.501.7649, Metropolitan Museum New York.

Persians for Cyrus's body (fig. 20). Hacking off his head, she plunged it into a kettle of blood drawn from the king's fallen men, crying, "I fulfill my threat! Here is your fill of blood!"[20]

Queen Tomyris's milk-drinking warriors from the steppes were unfamiliar with the effects of wine, which made Cyrus's strategy seem especially odious. In other instances, however, taking advantage of an enemy's careless overindulgence in food or liquor did not seem unfair, since it was assumed that a commander should be able to restrain his men's behavior, and also because of the element of free choice in the decision to indulge or not. Contaminating wine with poison substances was particularly treacherous, however, because it eliminated free choice, and offering poisoned wine as a gift was even more devious because it violated the principles of trust and fair gift exchange. And yet ever since the Trojan Horse trick took down Troy, vigilant generals and their armies should have been on guard against accepting "gifts" from enemies.

🖋 🖋 🖋

In Homer's *Odyssey*, we saw that the wicked suitors terrorizing Odysseus's wife, Penelope, and his son Telemachus express the fear that Telemachus might, like his father, use the toxic plant from Ephyra to poison their wine and then slaughter them while they were helpless (chapter 1). In historical times, two commanders, Himilco and Maharbal of Carthage, were credited with defeating North African tribes with poisoned wine. According to Polyaenus, Himilco, a "pertinacious soldier" who owed most of his victories to his enemies' errors (in the judgment of modern historians), had lost several battles when plague swept through his armies in 406 and 400 BC. With his forces severely reduced by this natural disaster, Himilco devised a biological strategy to conquer a rebellious North African tribe in 396 BC. Himilco defeated the Libyans by taking advantage of their fondness for wine. He tainted jugs of wine in his own camp with mandragora or mandrake, and then pretended to retreat.

Mandrake, a heavily narcotic root of the deadly nightshade family (chapter 2), originated in North Africa and so was a well-known *pharmakon* in Carthage. Mandrake was surrounded with ancient lore and danger. As with hellebore, there were two kinds of mandrake, white (male) and black (female), and the plant had to be gathered by shamans who knew the proper rituals. With their backs turned to the wind, the diggers first traced three circles around the plant with a sword and then dug it up while facing west. Some believed the root emitted screams as it was pulled from the ground, and to hear that terrible sound spelled instant death. To avoid hearing the screams, an herbalist tied the mandrake stem to the leg of a dog, which uprooted the plant when it was called from a safe distance. The strong-smelling roots were sliced and sun-dried, and then crushed or boiled and preserved in wine (this practice may have suggested to Himilco the idea of tainting barrels of wine).

According to Pliny, the mere fumes of mandrake made one drowsy, and those who inhaled too deeply were struck dumb. The tactician Frontinus described mandrake as a drug whose "potency lies somewhere between a poison and a soporific." A minute dose, either inhaled or drunk, could be used as a sleeping draught or anesthetic before surgery, but "those who in ignorance took too copious a draught" fell into a fatal coma. And indeed, the Libyans "greedily drank of the wine" while Himilco feigned his retreat. In what has become a timeworn tactic, the Carthaginians returned and killed the unconscious tribe.

During the Second Punic War (218–201 BC) Hannibal's hotheaded cavalry officer Maharbal also used mandrake against some unnamed "barbarians." Maharbal mixed up a large batch of wine with pulverized mandrake root and left it in his camp. The "barbarians captured the camp and in a frenzy of delight greedily drank the drugged wine." Maharbal came back and "slaughtered them as they lay stretched out as if dead."[21]

Julius Caesar may have been inspired by these Carthaginian ruses with mandrake during his tangle with pirates in Asia

Minor in about 75 BC. By Caesar's time, Cilician pirates (based on the coasts of Turkey and Syria) had become a serious threat in the eastern Mediterranean, and the Romans undertook several campaigns to wipe them out. On a sea voyage from Rome to Bithynia (in northwest Turkey), the young Caesar was captured near Cape Malea by the Cilician pirates prowling the treacherous waters around southern Greece. The pirates sailed on to Miletus, a wealthy Roman city on the coast of Asia Minor, and demanded a large ransom for Caesar's release.

Caesar managed to send a secret message to the Milesians requesting that they bring double the ransom money, along with provisions for a "great feast." According to Polyaenus, the Milesians sent the money, along with large jars of wine well-spiked with mandrake and another huge pot with swords hidden inside. "Overjoyed at the large amount of money," the unsuspecting pirates celebrated with the wine and collapsed en masse on the deck of the ship. The Milesians returned and stabbed them all to death, and Caesar returned the ransom money. He then coolly proceeded to catch another ship to Bithynia.[22]

Sometimes the people that the Greeks and Romans called barbarians used this biological tactic against other barbarians. When the Celts and Autariatae were locked in a long war, for instance, the historian Theopompus (fourth century BC) reported that the Celts "drugged their own food and wine with debilitating herbs and left them behind in their tents," then abandoned camp by night. The Autariatae, thinking the Celts had fled in fear, "seized the tents and freely enjoyed the wine and food." The effect was immediate: they "lay about powerless, undone by violent diarrhea. The Celts returned and murdered them as they lay helpless." We can make a good guess at the identity of the toxic herb. The symptoms recall those of hellebore, which we know was employed by the Celtic archers to poison their arrows, and which was used to similar effect by the Greeks when they poisoned the water supply of Kirrha.[23]

The ancient practice of poisoning wine or other tempting treats—turning what the Indian strategist Kautilya had termed the "enemy's physical enjoyments" into a weapon—turns up regularly in later history too. Some modern examples are vicious enough to make the ancient incidents seem almost quaint. The humanist physician Andrea Cesalpino reported that during the Naples Campaign of 1494–95, the Spanish abandoned a village to the French, leaving behind casks of wine that had been mixed with tainted blood drawn from leprosy and syphilis patients at Saint-Lazare Hospital. During World War II, Dr. Shiro Ishii, the Japanese master of biological weapons, reportedly handed out anthrax-laced candies to Chinese children in Nanking. A CIA plot to create exploding cigars for Fidel Castro in the 1960s is another example, and in the 1980s South African government agents poisoned beer, whiskey, cigarettes, chocolates, sugar, and peppermints to murder antiapartheid dissidents.[24]

* * *

In our reconstruction of the murky world of ancient biochemical warfare, many of the insidious weapons and stratagems were developed by experts in natural toxins who remained anonymous, with the credit going to the commanders they worked for, such as Himilco. The arrow poisons concocted from plants and vipers, and the hellebore and mandrake used to contaminate water and wine, for example, were gathered and prepared by shamans, witches, Druids, magicians, and other skilled practitioners of clandestine arts. "Those who possessed knowledge guarded it with jealous care" and encouraged ordinary people to believe "that it was obtained by supernatural means," remarks Vaman Kokatnur, in his article on chemical warfare in ancient India.[25] They usually worked covertly, behind the scenes, and their successes could be described as "revenge of the gods" or magic, to maximize the psychological terror of biochemical warfare. These specialists in early botany, zoology, pharmacology, toxicology—and magic—were actually the first biowar scientists, but their role has remained obscure to historians because of the secrecy that surrounded their arcane professions. As a result, the identities of only a few of the ancient biowar professionals can be pinpointed—such as the Psylli of Africa and the Agari snake-venom specialists of Scythia, hired by the military leaders Cato and Mithradates, respectively. Mithradates stands out as a unique example of a famous military commander who was himself learned in toxicology, and Kautilya, the adviser to King Chandragupta, is another military toxicology expert whose name has come down to us.

One very early example of rare notoriety for a bioweapons maker was Chrysame. She was a witch from Thessaly who devised a brilliant stratagem based on trickery and drugging the enemy with tainted comestibles. The legendary account, told by Polyaenus, is very old, set in about 1050 BC, the time of the Greek colonization of Ionia (western Turkey). Cnopus, son of Codrus, the king of Athens, was waging war with the Ionians who held Erythrae, a wealthy city on the Aegean coast. Cnopus consulted an oracle about how to achieve victory. The oracle advised him to send for Chrysame, a priestess of the goddess Hecate in Thessaly, to be his "general."

Thessaly, in northern Greece, was the center of ancient witchcraft, and Thessalian witches like Chrysame were renowned for their black magic spells, poison potions, and drugs. Their dark powers were said to come from Hecate, the sorceress-goddess of the Underworld, mistress of crossroads and the Hounds of Hell whose worship involved little cakes illuminated with burning candles and the sacrifice of puppies. Cnopus sent an ambassador to Thessaly, and Chrysame agreed to sail to Ionia to direct his battle strategies against Erythrae.

As a priestess of Hecate, Chrysame was an expert in poisonous herbs and deadly *pharmaka,* and once in Erythrae, she surveyed the situation and planned a complex plot based on her special knowledge. She selected the largest and finest bull from Cnopus's herds, decked it out in a purple robe embroidered with golden thread, gilded its horns with beaten gold, and hung garlands of flowers around its neck. Then she mixed madness-inducing drugs into its food. Meanwhile, in full view of the enemy encamped in the fields, Chrysame set up a great altar and all the regalia for an important sacrifice. Her plan was to stage a fake botched sacrifice for the Erythraeans.

Chrysame led the magnificently decorated bull toward the altar. "Crazy from the drug's influence and in a frenzy," wrote Polyaenus, "the bull leaped away and escaped," bellowing and bucking like the modern equivalent of rodeo rough stock (fig. 21). Pretending dismay, Chrysame watched with hidden satisfaction as the bull barreled into the enemy camp. Polyaenus described the success of her ruse: "When the enemy saw the garlanded bull with golden horns charging from Cnopus's

FIG. 21. The witch-priestess Chrysame of Thessaly devised a successful military strategy to defeat the Ionians. She drugged a sacrificial bull to deliver incapacitating intoxicants to the enemy. Sacrificial bull, Parthenon frieze, 438–432 BC. © The Trustees of the British Museum / Art Resource, NY.

camp into their own camp, they welcomed it as a lucky sign and an auspicious omen."

Thinking that the gods had rejected Cnopus's sacrifice, the Erythraeans captured the bull and sacrificed it to their own gods. Then, they feasted on the meat as though partaking of a "divine and miraculous omen" of their own victory. But as soon as they devoured the drugged flesh, they were seized by madness. "Everyone began to jump up and down, to run in different directions, to skip with joy." In this case, we can rule out the strong purgative hellebore. Rather, Chrysame's drug apparently had hallucinogenic properties; perhaps it was atropine from deadly nightshade, known in antiquity for causing "playful insanity" in certain doses. Whatever the *pharmakon* that Chrysame administered to the bull, it evidently retained enough potency after slaughter and cooking to affect the men who ate the meat.

As soon as Chrysame saw that the giddy guards had abandoned their posts and the whole camp was disordered and deranged, she ordered Cnopus and his army to take up their weapons and "speedily attack the defenseless enemy. Thus Cnopus destroyed them all and became master of the great and prosperous city of Erythrae."[26]

*　　　*　　　*

"We need something . . . like calmatives, anaesthetic agents, that would put people to sleep or in a good mood." "I would like a magic dust that would put everyone in a building to sleep, combatants and noncombatants." "It would surely be desirable to develop a mist that could put people to sleep quickly." These quotes from US military personnel and a major newspaper editorial describe special drugs, gases, or chemicals to be used against terrorists or to control crowds in civic unrest. Their words echo the ancient desire to disable adversaries with pacifying, sedating, or disorienting agents to produce stupor, enchantment, or a hypnotic state. Similarly, a Pentagon DARPA proposal sought a "system which would make an unfriendly crowd become friendly almost instantaneously."[27] The desire to develop some sort of "magic dust," calmative mists, and other crowd-control weapons (CCWs) to pacify or neutralize adversaries was long ago foreshadowed in the use of barrels of wine and Chrysame's drugged bull tactic in antiquity.

Modern efforts to find "nonlethal" ways of pacifying a foe began during World War II, with a bizarre initiative by the OSS (the forerunner of the CIA), whose agents attempted to find a means of chemically pacifying Adolf Hitler. They planned to surreptitiously inject his vegetables with female hormones. Then, in 1965–67, during experiments with LSD-like agents, the Pentagon secretly released on US citizens in Hawaii a hallucinogen that was being developed as a chemical weapon. And in 2002, it was reported that the Pentagon's Joint Non-Lethal Weapons Directorate (JNLWD) and the US Department of Justice began developing what they call "calmatives or chemical peacemakers." These "counterpersonnel" weapons in the form of sedatives or mind-altering agents could be placed in water supplies, sprayed as aerosol mists, or packed into rubber bullets. The idea was to use the weapons indiscriminately on large populations, such as dissidents, refugees, or "hostile mobs." Then US troops would sort through the mass of incapacitated people to identify enemies.

It's worth noting that in all of the ancient incidents of narcotizing or incapacitating enemies with intoxicants like wine or other drugs, wholesale slaughter of the unconscious victims, often including noncombatants, was invariably carried out. Indeed, the JNLWD has acknowledged the need for "training soldiers to refrain from killing persons unable to defend themselves."[28] It's also worth recalling that in Greek myth, even the master of devious ruses, Odysseus, rejected the option of drugging the enemies who had taken his family hostage, preferring to trick them into meeting him face-to-face.

The potential for lethal collateral damage with such agents in modern situations was vividly demonstrated in October 2002, when Russian troops pumped a powerful narcotic mist into a Moscow theater where more than 700 hostages were held by 40 Chechen rebels. The plan was to neutralize everyone in the building with the gas, so that special forces could enter and shoot the unconscious rebels at close range, and then save the hostages. As with the drug hellebore in the water supply of Kirrha in the sixth century BC, however, the effect of the gas proved impossible to control. In the Moscow theater, the gas was responsible for the deaths of 127 innocent hostages and impaired the health of hundreds more.

In defending the Pyrrhic victory (a victory won at excessive cost) over the Chechen rebels, the Russian health minister, Dr. Shevchenko, sounded like the apologists for the Greek doctor Nebros who indiscriminately poisoned all the citizens of Kirrha, and Winston Churchill's defense of the use of allegedly "nonlethal" gas on Kurdish villagers. Despite the high death toll, Dr. Shevchenko argued that the gas "cannot in itself be called lethal."[29]

"There is no such thing as nonlethal weapons," countered Mark Wheelis, an expert on biochemical arms, in the aftermath of the Moscow crisis. The military's attraction to such armaments may be understandable, he said, but one must consider the "grave risks and costs." Not only do such weapons generate "unrealistic expectations of bloodless battles" and the problems of overkill and friendly fire; Wheelis pointed out another drawback: the possibility of enemies obtaining and using the same technologies. That issue, of course, applies to all biological and chemical weaponry. And it echoes a statement attributed to King Eumenes of Pergamum, who was defeated in a naval battle (second century BC) by Hannibal's plan to catapult live snakes onto Eumenes's ships (chapter 6). Eumenes declared that he "did not think that any general would want to obtain a victory by the use of means which might in turn be directed against himself."[30]

CHAPTER 6

ANIMAL ALLIES

The elephant dreads a squealing pig.
—AELIAN, *ON ANIMALS*

THE PHARAOH OF EGYPT, deluded by visions of grandeur, had treated his warrior class with contempt, thinking he would never need their services. Now he was in deep trouble. The invincible Assyrian army, led by King Sennacherib, had just breached Egypt's borders (in about 700 BC). And now the pharaoh's warriors refused to fight for him. "The situation was grave," wrote the historian Herodotus.[1]

The great Assyrian army camped at Pelusium, in the salt flats and flax fields along the northeastern border of Egypt, poised to overtake the kingdom. The pharaoh, who was also a priest of Ptah, was desperate. Regretting his pride, "not knowing what else to do," he entered the god's temple and bemoaned "bitterly the peril that threatened him." The pharaoh fell asleep in the midst of his lamentations and the god appeared in a dream. Ptah instructed the pharaoh to forget his warriors. Instead, he said, call up all the shopkeepers, crafts- men, and market folk into an army, and boldly go out to meet Sennacherib's troops. The god promised to send "helpers" to ensure victory. Confident now, the pharaoh marched with his ragtag legions to Pelusium and took up a position facing the enemy host.

Night fell, and not a creature was stirring . . . except for thousands of mice. Into the Assyrian camp crept multitudes of rodents, gnawing through all the leather quivers, shield straps, and bowstrings. The next morning the Assyrians were horrified to find they had no weapons to fight with. In antiquity, mice eating leather military gear was an omen of imminent disaster, and hordes of rodents presaged epidemics (chapter 4). The terrible omen threw the men into chaos; the Assyrians abandoned camp and fled. The Egyptian ad hoc army pursued them, inflicting severe losses on Sennacherib's men.

Herodotus heard this tale personally from the priests at the temple of Ptah, who showed him a memorial statue of the pharaoh holding a mouse, and historians believe that a core of historical truth is embedded in Herodotus's story. Archaeologists at Nineveh have found a series of inscriptions from Sennacherib's reign recording his invasions of Egypt and Palestine. In these, the narrative of the war breaks off abruptly, implying that some sort of unexpected calamity took place during the campaign. Putting together the various literary and archaeological clues about the incident helps clarify what probably happened.[2]

Hebrew sources in the Old Testament also recount the sudden and ignominious defeat of Sennacherib's army in about 700 BC, but they set the event at the gates of Jerusalem. According to 2 Kings, "an angel of the Lord smote 175,000 Assyrian soldiers"—this is traditional scriptural wording for plagues that destroyed the Israelites' enemies. King Hezekiah, inside the walls of Jerusalem, was also struck by the pestilence.

Josephus, a Jewish historian writing in AD 93, added to Herodotus's account, saying that the omen of the gnawing mice was only one reason for the hasty retreat. According to Josephus's sources, Sennacherib had also heard that a large Ethiopian army was coming to aid the Egyptians. Then, citing Berossus, a Babylonian historian (300 BC), Josephus plainly states that "a pestilential plague killed 185,000 Assyrians" as they retreated from Egypt through Palestine.[3]

The Greek, Hebrew, Babylonian, and Assyrian evidence refers to a military campaign that was aborted after Sennacherib's army was beset by disease-carrying rodents (Ptah's "helpers" in Herodotus's account), who, incidentally, ate the leather parts of the soldiers' weapons at Pelusium. The bad omen and the rumor of the approaching Ethiopian army caused the Assyrians to abandon their invasion of Egypt and retreat through Palestine while the rodent-borne disease (perhaps bubonic plague or typhus) incubated in the men. As the army arrived at Jerusalem, the epidemic swept through the troops, killing tens of thousands.[4]

◢ ◢ ◢

In the ancient world, mice and rats were believed to be controlled by plague-bringing divinities, such as Apollo, Ptah, and Yahweh. In the Greek world, Apollo, the god who controlled pestilence, was worshipped as "Smintheus," master and killer of rodents. Statues of mice were set up in Apollo's temples at Chryse and Hamaxitus near Troy, and (as noted in the discussion of plague in chapter 4), the temple at Hamaxitus actually maintained a horde of live white mice. Three ancient Greek sources, the natural historian Aelian and the geographers Polemon and Strabo, tell the origin of the cult of Apollo's pestilential mice. That ancient myth has intriguing parallels to the biodisaster that befell the Assyrian army.

Long ago, mice arrived by the tens of thousands and ruined the crops in the region around Troy. The rodents also overran the camp of an invading army from Crete, and ate all of *their* leather shield straps and bowstrings. With no weapons to wage war, the Cretans settled at Hamaxitus. They built the temple to Apollo, to honor the god of mice—lowly creatures who possess the power to take down entire armies.[5]

In ancient times, writers did not differentiate among mice, rats, and other types of rodents, all of which can harbor plague, typhus, and other diseases. The modern chronicler of rodent-borne epidemics, Hans Zinsser, remarked in 1934 that long before any scientific knowledge "concerning the dangerous character of rodents as carriers of disease, mankind dreaded . . . these animals." The ancient Jews considered all varieties of rodents unclean, and Persian Zoroastrians so loathed rats that killing them was "a service to God."[6]

As Zinsser pointed out, "What rats can do, mice may also accomplish." Yet some modern scholars still take the ancient association of mice and epidemics as evidence of superstition rather than an understanding of a real source of pestilence based on observation. Apparently unaware that no distinction was made among rodents in ancient writings, and assuming that only mice were associated with disease in antiquity, some commentators assert that mice never carry bubonic plague. For example, the scholar of ancient religion Christopher Faraone suggested that "faulty reasoning" about the "curious coincidence of swarming mice and man-killing plague" must have led the ancients to believe that vermin "*cause* epidemic disease." Faraone labels this "a misunderstanding that arises from the frequency with which plague strikes close on the heels" of mouse infestations. But pathogens are carried by parasites, usually fleas or lice, of rodents, which can transmit the diseases to humans, and many ancient texts make it clear that periodic hordes of rodents of any sort were correctly recognized as harbingers of pestilence, although their authors were unaware of the role of parasites. The geographer Strabo remarked about infestations of vermin, "From mice pestilential diseases often ensue." He also noted that during a rodent-borne plague that attacked the Roman army on campaign in Cantabria, Spain (first century BC), the commanders offered bounties on dead mice.[7]

Further proof that the ancients understood the connection between rodents and epidemics can be found in the Old Testament story of the Philistines who were stricken by disease after they captured the Ark of the Covenant during a war with the Israelites in the twelfth century BC (chapter 4). In what may be the earliest account of rodent-borne bubonic plague, the Philistine lands were afflicted by an onslaught of mice that coincided with an epidemic marked by "swellings in the Philistines' private places." The classic sign of the Black Death is grotesquely swollen lymph glands in the groin and thighs. And 1 Samuel 5–6 clearly indicates that the Philistines *themselves* recognized a connection between the rodents and the disease.[8]

The rodent hordes that afflicted the Philistines and averted the Assyrians' invasion were natural disasters. Directing multitudes of infected rodents against the enemy would be nearly impossible. But the priests and populace who prayed to their gods of pestilence for deliverance from foes by means of mice or rats certainly *intended* to wage biological war, and when an enemy was routed by plague, they credited the gods with the biological victory. Those small creatures were considered zoological allies in war. In a striking continuity of the ancient cult of rodent allies, laboratory scientists rely on the very same "helpers" that were kept in Apollo's temple—white mice and rats—to develop today's germ warfare agents.

I include tales like Sennacherib's military disaster in this chronicle of early biowarfare because of the long-observed relationship between infestations of vermin and thwarted invasions. This association suggested the idea of praying to gods to send swarms of rodents and gave people the idea of deliberately trying to turn other noxious creatures against enemies. And, in fact, as the following episodes show, a remarkable variety of creatures from the animal and insect world were recruited to achieve victory in ancient times.

◢ ◢ ◢

Mice were not the smallest animal allies in waging biological war. One of the biblical Ten Plagues of Egypt was an infestation of lice that afflicted both animals and humans. Lice can carry typhus. That fortuitous infestation was attributed to Yahweh, but there is plenty of evidence from ancient texts that other insects, such as stinging bees, hornets, wasps, and scorpions (venomous arthropods), were purposefully used in wartime as agents for both offense and defense. Simply by doing what came naturally, these tiny creatures could inflict great damage and chaos.

Insects, with their sharp stingers and biochemical poisons, and their propensity to defend and attack, have long "served as models for man to emulate in . . . the art of war-fare," commented the military historian and entomologist John Ambrose. Bees were admired in antiquity as producers of honey, but they were also respected as aggressive crea-tures "of exceedingly vicious disposition." In one of the ear-lier examples of borrowing weapons from nature's armory, we saw how a relatively primitive tribe in Asia Minor dec-imated Pompey's Roman army by setting out toxic honey-combs (chapter 5). As Pliny noted, the baneful honey was the bees' defensive weapon against human greed. But the honeybees themselves—and wasps and hornets (the largest species of wasps)—were armed with stingers. Swarms had been known to invade towns, forcing entire populations to relocate.

Such a disaster had befallen the residents of Phaselis (cen-tral Turkey), and the people of Rhaucus, in Crete, had to aban-don their city when swarms of copper-colored killer bees from Mount Ida "inflicted the most grievous pain."[9]

Why not hurl entire hives filled with enraged, venomous insects at an enemy? The painful stings would send any army into wild confusion and retreat, and massive numbers of stings could be fatal. According to Pliny, it takes only twenty-seven hornet stings to kill a man (in fact, even one sting can cause death in individuals who are sensitive to the venom).[10]

Bees'-nest bombs were probably among the first projectile weapons, and the scholar of Mesopotamian history Edward Neufeld surmises that hornets' nests were lobbed at enemies hiding in caves as early as Neolithic times (fig. 22). Bees have figured in warfare in different cultures of many eras. The sa-cred text of the Maya in Central America, the *Popol Vuh*, for example, describes an ingenious bee booby trap used to repel

FIG. 22. Wasp nests and beehives were hurled at enemies from Neolithic times onward. Dover Pictorial Archives.

besiegers: dummy warriors outfitted in cloaks, spears, and shields were posted along the walls of the citadel. War bonnets were placed on the heads, which were actually large gourds filled with bees, wasps, and flies. As the assailants scaled the walls, the gourds were smashed. The furious insects homed in on the warriors, who were soon "dazed by the yellow jackets and wasps [and were sent] stumbling and falling down the mountainside."[11]

Were hornets and other venomous insects marshaled to scourge the Israelites' foes? Neufeld has written that in biblical times insects were "important military agents in tactics of ambush," guerrilla raids, and flushing out primitive strongholds. He also noted that ancient Hebrew and Arab sources refer to hordes of unidentified flying insects that were summoned by priests to attack the enemies' eyes with "acrid poison fluids," blinding or killing them. As Neufeld pointed out, these could belong to any of the dozens of species of noxious insects in the Near East. He suggested the gadfly or "eye fly" as the unknown insect that ejected blinding poison. Is it possible that some of the Near Eastern stories were about infestations of *Paederus* beetles? These rove beetles excrete the virulent poison *pederin*, a fluid that on the skin or mucous membranes causes suppurating sores and blindness, and in the bloodstream the effect is as deadly as cobra venom. Plagues of *Paederus* beetles periodically afflict populations in Africa and in the Mideast, but it is difficult to see how the swarms could ever have been directed effectively in a military campaign.

On the other hand, some biblical passages cited by Neufeld do seem to suggest a *planned* military use of stinging insects. Exodus states that hornets were "sent ahead" of the Israelites to drive out the Canaanites, Hittites, and other enemies, and in Deuteronomy hornets supplemented ordinary weapons against the Canaanites. In Joshua, hornets, in conjunction with swords or bows, drove out the Amorites. Proposing that these biblical narratives describe "massive assaults" with hornets' nests, "plotted and contrived deliberately," rather than reliance on spontaneous swarming insect behavior, Neufeld argues that the "texts clearly reflect an early form of biological warfare." Even the "crudest forms" of such warfare, simply throwing beehive bombs by hand, could inflict stings and ignite panic to rout an enemy hiding in caves (fig. 23).

Deploying stinging insects involved hazards for those who used them in war. The traditional practice of the Tiv people of Nigeria shows one clever method of directing bees at the enemy. The Tiv kept their bees in special large horns, which also contained a toxic powder. The poison dust was said to strengthen the bees' venom, but it is possible that it was a drug to calm the bees in the horn. In the heat of battle, the bees were released from the horns toward the enemy. It was not recorded how the Tiv avoided stings themselves, but it seems that the shape and length of the horns effectively propelled the swarm toward the enemy ranks.

Tossing beehive bombs at enemies also involved the potential for "blowback." Stinging insects had to be "kept peacefully

FIG. 23. A swarm of bees or hornets attacking men. Amphora from Vulci, about 550 BC. 1847.0716.1. © The Trustees of the British Museum / Art Resource, NY.

in their nests before the ammunition was used against the foe; the danger of premature explosion must have been considerable." To reduce "the chances of backfire," noted Neufeld, buzzing bombs had to be "hurled carefully at the enemy, wherein the bursting nest would release hundreds of very nervous hornets on the target." He suggested that hornets' nests may have been plugged with mud and transported in sacks, baskets, and pots, or perhaps bees were persuaded to colonize special containers.

One precaution against misdirected stings was smoke, which was recognized as a tranquilizer of bees very early in antiquity. Another method was to set up hives with trip wires along the enemy's route, a method used by both sides in Europe in World War I. Obviously, a great deal of skill and a variety of releasing devices were required for the entire operation, and it is possible that beekeeping shamans were involved in stunning the hornets with smoke or toxic dust, and in planning the attacks.[12]

There is historical evidence that the old strategy of hurling hives of stinging missiles at enemies continued to flourish even as more sophisticated methods of siege craft were developed. Catapults and trebuchets, for example, were a very effective delivery system for launching biological weapons of all sorts—including hornets' nests—while avoiding collateral damage. In fact, catapulting beehives at enemy troops became a favorite Roman tactic. In his survey of the use of bugs in battle from biblical times to the Vietnam War, John Ambrose even suggested that the Romans' extensive use of bees in warfare may partly account for the recorded decline in number of hives in the late Roman Empire. Ambrose also pointed out that heaving hives at foes retained popularity in later times: for example, Henry I's catapults lobbed beehives at the Duke of Lorraine's army in the eleventh century, a tactic used again in 1289 by the Hungarians against the Turks. In the Vietnam War (1961–75), the Viet Cong set booby traps with giant, ferocious Asian honeybees (*Apis dorsata*) against American soldiers. In retaliation, says Ambrose, the Pentagon began developing its own top-secret bee weapon to use against the Viet Cong, based on the bees' alarm chemical, a pheromone that marks victims for a swarming attack. Another device using insects to target enemy troops, the "Airborne Concealed Personnel Detector," was based on the green bottle fly and deployed on Huey helicopters over Vietnamese jungles.[13]

As the ancient Maya and many others have recognized, bees could provide a very effective *defense*, too. Defenders of the medieval castle on the Aegean island of Astipalaia, for example, fended off pirate attacks by dropping their beehives from the parapets. In Germany in 1642, during the Thirty Years' War, attacking Swedish knights were repulsed with beehive bombs. Armor protected the knights, but the clouds of stinging bees drove their horses crazy. In the same era, the village of Beyenburg ("Beetown") was named in honor of some quick-thinking nuns who overturned the convent hives to repel marauding soldiers. When Mussolini invaded Ethiopia in 1935–36, Italian planes sprayed a fog of mustard gas that devastated civilians and the landscape. The Ethiopians' only recourse was to drop beehives from ridges down onto the Italian tanks, terrorizing the drivers and causing crashes.[14]

Stinging insects helped to defend forts in antiquity. In the fourth century BC, Aeneas, in his book *How to Survive under Siege*, advised "besieged people [to] release wasps and bees into tunnels being dug under their walls, in order to plague the attackers." That tactic was employed against the Romans in 72 BC by King Mithradates in Pontus. Appian of Alexandria (a historian of the second century AD) relates that Lucullus, one of several Roman commanders who failed to capture the wily king, laid siege to Mithradates's strongholds at Amisus on the Black Sea, and at Eupatoria and Themiscyra. Lucullus's sappers excavated tunnels under the citadels, passageways so capacious that several subterranean battles were fought in them. But Mithradates's allies routed the Romans by drilling holes that intersected the tunnels, and releasing, not only swarms of angry bees, but also bears and other rampaging wild beasts.[15]

In AD 198–99, the emperor Septimius Severus began the Second Parthian War, in one of several Roman bids to control Mesopotamia. He failed, in two separate attempts, to capture the remote desert stronghold of Hatra, a city that derived great riches from its control of the caravan routes. Hatra's impressive remains, south of Mosul, Iraq, included an enormous double-walled fortress with 90 large towers and 163 small towers and a moat. The city was surrounded by barren desert (fig. 24).

Holed up inside their fortified city, King Barsamia and the citizens of Hatra prepared strong defense plans as the Roman legions advanced over the desert. One of their defenses was biological. Anticipating by seventeen hundred years the bombs of fragile porcelain filled with noxious insects that the Japanese dropped on China in World War II, the Hatreni filled clay-pot bombs with live "poisonous insects" and sealed them up, ready to hurl down at the attackers.[16]

FIG. 24. Ruins of the desert fortress of Hatra. Photo by Sgt. 1st Class Wendy Butts, Multi-National Corps Iraq Public Affairs, US Defense Visual Information Distribution Service, 2007.

Herodian, a historian from Antioch (Syria), who re-counted the story, did not specifically identify the venomous creatures, but simply referred to them as "poisonous flying insects." What sort of insects would have been collected by the Hatreni? In the wretched, waterless wilderness stretching for miles in every direction around Hatra, nothing grew but dragonwort and wormwood, and there were no bees, except for an occasional solitary ground bee. Scorpions, on the other hand, were and still are extremely abundant. In antiquity, the stinging arachnids were sacred to the local goddess Ishhara, and scorpion motifs abound in Mesopotamian mythology.[17]

In the deserts surrounding Hatra, deadly scorpions lurked "beneath every stone and clod of dirt," wrote the natural historian Aelian (fig. 25). They were so numerous that to make the land between Susa to Media safe for travel, Persian kings routinely ordered scorpion hunts, offering bounties for the most killed. Scorpions, declared Pliny, "are a horrible plague, poisonous like snakes, except that they inflict a worse torture by dispatching their victim with a lingering death lasting three days." The sting is intensely painful, followed by great agitation, sweating, thirst, muscle spasms, convulsions, swollen genitals, slow pulse, irregular breathing, and even death.

FIG. 25. Scorpions abound in the desert around Hatra, and they were apparently used as live ammunition against Roman besiegers. Dover Pictorial Archives.

Everyone "detests scorpions," as Aelian declared. The fear factor was put to symbolic military use among the ancient Greeks, who painted scorpion (and snake) emblems on their shields to frighten foes; by the early first century AD, the scorpion had been taken up as the official emblem of the dreaded Roman Praetorian Guard, the personal troops of the emperors. It's no coincidence that modern US military weapons carry names like "scorpion" and "stinger," "hornet," and "cobra" to instill confidence among the troops that man them and to inspire fear among the enemy.

According to Aelian, the sting of some scorpion species killed instantly, and in the Sinai Peninsula there were gigantic scorpions that preyed on lizards and cobras. Anyone who even "treads on scorpion droppings develops ulcers of the foot." Eleven types of scorpion were known in antiquity: white, red, smoky, black, green, potbellied, crab-like, fiery red-orange, those with a double sting, those with seven segments, and those with wings. Most of these species have been identified by entomologists, but others may have been venomous insects conflated with scorpions.

True scorpions lack wings, and Herodian referred to flying, stinging insects in his account. But many ancient authors consistently referred to winged varieties of scorpions, and winged scorpions are also depicted in ancient artifacts. The natural historian Pliny explained the error. Scorpions are given the power of flight by very strong desert winds, he said, and when they are airborne, the scorpions extend their legs, which makes them appear to have wings.[18]

The modern commentator on Herodian, C. Whittaker, considered Herodian's account of clay pots filled with scorpions to be a tall tale, an allusion to a special double-firing ballistic catapult that was called the *Scorpion*. But Herodian clearly described siege weapons in his Hatra account, so word-play allusions seem unlikely. Moreover, the abundance of scorpions in the Hatra desert, and the many other historical reports of hurling hornets' nests and earthenware pots filled with noxious creatures in ancient military engagements, make Herodian's account quite plausible. Notably, heaving scorpions by the basketful at attackers was specifically recommended by Leo VI (AD 862–912), in his famous military *Tactics* handbook.[19]

The Hatreni would have gathered the venomous insects and arachnids in advance. To avoid getting stung while preparing their live bioammunition, they would have followed several safety procedures. Aelian told of the "innumerable devices contrived for self-protection" against the giant Egyptian scorpions. He noted that there were multitudes of scorpions in North Africa, where people "devise endless schemes to counter scorpions." Wearing high boots and sleeping in raised beds with each bedpost in a basin of water were just two common defenses.

Scorpion stings were most deadly in the morning, declared Pliny, "before the insects have wasted any of their poison through accidental strikes." The Hatreni may have gathered them in the evening, and perhaps they teased the irascible scorpions into wasting stings before they placed them in the pots. Aelian pointed out that the stinger has a very slender hollow core, so one could temporarily block the tiny opening by very carefully spitting on the tip of the stinger. Another daunting trick would be to deftly grasp the scorpion by the tail just below the stinger. Alternatively, one could sprinkle scorpions with deadly aconite (monkshood) powder, which was said to cause the creatures to shrivel up temporarily. They

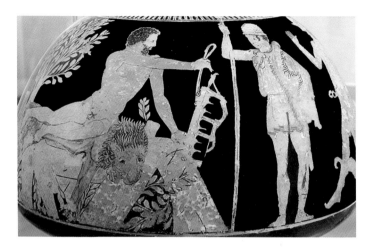

PLATE 1. Heracles on his funeral pyre, entrusting the quiver of Hydra-venom arrows to the young archer Philoctetes. Red-figure psykter, 475–425 BC, private collection, New York. Photo courtesy of VRoma.org, Paula Chabot, 2000.

PLATE 2. The Centaur Pholus curiously examining Heracles's poison arrows; the Centaur was one of several accidental victims of the Hydra-venom weapons. *The Wounded Centaur*, painting by Filippino Lippi, 1490. Christ Church Picture Gallery, Oxford.

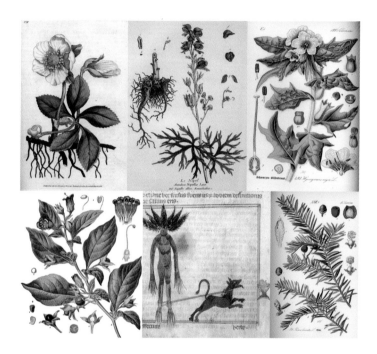

PLATE 3. Top, hellebore, aconite (monkshood), henbane; bottom, deadly night-shade (belladonna), mandrake, yew. Toxic plants used to poison arrows and water supplies in antiquity.

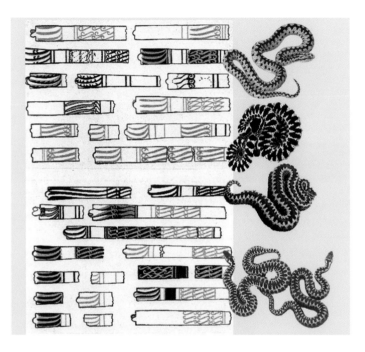

PLATE 4. Wooden arrow shafts for snake-venom arrows, painted with red and black designs, found in fifth century BC Scythian tombs. The designs resemble patterns of venomous Caucasus adders, used to poison projectiles. After Rudenko, *Frozen Tombs of Siberia*.

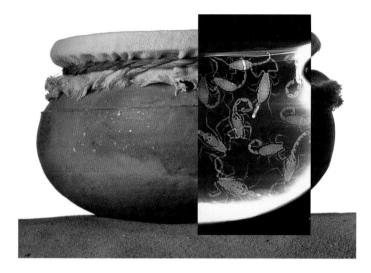

PLATE 5. Historical re-creation of a clay pot filled with live scorpions, like those hurled at Roman besiegers at the desert fortress of Hatra in AD 198. Photo Cary Wolinsky, X-ray Jim Doyle.

PLATE 6.
Assyrian war dog.
Painting,
Konstantin
Konstantinovich
Flerov, State
Darwin Museum,
Moscow. Alamy
stock photo.

PLATE 7. Some besiegers relied on the homing instinct of birds and cats to burn cities; the creatures were fitted with incendiary devices with long fuses. Franz Helm manuscript illustration, 1607.

PLATE 8. In antiquity the deposits of seeping, gushing, and flaming oil from Baku to Persia were known as the "lands of the naphtha fountains." Here, Alexander's Greek soldiers watch local people collecting naphtha in Persia. Painting by Bob Lapsley / Saudi Aramco World / SAWDIA.

PLATE 9. In Islamic legend, Alexander the Great (Iskandar) created a naphtha-spewing iron cavalry, to rout King Porus (King Fur) of India and his war elephants. *Iskandar's Iron Cavalry Battles King Fur of Hind*, illustrated folio in Great Ilkhanid *Shahnama*, AD 1335. 1955.167, Harvard Art Museums/Arthur M. Sackler Museum, Gift of Edward W. Forbes, © President and Fellows of Harvard College.

PLATE 10. Greek fire was a combustible incendiary weapon system based on naphtha and quicklime, perfected in the seventh-century Byzantine Empire. It ignited on contact with water. Greek fire in a naval battle, illustration Claus Lunau/Science Photo Library.

could be revived with poisonous white hellebore, once they were inside the earthenware containers (see plate 5).

It's possible that other venomous flying insects, such as assassin bugs, were associated with scorpions in antiquity. Assassin bugs (cone-nose bugs, *Reduviidae* family) were notoriously used by rulers in Central Asia for torturing prisoners. These predatory, bloodsucking insects cling tenaciously to a victim and push their sharp beaks into the flesh, injecting a lethal nerve poison that liquefies tissues. The bite can be extremely painful. Assassin bugs do have wings, and Herodian's description of the effects of the "poisonous flying creatures" also fits these insects' clinging, piercing attack. As Severus's men attempted to ascend the walls, the clay pots were rained down on them. "The insects fell into the Romans' eyes and the exposed parts of their bodies," wrote Herodian, "Digging in, they bit and stung the soldiers, causing severe injuries." Probably the best conclusion is that the earthenware bombs contained a potpourri of local deathstalker scorpions, assassin bugs, wasps, *pederin* beetles, and other venomous insects from the desert around Hatra.[20]

Military historians are perplexed over what caused Severus to give up his siege of Hatra after only twenty days, just as he had successfully breached the city walls and victory was within reach. Roman sieges were usually grueling ordeals, and they were expected to last several months or even years, but they were ultimately successful. Why did Severus give up? Citing the "insalubrious desert," mutinous troops, poor planning, disputes over plunder, a possible secret treaty, or other "unknown" factors, modern scholars seem to be unable to accept the ancient historians' clear indications that it was the brute effectiveness of Hatra's defensive biological and chemical weapons that overcame Roman morale, manpower, and siege machines.

Herodian gives a vivid account of the violent battle, in which every possible siege technique was tried. He makes it clear that the "scorpion bombs" were just one of many types of ammunition fired at the Romans. In the scorching desert sun, a great many legionaries had succumbed to the heat and unhealthy climate even before the battle, but the Romans sent their full forces and manned every kind of siege machine. The Hatreni "vigorously defended themselves" with their double-shot catapults, "firing down missiles and stones." Cassius Dio adds that the Hatreni also poured burning naphtha on Severus's army, which completely destroyed his siege engines and enveloped his men with unquenchable petroleum-fed flames (chapter 7).[21]

The last straw may have come when the defenders began firing the jars full of hideous insects down on Severus's soldiers as they assailed the walls. The terror effect would be quite impressive, no matter how many men were actually stung. Herodian states that these combined defense tactics caused Severus to withdraw "for fear his entire army would be destroyed." And the desert fortress of Hatra remained independent in "splendid isolation" until AD 241, when it was conquered by Iranian Sasanids.[22]

* * *

Harking back to ancient deployments of stinging insects, Pentagon experts not only investigated ways of using bees to attack the enemy in Vietnam, but they also tested the ability of assassin bugs (there are thousands of species around the world) to home in on prey at long distances. During the Vietnam War, the US Army carried out experiments using assassin bugs in special capsules to track down the Viet Cong in the jungle. The predatory bugs reportedly detected humans about two blocks away and emitted a "yowling" sound that was amplified to audible range. It is not known whether the assassin bug tracking device was ever actually used in the jungle. Research into other baneful insects' military capabilities begun in the Cold War era continues on a large scale today.[23]

The extremely ancient practice of enlisting bees as weapons has been taken to new levels in the US government's most advanced research. Since 1998, the Pentagon has sponsored experiments in "Controlled Biological Systems" to create sophisticated war technologies based on entomology and zoology. The research is overseen by the Defense Advanced Research Projects Agency (DARPA), the central research and development unit of the Defense Department. The mission is to exploit the natural traits of what they call "vivisystems," living creatures from insects to intelligent animals, in order to "turn them into war-fighting technologies." Just as the ancients learned to use the natural instincts of bees in waging war, scientists are studying insects whose attributes might be valuable for military purposes. For example, DARPA-funded laboratories train honeybees to detect minute amounts of substances that indicate the presence of biochemical or explosive agents. The hope is to deploy the hypersensitive insects as spies and sentinels in biochemical warfare.

We have come a long way from praying to plague gods to send mice and lobbing hornets' nests at foes. And yet the Defense Department's sophisticated insect research still relies on the timeless principle of exploiting bees' instincts. But living insects have disadvantages: for example, bees sting indiscriminately and they won't work when they are cold, or at night or in storms. Accordingly, DARPA scientists are improving on mere "vivisystems" by designing "Hybrid Biosystems" and "Biomimetics." With brain-computer interface technology, they can integrate living and nonliving components, for example by reengineering bee neurology or attaching real bee antennae to a cyborg bee.

In antiquity, biological strategies were often justified in self-defense, and modern treaties allow biochemical weapon research for defense, which has often served as a cover for clandestine development of biochemical agents with first-strike capabilities. The tendency to justify biological armaments "for defense only" is evident in the public explanations of DARPA's "vivisystems" mission. An ambiguous sentence in the DARPA "Objectives" statement of 2003 remarks that "other applications [of insect agents] might involve controlling the distribution of pest organisms to improve operational environments for troops," although the next sentence asserts that "all aspects of the program are for defensive purposes only."

Scientists stress the peaceful applications of their DARPA-funded research, but the military applications are obvious. The most recent Hybrid Biosystem creations, remote-controlled rats, are promoted in the media as "search and rescue" agents, but the project scientists admit that the cyber-rat would also be "an ideal delivery system for biological weapons." What nature (and the god Ptah) brought to Sennacherib's Assyrian army in Egypt back in 700 BC—a rodent-borne plague—could now be delivered by remote-controlled rats. The DARPA scientists have also successfully wired monkey's brains to control machines. Transforming animals into living war machines represents a giant step in the militarization of nature. And the use of intelligent animals in war has a very ancient history.[24]

* * *

In antiquity, mice were inadvertent allies in repulsing attackers, and even smaller allies were the stinging insects whose natural aggressive instincts could be directed against foes. But larger creatures, such as the ferocious bears sent against the Roman besiegers in Pontus in 72 BC, could also be drafted for war duty.

Hannibal's masterful use of animals during his invasion of Italy in 218 BC is an excellent example of how animals could be used for war. The well-known feat of Hannibal's war elephants crossing the snowy Alps was only the beginning, for the Carthaginian commander had other ad hoc animal tricks. For example, when he seemed to be trapped in a narrow valley guarded by the Romans, Hannibal terrified the enemy into wild flight by assembling herds of cattle and affixing burning torches to their horns. He made a safe getaway that night, by driving the herd before his army toward the Romans.

Four different historians related another creative zoological ploy thought up by Hannibal during a decisive naval battle against King Eumenes of Pergamum (Asia Minor) sometime between 190 and 184 BC. Hannibal and his allies were far outnumbered in ships. Therefore, explains the Roman historian Cornelius Nepos, "it was necessary for him to resort to a ruse, since he was unequal to his opponent in arms." Hannibal sent his men ashore to "capture the greatest possible number of venomous snakes" and stuff them into earthenware jars. When they had amassed a great many of these, he prepared his marines for the battle. The biological secret weapon boosted the confidence of the outnumbered men, reports Nepos. When the clash came and Eumenes's ships bore down on Hannibal's fleet, the marines let fly the jars, catapulting them onto the enemy decks.

The enemy's first reaction to the smashing pottery was derisive laughter. But as soon as they realized that their decks were seething with poisonous snakes, it was Hannibal's turn to laugh, as the horrified sailors leaped about trying to avoid the vipers. Eumenes's navy was overcome. It may have been this incident that led Eumenes to make his famous remark that an honorable general should eschew victory by underhanded means that he would not like to have turned against himself.[25]

Hannibal's idea was to terrorize Eumenes's crew so they were unable to fight. Similar ideas have occurred to commanders in other times and places. For example, in Afghanistan in about AD 1000, during the siege of Sistan, Mahmud of Ghazni ordered his men to catapult sacks of serpents into the stronghold to terrify the defenders of the fort. In an echo of the insect grenades created by the Hatreni against the Romans, in 2014 the terrorist group ISIS reportedly launched canisters packed with live scorpions on Iraqi villages to intimidate inhabitants.[26]

Animals could also be used to give the enemy an illusion of vast numbers of attackers, a ploy that was advised by Polyaenus and other ancient strategists. Alexander the Great, for one, was said to have resorted to this trick in Persia, tying branches to the tails of sheep to raise clouds of dust, which the Persians took as the sign of a massive army. He also tied torches to the sheep at night, so that the whole plain looked to be on fire. One of Alexander's successors, Ptolemy, did the same thing in Egypt in 321 BC, when he attacked Perdiccas, binding loads of brush to herds of pigs, cattle, and other domestic animals to raise dust as he approached with his cavalry. Perdiccas, imagining a very great cavalry was galloping toward him, fled and took heavy losses.[27]

Much earlier, in the sixth century BC, the Persian king Cambyses laid siege to Pelusium, which had remained the same entry point for invaders of Egypt since Sennacherib's mouse-borne disaster there in the eighth century BC. This time, the Egyptian defense was very well-organized, holding off the Persians with batteries of artillery that shot stones, bolts, and fire. Cambyses responded by placing a unique zoological shield before his ranks: a phalanx of yowling cats, bleating sheep, barking dogs, and mute ibexes. All these animals were worshipped by the Egyptians, and just as Cambyses hoped, the warriors halted their fire to avoid harming any sacred creatures. Pelusium fell and the Persians conquered Egypt.[28]

Cambyses exploited the religious beliefs of the Egyptians to his advantage. An interesting modern plan to play on Japanese folk superstitions about a legendary animal was devised by the US Office of Strategic Services (OSS, forerunner of the CIA) in 1943 during World War II. Code-named "Operation Fantasia" the plot called for destroying Japanese morale by sending eerie replicas of *kitsune*, fox-ghosts, to frighten soldiers and citizens. One idea was to spray live foxes with radium-containing glow-in-the-dark paint. In a test of the plan, thirty glowing foxes were released in a Washington, DC, park, which did indeed terrify passersby. Ultimately the plot proved impractical and was never implemented in Japan.[29]

So far, all the creatures dispatched against the enemy have been involuntary zoological allies, from Chrysame's poisoned bull (chapter 5), swarms of mice, and innocent sheep dragging branches, to venomous creatures whose aggressive nature leads them to attack human targets. But, unlike hordes of wasps or mice whose instincts might work to the advantage of one side in military contexts, large, intelligent animals could be specially prepared for war. Almost every army in antiquity maintained baggage animals (mules, oxen, donkeys, camels) and used dogs for sentry duty. But other large animals were trained to participate in the thick of battle: horses and camels served as cavalry mounts, and dogs and war elephants could be used to attack the enemy.

▰ ▰ ▰

Ever since dogs became our best friends, they have served as sentinels to warn of intruders. Their hunting instincts and acute senses, loyalty, vigilance, speed, and intelligence make them valuable for military purposes. To guard the citadel of Acrocorinth against Philip of Macedon in 243 BC, for instance, the great guerrilla general Aratos set out fifty dogs. An inscription from the small Greek city of Teos (on the Turkish coast) records that three dogs were to be purchased for sentinel duty at the garrison fort. The fourth-century BC tactician Aeneas referred frequently to dogs as sentries and messengers in wartime, but he also warned that their instinct to bark could backfire.[30]

Dogs also participated in combat. Large breeds can run twice as fast as humans, and they can be trained to bite and hold down victims. War dogs were extremely intimidating and the psychological effect was significant. Early evidence for dogs in hunting and warfare can be seen on a Babylonian clay relief showing a man with a shield and a large, collared mastiff, from about 1750 BC. Assyrian stone reliefs from about 600 BC (Birs Nimrud, Iraq), depict armed men with mastiffs (similar to the Molosser breed; see plate 6). At the Neo-Assyrian palace at Nineveh (about 645 BC), a set of small painted figurines of mastiff-type dogs with collars are engraved with their names ("Catcher of the Enemy," "Biter of His Foe," and so on). According to Pliny, the king of the Garamantes of Africa owned two hundred trained war dogs "that did battle with those who resisted him." In what is now Turkey, the cities of Colophon (in Ionia) and Castabala (Hieropolis, in Cilicia) maintained troops of war dogs that fought ferociously in the front ranks. These canines were their most loyal allies, joked Pliny, "for they never even required pay." The Hyrcanians of the Caspian Sea and the Magnesians (a mountain tribe of northeastern Greece) were also feared for the large hounds with spiked collars that accompanied them on the battlefield (by the Middle Ages, war dogs would sport full coats of mail). "These allies were an advantage and great help to them," remarked Aelian. At war with Ephesus, each Magnesian cavalryman had a dog, "fearsome, aggressive, and ferocious." These dogs were sent rushing forward in the first ranks, followed by javelin throwers, then cavalry.[31]

Just as using poison arrows, originally intended for hunting, to kill humans tended to raise the hackles of classical Greeks and Romans, siccing hunting dogs on human quarry might have seemed brutal and inhumane to many. But Polyaenus, the strategist who advised emperors on how to defeat the Parthians in the second century AD, recounted with approval how the "monstrous and bestial Cimmerians" were driven out of Asia Minor in the sixth century BC by the vicious hounds of King Alyattes of Lydia (west-central Turkey). The Cimmerians of the steppes had been driven west by the Scythians and invaded Lydia. King Alyattes set his "strongest dogs upon the barbarians as if they were wild animals"—which is exactly how Polyaenus characterized the invaders. The king's war dogs, he wrote, "killed many and forced the rest to flee shamefully."[32]

At the glorious Battle of Marathon in 490 BC, when the Athenians and their allies defeated the invading Persian army to the tune of 6,400 dead (only 192 Greeks perished), one Athenian dog accompanied his hoplite master. The dog, a "fellow-soldier in the battle," received honors "for the dangers it faced." It was seen fighting alongside the city's heroes Cynegirus, Epizelus, and Callimachus, according to Aelian. The heroic hound was featured in the famous mural of the victory in the Painted Stoa in the Agora of Athens.[33]

Dogs continued to participate in battles up to modern times, and the classical vignette of the trusty war dog hero at ancient Marathon could serve as the original K-9 Corps tale. Many dogs went to war in World War I, but war dog training in the US armed forces began on a large scale during World War II. By 1945 nearly ten thousand dogs served in K-9 war dog platoons in Europe and the Pacific. Thousands of dogs have worked as sentries and scouts, as well as pack, bomb-sniffing, and attack animals, in the Korean, Vietnam, Gulf, and Afghanistan wars.[34]

Since the 1990s, Apopo, a nonprofit organization based in Tanzania, has trained hundreds of giant African pouched rats as military allies, to detect the chemicals in landmines in Cambodia. It is estimated that there are about six million unexploded mines placed in the 1970s and '80s in Cambodia, so the rats' work saves countless lives. In 2021, the BBC and other news media celebrated Magawa, one of the top "Hero-RATs," who received a gold medal upon his retirement, for sniffing out more than seventy landmines in his five years of service.[35]

Canines, rats, and other mammals fall into the Defense Department's category of "Controlled Biological Systems" for waging war with the help of animals. The zoological scope of the program far exceeds Cambyses's military menagerie in the Persians' front ranks, used to stop the Egyptian artillery twenty-five hundred years ago. Since the Vietnam War's end in 1975, the Pentagon has funded the classified training and deployment of numerous species of mammals, including dogs, skunks, rats, monkeys, sea lions, dolphins, and whales. For example, in the 1980s, US Navy–trained dolphins were sent to the Persian Gulf to patrol the harbor for mines and to escort oil tankers; dolphins were deployed again in 2003 along with sea lions, trained to pursue and capture enemy divers with leg clamps, during the Iraq War. In 2007, the Navy Marine Mammal Program (NMMP) based in San Diego, California, planned to send dolphins and sea lions to patrol Puget Sound. In 2012, the marine mammals were to be replaced by under-water robots, but so far technology cannot compete with the animals' abilities; in 2019, about seventy dolphins, and thirty sea lions were still being trained in the NMMP project. The navy claims that no mammals have ever been trained to kill humans, in keeping with the ancient justification of biological weapons for defense only.[36]

* * *

The Greeks were astounded when they first encountered ranks of trained war elephants in action, at the battle on the Hydaspes River, where Alexander the Great defeated King Porus in India in 326 BC. The Macedonian soldiers were able to rally their spirits and prepared to fight the imposing beasts, but Alexander quickly realized that his cavalry horses would not face Porus's two hundred elephants. He found ways to outmaneuver the elephants with his infantry, by boxing in elephants and ordering his men to aim their long javelins to kill the mahouts. Hemmed in and without their drivers, Porus's elephants ran amok and trampled many of their own men. Alexander captured eighty of Porus's elephants, and he obtained one hundred more in subsequent campaigns in India.[37]

According to legends that grew up around the figure of Alexander, he had devised another brilliant plan to deflect the ranks of the living tanks. According to that story, Alexander piled up all the bronze statues and armor that he had taken as booty during his previous conquests and heated them over a fire until they were red-hot. (In reality, the Greeks brought very little booty with them over the Khyber Pass.) Then he set up the statues and shields like a wall in front of the elephants. When Porus sent forth his elephants, they made straight for the heated statues, taking them for enemy soldiers. As the beasts smashed into the statues, "their muzzles were badly burnt" and they refused to continue the attack.[38]

Alexander's Hellenistic successors, the Seleucids and Ptolemies, made heavy use of war elephants, which became *the* glamour weapon of the Hellenistic era. The elephants were carefully trained from birth by the traditional suppliers in India. Elephants were very effective, especially against men and horses who had never set eyes on such creatures before, and they could easily tear down wooden fortifications. Clanging bells were hung on the massive beasts; they were fitted with coats of armor and iron tusk covers, and carried crenellated "castles" with archers on top. An elephant could charge at fifteen miles per hour (though at that momentum, it had difficulty coming to a halt). The stampeding animals could plow through tight phalanxes of men, crushing them or causing them to scatter to avoid being trampled.

The Romans were first introduced to Indian war elephants when Pyrrhus of Epirus invaded Italy in 280 BC. The "bulk and uncommon appearance" of Pyrrhus's twenty pachyderms, each one carrying a tower manned by one or two soldiers with bows and javelins, undid the Romans, and their terrified cavalry horses refused to face the beasts. In the panic, many Roman soldiers were impaled by the elephants' tusks and crushed under their feet. Pyrrhus won, but with such excessive losses of his own men that he remarked that another victory would totally ruin him—thus the phrase "Pyrrhic victory." By 275 BC, Pyrrhus had lost many of his elephants and two-thirds of his original forces (fig. 26).

Hannibal's elephants crossed the Alps in the winter of 218 BC, during the Carthaginian's invasion of Italy. Hannibal's smaller North African forest elephants carried only a mahout—the beasts themselves were the weapons. In the alpine winter, however, all but one of the Carthaginian's thirty-seven elephants had died in the snow. Hannibal sent for more in 215 BC, but by then the Romans and their horses were not as terrified by the sheer sight of elephant phalanxes.

In the third century BC, the Hellenistic Seleucid king Antiochus routed the Galatians, Gauls who had invaded Anatolia. In the famous nonbattle, the Galatians were overwhelmed by the bizarre sight and loud clamor of Antiochus's sixteen trumpeting elephants with gleaming tusks advancing on the distant plain. The Galatian cavalry horses reared and wheeled in fright, and the foot soldiers were trampled under their hooves. In the first century BC, the Britanni surrendered to the Romans at

FIG. 26. War elephants could cause chaos in enemy ranks but sometimes trampled their own men in the melee. *Battle between Scipio and Hannibal at Zama*, engraving, 1550–78, Cornelis Cort, 59.570.439, Elisha Whittelsey Fund, 1959, Metropolitan Museum.

the sight of just one enormous elephant in gleaming armor. As many modern historians have noted, one of the advantages of biological weapons is the element of surprise and horror that can cause the challenged to capitulate without a fight.[39]

The war elephant could intimidate the enemy, but the cumbersome animals were so unpredictable that after a time they came to be regarded as a liability rather than an asset. The problems of friendly fire and collateral damage were serious. Drugs were sometimes administered before battle to make the beasts more aggressive, and if the elephant's mahout was killed, or the elephant was badly wounded or disoriented by something untoward, or in rut, the crazed behemoth would crash out of control, squashing its own men. Contemplating such bloody disasters with elephants in the first century BC, the Roman philosopher Lucretius surmised that perhaps other wild animals, such as lions, were "once enlisted in the service of war" in very early times, with similarly catastrophic results. The "experiment of launching savage boars against the enemy failed," he speculated, as did "advance guards of lions on leashes." The brute beasts, "enflamed by the gory carnage of battle," must have slashed their own masters with tusks, talons, and teeth, "just as in our own times war elephants sometimes stampede over their own associates."[40]

Safety procedures were developed to deactivate rampaging war elephants. Each mahout had a sharp chisel blade bound to his wrist, so that if his wounded elephant suddenly reversed direction, he could drive it into the beast's neck with a mallet, killing it instantly. This expedient was said to have been invented by the Carthaginian general Hasdrubal.

"Elephants, like prudent men, avoid anything that is harmful," noted Aelian. Unlike insects, intelligent creatures such as dogs, horses, camels, and elephants are subject to fear and rational instincts for self-preservation, which creates disadvantages and boomerang effects. It's an old problem that continued in modern times: in the Thirty Years' War (1618–48), the Swedish warhorses had fled from swarms of stinging bees unloosed by the enemy, and during World War II, British scout dogs, unnerved by heavy artillery fire, lost their sense of direction and failed to smell out the enemy.

In antiquity, guard dogs barked at the wrong time, and cavalry horses were spooked by elephants, while wounded war elephants panicked and crushed their own armies. Greek horses stampeded at the exotic scent of Persian baggage camels—who, for their part, "possessed an innate hatred for horses."[41] What if incompatible species, say, camels and horses, actually met on the battlefield? Pandemonium ensued—and that could work to a clever general's advantage.

◢ ◢ ◢

Some animal species instinctively loathed other species or panicked at the presence of unfamiliar beasts. An unexpected confrontation of incompatible or hostile animals often caused violent confusion on the battlefield. Drafting various members of the animal kingdom into human warfare, in order to take advantage of the antipathy between, say, horses and elephants, constituted a biological strategy, in the sense of manipulating natural forces against the enemy. These ingenious schemes had devastating consequences for an unprepared army, but animal ruses like these aroused few qualms about fairness in antiquity, whereas arrows coated in snake venom or clandestine poisoning of water supplies were reviled as dishonorable.

Ploys based on the natural antagonism between animal species were something an intelligent commander might anticipate and even prepare for. Nevertheless, a commander who understood which kinds of creatures would immediately send the enemy's trained war animals into a frenzy could often gain the upper hand. When interspecies conflict suddenly erupted during a military engagement, some spectacular reversals of fortune resulted.

In 546 BC, King Cyrus of Persia was about to meet the formidable cavalry of King Croesus, son of Alyattes, in Lydia. At the sight of the ranks of skilled Lydian cavalrymen armed with long spears massing on the plain, however, the Persian king's confidence plummeted. Cyrus knew his cavalry would be bested. Herodotus tells us that one of Cyrus's advisers came up with an emergency plan based on his knowledge of animal antipathy. Knowing that a horse naturally "shuns the sight and the scent of a camel," the Persians unloaded their baggage train of camels, and placed them in the front line, keeping their own camel-tolerant cavalry in the rear. Before the battle even began, Croesus's proud cavalry was "rendered useless." At the first sight and scent of the camels, the horses turned and galloped away, snorting in disgust and fear. Many of the Lydian foot soldiers were trampled in the melee. After that battle, most ancient armies kept a few camels among their horses, to acquaint them with their rank odor.

A couple of generations later, King Darius of Persia was galled and frustrated by the hit-and-run guerrilla tactics of the mounted Scythian archers, who made raids and then melted away, refusing to meet the Persians face-to-face. Darius knew that the Scythian cavalry was superior to his own, but felt certain that he could beat the nomads with his infantry, if only he could force them to stay and fight face-to-face.

Herodotus reports that the Persians enjoyed only one small advantage over the Scythians in skirmishes. Donkeys were completely unknown in Scythia, and during the battles the harsh hee-hawing of these Persian pack animals "so upset the nomads' horses . . . that they would constantly stop short, pricking up their ears in consternation." Darius, exasperated and running short on supplies, finally used his asses to cover his ignominious retreat from Scythia. As he slunk away by night, he left behind his donkeys, whose braying tricked the nomads into thinking the Persians were still there.[42]

As noted earlier, the psychological impact of using elephants was one key to their success in battle. The sight, sound, and odor of elephants threw untrained horses into chaos, and ancient military history records several disastrous defeats caused by horses (and men) turning tail at the novel appearance of elephants. The most famous example occurred in Britain in 55 BC, when the Britannis' chariot horses fled at the sight of Julius Caesar's monstrous war elephant covered in iron scales and clanging bells emerging from a river with a tower of archers balanced on its back.[43]

By the Hellenistic period, when war elephants became all the rage for the Ptolemies and Seleucids, commanders who faced them tried to obtain at least some elephants to condition their cavalry horses. In the second century BC, for example, Perseus, a son of the Macedonian king Philip V, knew how to prepare for an invasion by Romans who were bringing African and Indian war elephants. Perseus had artisans build and paint wooden models to resemble elephants, so that their size and shape would not intimidate his horses. Then he had pipers hide inside the huge mock-ups; as these were rolled toward the horses, the pipers played "harsh, sharp trumpeting sounds" on their pipes. By this means, the Macedonian horses "learned to disdain the sight and sound of elephants."[44]

Over time, elephants became less of a novelty, and creative gambits were discovered to neutralize them in battle. Alexander the Great was said to be the first to discover a surefire way to repulse elephants—by making use of elephants' natural aversion to pigs. Elephants were admired in antiquity as intelligent and as tasteful lovers of all things beautiful; they were said to appreciate perfumes, lovely women, flowers, music, and so on. By the same token, the wrinkled, gray, lumbering beasts, capable of ear-piercing trumpeting themselves, were thought to abhor ugly things and were themselves especially agitated by discordant sounds. Their highly developed aesthetic sensibilities could be turned against them in battle.

Legend has it that Alexander the Great learned this important bit of local folk knowledge from King Porus, who became Alexander's ally after Porus's defeat in 326 BC. Alexander had a chance to test the repellent effect of swine on elephants in India when his scout reported that about a thousand wild elephants were approaching the camp from the forest. On Porus's advice, Alexander ordered his Thracian horsemen to take some pigs and trumpets and ride out to meet the elephant herd. Porus assured Alexander that if the pigs could be caused to keep squealing, they could overcome the elephants. Indeed, as soon as the great beasts heard the harsh sound of the pigs combined with the Thracian trumpets, they fled back into the forest.[45]

Elephant behavior experts point out that elephants have very sensitive hearing and poor eyesight. This combination makes them averse to unexpected loud, discordant sounds, and smaller animals running around their feet can also spook them. This helps explain elephants' alleged fear of mice and their antipathy to a pack of squealing pigs suddenly rushing toward them (fig. 27).

In 280–275 BC, as noted above, the Romans had their first experience with war elephants, brought to Italy by Pyrrhus. In 279–275, as Pyrrhus was wearily marching the surviving twelve of his original twenty war elephants across Italy, the Romans noticed that the pachyderms were unnerved by the sight of rams with horns, and that they could not abide the high-pitched squeals of swine. Aelian says that both of these domestic

FIG. 27. A squealing pig was an effective weapon against war elephants. Terra-cotta pig, third century BC, 78.AD.346, Gift of David Collins, Courtesy of J. Paul Getty Museum Open Content Program.

animals were used to deflect the elephants of Pyrrhus, perhaps helping to account for his heavy losses of men and beasts in his Italian campaign.[46]

Notably, Cassius Dio included an interesting detail in his description of the terror evoked by Pyrrhus's elephants: he says the riders in the howdahs made a horrendous clatter and din. Perhaps the riders beat drums and banged spears. The combination of the sight and noise caused the Romans and their horses to panic and flee when the elephants appeared. On the other hand, during the Punic Wars, at the start of the Battle of Zama (202 BC) some of Hannibal's elephants were frightened by the shrill blasts of Roman war trumpets (fig. 26).[47]

In antiquity, the use of special sensory effects—sound, smell, and sight—to terrify war animals, or human foes, was considered an unconventional but fair tactic. For example, the Roman historian Tacitus described the psychological effects of the *baritus*, the hair-raising war cry of the Germanic tribes intended to demoralize the enemy. The chanting warriors produced a "harsh, intermittent roar," rising to a reverberating crescendo as they held their shields in front of their mouths to amplify the thunderous sound. A similar hair-raising effect was achieved by the Celtic war trumpet, the *karnyx*, used between about 200 BC and AD 200. The bronze tube in an elongated S shape had a wide bell shaped like a wide-open mouth of a boar, dragon, or other animal. The sound was eerie and harsh, "suiting the tumult of war," wrote Diodorus Siculus.[48]

"Whistling" arrows (in Chinese, *shaojian*, "screaming arrows") were used by mounted archers of the steppes, who attached a small, perforated bone, horn, or wood compartment or chamber on the shaft behind the arrowhead or on the arrowhead itself. Whistling arrows were used in hunting to startle various animals in predictable ways. In battle, the shrill, shrieking sound accompanying the arrow would have a terrifying psychological effect on the enemy and their horses.[49]

Ways of producing "horrible sounds," optical illusions, and explosive noises to disorient and frighten enemies were also described in ancient Indian and Chinese war manuals. As we've seen, assaults on sensitivity to odors—the stink of unfamiliar or hated species—could send an enemy's war animals into chaos, but offensive smells could be directed against humans as well. Strabo, for instance, described the overpowering reek of the poison arrows of the Soanes of Colchis as injurious to victims even if they were not wounded (chapter 2).[50]

The ancient experiments with unbearable noise and odors used against enemies and their war animals have been revived with modern research into "nonlethal" weapons directed against humans. Military scientists have created malodorants (repulsive smells to trigger incapacitating nausea). They have also developed crude as well as sophisticated ways to project very loud, low-frequency sounds. The weaponization of music occurred during World War II, when the Soviets played Argentine tangos through loudspeakers all night to keep German soldiers awake. Deafening hard rock music (including The Doors, Alice Cooper, and The Clash) was blasted day and night by US psyops Loudspeaker Teams during the siege against Panamanian general Manuel Noriega in 1989. Aggravating, loud music was used again by the United States during the Gulf War of 1991. Police deployed shrill, pulsating Long-Range Acoustic Devices (LRADs) against, for example, civilian protests in New York in 2011 and 2020, as well as in Missouri in 2014, and they were used by US forces in the Iraq War in 2004. High-decibel and high- and low-frequency technologies also include the Magnetic Acoustic Device (MAD) called "the mosquito" and gas-powered sonic-vibration guns, both handheld portable versions and large sound-wave "guns" mounted on tanks, invented by the Chinese in 2019. The most advanced sonic weapons are infrasound wave transmitters, which induce dizziness, hallucinations, incapacitating nausea and vomiting, damage to inner ears, cavitation, and possibly internal injury and death. The mysterious neurological symptoms and brain injuries similar to concussion that incapacitated US diplomats and CIA officials in Cuba and China beginning in 2016 ("Havana Syndrome") are thought to have been produced by directed microwave or targeted sonic energy.[51]

▰ ▰ ▰

Alexander the Great reportedly used fire—red-hot bronze statues—and noisy pigs in separate incidents against elephants. Not long after Pyrrhus's retreat from Italy in 275 BC, fire and pigs were combined into a single devilish plan to repel war elephants.

In about 270 BC, Antigonus Gonatus, the Macedonian ruler of Greece, massed his Indian war elephants to besiege the city of Megara (between Athens and Corinth). The resourceful Megarians already knew the folk wisdom that elephants had a terror of squealing hogs. They smeared a bunch of pigs with pine pitch resin, set them on fire, and released them. These living torpedoes made a beeline for Antigonus's lines of war-trained elephants. As the shrieking, flaming pigs rushed the elephants, the behemoths panicked. Made frantic by the sight, the noise, and the smell of the desperate burning pigs, the elephants fled trumpeting in all directions, breaking the siege. Antigonus's confused rout at Megara must have been one of the most spectacular retreats on record.

The sticky pitch-fueled flames that tortured the pigs at Megara were intended to maximize their squealing, rather than to burn the enemy forces. But one could say that the Megarian stratagem of setting pigs afire with combustible resin created the first hybrid biological-chemical weapon. "In the future," commented Polyaenus, "Antigonus ordered his Indian suppliers to raise the young war elephants in the company of pigs," so the beasts would become accustomed to their appearance, smell, and shrill voices.[52]

The Megarians were unique in setting pigs afire against elephants. But the last recorded use of a pig against a war elephant was said to have occurred at the siege of Edessa, held by the Romans in the time of the emperor Justinian (sixth century AD). Chosroes, king of the Persians, stormed the city, sending his biggest elephant with many soldiers on top right up to the circuit wall. Just as the Persians were about to clamber over the wall and capture the city, the quick-witted Romans grabbed up a pig and suspended it directly in the face of the startled elephant. The dry-witted historian Procopius writes, "As the pig was hanging there, he very naturally gave vent to sundry squeals, and this angered the elephant so that he got out of control." Confusion swept back in waves through the entire Persian army, and, panic-stricken, they fled in great disorder.[53]

Fire plus animals was a combination guaranteed to wreak havoc against the enemy, as Frontinus and Appian proved in their description of a Spanish strategy against Hannibal's father, Hamilcar Barca, in 229 BC. The Spanish front lines consisted of steer-drawn carts filled with combustibles: pitch, animal tallow, and sulfur. These carts of fuel were set afire and driven into the Carthaginian lines, causing screaming panic. Nine-year-old Hannibal went along with his father on the conquest of Spain. Perhaps he recalled the combination of steers and fire when he engineered his own rout of the Romans in 218 BC, by means of the cattle-horn torches, described earlier.[54]

The use of animals as a delivery system to carry flammable materials occurred elsewhere in the ancient world. For example, Kautilya's *Arthashastra*, the Indian military manual, recommended attaching incendiary powders to birds, cats, mongooses, and monkeys. The flammable packages were lit on a long fuse and the creatures were dispatched to burn down thatched-roof structures and wooden forts. It's not clear how these involuntary suicide bombers were persuaded to zero in on the right targets (this is precisely the problem that has now been solved with the modern creation of remote-controlled rats and other species that can be directed to specific targets, described above). Kautilya anticipated the problem, though: he suggested capturing only the vultures, crows, and pigeons that nested in the besieged city walls. They could be trusted to fly back to their nests with the flammable powders.[55]

Genghis Khan relied on the same "homing" principle on a large scale during his conquest of China in AD 1211. During his siege of several fortified cities, it is said that he offered to lift the siege in exchange for the town's cats and swallows. "These were duly handed over," writes the historian David Morgan, and the Mongols tied flammable materials to the tails of the birds and cats and ignited them (see plate 7). When the creatures were released, they naturally fled home, setting each city on fire, and Genghis Khan easily stormed the burning cities.[56]

Chinese and Arabic military manuals suggested smearing crows and other birds with incendiary substances or attaching flammables to expendable animals to set fire to enemy tents. The Chinese military treatise *Wu Jing Zong Yao* (AD 1044) has illustrated instructions for making a "Fire Bird" incendiary, by lighting gunpowder in a hollow peach pit hung around a bird's neck and sending it forth in the hope that it would ignite enemy structures.[57]

Perhaps some intelligent animals were trained for tasks beforehand, to offset the potential for serious backfire. There is a Chinese account from AD 1610 claiming that the General Tseh-Ki-Kwang trained several hundred monkeys from Mount Shi-Chu in Fu Tsing to shoot firearms. When the monkey militia was ordered to fire on Japanese raiders, the marauders were so terror-stricken that the Chinese general's soldiers hiding in ambush were able to slay them all. The animal guerrillas must have been taught not to shoot at their Chinese handlers.[58]

Friendly fire accidents caused by confused creatures carrying incendiaries are represented by a category of medieval folklore and modern urban legends collectively known as "the revenge of the exploding animal." These tales recount the ironic consequences of tying dynamite, firecrackers, or other burning material to dogs, cats, or birds, or tossing live grenades at sharks, and so on, who inevitably circle back toward their tormentors. One Indian folktale, for example, about a flaming cat burning down a village, was collected in Kashmir. A medieval European tale tells of a flock of birds set afire by besiegers to burn down a city. The actual use of such tactics in antiquity may be the origin of these folk motifs.[59]

Perhaps the last instance of an animal-on-fire weapon was used by Tamerlane (Timur), the great Mongol conqueror, in 1398 to sack Delhi, which was protected by the Indian sultan's 120 war elephants. Tamerlane's warriors were usually mounted on war camels, but for this battle Tamerlane loaded the camels with straw and ignited the bundles. As the flaming camels raced forward, the sultan's elephants fled in panic.[60]

The image of terrified burning pigs or awkward flaming camels may seem amusing in a macabre way, but it takes only a slight shift of perspective to imagine the terror and pain that would be experienced by human beings set afire with unquenchable, corrosive flames. And that brings us to the final chapter, about ancient chemical incendiaries, culminating in some of the most inhumane weapons ever devised.

CHAPTER 7

INFERNAL FIRE

Attacked by a terrible stream of consuming fire,
her flesh fell from her bones like resin from a pine-torch,
a sight dreadful to behold.

—EURIPIDES, *MEDEA*, 431 BC

THE PRINCESS DONNED THE GOWN, a gift from the sorceress Medea, and twirled to admire it. Suddenly the gown burst into flames. Like Heracles in his envenomed tunic, the princess tried to tear off the flaming dress, but the material stuck to her skin, creating a fire so hot that it melted the flesh from her bones. Engulfed by "clinging streams of unnatural, devouring fire," she dashed outside and threw herself into a fountain. But water only made the fire burn more intensely. Her father, King Creon, tried to smother the flames, but he too caught fire. Both perished, immolated alive. The blaze spread, destroying the entire palace and everyone inside.

This scene from Euripides's tragedy *Medea* was performed in Athens in 431 BC. Based on ancient Greek myth, the scene describes a terrible fire weapon concocted by Medea of Colchis, who had helped her lover Jason, and his Argonauts, win the Golden Fleece. When Jason later abandoned Medea, she took revenge on his new love, the Corinthian princess Glauke.

Medea treated a beautiful gown with secret substances that "stored up the powers of fire." She sealed the gift in an airtight casket and delivered it to the unsuspecting princess.

How did Medea create such an extraordinary conflagration? The graphic details—and the popularity of the story in Greek and Roman literature and art—suggest that some real but unusual fire phenomenon inspired the legend. The notion that materials could be made to suddenly combust in the presence of water or heat must have been plausible to audiences as early as the fifth century BC.

According to Euripides, Medea combined special volatile substances that had to be sealed from air, light, moisture, and heat. The violent combustion resulted in flames that were clinging, corrosive, extremely hot, and unquenchable by water—much like napalm in its ghastly effects. The myth alludes to knowledge of chemical petroleum-based weapons more than a thousand years before the invention of Greek Fire in the seventh century AD.[1]

Fire itself has been a weapon "from the first time an angry hominid snatched a burning brand from a campfire and threw it at the cause of his wrath," writes historian Alfred Crosby in *Throwing Fire.* More than two millennia before Crosby, the Roman philosopher Lucretius had written that fire became a weapon as soon as men learned to kindle sparks. In Greek myth, we saw how the hero Heracles used burning arrows and torches to destroy the Hydra monster (chapter 1).[2]

Fire arrows were a very early invention in human history. Assyrian reliefs from the ninth century BC show attackers and defenders exchanging volleys of burning arrows, and firepots, apparently filled with local petroleum, hurled over fortified walls. In ancient India, fire weapons were common enough to be forbidden in the *Laws of Manu*, which, addressing kings. proscribed "weapons made red-hot with fire or tipped with burning materials." Yet the *Arthashasta* and several other Indian treatises of the same era give many recipes for creating chemical fire projectiles and smoke weapons. Meanwhile, in China, during the Warring States period of feudal conflicts (403–221 BC), Sun Tzu's *Art of War* and other military treatises advocated ways to deploy fire and smoke to terrify foes.[3] The inventory of fire armaments devised in antiquity is impressive in its variety, beginning with burning arrows and progressing to chemical additives and sophisticated incendiary technologies.

▰ ▰ ▰

The first incendiary missiles were arrows wrapped with flammable plant fibers (flax, hemp, or straw, often referred to as tow) and set afire. Burning arrows of these materials could be very effective in destroying wooden walls from a safe distance.

Athens was captured by flaming hemp arrows in 480 BC, when the Persians invaded Greece. Xerxes had already destroyed many Greek cities with fire and, as the Persian army approached Athens, the populace was evacuated to the countryside. A few priests and poor and infirm citizens were left behind to defend the Acropolis. These defenders put up barricades of planks and timber around the Temple of Athena and managed to hold off the Persians for a time by rolling boulders down the slopes of the Acropolis. But, in the first recorded use of fire projectiles on Greek soil, the Persians shot fiery arrows to burn down the wooden barricades. The Persians swarmed over the Acropolis, slaughtering all the Athenians in the temple and burning everything to the ground.[4]

But simple flaming missiles of straw were "insufficiently destructive and murderous" to satisfy ancient strategists for long, notes Crosby. They were not much use against stone walls, and ordinary fires could be doused with water. "What was wanted was something that would burn fiercely, adhere stubbornly, and resist being put out by water."[5] What kinds of chemical additives would produce fires strong enough to burn walls and machines, capture cities, and destroy enemies?

The first additive was a plant chemical, pitch, the flammable resin tapped from pine trees. Later, distillations of pitch into crude turpentine were available. Resinous fires burned hotly and the sticky sap resisted water. Arrows could be dipped in pitch and ignited, or one could set fires fueled with pitch to burn the enemy's equipment. Other mineral accelerants for making hotter and more combustible weapons were discovered too.[6]

The earliest evidence that flaming arrows were used by a Greek army appears in Thucydides's *History of the Peloponnesian War*. In 429 BC, the Spartans besieged the city of Plataia (Plataea), an ally of Athens, and they used a full panoply of siege techniques against the stubborn Plataians. We know the Spartans planned to use fire arrows, because the Plataians protected their wooden palisades with what would later become the standard defense against fire projectiles, by hanging curtains of untanned animal hides over the walls. The Plataians lassoed the Spartans' siege engines, winching them into the air and letting them crash to the ground. With their machines smashed and with their archers unable to ignite the rawhide-covered walls, the Spartans advanced beyond mere flaming arrows, into the as-yet-unexplored world of chemical fuels. This event occurred just two years after Euripides's play about Medea's mysterious recipe for "unnatural fire."

First, the Spartans heaped up a massive mound of fire-wood right next to the city wall. Then they added liberal quantities of pine-tree sap and, in a bold innovation, lumps of sulfur. Sulfur is the chemical element found in acrid-smelling, yellow, green, and white mineral deposits in volcanic areas, around hot springs, and in limestone and gypsum matrix. Sulfur has been called brimstone, which means "burning stone." Volcanic eruptions were observed to create flowing rivers and lakes of burning sulfur, scenes that corresponded to biblical visions of Hell with its lakes of fire and brimstone. Clods and liquid forms of sulfur had many uses in antiquity, from medicine and pesticides to bleaching cloaks and togas. Sulfur's highly flammable nature also made it a very attractive incendiary in war. "No other substance is more easily ignited," wrote Pliny, "which shows that sulfur contains a powerful abundance of fire."

When the Spartans ignited the great woodpile at Plataia, the combination of pitch and sulfur "produced such a conflagration as had never been seen before, greater than any fire produced by human agency," declared Thucydides. Indeed, the blue sulfur flames and the acrid stench must have been sensational, but the fumes would also have been quite destructive, since the combustion of sulfur creates toxic sulfur dioxide gas, which can kill if inhaled in large enough quantities. The Plataians abandoned their posts on the burning palisades. Much of the wall was destroyed, but then the wind reversed and the great fire eventually subsided after a severe thunderstorm. Plataia was saved by what must have seemed to be divine intervention against the Spartans' technological innovation. Notably, this first record of Greeks using flaming arrows also happens to be the earliest recorded use of a chemically enhanced incendiary that created a poison gas, although it is not clear that the Spartans were aware of that deadly side effect when they threw sulfur on the flames.[7]

Defenders quickly learned to use chemically fed fires against besiegers. In his manual on how to survive sieges, written in about 360 BC, Aeneas devoted a section to fires supplemented with chemicals. He recommended pouring pine resin pitch down on the enemy soldiers or onto their siege machines, followed by bunches of hemp and lumps of sulfur, accelerants that would stick to the coating of pitch. Next, one immediately let down burning bundles of kindling by ropes to ignite the pitch and sulfur. Aeneas also described a kind of spiked wooden "bomb" filled with blazing material that could be dropped onto siege engines. The iron spikes would embed the device into the wooden frame while it burned. Another defense strategy was to fill bags with pitch, sulfur, tow fiber from flax or hemp, powdered frankincense gum, pine shavings, and sawdust. Set afire, these sacks could be hurled from the walls at men below.[8]

During the grueling year-long siege of the island of Rhodes by Demetrius Poliorcetes ("The Besieger") in 304 BC, both sides hurled resinous fiery missiles—firepots and flaming arrows. On moonless nights during the siege, wrote Diodorus of Sicily, "the fire missiles burned bright as they hurtled violently through the air." The morning after a particularly spectacular night attack, Demetrius Poliorcetes had his men collect and count the fire missiles. He was startled by the vast resources of the besieged city. In a single night, the Rhodians had fired more than eight hundred fiery projectiles of various sizes, and fifteen hundred catapult bolts. Rhodes's resistance was successful. Demetrius Poliorcetes withdrew with his reputation tarnished, and he abandoned his valuable siege equipment. From the sale of his machines, the Rhodians financed the building of the Colossus of Rhodes astride their harbor, one of the Seven Wonders of the Ancient World.[9]

Technological advances in fire arrows were reported by the Roman historians Silius Italicus and Tacitus, who describe the large fire bolt (*falarica*), a machine-fired spear with a long iron tip that had been dipped in burning pitch and sulfur. (The opening scene of the 2000 Hollywood film *Gladiator* showed the Roman *falarica* in action in a night battle in Germany.) The burning spears were "like thunderbolts, cleaving the air like meteors," wrote Silius Italicus. The carnage was appalling. The battlefield was strewn with "severed, smoking limbs" carried through the air by the bolts, and "men and their weapons were buried under the blazing ruins of the siege towers."[10]

Machine-fired fire bolts and catapulted firepots of sulfur and bitumen were used to defend Aquileia (northeastern Italy) when that city managed to hold off the long siege by the emperor Maximinus in AD 236. The Aquileians set out pots of tar and sulfur around the walls, ready to be ignited and either hurled or poured as flaming cascades onto the attackers on ladders. Herodian described the horrendous effects: men were blinded and burned by the sticky substance; their metal chest plates became red-hot as the leather straps and buckles "hissed and shrunk" in the fire. Maximinus's men fled, "leaving their cuirasses piled up at the foot of the walls." The demoralized soldiers then found the emperor in his tent outside the city walls and killed him along with his family and officers.[11]

Later, incendiary mixtures were packed *inside* the hollow wooden shafts of the fire bolts. Vegetius, a military engineer of AD 390, gives one recipe for the ammunition: sulfur, resin, tar, and hemp soaked in oil.[12]

Ammianus Marcellinus (fourth century AD) described fire darts shot from bows. Hollow cane shafts were skillfully reinforced with iron and punctured with many small holes on the underside to provide oxygen for combustion. The cavity was filled with bituminous materials. (In antiquity, *bitumen* was a catchall term for petroleum products such as asphalt, tar, naphtha, and natural gas.) These fire darts had to be shot with a weak bow, however, since high velocity could extinguish the fire in the shaft. Once they hit their target, the fire was ferocious. They flared up upon contact with water, marveled Ammianus, and a defender could put out the flames only by depriving the blaze of oxygen, by smothering it with sand.[13]

The fire dart resembles the Chinese fire lance, invented in about AD 900. This was a bamboo (later, metal) tube with one opening, packed with sulfur, charcoal, and small amounts of the "fire chemical" (explosive saltpeter or nitrate salts, a key ingredient of gunpowder). The tube was affixed to a lance with a kind of pump, which Crosby describes as "a sort of five-minute flame thrower." At first, they "spewed nothing but flame," but soon the Chinese added sand and other irritants like sharp shards of pottery, sand, and metal shrapnel, and many different kinds of poisons, such as toxic plants, arsenic, and excrement, to the saltpeter mixture. As Robert Temple, historian of ancient Chinese science, remarked, "Bizarre and terrible poisons were mixed together" to make bombs and grenades. "Practically every animal, plant, and mineral poison imaginable was combined," for "there hardly seemed to be a deadly substance unknown to them."[14]

Tracing the history of gunpowder weapons to early guns in China from about AD 1000 to 1250, Tonio Andrade surveyed a variety of gunpowder "eruptors" that evolved from the fire lance, described in the Ming-era military manual *Book of the Fire Dragon*. The vivid names allude to their capabilities: the "filling-the-sky erupting tube" shot out poisonous gas and shards of porcelain; the "flying sand magic mist tube spewed forth sand and poisonous chemicals"; gunpowder gourds propelled flames and toxic gas at foes forty feet away; and "flying rats" unpredictably jumped about, spattering fiery sparks.[15]

In India, an early military manual, the *Nitisara* (date uncertain), describes tubular projectiles thrown by devices used by the infantry and cavalry. The tube, about three feet long, contained saltpeter, sulfur, and charcoal, with other optional ingredients, such as iron filings, lead, and realgar (arsenic). The tubes shot iron or lead balls by "the touch of fire" ignited "by the pressure of flint." The author remarks that "war with [these] mechanical instruments leads to great destruction."[16]

🐾 🐾 🐾

In practice, early fire weapons were probably used at close range against large, combustible targets such as wooden walls and ships. Indeed, the Spartans' great sulfur and pitch conflagration at Plataia was piled next to the wooden walls of the fort. Lucan (a Roman writer of the first century AD) writes of casting burning torches dipped in oil and sulfur onto ships' decks and shooting arrows smeared with burning pitch or wax to ignite the flaxen sails. To make the arrows "burn even more vehemently," the archers soon learned to melt a mixture of varnish, oil and petroleum, colophon (dense black residue of turpentine boiled down with "sharp" vinegar), and sulfur. Lucan's description of a firefight at sea is harrowing. Fire, fed by chemicals and the extremely flammable wax caulking of the ships, coursed swiftly through the riggings. It consumed the rowers' wooden benches and spread everywhere, even over the water itself. Houses near the shore also caught fire, as wind fanned the conflagration. Such fire weapons were clearly intended to destroy the ship and the crew, and the victims faced the choice of burning or drowning. Some sailors clung to blazing planks in the waves, terrified of drowning, while others, wishing to go down fighting, grappled with the enemy amid the burning wreckage.[17]

Wooden ships were not just good targets; their flammability also made them attractive delivery systems for fire. During the ill-fated Athenian attack on Sicily in 413 BC, for example, the Syracusans came up with a creative deployment of resinated fire in a naval battle. They loaded an old merchant ship with faggots of torch pine, set it alight, and simply let the wind blow the ship of fire toward the Athenians' fleet of wooden triremes. Frontinus, the Roman strategist, reported that in 48 BC, the commander Cassius, also campaigning in Sicily, copied the Syracusans; he filled several decrepit transport vessels with burning wood and "set them with a fair wind" to destroy the enemy fleet. Fireship tactics required favorable winds, of course, or else the boomerang effect could be disastrous.[18]

The most stupendous fireship of all was manufactured in 332 BC, by the Phoenicians during Alexander the Great's famous siege of Tyre (an island city on the coast of Lebanon).

The historians Arrian and Quintus Curtius described the ship as a floating chemical firebomb. The Phoenician engineers fitted a very large transport ship (originally used for carrying cavalry horses) with two masts and yardarms. From these they suspended four cauldrons brimming with sulfur, bitumen, and "every sort of material apt to kindle and nourish flame." The foredeck of the ship was packed with cedar torches, pitch, and other flammables, and the hold was filled with dry brush liberally laced with more chemical combustibles.

Waiting until the wind was favorable, Phoenician rowers towed the great fireship right up to the offensive mole (a pier extending from the shore to the fortified island) erected by Alexander's men. The mole had two movable towers and many ballistic engines behind its palisades, all protected with curtains of raw hides in case of flaming arrows. But the Macedonians were unprepared for the unstoppable ship of flames. The Phoenicians ignited the transport and then rowed like mad to crash the burning mass into the mole. They escaped by jumping overboard and swimming to skiffs that returned them to safety. On impact with the mole, the cauldrons on the burning ship spilled their flammable contents, further accelerating the flames. Propelled by the wind, the raging chemical fire incinerated Alexander's palisades and his siege engines. The Macedonians on the mole either were consumed by flames or leaped into the sea. The Phoenicians chopped at the desperate swimmers' hands with stakes and rocks until the men drowned or were taken prisoner.[19]

The casualties and destruction of the mole did not end Alexander's siege, nor was the fireship the last of the fiendish incendiary devices thought up by the Phoenician engineers of Tyre. The Phoenicians realized that the Macedonians

possessed superior hand-to-hand fighting abilities, commented Diodorus of Sicily. They needed an antipersonnel
weapon to "offset such a courageous enemy." There is a clear
sense of disapproval in Diodorus's account, deploring the
cowardice of those who turn to chemical weapons to defeat
honorable warriors.

The Phoenician engineers "devised an ingenious and horrible torment which even the bravest could not deflect," wrote
Diodorus. They filled enormous shallow bowls of iron and
bronze with fine sand and tiny bits of metal. These pans they
roasted over a great fire until the sand glowed red-hot. "By
means of an unknown apparatus" (a catapult of some sort),
the Phoenicians cast the burning sand "over those Macedonians who were fighting most boldly and brought them
utter misery." There was no escape for anyone within range
of the sand. The molten grains and red-hot shrapnel "sifted
down under the soldiers' breastplates and seared their skin
with the intense heat, inflicting unavoidable pain." Alexander's men writhed, trying to pull off their armor and shake
out the burning sand. "Shrieking like those under torture,
in excruciating agony Alexander's men went mad and died."
The historical scene at Tyre brings to life in astonishing detail
the mythic image of Heracles struggling to escape from his
burning tunic.[20]

The rain of burning sand at Tyre, devised more than two
millennia ago, also has an uncanny resemblance to the effects
of modern metal incendiaries, such as magnesium and thermite bombs of World War II. Burning particles of the magnesium and molten iron were dispersed by the combustion
of these intensely hot metal bombs and splattered on victims,
making myriad small but extremely deep burns. The high-

temperature metallic embers, just like the red-hot sand, penetrate far into the skin and keep on burning, causing deep tissue injury and death. Thermite bombs have now been replaced by mortar rounds of white phosphorus (WP), which release a shower of flaming chemical particles that ignite on exposure to air. The US forces reportedly used WP against Fallujah in 2004 in the Iraq War and again in 2016 against ISIS in Iraq; Israel used WP against Palestinians in Gaza in 2008–9; Saudi Arabia used WP in Yemen in 2016; Turkey reportedly used WP in Syria in 2019. Military commanders claim WP is used only to illuminate and create smoke screens, but in fact it causes horrific injuries, melting flesh and burning bone-deep.[21]

▰ ▰ ▰

A century after Alexander's tribulations with burning weapons at Tyre, the Syracusans invented a long-range thermal weapon of amazing effectiveness. During the Roman siege of Syracuse in 212 BC, Archimedes, the brilliant philosopher-mathematician, was commissioned by King Hiero to devise ingenious ways of defending Syracuse. Archimedes developed an array of formidable weapons that were used against the Romans, from catapults that hurled burning fireballs to gargantuan grappling cranes (the "Snatcher" or "Iron Claw") that lifted warships completely out of the water and smashed them down with such force that they sank.[22]

Another celebrated weapon invented by Archimedes was essentially a heat ray used against the Roman navy commanded by Claudius Marcellus. According to ancient accounts, Archimedes had soldiers polish the concave surfaces of their bronze shields to a mirror finish. Then he assembled them to stand in a parabola shape and tip their shields to create a huge reflective surface to focus the sun's rays onto the Roman ships' riggings. Just as paper or matchsticks can be burned with a magnifying glass, the intense heat of the concentrated rays caused the sails and wooden masts to catch fire instantaneously. Marcellus's fleet was reduced to ashes. The Roman commander gave up the naval blockade and finally captured Syracuse "by thirst."

Marcellus ordered his men to capture Archimedes alive, thinking that the Romans could learn from him. This appears to be the first recorded instance of the practice of capturing or giving immunity to enemy biochemical weapons scientists. But the old engineer was killed by Roman soldiers during the brutal sack of the city. Marcellus buried the scientist with honor, decorating his tomb with a geometric cylinder and sphere. Archimedes's grave was long forgotten, until it was discovered in a bramble patch outside the gates of Syracuse by the Roman orator Cicero, more than a century later.[23]

About seven hundred years after Syracuse, in AD 515, the philosopher Proklos was said to have used Archimedes's mirror technique to burn the ships sent by the rebel Thracian leader Vitalianus against the Byzantine emperor Anastasios I. Since the Enlightenment, many scientists have undertaken complex calculations and experiments to learn whether Archimedes's method could have worked. The first series of experiments, by Count Buffon of the Paris Museum of Natural History in 1747, used mirrors to ignite a pine plank 150 feet away. A more recent test was carried out in 1975 by a Greek scientist, Dr. I. Sakkas. He lined up sixty Greek sailors each holding a mirror shaped like an oblong shield. In concert, they tilted the mirrors to direct the sun's rays at a wooden ship 160 feet away. It caught fire immediately. A similarly successful re-creation was enacted in 2005 for the popular TV show *MythBusters*, when Dr. David Wallace of the Massachusetts Institute of Technology used mirrors to ignite a 1924 wooden fishing boat in San Francisco Bay.[24]

According to the Latin sources, Marcellus's Roman sailors were sent into deepening panic at each new weapon deployment, with many believing that the Syracusans were being aided by the gods or magic. The burning ray that caused their ships to suddenly burst into flame must have seemed like a bolt from the heavens. Indeed, the impressive effects of long-range thermal-ray weapons are not just the stuff of science fiction but are sought by real-life weapons designers today. A burning ray in the form of a laser gun that incinerated victims was apparently one of many sophisticated secret weapons tested by the United States during its invasion of Panama in 1989, according to interviews with medical personnel and eyewitnesses. Some years later, in 2001, the Pentagon unveiled an antipersonnel weapon that fires a beam of intense heat more than a third of a mile. The painful burning sensation, caused by the same microwave energy used to heat food but more intense, was supposed to disperse crowds without actually cooking or killing anyone.[25]

The idea of this "Active Denial System," designed by Raytheon, is to mount the microwave ray gun on a military vehicle and point it at individuals or groups. By sweeping "menacing crowds" from a safe distance, the ray is supposed to cause excruciating pain without damage—as long as people are able to move out of the beam. The directed energy ray penetrates a victim's skin, heating it to 130°F, creating the agonizing sensation of being on fire. In 2007, another version of the heat-ray gun discharged electromagnetic radio-frequency beams at five hundred yards. We need "weapons like this," said the head of DARPA's Non-Lethal Weapons Directorate, "because distinguishing between combatants and non-combatants is difficult." Indeed, these thermal weapons were precisely designed for controlling crowds, which often include civilians and involve densely populated areas. The US military decided not to deploy mounted heat-ray tanks in Iraq that year, to avoid accusations of torture. In 2010, the weapon was sent to Afghanistan, but controversies about ethics and burn injuries mounted and it was withdrawn. Continuing development aims at making directed-energy weapons that can be operated from the air as well as from tanks and ships.[26]

"It's safe, completely safe," declared Colonel George Fenton, the director of the US Joint Non-Lethal Weapons Directorate in 2001. "You walk out of the beam [and] there's no long-term effect, none, zero, zip." But the potential for grave damage is obvious. Critics point out that severe burns result if the beam is focused on someone long enough, say, someone already incapacitated by other "nonlethal" weaponry such as tear gas or calmative mists, or immobilized in a crowd, or injured. That person might be as unable to escape as one of the Macedonians trapped in the range of the burning sand at Tyre or a Roman sailor who happened to be in the rigging when Archimedes aimed his heat ray.[27]

▰ ▰ ▰

The bow and arrow, Archimedes's mirrors, and burning ships proved to be good systems for delivering fire. Torsion catapult technology (based on the spring tension of ropes made of elastic materials such as sinew or hair) was invented in about 350 BC, and greatly expanded the horizons for hurling firepots and fiery projectiles over the walls of cities, and onto vessels. But yet another invention for propelling fire, a remarkable flame-blowing contraption, was created at a very early date, in 424 BC, by Sparta's allies during the Peloponnesian War, the Boeotians.

The invention came just four years after the Spartans had created the superconflagration at Plataia, which had ultimately failed owing to shifting wind. The design of the primitive Boeotian flamethrower got around the problems encountered by the Spartans at Plataia by creating man-made wind. The device had a large capacity but a short range, like modern flamethrowers. Thucydides described how the flame-thrower destroyed the wooden fortifications at Delium, held by the Athenians.

The Boeotians hollowed out a huge wooden log and plated it with iron. They suspended a large cauldron by a chain attached to one end of the hollow beam, and an iron tube was inserted through the length of the hollow beam, curving down into the cauldron, which was filled with burning coals, sulfur, and pitch. The apparatus was mounted on a cart and wheeled right up to the wall. At that point the Boeotians attached a very large blacksmith's bellows to their end of the beam and pumped great blasts of air through the tube to direct the chemical fire and gases in the cauldron at the wall. The walls were incinerated, as were many defenders as they attempted to flee their posts, and Delium was captured.[28]

A similar flame-throwing device—with the surprising addition of vinegar to the combustibles—was devised by

Apollodorus of Damascus, the military engineer for Roman emperors in the second century AD. The addition of vinegar reputedly allowed the flamethrower to destroy fortification walls of stone. Other Roman historians, for example Cassius Dio and Vitruvius, also reported that vinegar and fire in combination could shatter rock. But modern scholars have puzzled over how vinegar could accomplish this.[29]

The use of vinegar and fire for breaking up stone was first described by the historians Livy and Pliny, in their accounts of how Hannibal's engineers solved a logistics problem while crossing the Alps in 218 BC. To clear a landslide obstructing Hannibal's route in the mountains, the Carthaginians felled large trees into a pile on top of the rock slide, then set them on fire. When the huge bonfire had caused the rocks to glow red, they poured vinegar (acetic acid contained in sour wine) on the rocks, which instantly disintegrated.

The ancient claims that vinegar and fire could destroy walls and the story of Hannibal's feat were long ridiculed as legends, until scientific experiments in 1992 proved that rocks heated to high temperatures will indeed fracture if a considerable quantity of acidic vinegar is splashed on the hot stone. Further experiments with sour red wine (the source of vinegar in antiquity) produced even more violent results, as the hot rocks sizzled and cracked apart. The scientists found that the chemical reaction worked best on limestone and marble, which happened to be the favorite building stone for ancient fortification walls. Now we can understand the principle of Apollodorus's machine, which directed very hot, chemically intensified flames at stone walls. When the stones were red-hot, buckets of vinegar were poured on the walls, which immediately cracked apart.[30]

With the multitude of types of fire weapons proliferating through the ages, methods of defense against them were sought. Aeneas, for example, advised that those encountering flaming weapons should shield their faces if possible. He also recommended covering wooden parapets or walls with wet felt or raw animal hides, the practice carried out by the Plataians defending against Spartan fire arrows and by the Macedonians besieging Tyre.[31]

Alum (double sulphate of aluminum and potassium) was known in antiquity as a fire retardant that could prevent wood combustion. Alum was mined in Egypt and Pontus. After the temple of Delphi burned down in 548 BC, for example, King Amasis of Egypt sent a large quantity (one thousand talents) of alum to fireproof the timber used for rebuilding. King Mithradates of Pontus fireproofed the wooden towers of his fortresses with alum in 87 BC, and in AD 296 the emperor Constantine fireproofed his siege engines with alum against Persian incendiaries.[32]

Sand, earth, and mud were used to extinguish water-resistant chemical fires. Incendiaries containing sulfur, resins, tar, or petroleum would stick tenaciously to any surface and could be put out only with difficulty, using sand or dirt, wrote Aeneas. To protect siege machines from chemical fires or melted lead poured from above, he suggested that the housings should be covered with clay mixed with hair, or wet mud. Advice on protecting men from chemical burns is notably nonexistent in Aeneas and other ancient Greek and Roman military manuals. In India, however, it was believed that certain ointments rubbed on the skin could protect a soldier from burns. Kautilya's military treatise of the fourth century BC told how to make fire-resistant salves from sticky plant juices and frog skin. Muslim military fire books gave fire-retardant recipes calling for a paste of talc, egg whites, gum, and "salamander-skin" (an early name for the fire-resistant mineral asbestos).[33]

A well-known fire retardant in antiquity was vinegar, despite its ability to shatter stone when heated. "If the enemy attempts to set fires with highly combustible materials" such as pitch and sulfur, water cannot soak into or wet the fire, wrote Aeneas. Only "vinegar will put it out and also makes it difficult to restart the fire." In 73–72 BC, the city of Cyzicus on the Black Sea was besieged by Mithradates of Pontus. The defenders draped their walls with water-soaked hides and, as Aeneas advised, they doused the stone walls with vinegar against Mithradates's fiery missiles. But Mithradates understood the vulnerability of this defense, perhaps from his study of the chemical reaction exploited by Hannibal, described above. If vinegar-soaked limestone is heated sufficiently, the stone will crumble. The intense heat of Mithradates's fire bolts breached a section of the city's walls.[34]

Besiegers could also use vinegar to resist burning materials thrown down on them by defenders. To protect siege equipment, Polyaenus recommended that vinegar, "particularly good at extinguishing every kind of fire," should be poured or sponged periodically onto wooden siege machines. Vinegar could also help neutralize choking fumes from fires: Pliny noted its beneficial effects on sneezing and other respiratory problems.[35] In an interesting modern variation on the ancient defensive uses of vinegar, in skirmishes between political dissidents and riot police today the sharp odor of vinegar often hangs in the air. Protesters routinely soak hand-kerchiefs in vinegar and hold them over their faces to coun-teract the pepper spray and tear gas deployed by the police.

✶ ✶ ✶

Clouds of dust or smoke could give commanders an advan-tage. In World War II, the German general Rommel, popularly known as the Desert Fox, was a master of "military dust" in North Africa. More than two thousand years earlier, the Car-thaginian general Himilco created fires with thick black smoke that blew into the eyes of his enemies at Cromium, Sicily, in about 397 BC; he also used smoke to send a deceptive signal, enabling him to overtake Agrigentum. In the fourth century, the innovative generals Epaminondas and Pelopidas of Thebes and Iphicrates of Athens created smoke screens to cover troop movements. Aeneas advised city defenders to build smoky fires and channel the smoke toward besiegers attempting to tunnel under walls. This, he promised, "will be injurious to the men inside and may even kill many of them." A Chinese historical text, *Mo Zi*, written around the same time, told how to lower burning bundles of kindling, hemp, and reeds by chains into tunnels to smoke out diggers: "The enemy will immediately die."[36]

Smoke from ordinary fires could be harmful, even deadly, but sulfurous fumes from chemically activated fires, like the one the Spartans created at Plataia in 429 BC, would be se-riously toxic and lethal (fig. 28). One could create irritating, choking, chemically toxic gases by burning particularly noxious substances. As early as the seventh century BC, the Chinese destroyed insect pests by fumigating with poisonous smoke

FIG. 28. Noxious substances could be burned to create toxic smoke. Here two men create a smoky fire. Attic vase painting, 510 BC. Toledo Museum of Art, Libbey Endowment, Gift of Edward Drummond Libbey.

clouds, which they created by burning sulfur and arsenic; this practice may have led to their interest in developing toxic gases for military use. Ancient Chinese writings contain hundreds of recipes for producing irritating fogs and fumes. As early as the fourth century BC, defenders of fortresses in China burned toxic substances and plants such as mustard seeds in furnaces connected by pipes to oxhide bellows in order to pump poison gases into tunnels dug by attackers. Chinese incendiary-weapons manuals also give directions for making poisonous smoke balls. One extremely effective smoke-ball compound called for powdered aconite root and wolfbane (monkshood), croton beans (a drastic purgative that also causes skin pustules), the poisonous mineral arsenic, hallucinogenic cannabis, blister beetles, and toxic sulfur, plus charcoal and resin.[37]

In India, turpentine and tree resins, charcoal, and wax were some flammable components of smoke powders. In the fourth century BC, the *Arthashastra* provided formulas for creating burning powders whose fumes were supposed to drive enemies mad, blind them, or cause them to catch a disease or even perish immediately. Different smoke powders were concocted from the droppings of certain reptiles, animals, and birds, mixed with genuine poisons and intoxicants. One lethal cloud was created by burning the bodies of venomous snakes and stinging insects along with the seeds of toxic plants and hot peppers. Notably, hot peppers, which contain capsaicin, were used against enemies in the New World too: in the sixteenth and seventeenth centuries, Caribbean and Brazilian Indians produced an early form of pepper spray against the Spanish conquistadors by burning piles of ground-up hot pepper seeds.[38]

In Japan during the medieval feudal period (beginning in the twelfth century), ninja and samurai used *metsubushi* ("eye-closers") to disorient or permanently blind attackers or captive enemies. The device evolved from bamboo tubes or hollow eggs to handheld lacquer or brass boxes with a mouthpiece and an opening or pipe on the other end. These were filled with ashes, powdered pepper, dirt, or even finely ground glass to be blown into the enemies' eyes. Medieval ninja placed pepper, dust, and iron filings in the scabbard of their katana, to blind opponents. Metal weapons could be tipped with poison, such as spiked rings (*kakute*) and the talons of iron gloves (*neko te*). Ninja also wielded tubes that spurted acid, poison darts, explosives, and smoke grenades.[39]

Poisonous smokes that combined magical and toxic ingredients intended to kill or disorient enemies also appeared in ancient Greek and early medieval alchemy treatises. For example, Hippolytus (AD 230) claimed that burning powdered iron magnets would produce a deadly smoke. The addition of weasel feces to the magnets was supposed to create the sensation of an earthquake to terrify the foe.[40]

Noxious smoke was hard to control and direct, and therefore most effective when employed in confined spaces like tunnels. In western Greece in AD 189, during the long Roman siege of Ambracia, the defenders invented a novel smoke machine to repel the Roman sappers attempting to tunnel under the city walls. The Ambracians "prepared a jar equal in size to the tunnel, bored holes into the bottom, and inserted an iron tube." They packed the giant pot with layers of fine chicken feathers and smoldering charcoal and capped the jar with a perforated lid. Chicken feathers are composed of keratins containing cysteine, a sulfuric amino acid. Feather combustion actually releases poisonous sulfur dioxide, the kind of gas created by the Spartans at Plateia, described above. The Ambracians were not aware of the scientific explanation; they knew only that burning chicken feathers produced a notoriously nasty effect, especially in a confined space. To repel the Romans, the Ambracians aimed the lidded end of the jar of burning feathers at the tunnelers and fitted blacksmith's bellows to the iron tube at the other end. With this device—which calls to mind the primitive flamethrower at Delium—

the Ambracians filled the passage with clouds of acrid, toxic smoke, sending the choking Romans hurrying to the surface. "They abandoned their subterranean siege," was Polyaenus's succinct comment.[41]

During sieges, tunnelers mining under towers would employ wooden timbers to temporarily prop up the structure and then set them afire so the tower caved in, while they themselves escaped. Opponents defending the fortresses dug countermines, and sometimes battles with incendiaries took place in the tunnels. A fascinating archaeological discovery in 1935 at the Roman-held fortified city of Dura-Europos in Syria revealed evidence of just such an underground battle. The Sasanian Persians besieged the Romans at Dura-Europos in AD 265, and each side dug tunnels. The early archaeologists found many weapons, piles of skeletons, and a jar containing the telltale burned residue of sulfur and pitch that the Sasanians had added to a fire they set to repel the Roman sappers. In 2011, archaeologist Simon James reinvestigated the site's twenty human remains and forensic evidence to show that the fire plus accelerants had indeed created a toxic sulfur dioxide gas. His "crime scene" reconstruction, with photos and diagrams, explains the combat, the chemical gassing, and the death struggle inside the tunnel. One of the skeletons, still clad in Persian chain mail, appears to have been a Sasanian victim of "friendly fire" (fig. 29).[42]

Plutarch (writing in about AD 100) described another chemical weapon—an aerosol of particulates suspended in air. This cunning use of dust was employed by the Roman general Sertorius when he was trying to defeat the Characitani of Spain, in 80 BC. The Characitani lived in caves carved out of an impregnable mountainside. Frustrated, Sertorius rode

FIG. 29. Skeleton of soldier in tunic of iron mail, apparently a Sasanian attacker who failed to escape in the Sasanian gas attack on the Romans in the tunnels under the fortress at Dura-Europos, AD 265. Yale University Art Gallery, Dura-Europos Collection.

around the hill "muttering empty threats." Then, he noticed that his horse was kicking up clouds of caustic dust from the fine white soil at the foot of the caves. The soil may have been soft limestone or gypsum, since Plutarch compared it to "ash or unslaked lime powder." Limestone or gypsum powders are severe irritants to the eyes and mucous membranes; Sertorius would have experienced this effect. Sertorius also noticed that the prevailing winds blew each day from the north, and that the cave entrances faced north. Putting these natural facts together, Sertorius ordered his men to pile great heaps of the powdery soil in front of the caves. The next day as the north wind gathered force, the Romans, probably wearing ad hoc masks, stirred up the mounds and rode their horses over the powder, raising great clouds that blew into the cave entrances. The Characitani surrendered after three days of enduring the choking, blinding dust.[43]

In China, lime dust was used to make an early form of tear gas to quell riots. In AD 178, for example, an armed peasant revolt was quelled by horse-drawn "lime chariots" equipped with bellows to blow fine limestone dust "forward according to the wind." This very effective fog was followed by stampeding horses, sent forth with burning rags tied to their tails, accompanied by loud drums and gongs, backed up by ranks of archers and crossbowmen. The rebels were blinded, thrown into chaos, and "utterly destroyed." When lime powder interacts with the moist membranes of the eyes, nose, and throat, the effect is corrosive. A poison aerosol described in *Tactics*, the Byzantine emperor Leo's military treatise, was based on the same principles: pots of powdered quicklime (burned lime) were thrown to form a caustic cloud that blinded and suffocated the enemy as they inhaled the dust.[44]

Wind-borne weapons could be capricious. Those who made use of toxic powders and smoke had to beware of unpredictable, reversing winds. Kautilya was highly aware of the danger. In his chapter on poison smokes, he warned that the army must keep their "eyes secure" with applications of protective salves before deploying chemical aerosols. Only after "having applied these remedies to ensure the safety of himself and his army, should the king make use of poisonous smokes and other mixtures" against an enemy.[45]

An Islamic manuscript from the early Middle Ages suggested the use of "smokes, prepared liquids, and ill-smelling deadly odours for causing damage to forts and castles and horrifying the enemy." In 1241, Mongol armies invading Poland and Hungary released evil-smelling poison vapor and smoke to overcome Hungarian, Polish, and German troops; the unbearable vapor was shaken from an image of a large, black-bearded head mounted on a lance or standard. Noxious smokes have not gone out of style in modern arsenals. Dense clouds of smoke and irritant chemical weapons like mustard gas, pepper sprays, and tear gas still present blowback problems, however, requiring the users to don gas masks to avoid eye injury and inhalation. Such weapons are indiscriminate, too, affecting combatants and noncombatants alike.[46]

▰ ▰ ▰

By the time of the Peloponnesian War, three combustible chemicals were known in the Mediterranean world—pitch, sulfur, and quicklime—and the first two were definitely used in warfare in that era. Pitch, the highly flammable resin from pine trees, has a sticky consistency and burns hotly. Sulfur, a mineral characterized by corrosive combustion, burns at extremely high temperatures and creates sulfur dioxide gas, and as it liquefies, it releases corrosive vitriol, sulfuric acid.

The choking effects of lime powder were weaponized by Sertorius in the first century BC, but lime's ability to spontaneously burst into flame was known centuries earlier. As Pliny remarked, lime "possesses a remarkable quality: once it has been burnt, its heat is increased by water." Roasting limestone produces a crumbly residue called *calx*—caustic quicklime or calcium oxide. Sprinkled with water, quicklime becomes slaked lime (calcium hydroxide), which generates enough heat to cause spontaneous combustion, and more water feeds the blaze. Fullers in ancient Greece and Rome sprinkled quicklime on clothes to clean and whiten them, and new woolen garments were commonly brushed with lime and sulfur, which served to bleach them. Theophrastus, a natural philosopher of the fourth century BC, remarked on the "fiery nature" of lime, which was especially dangerous when wet. As an example, Theophrastus reported that a ship laden with a cargo of new clothing treated thus went down in flames when water splashed on the lime-treated wool. Such accidents were rare, but they would have demonstrated to observers the concept of mixing spontaneously combustible materials for use as weapons.[47]

Sulfur, quicklime, and other substances were combined to make what was known in Latin as *pyr automaton*, "automatic or self-lighting fire." The combination was first used to produce pyrotechnic tricks staged by priests and magicians. In 186 BC, for example, the historian Livy reported that during a religious ceremony, torches drenched in sulfur, tar, and quicklime continued to burn after being plunged into the Tiber River. Other Latin authors provided recipes for *pyr automaton* in which sulfur, pitch, quicklime, and naphtha were tightly sealed in containers and then ignited with a single drop of water. Naphtha is the highly flammable light fraction of petroleum, an extremely volatile, strong-smelling vaporous or gaseous liquid common in oil deposits of the Near East. It was the quicklime that caused the mixture to ignite with a drop of water. In the Old Testament, a self-lighting fire trick was described as a miracle performed by the prophet Elijah to impress the priests of Baal, in about 875 BC.[48]

The potential of combining these substances as an implement of warfare was not realized until much later. A remarkable automatic incendiary weapon, ignited by morning dew, appears in a compilation often attributed to Julius Africanus, a philosopher born in about AD 170 near Jerusalem, who wrote on magic and military tactics. His recipe calls for sulfur, salt, resin, charcoal, asphalt, and quicklime to be very carefully mixed into a paste during the day, and then tightly sealed in a bronze box, protected from moisture and heat. In the evening, the paste was to be surreptitiously smeared on enemy siege engines. At sunrise, the paste was supposed to combust, ignited by heavy dew or light mist. Such an unpredictable weapon with serious backfire issues was "probably not viewed with favour by military commanders," commented the British historian of ancient incendiaries James Partington. But the elaborate combination of the chemical reactions of sulfur, petroleum, and quicklime hydrated by the natural condensation of dew was one of many experiments that eventually led to the development of complex incendiary weapons like Greek Fire.[49]

A paste like the one attributed to Julius Africanus would have allowed Medea to turn Princess Glauke's gown into a murder weapon in the Greek myth. By the first century AD,

Roman authors who were familiar with "automatic fire" magic tricks and the destructive properties of petroleum had begun to speculate on Medea's formula. In his version of the Medea legend, the Stoic philosopher Seneca named "the fire that lurks in sulfur" as one of the components that ignited Glauke's gown, and Seneca also referred to Medea's knowledge of "fire-breathing" natural petroleum wells in the Caucasus region, around Baku, Azerbaijan. Indeed, both Pliny and Plutarch also concluded that naphtha must have been one of Medea's secret ingredients.[50]

* * *

The extraordinary conflagration created by Medea, which adhered to the victims' clothing and skin and burned them alive, has striking similarities to modern napalm. A mixture of a volatile naphtha (or gasoline, another petroleum derivative) and a thickening agent to make it jell, napalm burns at more than 5,000°F. Invented in the 1940s at Harvard, napalm was used widely against combatants and civilians by US and South Vietnamese forces in the Vietnam War. One of the most unforgettable images of that war was the 1972 photograph of a girl fleeing an aerial napalm attack on South Vietnamese villagers. The jellied, liquid fire consumed her clothes and clung to her body, as she and the other victims ran away in pain and terror. The searing, sticky flames burned down to the bone, and water was of no avail. The ghastly scene could have been written by Euripides twenty-five hundred years ago. Just as the use of napalm was an intensely fraught issue during the Vietnam War and "came to symbolize the horrific nature" of advanced war technologies, so the fate of Glauke burned alive by liquid fire symbolized for the ancients the horrors of nefarious toxic weapons.[51]

The young Vietnamese girl and the Corinthian princess in the burning dress were separated by millennia, but the historical and mythic weapons appear to be related. The legendary unquenchable substance wielded by Medea was based on her arcane knowledge of the destructive burning nature of petroleum. Medea's homeland was located in the region between the Black and Caspian Seas known for the rich oil deposits of Baku, where burning gas wells were worshipped as early as the sixth century BC. Medea was also associated with Persia. In antiquity, the Greek name for petroleum—Medean oil—could refer either to Medea or to the land of the Medes (Persia), which also has abundant oil deposits.[52]

Petroleum hydrocarbons come in many forms, all combustible, from the vaporous light fractions, volatile natural gas and liquids like naphtha, to heavier crude oils and tarry bitumen or asphalt. A few rare deposits of petroleum exist in the Mediterranean, but very rich petrochemical resources exist throughout the Middle East (some deposits occur in China and India too). In the deserts, oily and highly flammable liquid petroleum wells up from the sand and seeps from bedrock (*petroleum* means "rock-oil" in Latin), and natural gas wells send up cascading flames and burn under water.

Ancient texts from Mesopotamia show that spontaneously burning lakes and fountains of fire—fire that behaved like water and was unquenched by any liquid—evoked awe from earliest times. Persians, Babylonians, Jews, and other peoples of the ancient Near East had special reverence for the mystifying phenomena of "liquid fires." As they did in Baku by the Caspian Sea, the ancient worshippers in Persia and

Babylonia built temples at sites where natural gas wells burned perpetually. For example, the so-called Eternal Fires, a naphtha fountain at Baba Gurgur (near Kirkuk in northern Iraq), had burned continuously since 600 BC before it was tapped to become the first modern oil well in Iraq in 1927.[53]

Naphtha figured in Jewish history too. Elijah's self-lighting fire trick was mentioned above. In about 169 BC, Nehemiah, the governor of Judea during the Persian rule of Artaxerxes I, performed a similar display. He gathered a thick liquid from Persia, called *nephthar*, to create miraculous self-lighting fire that astounded witnesses. Nehemiah's trick was analyzed by Partington, who pointed out that spontaneous combustion would occur if naphtha and water were poured over quicklime, or if water was poured onto wood soaked in petroleum and quicklime, or onto sulfur and quicklime. All these components were known and available for experimentation from earliest times. This simple chemical reaction could have produced the effects of Medea's mythical murderous gown, and it lent itself to weaponization.[54]

Archaeological evidence shows that surface deposits of oil in the Near East were exploited—for lamps, torches, pigments, waterproofing, cleaning, magic fire rituals, and weapons—as early as 3000 BC. Evidence from cuneiform tablets and inscriptions indicates that even the dangerously volatile liquids and gases were used at early dates. Ancient Assyrian texts indicate that burning petroleum was used to punish criminals, and *naft* (naphtha) was apparently a siege incendiary in Mesopotamia at an early date, as shown in Assyrian reliefs of flaming firebombs of the ninth century BC.[55]

But the origins and uses of the petroleum of exotic lands were not well understood by the early Greeks and Romans.

Herodotus was the first Greek historian (about 450 BC) to describe the awesome powers of the "dark and evil smelling oil the Persians call *rhadinace*." Around the same time, Ctesias, the Greek physician who lived in Persia and wrote sometimes-garbled accounts of wonders from the strange lands further east, described a curious fire weapon of India. The method of gathering this combustible substance was cloaked in fable, probably created to keep it a state secret. Only the king of India was allowed to possess the special oil that derived from giant "worms" lurking in the Indus River, reported Ctesias. The power of the oil was marvelous: "If you want to burn up a man or an animal, just pour some oil over him and at once he is set on fire." With this weapon, Ctesias heard, the Indian king captures cities without the use of battering rams or siege engines. He simply fills clay vessels with the oil, seals them up, and slings them against the city gates. Upon impact, the oil oozes down and fire pours over the doors. The miraculous oil consumes enemy siege machines and covers the fighting men with fire. Water cannot put it out; the only hope is to smother the flames with dirt.[56]

Philostratus's biography of Apollonius of Tyana, a Greek sage who traveled to India in the first century AD, also described a mysterious substance said to resemble a "white worm" in the River Hyphasis (Beas) in Punjab. This substance was melted down to render a flammable oil, which could be kept only in glass vessels. Once ignited, it was inextinguishable, and it was the king's exclusive secret weapon against enemy battlements. The mystical "worm" oil of India in these accounts certainly appears to allude to weapons of volatile petroleum, ignited by various means.[57]

These and other reports about the remarkable effects of liquid fire from the East filtered back to Greece and Italy, but the true sources and ways of controlling the substances remained shrouded in mystery until Roman armies began besieging cities in the Middle East to expand their empire and encountered weapons made from local naphtha.

▰ ▰ ▰

Alexander the Great was introduced to the wonders of petroleum "magic" after he captured Babylon in 324 BC. *Naft* was the most singular of these substances, wrote the geographer Strabo, for "if it is brought near fire it instantly catches fire; and if you pour the liquid on a body and bring a flame near, the person will burst into flames. It is impossible to quench those flames with water, which makes them burn more violently." His description replicates what happened to Glauke in the treated gown. Strabo remarked that the only recourse was to suffocate the fire with mud, vinegar, alum and glue, or enormous volumes of water.[58]

To impress Alexander, one night his Persian hosts at Ecbatana sprinkled a street with naphtha and set fire to one end—the flames flashed instantaneously to the other end. Intrigued, Alexander, "for an experiment," poured some naphtha on a young singer named Stephanus and then brought a lamp near him. Sure enough, the boy was immediately enveloped in flames and would have burned to death, like Glauke in the myth, had not bystanders quickly smothered the fire. Even so, the boy was severely burned.[59]

For Alexander and the Greeks of the fourth century BC, naphtha was an exotic marvel of Babylonia, not a weapon (see plate 8). Although bituminous materials were used in the fireship at Tyre, no historian recorded the use of petroleum weapons against Alexander in Mesopotamia or India. Curiously, however, Philostratus—who wrote about the flammable "worm" gathered at the Hyphasis River, above—recorded an Indian explanation for why Alexander refrained from attacking a fortress of the warlike Oxydrakae across the Hyphasis River. The Indians said he knew that the defenders typically would wait until attackers began an assault with siege engines; then they would suddenly let loose "rockets and bolts of fire" that rained down on the enemy's armor.[60]

A remarkable discovery in 2006 by archaeologists indicates that Alexander may have encountered incendiary weapons during his campaign in India, in Gandhara (between Pakistan and Afghanistan), where he besieged and sacked several forts in 327 BC. During their excavation at one of the forts, the archaeologists recovered a strange object in the defensive ditch. It was a charred, man-made ball composed of organic pitch and the minerals barite and sulfur. It resembles other incendiary balls of bituminous materials found in ancient Mesopotamian sites. The archaeological team proposed that the sphere was a surviving specimen of fireballs that had been ignited and propelled by slingers at the Macedonian invaders.[61]

Interestingly, among the incendiary formulas in the *Arthashastra*, the Indian war manual written during the time of Alexander's invasion, there are instructions for preparing "small balls" to be hurled at the enemy, as well as fire arrows. The balls and arrows were made flammable with a paste of powdered plant fibers mixed with resins, dung, charcoal, zinc, "red metals" (perhaps the red mineral realgar, the source of arsenic, or "red lead," lead tetraoxide, an oxidizer used in py-

rotechnics and explosives), lead, and wax. Other Indian recipes for making naphtha arrows and fireballs included magical
herbs and ground-up reptiles and worms—as well as highly
effective pitch, charcoal, and petroleum.[62]

▰ ▰ ▰

Burning naphtha could easily destroy siege engines. But unlike
fire arrows aimed at wooden walls, the liquid petroleum incendiaries were chiefly intended to burn humans alive, re-creating
the mythical deaths of Heracles, Glauke, and Creon, and causing extreme suffering and injury for real-life soldiers. Plutarch,
Pliny, and Seneca, the historians who identified naphtha as
Medea's secret weapon, based their speculation on firsthand
accounts of liquid-fire weapons from Roman army veterans
who had seen action in the Middle East in the first century
BC. The armies that pursued Mithradates and his allies, from
the Black Sea to Mesopotamia, were the first Romans to experience naphtha attacks. And Roman soldiers faced naphtha weapons over the next two centuries as the emperors attempted to maintain their rule in the Middle East (fig. 30).

Hatra was one of many Mesopotamian strongholds that
relied on nearby petroleum seepages to defend itself against
Rome. Ammianus Marcellinus described the lakes of naphtha
found in the region (the rich oil fields of northern Iraq). The
liquid was prodigiously sticky, he said, with heavy, "mortally
noxious fumes." Once it begins to burn, "human intelligence
will find no means of quenching it other than covering it
with earth."[63]

In AD 199, as we saw in chapter 6, Severus's soldiers at
Hatra were assailed by a panoply of terror weapons, including

FIG. 30. Naphtha, known as liquid fire, *maltha*, burning mud, was feared by Roman besiegers in the Near East. Here Queen Zenobia is using naphtha to defend her fortress at Palmyra, Syria, in 240 BC, drawing by Fortunino Matania, 1928.

scorpions and streams of burning naphtha. Because of its invisible but highly flammable fumes, the naphtha appeared to jump toward any spark, igniting the intervening air, and it was so sticky that it "pursued" anyone who tried to flee. Water offered no hope but fed more flames of intense heat. According to Cassius Dio, at Hatra the cascades of burning naphtha "inflicted the greatest damage, consuming the engines and all the soldiers on whom it fell." A horrified Severus gave the order to retreat even as his men breached Hatra's walls.[64]

Conventional weapons of antiquity—arrows, spears, and swords—wounded or killed by penetrating the skin and damaging internal organs. One could depend on training, skill, courage, and armor for protection. But there was almost no way to prepare for or deflect weapons of fire. Ordinary fire was bad enough, causing severe injury or death from smoke inhalation and destruction of skin, measured in degree (depth) and extent of burns over body surface. But accelerants greatly increased the scale of damage by fire. Fire weapons fueled by exothermic chemicals, because of their adhering nature and extremely high temperatures, intensified the degree of destruction of skin, deep tissue, and even bone, and prolonged the victim's death or else inflicted torturous pain and lifelong injuries. For all these reasons, incendiary weapons have generally been considered exceptionally cruel and abhorrent.[65]

* * *

In the sixth century AD, Parthians and Sasanians used naphtha incendiaries and ballistics called *naft-andazan* ("naphtha-throwers") in battles. Combined with archery, these were especially effective against war elephants. For example, the Sasanian commander Bahram Chobin reportedly used naphtha-throwers against two hundred elephants manned by the Turks in the Battle of Herat, AD 588. The naphtha and arrows aimed at the elephant's eyes and tusks caused them to run amok and flee back toward the Turkic lines.[66]

By the time of Muhammad, in the seventh century AD, naphtha projectiles had become favored siege weapons in the Middle East. Interestingly, some Arabic, Persian, and Mongol traditions and treatises on military incendiaries credit

Alexander the Great (and his "grand vizier," the philosopher Aristotle, Alexander's teacher and friend) with the invention of several infernal naphtha fire weapons. Two of those naphtha legends were recounted in the *Shahnama* epic by the Persian poet Firdawsi (AD 940–1020).

According to one legend, during his Indian campaigns Alexander forged thousands of life-sized horses and riders of hollow iron on wheels, each filled with naphtha. When these were rolled toward Porus's war elephants, the eerie black metal figures spewed streams of fire (apparently ignited by a fuse or quicklime and water, since naphtha alone is not self-lighting). A dramatic color illustration of this battle appears in the elaborate Mongol version of the *Shahnama* (see plate 9). The tale is a curious combination of the old Homeric myth of the Trojan Horse and the later Greek legend of Alexander's red-hot bronze statues deployed against Porus's war elephants. In the other illustrated legend of Alexander's ingenious inventions of chemical weaponry, Alexander constructed an invincible double wall of iron and copper, and filled it with charcoal, sulfur, and naphtha. When savage tribes attacked, the naphtha inside the wall could be ignited, to produce a shield of awesome flames and heat.[67]

The first use of catapulting naphtha by an Islamic army reputedly occurred during one of Muhammad's last campaigns, in AD 630. At the siege of Ta'if, a fortified city in the mountains east of Mecca held by the pagan Thaqif tribe, Muhammad ordered a catapult attack with fire. The Thaqif responded with catapult fire that rained red-hot scraps of metal on Muhammad's army, a reprise of the catapult loads of red-hot sand and shrapnel first used by the Phoenicians against Alexander the Great's men besieging Tyre, more than a thousand years earlier.[68]

In the civil wars after the death of Muhammad (AD 632), a specialized siege machine for delivering naphtha bombs was mentioned for the first time by name in Muslim annals. Created for the Umayyad caliph in Damascus (Syria), the *manjaniq*, or mangonel, was a heavy-duty catapult specifically designed to bombard cities with blazing naphtha. Prototypes were reportedly first manned at the siege of Alexandria in AD 645, but the mangonels saw massive use in AD 683, when the Umayyad army set out to take Medina and Mecca. In Damascus, the soldiers loaded a camel caravan with great numbers of the heavy catapults and containers of volatile naphtha and accomplished the astonishing feat of crossing the searing Nafud Desert in high summer to make surprise attacks on the two holy cities.

In AD 813, Baghdad, the Islamic capital, was totally destroyed by a new type of special forces to wield petroleum weaponry. Naphtha troops called *naffatun* manned hundreds of mangonels catapulting thousands of barrels of liquid fire. By AD 850, every Islamic army maintained regular *naffatun* units, and they were now protected by special fireproof uniforms and padding. Their gear was woven of the mysterious substance they called *hajar al-fatila*, asbestos, the fibrous rock impervious to flame discovered by Muslims in Tajikistan in the 800s. The invention of the fireproof uniforms led to a novel form of Islamic psychological warfare that brought Alexander's legendary naphtha-filled iron horses and riders to life. In an innovation worthy of today's Hollywood stuntmen on fire, Muslim riders and horses were covered with asbestos padding and then doused in naphtha and set afire to terrify the enemy cavalry. Spectacular "burning men on horseback" feats are now featured in the World Nomad Games.[69]

In AD 1167–68, an extreme example of the "scorched earth" policy of denying resources to an invading army occurred. In this case, when Cairo faced attack by Frankish Crusaders, the Muslims used their own petroleum weapons to destroy their own city (fig. 31). As the Crusaders advanced across Egypt, the Islamic ruler turned the entire city into a raging inferno in order to leave nothing but rubble for the Christians. As the terrified populace fled, twenty thousand naphtha pots and ten thousand petroleum grenades were ignited, and flames engulfed the city for fifty-four days.[70]

FIG. 31. Naphtha grenades. Ceramic pots were filled with volatile naphtha, lit with a fuse, and hurled at the enemy. Heeresgeschichtliches Museum, Vienna, Austria. Erich Lessing / Art Resource, NY.

This historical incident in Egypt gives us an example of enormous stockpiles of volatile petrochemical weapons stored in military warehouses in the Middle East at a surprisingly early date. The desperate Cairo option during the Crusades set a precedent for the threat, anticipated by US intelligence in 2003, that Saddam Hussein would torch Iraq's 1,500 oil wells, in order to deny them to US invaders. In the earlier 1991 Gulf War, Saddam's retreating Iraqi troops had set fire to 650 oil fields in Kuwait, creating fires of stupendous magnitude that burned for eight months.[71]

Remarkable archaeological evidence of the destruction of Cairo in AD 1167–68 by its own chemical weapons came to light in 1916. French and Egyptian archaeologists uncovered troves of the ceramic, fist-sized naphtha pots in the ruins of the old city. The grenades were of astonishing sophistication: they had been filled with volatile jellied naphtha (similar to napalm) and a crude gunpowder made of nitrates and sulfur.[72]

▬ ▬ ▬

The dangers of backfire for the early users of weaponry based on pyrophoric chemicals were daunting. As Kautilya remarked in his discussion of how to use incendiaries to capture cities, "Fire cannot be trusted." In the case of quicklime, sulfur, and petroleum and naphtha, ensuring safety in collecting and storing the combustible substances was difficult, because volatile vapors and liquids had to be kept away from moisture, oxygen, heat, and sparks. Notably, in the myth recounted at the beginning of this chapter, Medea followed these precautions in treating the combustible gown by sealing it in an airtight container. Somehow, during the chaos of battle, one had to mix the unstable, sticky materials, ignite them, and then aim them at the enemy, without allowing the rapacious flames to leap back toward the source of the spark or toward combustible fuel or water in the vicinity of the user.

One precaution when using combustibles, advised by Aeneas in 360 BC (mentioned above), was to hurl or otherwise emplace the unlit fuel first and then fire a blazing arrow or throw a burning pot to ignite it. That technique was used in the Third Crusade, in AD 1189–91, by Saladin's Muslim army besieging the Crusaders' castle at Acre (Acca, Israel). The Muslims tossed pots of naphtha without fuses against the Crusaders' towers. When nothing happened, the Christians crowded onto the towers and mocked the besiegers. The Muslims held their fire and waited for the naphtha to soak in. Then they threw a lighted pot, and the whole edifice and all the Christians exploded in flames.[73]

With vaporous naphtha and other combustibles, the chances of accidental explosions were extremely high, as acknowledged in Byzantine warfare manuals. Volatile compounds were always prepared outdoors for fear of fire and ease of escape. Chinese texts warned that heating sulfur, arsenic, carbon, and saltpeter indoors had resulted in severe burns to the alchemists' hands and faces, and even burned down the buildings where they were working. Naphtha bombs were especially difficult to aim and control, as the Umayyad Muslims learned during their siege of the holy city of Mecca in AD 683. In that battle, as they catapulted naphtha projectiles into the city, they tried to avoid the Ka'aba, the sanctuary of the Black Stone worshipped by Muslims. But the covering was struck and caught fire. The intense heat split the sacred Black Stone of Mecca into three pieces.[74]

And, of course, wind could also betray wielders of liquid fire. In a famous military disaster on the Yangtze River in AD 975, the Chinese admiral Chu Ling-Pin watched in horror as the liquid fire his troops were propelling toward the enemy fleet of the Song emperor was suddenly swept up by a strong contrary wind. The "smoke and flames were blown toward his own ships and men," immolating more than 150,000 sailors and soldiers. "Overcome with grief," the admiral "flung himself into the flames and died."[75]

Petroleum bombs and naphtha flamethrowers posed hazards to the users because of the low viscosity and vaporous light fractions: the fuel tended to explode prematurely. The use of soaps and other agents to thicken and stabilize naphtha and/or gasoline in the 1940s is what led to the formulation of napalm, allowing it to adhere to targets and burn at very high temperatures over a prolonged time. In antiquity, it was discovered that liquid naphtha could be somewhat stabilized with heavier oils, tar, or pitch, but those additives are themselves flammable. Handlers of such weapons always had to exercise great caution, even after the discovery of distillation techniques to remove the flammable vapors—a technique that led to the creation of the fearsome weapon known as Greek Fire.

◢ ◢ ◢

Greek Fire's origin is surrounded by fable. According to one legend, an angel whispered the formula to Constantine the Great, the first Christian emperor, in AD 300. But Greek Fire did not suddenly burst on the scene out of nowhere. Centuries of observations, insights, discoveries, and experiments with combustible sulfur, quicklime, and naphtha, under various names (liquid fire, *maltha*, *pyr automaton* or automatic, artificial, or prepared fire, sea fire, wild fire, flying fire, *oleum incendiarium*, fierce fire oil, water-white, *naft abyad*, and so on), ultimately led to the invention of the naval incendiary that was dubbed "Greek Fire" by the Crusaders in the 1200s. Naphtha had been a tool of siege craft since Assyrian times. With mangonels and *naffatun*, naphtha weaponry reached its peak performance in land engagements, but inventions in Syria and Constantinople (modern Istanbul) perfected naphtha armaments for battles at sea.

According to what survives in Islamic and Byzantine chronicles, it was the development of effective distillation and siphon pump technologies that enabled a flammable petroleum mixture to be stored and then propelled under pressure from boats, thus introducing the deployment of "something new, dreadful, launchable, and flammable," in the words of the historian Alfred Crosby.[76]

What exactly was the "terrible agent of destruction" known as Greek Fire? The story of how the Byzantine and Islamic formulas, once heavily guarded state secrets, were lost, and the evolution of similar weapons in Indian and Chinese warfare, has been recounted in detail in modern military literature. Basically, Greek Fire was a *weapon system* for blasting ships in naval engagements. The complex weapon consisted of a refined chemical *ammunition* and an ingenious *delivery system* of cauldrons, siphons, tubes, and pumps.

The main ingredient of the ammunition was naphtha, originally used as an incendiary poured over or hurled in pots at besiegers in Mesopotamia, and later in firebombs catapulted by mangonels invented in Damascus and used by Muslims to bombard fortifications, as described above. The Byzantines had used small siphons and syringes to squirt petroleum incendiaries as early as AD 513. But the new technology of pumping pressurized, distilled naphtha through bronze tubes at ships was achieved through brilliant chemical engineering by a Greek "petroleum consultant" named Kallinikos. Fleeing the Muslim occupation of Syria, Kallinikos sought refuge in Constantinople in about AD 668 and taught the Byzantines his invention. Greek Fire was first used to break the Muslim navy's seven-year siege of Constantinople begun in AD 673, and the weapon saved the city again from the Muslim fleet in AD 718.[77]

The exact details of Kallinikos's formula and delivery system are lost to modern science, and historians and chemists who try to reconstruct how the device worked disagree on the exact composition of the naphtha ammunition and the system design. We know that Greek Fire burned in water and may have been ignited by water, and it adhered to victims. Besides distilled naphtha, the ingredients may have included thickeners such as resin or wax, quicklime, sulfur, turpentine, and saltpeter. The precise formula of the ammunition matters less than the amazing delivery system, which was capable of shooting liquid fire from swiveling nozzles mounted on small boats without the benefit of modern thermometers, safety valves, and pressure gauges (see plate 10).[78]

The only recourses available to crews facing Greek Fire—draping ships with masses of heavy, wet hides; sailing only in stormy weather; and attempting rapid, evasive maneuvers—were rarely successful and were dangerous in themselves. "In short," writes military historian Alex Roland, "there was no adequate countermeasure to Greek Fire." From the seventh century on, the Byzantines and Arabs formulated variations on Greek Fire, which resembled napalm in the way "it clung to everything it touched, instantly igniting any organic material—ship's hull, oars, sails, rigging, crew, and their clothing. Nothing was immune." Even "jumping into the sea failed to quench the flames." The weapon caused enemies to "shiver in terror" and capitulate in despair.[79]

Greek Fire was the ultimate weapon of its time. "Every man touched by it believed himself lost, every ship attacked with it was devoured by flames," wrote a crusader in AD 1248. Partington, a historian of Greek Fire, compared the ancient reaction of horror to the modern dread of the atomic bomb. In 1139, the Second Lateran Council, following ideas of chivalry and honorable war, decreed that Greek Fire or similar burning weapons were "too murderous" to be used in Europe. The council's decision was respected for some centuries, but the issue may have been moot since the formula for Greek Fire seems to have already been lost by then. The recipe was rekindled in a treatise published for Napoleon, with the chilling title *Weapons for the Burning of Armies*.[80] But centuries before the invention of Greek Fire, naphtha was already an ultimate weapon of devastating destructive power. The early precursors of Greek Fire, first described so graphically in the ancient Greek myth of Medea and Glauke, and then experienced in real battles during the Roman Empire, were the most dreaded, fearsome weapons of their day. There was no adequate countermeasure, no way to withstand such infernos. Neither extraordinary valor nor a suit of bronze armor could save a soldier enveloped by cascades of corrosive flames that melted both metal and flesh. The experiences of Lucullus and his Roman legions in the first century BC serve as a compelling case study of the effects of liquid fire.

▗ ▗ ▗

Veterans who served with Licinius Lucullus had nightmarish tales to tell of their campaigns in Asia: they were among the first Romans to undergo naphtha attacks. The story of Lucullus's campaign is a fitting conclusion to this chapter on infernal fire weapons—and it also draws together a full range of the biochemical weapons described in the preceding chapters. Lucullus's army faced a panoply of bioterrors, from poison arrows, stinging bees, savage bears, and scorpion bombs to unquenchable, burning mud.

In the Third Mithradatic War of 73–66 BC, the Roman general Lucullus continued the frustrating pursuit of King Mithradates, the wily ruler of the Pontic Kingdom and master of poisons, whose dream was to create the ultimate personal antidote to biotoxins. Mithradates and his allies invented a stunning array of terror strategies directed at the Romans. He had begun his challenge to Roman power in 88 BC, with a shocking atrocity. He secretly ordered the massacre of every Italian man, woman, and child living in the new Roman Province of Asia, to take place on a specified date. So hated were the imperial colonists that more than eighty thousand Romans were reportedly slaughtered on a single day. Mithradates's armies then swept west through Greece and even threatened to invade Italy, while his client princes took control of significant cities in Rome's Asian Province.[81]

The first battle with Mithradates in Bithynia ended very badly for the Romans and their allies. When Mithradates's vicious scythe-bearing chariots plowed at high speed through the ranks, the soldiers were overwhelmed by the sight of their companions "chopped in halves but still breathing, and others mangled and cut to pieces" by the whirling blades. It was the "hideousness of the spectacle," not the losses, that sent the troops fleeing in horror, commented the historian Appian.[82]

Next, Mithradates captured the Roman legate Manius Aquillius, the son of the brutal Roman commander who had been criticized for poisoning wells in Asia in an earlier war (chapter 3). Mithradates paraded the official on an ass, and then executed him in a particularly horrid way—by pouring molten gold down his throat. These acts ushered in the long Mithradatic Wars (90–63 BC), in which a succession of Roman generals achieved victory after victory on land and sea against the monarch and his allies, but failed to capture Mithradates, who eluded their grasp like quicksilver.

Beginning in 73 BC, Lucullus relentlessly attacked and sacked the monarch's allied kingdoms from Pontus to Mesopotamia and back again. After difficult sieges of several cities near the Black Sea, where the defenders let loose swarms of bees and rampaging bears to assault the Roman tunnelers, Lucullus tracked Mithradates south, to Armenia. There, Lucullus laid siege to Tigranocerta on the Tigris (eastern Turkey), where Mithradates had taken refuge with his son-in-law King Tigranes. The new fortifications were only half-built and the city was captured, but the two monarchs slipped out of Lucullus's hands and began to gather up new armies.

Despite his victory at Tigranocerta, "the barbarians did Lucullus serious injury" with a new weapon of unexpected savagery. Cassius Dio described how the Tigranocertans poured streams of fire on the Romans and their siege engines. The extraordinary fire flowed over and consumed everything: wood, leather, metal, horses, and human bodies. "This chemical," marveled Cassius Dio, "is full of *bitumen* and is so fiery that it burns up whatever it touches and cannot be extinguished by any liquid." The weapon was naphtha, gathered from the rich local petroleum deposits. This event and similar attacks on Roman armies in the region counter the suggestion by biochemical warfare historian Eric Croddy that "the combustible properties of naphtha and its utility as a weapon" first came to the Romans' attention much later with the invention of Greek Fire in AD 668.[83]

In the Armenian countryside, the Romans suffered another kind of bioattack by Mithradates's allies. In skirmishes, Lucullus lost a great many men to the skilled mounted archers, who shot arrows backward as they galloped away from the pursuing Romans. His men's wounds were "dangerous and incurable," wrote Cassius Dio, for the archers, like the Scythians described above, used "double arrow-points of iron and moreover, they poisoned them." With so many dead and dying from the poison arrows, Lucullus retreated.[84]

After facing these weapons of extraordinary brutality in battles of dubious outcome in 69–68 BC, Lucullus's legionaries began to revolt. But Lucullus forged on, intending to conquer another ally of Mithradates, the Kingdom of Commagene in the oil fields along the Euphrates (on the border of southeastern Turkey and Syria). Samosata, the wealthy fortified capital of Commagene, guarded the Euphrates river traffic, the strategic crossroads from Damascus to Pontus, and the east-west trade routes.[85]

When Lucullus stormed the fortified city in 69 BC, he was unaware that the Samosatans had a secret weapon to defend their walls. They had collected "a flammable mud called *maltha* that exudes from nearby marshy pools," wrote Pliny, who described the battle. *Maltha* was apparently a very viscous form of naphtha skimmed from great pools of *asphaltum,* petroleum tar that oozes from fissures in sandstones in the region.

When the Samosatans poured the flaming mud over the Roman soldiers, the effect was horrendous. *Maltha*'s ravenous appetite makes it "cling stubbornly to anyone who tries to flee," Pliny declared, "and water only makes it burn more fiercely." Only covering the flames with earth could extinguish the blaze. At Samosata, the voracious flames burned up the men in their armor, and the extreme heat even turned the Romans' own armaments against them. "They were repeatedly burned by their own weapons," wrote Pliny.[86]

In later times, other besieged populations in the region would capitalize on the unique ability of high-temperature incendiaries to turn an attacking soldier's weapons and armor against him. We already saw how the Phoenicians, with a rain of hot sand at Tyre, had turned the bronze chest plates of Alexander's Macedonians into red-hot torture devices. And in AD 630, during the siege of Ta'if near Mecca, Muhammad's army had advanced on the walls under a "testudo" (turtleshell) of interlocking shields held over their heads to deflect the arrows of the defenders. But they were unprepared for the rain of red-hot clay balls that heated their shields to intense temperatures. As they dropped the burning shields, the men were cut down by a barrage of arrows.[87]

The terror of the burning *maltha* at Samosata forced Lucullus to withdraw again. His army, never very loyal, now began to mutiny and desert in significant numbers. And Samosata, like Hatra, remained an independent desert stronghold for another century.

Mythic parallels were beginning to accumulate for Lucullus, eerie reminders of the old stories of Heracles and Medea.

First, the poison arrows of the Armenians caused torturous death and incurable wounds, and then the burning mud coated the soldiers, like the corrosive tunic that tormented Heracles. The scene at Samosata also replicated the deaths of Glauke and Creon and the Corinthians in the palace, in the unnatural conflagration engineered by Medea. Pliny was certainly struck by the coincidence, for in his description of the Roman disaster at Samosata, he suggested that some form of *maltha* must have been Medea's secret weapon.

During his campaigns against Mithradates, Lucullus discovered an art treasure with haunting mythical resonance: a large bronze statue of Heracles, showing the mighty hero contorted in pain, trapped in the garment that turned his own poison weapons against him. Lucullus wrapped the magnificent bronze statue in a linen shroud and brought it back to Rome. The statue was paraded along with the rich booty he had raided from Mithradates's kingdoms, and then placed on permanent public display, next to the Temple of the Divine Julius. About a century later, Pliny recorded the layers of inscriptions that had been carved into the base of the highly valued artwork by the unknown sculptor of Asia Minor. Known as "Hercules in the Burning Tunic," the statue was admired by the Romans as a powerful evocation of the hero's final agony (fig. 32).[88]

Yet another event with mythic echoes occurred during Lucullus's campaign. After capturing a string of cities loyal to Mithradates, Lucullus chased Mithradates's navy—led by three of the king's major allies, Varius, Alexander, and Dionysius—down the coast of Turkey. The historian Appian described how, at the same harbor where the Greeks had landed to attack Troy in Homer's *Iliad*, Lucullus captured thirteen of Mi-

FIG. 32. Heracles struggling to tear off the burning, poison tunic. Bronze sculpture, 1680. 49.7.61, Jules S. Bache Collection, 1949, Metropolitan Museum, New York.

thradates's ships; he overtook the rest of the fleet on a small, barren island near Lemnos. The trio of captains escaped, but Lucullus discovered them hiding in a cave on the small island. Varius he killed; Alexander he captured; but Dionysius, a true follower of Mithradates, took the poison that he always carried with him and died by his own hand.[89]

As Appian pointed out, the tiny island was none other than Chryse, the desert isle where, according to myth, Philoctetes was abandoned after having suffered an accidental wound from Heracles's Hydra-venom arrows, the original biological weapons (described in chapter 1). Philoctetes was marooned in misery for ten years in a cave on the island, perhaps in the very cave where Mithradates's allies took refuge. Chryse was a well-known landmark, where many ancient travelers stopped to pay their respects to Philoctetes's shrine. A learned scholar of Greek mythology, Lucullus would certainly have been aware of the island's fame, and it was common for Roman commanders to visit mythological landmarks during their campaigns. In 191 BC, for example, after his victory over Antiochus in Greece, the Roman commander Manius Glabrio sought out the sacred site of Heracles's pyre, where Philoctetes had inherited the poison arrows. Did Lucullus pay a visit to the shrine on the isle of Chryse after his major victory there, to admire Philoctetes's bow and breastplate and the bronze serpent symbolizing the envenomed arrows?

Ancient authors describe Lucullus as a compassionate and generous man: early in his campaigns he burst into tears at the sight of a city he had reduced to ashes. Perhaps his war experiences with poison arrows and all-consuming fire gave him a unique appreciation for Philoctetes's and Heracles's sufferings. On the other hand, maybe the beleaguered commander wished that Philoctetes could miraculously appear with a quiverful of Hydra arrows to turn the tide against Mithradates.

Had Lucullus been able to peer into the future, he would have seen his successor Pompey sabotaged by poison honey and his archenemy Mithradates done in at last by his own reliance on poisons. Lucullus's own end came in 57 BC, after a descent into insanity, ironically brought about by poison—by deadly drugs administered by his freedman.

There is no evidence that Lucullus or other Roman commanders of the republic ever fought "fire with fire," or retaliated with naphtha in Mesopotamia—probably because their enemies controlled the petroleum resources there. But, eventually, the Romans did turn to a morally repugnant use of the frightening chemical weapon. In the Roman arena, one could witness the spectacle of prisoners condemned to reenact the fiery fate suffered by so many Roman soldiers at Tigranocerta and Samosata, and later at Hatra and other Mesopotamian cities. Inspired by the dramatic death of Heracles and the celebrated statue of Heracles displayed in Rome after Lucullus's campaign, and probably influenced by veterans' tales of burning *maltha*, public executions by the *tunica molesta* became a popular diversion. The gruesome death sentence by means of the naphtha-soaked "tunic of torture" was first devised by the emperor Nero in AD 64, as one of many inventive execution methods he designed to re-create mythic death scenes. Executions mirroring Heracles's death continued to be staged for the amusement of Roman audiences through the third century AD.[90] Meanwhile, in distant Mesopotamia, Rome's own soldiers, pursuing the imperial agenda demanded by their emperors, were compelled to endure the very real ordeals of hellfire.

THE MANY-HEADED HYDRA

Chopping off the immortal head of the venomous Hydra,
he buried it alive, and placed a heavy rock over it.
—MYTH OF HERACLES

LUCULLUS AND HIS ROMAN SOLDIERS were not the first army to face weapons of poison and hellish fire, nor were they the last. But theirs is a story brimming with mythic parallels. Not only did they encounter biological and chemical weapons on their campaigns, but they discovered the celebrated statue of the dying Heracles and visited the famous desert island of Philoctetes, two mythic biowarriors who exemplified the unforeseen consequences of toxic weapons. Lucullus's experiences in the first century BC help show how the ongoing history of biochemical weapons continually harks back to its mythological beginnings.

From antiquity onward, the annals of toxic weaponry form a widening gyre of myth reflecting history, and history mirroring myth. And just as the Hydra's heads multiplied at a drastic rate, so human ingenuity in waging biochemical warfare has proliferated at a dreadful pace. "And so," wrote the Roman philosopher Lucretius, contemplating that murderous progression in his own lifetime (first century BC), "tragic discord gave birth to one invention after another and added daily increments to the horrors of war." The race was on to develop more and more fearsome weapons to intensify psychological dread and ensure agonizing death, suffering, and destruction on a scale far beyond that wrought by the simple sharp and blunt weapons of old. The terse words of Appian, historian of the Mithradatic Wars, are fitting: "They left nothing untried that was within the compass of human energy."[1]

The basic concepts of the diverse biochemical weapons that were wielded in historical battles—from poisons and contagion to animal allies and hellish fire—were first imagined in ancient mythology. The archaic myths even anticipated the moral and practical quandaries that have surrounded biological and chemical armaments since their invention. Far from fading over millennia, the age-old problems of controlling toxic agents of war and avoiding unintended consequences have intensified with the advance of science in the service of war. Heracles thought he could control the poison arrows he created from the Hydra's venom, but they brought death and tragedy to his friends and ultimately destroyed Heracles himself. The poison weapons were inherited by Philoctetes and dealt him great misfortune too, even though they turned the tide in favor of the Greeks at Troy.

Once created, toxic weapons take on a life of their own, resistant to destruction and threatening harm over generations. Consider the thousands of tons of still-active biological and chemical weapons from World Wars I and II and later, lurking in long-forgotten dumping areas, releasing toxins and posing grave risks to unwitting finders. These weapons, and the

countless vials of smallpox, anthrax, and other superpatho-
gens stored in laboratories around the world, ripe for weaponization, have their antecedents in the "plague demons"
imprisoned in jars buried under the temple in Jerusalem, and
the pestilence locked inside the golden casket in Babylon.
Centuries later, those containers were broken open during
wartime, and plague spread over the land (chapter 4).

Long before the invention of Greek Fire, and two millennia before the invention of napalm and nuclear bombs, the
Greeks and Romans confronted new chemical fire weapons
whose awesome powers of destruction could not be checked
by normal means. Over and over, the ancient commentators
repeated the refrain: the only hope of quelling the ghastly
fire weapon was to cover it with earth. That solution echoed
Heracles's method of getting rid of the monstrous Hydra's
head, by burying it underground (fig. 33). Now, those desperate attempts to bury poison and fire weapons seem to

FIG. 33. The many-headed Hydra, a symbol of the proliferating dilemmas of biological warfare. Caeretan hydria, 520 BC, attributed to the Eagle Painter, 83AE.346.
Courtesy of the J. Paul Getty Museum Open Content Program.

foreshadow our own efforts to dispose of dangerous weapons underground, out of sight but never completely out of mind.

As the myths forewarned, a tragic myopia afflicts those who resort to poison weapons. Even as modern adversaries threaten to attack and retaliate with terror weapons that would bring mass destruction of innocents, nations are forced to seek safe ways to dispose of the stockpiles of biochemical munitions and radioactive nuclear waste they have already brought into being. But burning, dumping at sea, burying in the ground—each method poses contamination hazards for present and future generations. Sites where biochemical and radioactive weapons have been buried, tested, or accidentally released remain deadly to all life-forms. The menacing situation recalls the ancient dread of places corrupted by *miasma*, exhalations of deadly vapors.

The human cost is incalculable. Take, for instance, the anthrax, bubonic plague, smallpox, and other supergerms created, tested, and dumped at the world's largest bioweapons laboratory, established in 1948 on Vozrozhdeniya Island in the Aral Sea. The lab was one of eighteen weaponized pathogen Biopreparat centers scattered around the former Soviet Union. At the time, the Aral Sea was the fourth largest lake in the world. But by 2014, the Aral Sea had almost completely dried up and is now called the Aralkum Desert. The pathogenic weapons thought to be confined to the island have poisoned the air and water of Uzbekistan and Kazakhstan. Of the environmental disasters in the region that have been made public, the sudden death of five hundred thousand steppe antelopes in just one hour in 1988 is striking, and the Aral Smallpox Incident of 1971, affecting humans in the region, came to public notice only in 2002. That same year, ten of

Vozrozhdeniya's anthrax dumps were reportedly decontaminated. But animals and humans could still contract and spread the hypervirulent plagues buried in what was once an island.[2]

In the United States, plans to incinerate tons of obsolete chemical weapons pose serious safety hazards, and accidents have been documented at furnace sites in the Pacific and the United States. After years of debate, Congress mandated the Centers for Disease Control (CDC) to neutralize five hundred tons of chemical munitions still stored in concrete bunkers underground at Blue Grass Army Depot, Kentucky, in accordance with the International Chemical Weapons Convention Treaty ratified in 1997. The weapons, including mustard gas, sarin, and nerve agents, were created between 1917 and 1968. For safety, a massive complex for destruction and an intensive training program for more than a thousand workers was required, costing more than $5 billion. Destruction began in January 2019. Another storage site holds twenty-six hundred tons of chemical weapons at Pueblo Chemical Depot, Colorado: in April 2020 the US government extended the destruction completion date to 2023.[3]

The search for other options for the disposal of nuclear weapons, such as chemical neutralization or vitrification (encasement in glass), continues. Meanwhile, scientists agree that the "geological solution"—entombing lethal, indestructible weapons under mountains of rock—is the best option for disposal. One cannot help but picture the eerily prescient parallel from myth. After he had created his poison weapons, Heracles hit upon his own "geological solution" to dispose of the Hydra's immortal head. He buried the evil thing alive deep in the ground and placed a massive boulder over the spot, to warn away future generations. Indeed, the Hydra's head with fangs eternally dripping poison into the earth is a perfect symbol for indestructible biochemical and radioactive armaments emitting moral and physical pollution in the world today.

In 1999, the world's first underground repository for the "safe and permanent disposal" of radioactive weapons material was dug in a salt bed more than two thousand feet deep, in the Chihuahuan Desert near Carlsbad, Mexico (Waste Isolation Pilot Plant, WIPP). In 2014, an explosion and airborne release of plutonium at WIPP cast doubts on this solution and resulted in a growing backlog of nuclear waste, indefinitely stored in concrete and steel casks.[4]

A geologic solution on a massive scale was proposed in 2002, when plans were developed to bury a huge cache of radioactive material deep under Yucca Mountain in Nevada, in the desert about a hundred miles northwest of Las Vegas. The seventy thousand tons of nuclear material (requiring forty miles of tunnels) are expected to remain dangerously radioactive for one hundred thousand years. The idea was to make the toxic sepulcher impregnable for at least ten thousand years, until the year AD 12,000.

Scientists who opposed the plan pointed out that the man-made containers, seals, and barriers buried under the rock cannot safeguard the material against seismic faulting, volcanic activity, erosion, groundwater seepage, and climate changes over ten thousand years. Ominous evidence at Rocky Mountain Arsenal near Denver, Colorado, where chemical weapons were disposed of in deep wells in the mid-twentieth century, suggested that the deep dispersal of toxic fluids actually caused earthquakes in the area. Nevada is already fourth in the nation for seismic events. In 2011, the controversial plans and the funds to develop Yucca Mountain nuclear waste repository were withdrawn; the site remains in limbo as of this writing.[5]

Similar Herculean "geological solutions" are under way in Europe. Germany maintained two geological repositories for radioactive materials, Morsleben and Schacht Asse II salt mines, both deeper than WIPP in New Mexico, but both sites are jeopardized by geological instability. Storage at Morseleben was suspended in 1998; costly attempts at remediation continue. Another site, Gorleben, has similar issues; the iron ore mine Schacht Konrad was proposed to begin in 2013, funded until 2043. Finland began constructing a geological repository called Onkalo in 2004, to begin operations in 2023 and expected to be filled to capacity by 2120. The French National Radioactive Waste Management Agency, Andra, plans to deposit eighty thousand cubic meters of nuclear waste at a site called Cigéo, in northeastern France, beginning in 2025.[6]

Beyond the grave problems of trying to safely imprison perilous materials of mass destruction under rock for one hundred centuries, there is also the necessity of preventing inadvertent human intrusion into such storage sites. Immediate problems of keeping uninformed people or terrorists away from deadly weapons burial grounds are compounded by the long-term dilemma of devising warnings for eternity. Notably, the ancient Greek myth of the Hydra anticipated this concern: Heracles placed a great rock over the place where the immortal venomous serpent's head was entombed, to warn people away.

Since 1992, when the Russians abandoned the biochemically contaminated Vozrozhdeniya Island, mentioned above, people living around the desiccated Aral Sea continue to salvage tons of military equipment and valuable scrap materials despite the health risks. In Denver, the Rocky Mountain Arsenal National Wildlife Refuge is contaminated with napalm, mustard gas, sarin, and other biochemical weapons dumped in the 1940s and '50s. Public access to the popular wildlife refuge had to be suspended in 2000, while ways to deal with the pernicious miasma were investigated. In 2010, decontamination was said to be complete.

Examples of the dangers of buried or sunken biochemical weapons can be multiplied. In the 1960s and '70s, the United States simply filled old ships with disposed chemical weapons and sank them in the oceans. Other chemical munitions were buried and forgotten. In 1993, live munitions containing viable mustard gas were unearthed at the site of a luxury housing development in Washington, DC. In 1997, a fishing crew in the Baltic Sea suffered serious burns when their nets brought up a greasy yellowish lump of mustard gas, from the forty thousand tons of German chemical munitions dumped at sea after World War II. An archaeological discovery with disquieting echoes of the vessels of plague in ancient temples occurred in San Francisco in 2003. During excavations of the historic fort at the Presidio, the archaeologists unearthed a cache of glass vials. The strange "artifacts" turned out to contain still-toxic mustard gas buried by the US military during World War II. These incidents are only the tip of the iceberg: it is estimated that hundreds of thousands of deteriorating chemical munitions lie in unmarked burial sites around the world.[7]

At nuclear waste sites like that proposed for Yucca Mountain and already in existence at WIPP in New Mexico and other sites around the world, the enormity of geologic scale and the vast time frame of toxicity take on cosmic proportions. In other words, the authorities must face the ramifications of their actions on future generations in *mythic* terms. To that end, government agencies have turned to *mythic* solutions. To forge this crucial new interdisciplinary field of "nuclear semiotics," folklorists, anthropologists, linguists, architects, archaeologists, artists, science fiction writers, behavioral psychologists, philosophers, and other scholars and scientists work to figure out how to ensure that the buried, indestructible Hydra's heads of radioactive doom will remain undisturbed by human beings over time measured in eons.[8]

What if, over the ages, WIPP and other underground repositories for biochemical and nuclear waste around the world take on a mysterious allure? What if future underwater archaeologists and treasure hunters decide to dive to explore shipwrecks, and come upon forgotten ships filled with chemical weapons that were sunk in the seas during the Cold War? What if the doom-laden sites, surrounded by the mystic aura of adventure, exert an attraction for vision quests, spiritual seekers, or extreme risk takers of some future age? What if the forbidden places come to be seen as locations where fabulous treasure must have been hidden in the remote past, like the Pyramids of Egypt or the secret tomb of Genghis Khan? How can treasure hunters, archaeologists, scientists, prospectors, adventurers, and other explorers in the future be prevented from breaking the seals of the secret chambers and tunnels deep inside mountains? They might unwittingly release the "spirits of death," as occurred in the ancient temples where plague was once stored (chapter 4).

Some experts have suggested that frightening legends should be disseminated about the doomsday weapons, in the hope that these tales will become long-lasting oral traditions, like Homer's *Iliad* or biblical stories, retold for generations.

Perhaps an "atomic priesthood" could preserve the message of danger through rituals. Perhaps warning messages could be encoded in the DNA of plants at dangerous sites. Another creative idea involves genetically engineering cats to change color in the presence of lethal radiation and reinforcing their role with myths about lifesaving "ray cats."[9]

Inspired by ancient Babylonian inscriptions carved on stone in the eighteenth century BC, some archaeologists proposed that stone tablets inscribed with sinister warnings in seven languages should be randomly buried in the surrounding deserts. These messages would explain what is entombed deep under the mountains or deserts, and why the sepulchers should never be disturbed. But linguists point out that it is doubtful that present-day languages and cultures will exist ten thousand years from now.

To back up verbal warnings in what will surely become dead languages, other consultants suggest foreboding, repellent symbolism. One could surround such places with menacing earthworks, such as gigantic concrete thorns or jagged lightning bolts emerging from the ground to convey a sense of dread and mortal danger to the body. Another plan calls for a "spike field," tall towers of granite, engraved with ominous symbols. Human faces expressing horror and nausea (along the lines of Edvard Munch's famous painting *The Scream*) and pictographs indicating mass death and destruction have been proposed (fig. 34). Backfiring potentials loom, however. The drawback is based on human nature. Such a landscape—"a strange, disturbing wonder—would probably attract rather than repel." Florian Blanquer, a semiotician for Andra, remarks: "We are adventurers. We are drawn to conquer forbidding environments." As with the tombs of the pharaohs, the

FIG. 34. Landscape of Thorns, one of the designs intended to warn future civilizations away from nuclear materials burial sites like WIPP and Yucca Mountain. Concept by architect Michael Brill, art by Safdar Abidi, SAND92-1382. Sandia National Laboratories.

placement of grandiose warnings, mystic symbols, elaborate booby traps, and terrifying curses could attract adventurers. As with the golden casket in the ancient Babylonian temple plundered by the Roman soldiers, valuable materials such as industrial titanium, platinum, and sapphire might also lure looters.[10]

The essential concept, suggests one anthropologist, is to identify the place itself as an urgent message for future civilizations: "We considered ourselves to be a powerful culture. But this place is not a place of honor." What lies buried here "was dangerous and repulsive to us." The warning should somehow convey that the peril is still present, a mortal danger, an emanation of evil energy that will be unleashed if anyone physically disturbs this place. People should shun and run from this place. Here is a place "you must always remember to forget."[11]

This kind of message would have struck a chord with ancient Greeks and Romans who visited the shrine where Philoctetes had dedicated his poison arrows, or with those who marveled at the tragic statue of Heracles in the burning cloak, listened in awe to the story of Glauke's death, or pointed out the rock marking the place where Heracles had entombed the Hydra's hideous head.

If only it were so easy to extinguish the poisonous miasma of biotoxic weapons, invented so long ago, by hiding them under mountains of solid rock. If only mythology really does possess the power to warn against the relentless advance of the dark sciences of war. Perhaps there is a ray of hope in the myth of Philoctetes, in his decision to dedicate the dreadful bow and arrows to a memorial of divine healing rather than pass the weapons on to a new generation of warriors. His act anticipates modern efforts to forge treaties in which nations could agree to halt the proliferation and deployment of bio-chemical and nuclear arms, and turn technological efforts to alleviating human suffering.

One can only hope that a deeper understanding of toxic warfare's mythic origins and earliest historic realities might help divert the drive to transform all nature into a deadly ar-senal, redirecting it into the search for better ways to heal. Then Appian's sorrowful words about war, "They left nothing untried that was within the compass of human energy," could instead refer to human ingenuity striving to turn na-ture's forces to good.

ACKNOWLEDGMENTS

MANY SCHOLARS, SCIENTISTS, AND FRIENDS helped this project take form. For expert knowledge, valuable references, critical support, and/or substantive comments, I thank Aaron Bauer, Steve Casey, Scott Chesworth, Simon Cotton, Kaveh Farrokh, Lori Hamlett, Kyle Harper, Sohail Hashmi, Arthur Keaveney, Will Keener, John Kelsay, Milton Leitenberg, Mike Loades, John Ma, Michelle Maskiell, David Meadows, Antoinette Morris, Ian Morris, Robert Murphy, Josiah Ober, Robert Peterson, Serguei Popov, David Rafferty, Roshni Rajadorai, Julian Perry Robinson, Paula Saffire, Alexander Samuel, Jack Sasson, Rose Mary Sheldon, Matt Simonton, Barry Strauss, Philip Thibodeau, Tod Todeschini, Dolores Urquidi, Kathleen Vogel, Philip Wexler, and Mark Wheelis. Thanks to Michele Angel for creating excellent new maps.

I'm grateful that my interest in investigating the hidden scientific depths of classical legends received encouragement at very early stages from Gerald Erickson, William Hansen, and Henrietta Warwick. Thanks to *MHQ: Quarterly Journal of Military History* (Autumn 1997) and *Archaeology* (November–December 1995 and March–April 1997) for publishing some of my preliminary research on ancient unconventional weapons and tactics.

It gives me great pleasure to thank Javier Gómez Valero, editor at Desperta Ferro Ediociones for publishing the Spanish translation, *Fuego Griego, Flechas Envenenadas y Escorpiones: La guerra química y bacteriológica en la Antigüedad* (Madrid, 2018). I also thank Álvaro López Franco, editor at *Descubrir la Historia* 19 (2019) for interviewing me about biological and chemical weapons in ancient times.

Special thanks to my wonderful agents, Sandra Dijkstra and Andrea Cavallaro, for placing the updated and revised edition of this book into the hands of my splendid editor, Rob Tempio, at my favorite press. I'm also thankful for astute and constructive suggestions for revision and bibliography from the anonymous reviewers for Princeton University Press. Also at PUP, I appreciate the artistic advice of Dimitri Karetnikov, the excellent copyediting by Lauren Lepow, and the amazing cover design by Chris Ferrante.

Eternal thanks to Josiah Ober, my heart's companion: Long may our conversation continue.

NOTES

PREFACE

1. Evidence for various conspiracy hypotheses about COVID-19, through early 2020, was gathered and analyzed by Health Feedback organization, a worldwide network of scientists on health and medical information in media coverage. A WHO investigation reported on February 9, 2021, that the reservoir host species could not yet be identified; but accidental escape of the zoonotic virus from the Chinese lab at Wuhan in 2019 has not been ruled out, as of this writing. The lab's controversial and risky secret experiments with making bat coronavirus with capabilities of "spillover" to humans was partially financed by the United States National Institute of Health (NIH) in 2017. See Teoh 2020; Guterl et al. 2020; "Spore Wars" 2020; "Origin of Covid-19" 2020.

2. By January 2022, COVID had killed more than five million people worldwide. See chapter 4 for deliberate plague fears. I was interviewed about the ancient history of biological weapons for an episode of ABC Australia's *Rear Vision* radio show, "Biowarfare—Can It Tell Us Anything about the Corona Virus?" June 7, 2020. Genetically targeted and DNA hybrid weapons, Ahmadi 2020.

3. In an act of unconventional warfare, the World Trade Center was demolished by terrorists who commandeered a US passenger plane and flew into the top of the skyscraper. Mayor 1995a (toxic honey); Mayor 1995b and 1997b; Maskiell and Mayor 2001 (clothing imbued with contagion or chemicals); Mayor 1997a ("Dirty Tricks in Ancient Warfare").

4. The case of the anthrax letter attacks of 2001 remains unsolved; the prime suspect, a US government anthrax/bioweapons researcher,

committed suicide in August 2008. Ali Hassan al-Majid was tried and executed in 2010. For Iraq's biological weapons program of the 1980s and '90s, see Colvin and Mahnaimi 1998. In 2008, a US missile strike killed al-Qaeda biochemical weapons mastermind Abu Khabab al-Masri, whose projects in the Afghanistan War included an anthrax weapon and poisons that would be absorbed by skin. Osama bin Laden was killed by a US special operations unit in Pakistan in 2011.

5. *Newsweek*: Carmichael 2003. By 2004 it was evident that Iraq had no biochemical or nuclear WMD.

6. Newman 2005; Eveleth 2012; Lockwood 2014. ISIS use of scorpion bombs: Grossman 2014.

7. Disease as weapon, chapter 4; venom, chapter 2; incendiaries and poison gas, chapter 7; Dura-Europos, James 2011; for counterarguments, see Farrokh 2017, 257–59.

8. Ciaraldi 2000; Ciaraldi 2007.

9. Mithradates's experiments with toxins, his "universal antidote," and the antidote's later appearances in Rome, chapter 5, and see Mayor 2010, 237–47; Mayor 2019a.

10. BioSecurity 2003, October 20–22, 2003, Washington DC, was organized by Harvard Medical School, Harvard School of Public Health, and Harvard Medical International, in conjunction with the RAND Center for Domestic and International Health Security and Jane's Information Group. International biosecurity experts conferred on how to respond to biological events involving anthrax, smallpox, SARS, etc. The talk show was A&E History Channel International, "Global View," December 23, 2004. Beginning in 2004, Serguei Popov worked at the National Center for Biodefense, George Mason University, with his former Biopreparat supervisor Ken Alibek, author of *Biohazard* (2000). Their research in the Soviet Union and in the United States is described in Williams 2006. Holy grail: Dan Kaszeta quoted in "Spore Wars" 2020.

11. Newman 2005.

12. Vaughan 2011. Koblentz 2011; Valente 2019; Balmer 2016; Cotton 2013. "Five References to the Ancient and Late Roman World within *Game of Thrones*," by Sarah Bond, *Forbes*, July 24, 2017. *Blowback*, Hannibal's

secret weapon: "After reading Adrienne Mayor's book about chemical and biological warfare in the ancient world and John Prevas's book about Hannibal's crossing the Alps, I knew I had to take my novel in an entirely different direction." Brad Thor, "Behind the Book," www.bradthor.com. *Greek Fire* is a "fascinating and pretty horrifying read . . . and a resource of pure gold if you are a writer," noted Dana Stabenow in 2020.

13. Armbruster 2009, fig. 5, from Arzhan 2, Tuva.

14. Smithsonian Channel's *Epic Warrior Women* series, episode 1, "Amazons," 2018. https://www.smithsonianchannel.com/shows/epic-warrior-women/amazons/1004515/3437447.

15. Mayor 2019b.

16. Lorenzi, 2007. Trevisanato 2007.

17. Barker 2021. For the history of the Kaffa claim, Zanders 2021.

18. Federal Protective Service, US Department of Homeland Security, Weekly Intelligence Briefing, February 17–24, see Walker and Winter 2020. Ahmadi 2020.

19. The molecular biologist and Soviet general Igor Ashmarin ordered Biopreparat scientists to splice human neurotransmitters, opioid beta-endorphins produced in response to pain and other stressors, into infectious viruses beginning in 1979. Bioweapons that target enemy personality and behavior, and cobra venom delivered by virus, Williams 2006. Ahmadi 2020.

20. DARPA, Defense Advanced Research Program Agency, announced in March 2006 that the Hybrid Micro Electronic Mechanical Systems (HI-MEMS) program "seeks innovative proposals to develop technology to create insect-cyborgs, possibly enabled by intimately integrating microsystems within insects, during their early stages of metamorphoses." Once these insect-machine hybrid "platforms are integrated, various microsystem payloads can be mounted on the platforms with the goal of controlling insect locomotion." History of DARPA projects, see Weinberger 2017.

21. Flaming pigs: Activision's *Rome: Total War* video game, developed by Creative Assembly, was released in 2003; flaming pigs were added in 2004, totalwar.com. Per totalwar.fandom.com: "Incendiary pigs are 'one shot' weapons intended to spread panic and terror amongst

enemies, particularly mounted troops." Each Greek city unit has ninety-six pigs and twenty-four handlers. "The pigs are coated in pitch, tar and oil, and herded towards the enemy. At the right moment, the pigs are ignited by their handlers and, not unnaturally, they run away in pain and terror—hopefully towards the enemy. Apart from goring anyone foolish enough to get in their way, the pigs are tremendously disruptive to formations. They are also very frightening for elephants in particular, and this is their main use in warfare. Pigs can only be fired up once a battle, and few survive for long." Reviewed by Dave "Fargo" Kosak, gamespy.com, May 19, 2004; also reviewed by Burns 2005.

22. Painted examples of the flaming pig skirmish unit by Xyston (2013), www.scotiagrendel.com: http://dreispitz.blogspot.com/2013/05/rome-republican-army-triarii-and-war.html. "Flaming Pigs and Anti-Elephant Tactics Documentary," Invicta, June 25, 2020. https://www.youtube.com/watch?v=8Bdk82xTNm8.

23. Archimedes's mirror weapon was reproduced successfully by Dr. David Wallace and his students from Massachusetts Institute of Technology, in San Francisco harbor, igniting a 1924 wooden fishing boat, on October 22, 2005, Discovery Channel's *MythBusters*, January 25, 2006. http://web.mit.edu/2.009/www/experiments/deathray/10_Mythbusters.html. Steam cannons and chemical incendiary: Hsu 2010.

24. DARPA's "active denial" system (ADS) heat-ray research began in 1995. The new ray gun was widely reported in 2007. "Pentagon Looks to Sci-Fi Weaponry," Agence France Presse, January 30, 2007. The Pentagon decided not to deploy the weapon in Iraq in 2007, for fear it "might be seen as a torture device." "Pentagon Denied U.S. Calls for Ray Gun Weapon in Iraq," AP news story, August 30, 2007. Later developments, Shachman 2010; "Rise of the Ray Gun" 2020.

25. *How Greek Fire Was Used to Target Enemy Ships*, Smithsonian Channel, *World of Weapons: War at Sea* series, April 13, 2020, demonstrated by chemical weapons expert Stephen Bull. https://www.youtube.com/watch?v=lPUgvYZ5UDk.

26. Gordon 2019.

27. Dr. Leonard Cole, professor of political science, Rutgers, appeared in the "Silent Killers: Poisons and Plagues" episode of PBS's *Avoiding*

Armageddon TV series, spring 2003. See also Balmer 2016, on secrecy and biological and chemical weapons programs in Cold War Britain.

INTRODUCTION. WAR OUTSIDE THE RULES

1. Epigraph: Thucydides 3.82.2. The chimerical adjective "biochemical" is often used as a catchall term to denote biological and chemical agents in general. Poupard and Miller 1992, 9. Other historians of biochemical warfare accept the common assumption that there is very little ancient evidence for biological and chemical strategies. "Given the potential advantage that could accrue from biological weapons," comments the historian of biological and chemical warfare Mark Wheelis (1999, 8), "it is surprising that there are so few recorded instances of their use." The noted biological and chemical warfare authority Julian Perry Robinson (2002) remarks that "the exploitation of disease as a weapon of war is exceedingly rare in the historical record," as were the uses of poison and chemicals. In her study of smallpox in colonial America, Fenn 2000, 1573, is typical in claiming that ancient Greeks lacked technical knowledge for carrying out biowar. According to biological and chemical warfare scholar Leonard Cole (1996), the frequency of poison weapon use in antiquity was "minimized" because of ancient taboos.

2. For example, army troops in Burma (Myanmar) carried out systematic rape as a "weapon of war" to crush ethnic rebellion: *New York Times*, December 27, 2002. In 2014 Islamic State (IS) jihadists killed about 5,000 Yazidi men and enslaved and raped 5,000–7,000 Yazidi women in Kurdistan. "The Yazidis" 2020. Ahmadi 2020.

3. A pseudo-fact cited in some histories of biological warfare (e.g., Miller 1998; Harris and Paxman 2002, 190) asserts that the ancient Assyrians (whose civilization began around 2400 BC in modern Turkey, Iran, Syria, and Iraq) poisoned enemies' wells with LSD-like ergot, a fungus of rye, wheat, and other grains. It appears that ergot is referred to in Assyrian texts, but there is no basis for the notion that the hallucinogen was deliberately used against foes.

4. On harm resulting from modern "nonlethal" weapons, see *Lethal in Disguise* 2016. Chrysame's plot, see chapter 5.

5. Definitions of biological and chemical warfare: the 1972 Biological Weapons Convention (BWC) bans "microbial or other biological agents, or toxins whatever their origin or method of production, of types or quantities that have no justification for prophylactic, protective, or other peaceful purposes." This includes living agents such as insects, and toxins produced from them. The BWC states that the use of bioweapons is "repugnant to the conscience of mankind"; Koblentz 2011, 49. For a comprehensive definition of biological weapons, see GlobalSecurity.org's sections on biological and chemical weapons: https://www.globalsecurity.org/wmd/intro/bio.htm and https://www.globalsecurity.org/wmd/intro/cw.htm. Definitions of chemical weapons: Stockholm International Peace Research Institute (SIPRI) 1971 and 1975, 202–6. See also Arms Control Association reports: https://www.armscontrol.org/factsheets/cbwprolif. Robertson and Robertson 1995, 369, exclude forcing enemies into "unsanitary" areas and bioterrorism from their definition of biowar. Poupard and Miller 1992, 9, separate biological weaponry that uses "viable organisms" from "bacterial toxins and related chemical derivatives of microorganisms," which they believe should be categorized as chemical weapons (CW). Biological warfare is defined as "the use of pathogens, . . . disease-causing bacterial and viral agents, or biologically derived toxins against humans, animals, and crops," according to Croddy 2002, 219; on 130, Croddy notes that "while purists would not consider Greek Fire" and ancient incendiaries to be "true CW, these early flame- and smoke-producing techniques have direct [and indirect] connections with the modern use of toxic substances on the battlefield." History of chemical weapons, Valente 2019.

6. Every arms innovation in antiquity was regarded as inhumane and dishonorable at first. When the new catapult technology of the fourth century BC was demonstrated to the Spartan general Archidamus, for example, he exclaimed, "Now what will become of valor?" Plutarch, *Moralia* "Sayings of Spartans" 219. In the 1100s, the crossbow was singled out as inhumane; gunpowder raised similar criticism in the 1300s. But "today's secret weapons had the nasty habit of becoming tomorrow's universal threat," notes O'Connell, "Secret Weapons" in Cowley and Parker 1996, 417–19. For the history of chemical warfare in the Mid-

east, historical qualms about poison weapons, and "force multipliers," Zimeta 2013. History of biological warfare: Koblentz 2011. On modern asymmetric warfare and warrior "honor" ethic, see Renic 2020.

7. Criteria for evaluating attempts to deploy disease as a weapon since the Middle Ages are discussed by Wheelis 1999, 9, who restricts his discussion of biological warfare before 1914 to the intent to transmit contagion, leaving out the use of toxins and pollution of wells.

8. Poison weapons have "long been regarded as peculiarly reprehensible [and] subject to express prohibition since ancient times," in Greece, Rome, and India, and in the Quran, remarks Robinson 2002. He suggests that this "ancient taboo" reflects a "human impulse against the hostile use" of disease and chemicals that is "multicultural, multiethnic, and longstanding." Banning biochemical arsenals today "goes to the roots of what humankind finds acceptable and unacceptable." Indeed, the ancient "taboo may be our one remaining hope" as science and commerce push biotechnology still more deeply into developing "immensely threatening new weapons." Leonard Cole, discussing the ancient "poison taboo," proposed that the "moral repugnance [and] deep-seated aversion" to such weapons going back thousands of years helps explain their rarity in the past. But Cole's claim that "the Greeks and Romans condemned the use of poison in war as a violation of . . . the law of nations," projects a seventeenth-century concept ("law of nations") into classical antiquity. "Poisons and other weapons considered inhumane were forbidden [in] India around 500 BC and among the Saracens 1,000 years later," continues Cole 1996, 64, 65. Neufeld 1980, 46–47. Moral, practical, and strategic reasons against using biological weapons: Koblentz 2011, 49–51.

9. Strabo, 10.1.12–13. Creveld 1991, 23, points out that what is "considered acceptable behavior in war is historically determined, neither self-evident nor unalterable." See also Fenn 2000, 1573–74. For differing views of the development of Greek conventions of war and military protocols from Homeric epic to the Peloponnesian War, see Ober 1994; Krentz 2002; and Lanni 2008. On the moral dilemmas of asymmetrical warfare, see Renic 2020.

10. Krentz 2002, 25. Ober 1994, 14; on hoplite battle, 14–17. Lanni 2008 demonstrates that religious beliefs and humanitarian norms were not a

check on inhumane warfare in classical Greece, 486; and see Sheldon 2012, xxi–xxvi. Nostalgic notions of the ancient "poison taboo" were evident in the late Middle Ages. The great artillery engineer Kazimierz Siemienowicz (ca. 1600–1651) considered poison weapons dishonorable, and wrote that "the first inventors of our art thought such actions as unjust [and] as unworthy of a man of heart and a true soldier."

11. On classical Greek warfare, see Lendon 2006; Konijnendijk 2018; Wrightson 2019. Sallust, *Jugurthine War,* chap. 11, 101.

12. "Reciprocal risk" also determined ethical legitimacy of combat; see Renic 2020, 60–66 for a dated discussion of ancient Greek and Roman attitudes to asymmetrical warfare as prelude to his powerful consideration of modern long-distance and drone warfare.

13. On ambush and deception in Homer's *Iliad* and *Odyssey,* Sheldon 2012, chaps. 1 and 2. Moral tension between the warrior ethos and the "Odysseus ethos" (Wheelis) continues today; see Renic 2020, 63.

14. Lanni 2008; Sheldon 2012. See Krentz and Wheeler, introduction to Polyaenus 1994, 1:vi–xxiv, esp. vii and xii, on advising Roman emperors to use brains over brawn, to value pragmatic, subtle deceit, inventive trickery, and resourcefulness to avoid the risk of direct combat.

15. As Creveld 1991, 27, points out, "war by definition consists of killing, of deliberately shedding the blood of fellow creatures." Killing cannot be tolerated unless it is "carefully circumscribed by rules" defining what is permissible and what is not. The line between murder and war is essential but never precise. Hugo Grotius, considered the originator of international law (1625–31), condemned the use of poison in warfare as a violation of what he called the Laws of Nations and Natural Law. He argued, citing various ancient Greek and Roman writers (Livy, Claudian, Cicero, Gellius, Valerius, Florus, and Tacitus), that by general consent war is murderous enough without making it more so by poisons. On Grotius and ancient rules of war, see Penzer 1952, 5–6. Drummond 1989 notes that "laws of war are currently recognized as customary practices which are intended to reduce the amount of suffering in wartime to a minimum and to facilitate the restoration of peace." There is a sense that the level of destruction in wartime should be limited to "minimum necessary force." On Western laws of war from ancient Greece to the late twentieth century, see Howard,

Andreopoulos, and Shulman 1994; Stockholm International Peace Research Institute 1975, 18–20. On ethics of war, see Nardin 1996; Hashmi and Lee 2004.

16. "Spoiling the grass" and pastures of the enemy foreshadows the American use of defoliants, such as Agent Orange, to destroy forests and jungles during the Vietnam War. Righteous warfare, *dharmayuddha*, was opposed to *kutayuddha*, crafty, ruthless strategies. *Laws of Manu* 7.90; 92; Buhler 1886, 195. Hindu war ethics: Hashmi and Lee 2004.

17. *Arthashastra*: Kautilya 1951, 436–37; Kautilya 1992. Ishii: Lesho, Dorsey, and Bunner 1998, 516.

18. Cowley and Parker 1996, s.v. "Sun Tzu," and see review by Sienho Yee, of Zhu Wen-Qi, *Outline of International Humanitarian Law* (Shanghai: International Committee of the Red Cross, 1997, in Chinese, with an English abstract), https.www.icrc.org/en/doc/resources/documents /article/other/57jnzc.htm. "Unorthodox" warfare in Chinese history: Sawyer 2007. Confucian and Buddhist war ethics: Hashmi and Lee 2004.

19. Deuteronomy 19–20. Jericho: Joshua 6.21, 24. On ancient Jewish rules of war, see Nardin 1996, 95, 97–98, 106–9; Hashmi and Lee 2004. The Ten Plagues in Exodus are discussed in chapter 4.

20. Quran 2.11–12; 2.190–94; 3.172; 22.19–22; 22.39–40; and later Islamic traditions in the Hadith. John Kelsay, personal correspondence, February 2, 2003, and see Kelsay's chap. 18 in Hashmi and Lee 2004. Farrokh 2017, 174, 353–54, 573. Abu Bakr al-Siddiq's decree, "Islamic Law and the Rules of War," *New Humanitarian*, April 24, 2014, Dubai, https://www.thenewhumanitarian.org/2014/04/24/islamic-law-and -rules-war.

21. Sheikh Hamza Yusuf interviewed by Goldstein 2001. See Nardin 1996, 129–33, 161–64, 166 nn. 25 and 26. For a full discussion of debates over incendiaries and permissible tactics among Muslims, see Hashmi 2004.

22. Hashmi 2004. El Fadl 2007, 144.

23. El Fadl 2007, 144–45, 156. History of Muslim fire weapons: Bilkadi 1995.

24. Polybius 13.3.1–8. Krentz 2002, 25. Lanni 2008, 485–86. Strabo 10.1.11–13. See chapter 3 for the destruction of Kirrha by poison in the water supply.

25. Ober 1994, 12, 14.
26. Drummond 1989, introduction. Thucydides 1.49; 3.82–83, atrocities against noncombatants and children, e.g., 3.81–82; 7.29–30.
27. For Aeneas, see chapters 3 and 7. Other ancient Greek and Roman expressions of disapproval of underhanded tactics, Renic 2020, 61–66.
28. Cicero discussed just war in *On Duties* 1.34–36, and in his *Republic*, which survives only in paraphrases in later sources. According to Cicero, war was justified for self-defense, defense of allies, and vengeance. Ovid and Silius Italicus, see chapter 2; Florus, chap. 3. Tacitus, *Germania* 43.
29. Vegetius, *On Military Matters* 3. On changing rules of war in the Roman Empire, see Drummond 1989, a case study of the period AD 353 to 378. For Roman attitudes toward deception in war, Sheldon 2007.
30. Self-defense in extremity and last resorts: Nardin 1996, 28–29, 86–88. Roman Stoic commanders idealized Odysseus: Krentz and Wheeler introduction to Polyaenus, 1:vixxiv, esp. vii, xii. On use of inhumane weapons against "cultural others," see Mayor 1995b; Fenn 2000, 1574. On challenges to rules of war through history, and situations that encourage violations, see chap. 12 of Howard, Andreopoulos, and Shulman 1994; Hashmi and Lee 2004; on risk avoidance, see Renic 2020. For the history of a culture in which a deadly poison was a valuable resource commodity, and its use normalized within the society and as a weapon of war, see Carey 2003 on the "political economy" of poison in Makassar, Southeast Asia. Poison arrows for war and hunting and poisonings were common within many Native American groups, Jones 2007.
31. "Greek mythology, always a good source of insight," depicted warriors punished for breaking conventions of war or committing excessive brutalities, notes Creveld in his article on changing rules of war since the Gulf War of 1991 (1991, 27). Whirlwind: O'Connell, "Secret Weapons," in Cowley and Parker 1996, 419. One reason for hope expressed by military historian Jonathan Roth is that "as technology becomes more sophisticated and more expensive, there are more barriers to technological spread" of complicated superweapons. Vaughan 2011, 61.

CHAPTER 1. HERACLES AND THE HYDRA:
THE INVENTION OF BIOLOGICAL WEAPONS

1. Epigraph: Ovid *Metamophoses* 9.159–210. Pliny the Elder 16.51 gives the folk etymology associating yew and poison: see Harrison 1994. See also Reinach 1909, 70.

2. Dioscorides's statement appears in bk. 6 of *Materia Medica*, an extensive collection of medical and pharmacological texts attributed to the physician Dioscorides. Majno 1991, 145, 147 and n. 38.

3. On pitch from pine trees in antiquity, see Pliny 16.52–61; pine resin is the source of the flammable solvent turpentine.

4. Heracles's struggle with the Hydra is one of the earliest and most popular myths depicted in Greek art, appearing by the eighth century BC. The Hydra myth is recounted in Ovid, *Metamorphoses* 9.62–75; Apollodorus, *Library* 2.5.2; Diodorus of Sicily 4.11, and other sources; for a full discussion of the myth in ancient literature and art, see Gantz 1993, 1:23, 384–86.

5. Herodotus 4.1–82.

6. The foregoing description of the deaths of Chiron and Pholus, and the wounding of Telephus, are found in Apollodorus, *Library* 2.5.4; *Epitome* 3.17–20, and see Frazer's nn. 1 and 2, 2:186–89. Centaurs dying of Heracles's poison arrows were featured in many famous sculptures and paintings in antiquity. Places where they had died, polluting waters with the poison, were also pointed out. Telephus's wounding was the subject of several ancient plays and paintings. Pliny 25.42; 34.152. Gantz 1993, 1:147, 390–92; see also 2:579. Telephus's infected wound was healed by rust scrapings from Achilles's spear; see chapter 2.

7. For the death of Heracles in the poisoned tunic, see Apollodorus, *Library* 2.7.7, with Frazer's n. 1, 1:270–71; Sophocles, *Trachinian Women* 756ff.; Diodorus of Sicily 4.38; Ovid, *Metamorphoses* 9.100–238; and see Gantz 1993, 1:458.

8. For the burning, corrosive symptoms of the bite of the *dipsas* ("thirst") viper, Lucian of Samosata 4–6.

9. On Troy, and the cycle of stories about the Trojan War, see *Oxford Classical Dictionary*, entries for "Troy" and "Homer"; Gantz 1993, 2:576–657; Rose 1959, 230–53.

10. Homer, *Iliad* 1.50–70, 376–86; 2.731–33; 4.138–219; 11.812–48. Reinach 1909, 70, points out other linguistic hints of empoisoned arrows in Homer, who often uses words that evoke the imagery of snakebites to describe arrows, such as "biting, burning, and bitter." See Majno 1991, 145–47 and n. 35, on "sucking out of snakebite wounds" in antiquity; see also 271, on black blood indicating poison arrows; for ancient treatment of snakebite by sucking out the venom and cautery, see 280. See Scarborough 1977, 6, 8-9, for vivid and accurate ancient descriptions of the sequelae of snake envenomation.

11. Homer, *Iliad* 2.725–39. That Philoctetes's ships were rowed by archers was considered historical by the fifth-century BC Greek historian Thucydides 1.10.

12. Gantz 1993, 1:459–60; 2:589–90, 625–28, 635–38, 700–701, surveys the Philoctetes stories in literature and art. Apollodorus, *Epitome* 3.26–27, 5.8–10, and see Frazer's n. 2, 2:194–97, and n. 1, 2:222–23. See Sophocles's play *Philoctetes* (409 BC); Euripides, Aeschylus, and two other playwrights also wrote *Philoctetes* tragedies, now lost. Quintus of Smyrna, *Fall of Troy* 9.334–480. Philoctetes's suffering was depicted in vase paintings and other artworks, with the earliest known art dating to 460 BC. The shrine to Philoctetes on Chryse could be visited through the first century AD, but in about AD 150, the island was submerged by earthquakes. Appian, "Mithridatic Wars" 12.77; Pausanias 8.33.4. Scarborough 1977, 7, 9.

13. Quintus of Smyrna, *Fall of Troy* 3.58–82 and 148–50; 9.353–546. Ovid, *Metamorphoses* 12.596–628.

14. See Sheldon 2012, chaps. 1 and 2, on ambush in classical antiquity; Renic 2020 on risk avoidance in modern warfare. On negative opinions about projectiles in war, see *Oxford Classical Dictionary*, s.v. "archers." The bow and arrow as "unheroic weapon": Faraone 1992, 125.

15. On the ideal of fighting up close, not "at long range" (i.e., with arrows), in the "front ranks for action and for honor," and avoiding blows "from behind on nape or back, but [taking them] in the chest or belly as you wade into . . . the battle line," see, e.g., Homer, *Iliad* 8.94f.; 12.42; 13.260–300; 16.791, 806f. See Salazar 2000, 156–57, for a good discussion of the criticism of archers and the ideals of fighting face-to-face and avoiding wounds in the back.

16. Virgil, *Aeneid* 9.770–74.

17. Philoctetes after Troy and his last years: Gantz 1993, 2:700–701. Philoctetes's dedication of the weapons: Euphorion cited by Apollodorus, *Epitome* 6.15b; Pseudo-Aristotle, *On Marvelous Things Heard* 107 (115), says that Philoctetes dedicated the weapons in the Temple of Apollo at Macalla, near Krimissa, and that the citizens of Croton later transferred them to their own temple of Apollo. Ancient vases, coins, gems, and sculptures depicted Philoctetes receiving Heracles's quiver, wounded and abandoned, taking arrows from his quiver, shooting birds, fanning flies from his unhealing wound, shooting Paris, and so on.

18. Homer, *Odyssey* 2.325.

19. Herodotus 5.92. Homer, *Odyssey* 1.252–66; 2.6. On the moral and historic meaning of this passage, see Dirlmeier 1966. Gantz 1993, 2:711–13; 732 (Circe). Ovid, *Metamorphoses* 7.406–25 (Cerberus), 14.41–68, 264–302 (Circe). Circe, Homer, *Odyssey* 10.212. Birds killed by fumes: Pliny 4.2.

20. The stingray spear was made by Hephaestus, god of fire and invention, at Circe's request. Odysseus's death: Ganz 1993, 2:710–13. The ray was probably a marbled blue stingray common in the Mediterranean: see chapter 2 for the story and evidence of the actual use of stingray spines as weapons.

21. Sophocles, *Trachinian Women* 573–74. The paradoxical figure of Heracles is discussed by Faraone 1992, 59.

22. The "poisoner poisoned" folk motif is a widespread and ancient theme: for examples, see the standard folklore reference work, Stith Thompson's *Motif-Index of Folk-Literature*, motifs K1613. The reason for the deaths at Bari was covered up by the US military: Harris and Paxman 2002, 77–79, 119–25. The US troops' health problems have also been attributed in part to vaccinations and prophylactics against biochemical arms in 1991; see chapter 5. On the origins of Iraq's biological weapons, see Shenon 2003; Colvin and Mahnaimi 1998. Cf. US funding of Chinese zoonotic-human coronavirus "spillover" before the COVID-19 pandemic: Guterl et al. 2020.

23. Faraone 1992, 125, on combined plague and fire imagery. Poisons and incendiaries combined: see chapter 7 and Partington 1999, 149, 209–11, 271, 273, 284–85.

24. Quintus of Smyrna, *Fall of Troy* 9.386–89. On Greek atrocities during the sack of Troy, see Gantz 1993, 2:650–57; for ancient sources, see n. 3 in chap. 3. Painting on the Acropolis: Pausanias 1.22.4. Ovid, *Metamorphoses* 9.170–204; and Ovid, *Tristia*.

CHAPTER 2. ARROWS OF DOOM

1. Epigraph: Ovid, *Tristia* and *Letters from Pontus*; Silius Italicus, *Punica* 1.320–415, 3.265–74. Galen (ed. C. G. Kuhn) XIV, 230–31 (second century AD).
2. See Scarborough 1977 for discussion of the ancient dread of venomous snakes and the many Greek and Roman treatises on plant and animal poisons and antidotes, some effective and some bizarre. Homer, *Iliad* 3.35–47.
3. Aelian, *On Animals* 9.40, 1.54, 5.16, 9.15. Pseudo-Aristotle, *On Marvelous Things Heard* 844 b 80 (140), claims that wasps that have feasted on poisonous adder's flesh have a sting worse than the adder's bite.
4. Quintus of Smyrna, *Fall of Troy* 9.392–97. Diodorus of Sicily 4.38. Pausanias 2.37.4.
5. On symptoms of snakebites and Nicander, see Scarborough 1977, 6–9. *Dipsas, seps, aspis, kerastes, echis* are a few of the names for Viperidae in ancient texts. *Vipera ammodytes, Cerastes* species, *Vipera berus, Echis carinata* are some of the poisonous snakes known to Greeks and Romans.
6. Prehistoric and prescientific poison arrows: Borgia 2019; Jones 2007. Quintus of Smyrna, *Fall of Troy* 9.392–97. Heracles shooting the deer, the Centaurs, and the man-eating Stymphalean birds: Gantz 1993, 1:387–88; 390–92, 394.
7. According to Grmek 1979, 143, and Reinach 1909, 56, classical Greek authors felt that using weapons intended for hunting animals in battles with men was an odious practice, rather than an acceptable military stratagem. This attitude explains why Homer depicted King Ilus refusing to give Odysseus poison for "murdering men."
8. See Lesho, Dorsey, and Bunner 1998, 512, on the psychological terror of poisonous projectiles.

9. Galen and Paul of Aegina referred to Dacian and Dalmatian arrow poisons, Salazar 2000, 28. Hellebore: Majno 1991, 147, 188–93. Pliny 25.47–61.

10. Celts: Pseudo-Aristotle, *On Marvelous Things Heard* 837 a 10 (86). Hadzabe tribe of Tanzania: Martin 2001.

11. For a survey of Celtic and other ancient arrow poisons and antidotes, see Reinach 1909.

12. Ovid, *Metamorphoses* 7, origin of aconite. Aelian, *On Animals* 9.18, 4.49. Pliny 6.4 (the town of Aconae on the Black Sea was of "evil repute for the poison called aconite"); 8.100; 22.18 (nature's weapons); 27.4–10; for antidotes, see 20.132; 23.43, 92, 135; 25.163; 28.161; 29.74, 105. Jones 2007, 5, effects of aconite.

13. Aconite in India: Penzer 1952, 11.

14. Jones 2007, 23–25; Ainu, 21–22; Inuit, 47; China, 23. Moors and aconite: Partington 1999, 231 n. 103. Aconite in China, Wexler 2019, 431–39. Aconite bullets: Harris and Paxman 2002, 63. On septic bullets, see Wheelis 1999, 34. Native American tribes, such as the Tonkawa, Sioux, Blackfoot, Cree, Apache, and Nootka, coated rifle bullets with a variety of poisons, Jones 2007, 48.

15. Henbane: Aelian, *On Animals* 9.32. Pliny 23.94; 25.35–37. See also Majno 1991, 387.

16. Poison arrow frogs: thanks to Lori Hamlett, Nashville Zoo, Tennessee; and Jones 2007, 30. Psylli: Pliny, 25.123; Aelian, *On Animals* 1.57; 16.28.

17. Curare: Jones 2007, 26–20. On Iroquois, Apache, Navajo, and many other tribes' poison arrows: Reinach 1909, 52–53 and n. 1; and Jones 2007, for numerous recipes and historical cases of arrow poisons of Native Americans and other indigenous peoples. Agari shamans twice saved the life of Mithradates when he was wounded in battle by using snake venom to staunch bleeding: Mayor 2010, 101, 240–41, 289, 309–11.

18. Hemlock: Aelian, *On Animals* 4.23. Rolle 1989, 65.

19. Aelian, *On Animals* 9.27. Pliny 16.51. Majno 1991, 488 n. 38. Also see Harrison 1994. Lucretius, *On the Nature of the Universe* 6.780–86, may have been speaking of yew when he mentioned a tree whose "shade was so oppressive as to provoke a headache in one who lies under it."

The chemotherapy drug taxotere was originally derived from European yew, *Taxus*.

20. Pliny 21.177–79. Ancient *strychnos* is not related to modern strychnine, which is derived from the *Strychnos nux-vomica* tree of South Asia. See Carey 2003. Arrow poisons can be very long-lived. Recent toxicological analysis of desiccated poison paste on arrows collected in the 1900s in Assam, India, and Burma, stored in the Victoria and Albert Museum, London, revealed that the longevity of some of the toxins was more than thirteen hundred years. http://www.vam.ac.uk/content/articles/p/poisoned-arrows/.

21. Aelian, *On Animals* 1.56; 2.36 and 50; 8.26. Pliny 9.147 on the "burning sting" of jellyfish and sea urchins.

22. Ancient sources for the story of the stingray spear, see Apollodorus, *Epitome* 7.36–37 and Frazer's n. 2, pp. 303–4; Ganz 1993, 2:710–13. Scholion ad Homer *Od.* 11.134 (Dindorf 1:6): "Hephaestus at the pleading of Circe fashioned for Telegonus a spear out of the sea-going stingray, which Phorcys killed." Cf. Oppian, *Halieutica* 2.497–500; Homer, *Odyssey* 11.134; Philostratus, *Apollonius of Tyana* 6.32; Philostratus, *Heroes* 3.42.

23. Thanks to Dolores Urquidi, Austin, Texas, for sharing her research into the use of stingray spines as arrowheads in Central and South America. The spines were also made into weapons in the South Pacific: Schultz 1962, 130, 132.

24. Ancient writers on poison archery: Reinach 1909, 54–56 and nn. Hua T'o removed a poison arrow that pierced the arm of General Kuan Yu, about eighteen hundred years ago: Majno 1991, 249–51, fig. 6.19. Bradford 2001, 160. *Gu*: Hanson 2012, 80–83.

25. Strabo 16.4.10. Silius Italicus, *Punica* 1.320–415, 3.265–74. Ancient Greek and Roman authors who mention arrow poisons: Salazar 2000, 28–30. Poison arrows were reportedly used in violent uprisings in Kenya in August 1997, according to CNN news reports. Lesho, Dorsey, and Bunner 1998, 512, note that the use of "biological projectiles . . . persisted into the 20th century during the Russian Revolution, various European conflicts, and the South African Boer wars."

26. Herodotus 4.9–10; hooks and cups, see commentary in Murray and Moreno 2007, 579. A miniature golden vial with a gold chain was

recovered from the grave of two warriors of ancient Scythia, male and female, buried with a rich cache of golden treasures, quivers of arrows, and other weapons, from the seventh century BC. Armbruster 2009, fig. 5. A grave in Tillya Tepe (Bactria, first century BC) yielded a similar tiny gold vessel with a lid and chain. The flasks are about 1 inch (ca. 2.5 cm) high, with narrow neck. Compare the vial held out by Athena to collect the Hydra venom in a Corinthian vase painting of about 590 BC (Antikenmuseum, Basel, Switzerland) and in fig. 3, chapter 1.

27. On the history of the bow and arrow and advances in archery technology, see Crosby 2002, 37–39, and his chap. 5. Herodotus's bk. 4 describes the Scythians; see esp. 4.9. Rolle 1989, 65. Akamba poison arrows information from Timothy F. Bliss, former resident of Kenya; descriptions of Akamba bow, quiver, and poison arrows from the 1970s offered for sale in 2002 by the now-defunct Krackow Company, New Wilmington, PA, specializing in traditional, worldwide archery equipment.

28. The recipe in Pseudo-Aristotle, *On Marvelous Things Heard* 845 a 5 (141), states that human blood was buried in a dunghill until it putrefied; then the contaminated blood was mixed with the rotten venom. Aelian, *On Animals* 9.15, citing a lost work by Theophrastus. Dioscorides also mentions the *toxicon pharmacon* of the Scythians, 1.106, 2.79. See Reinach 1909, 54–55. Many Native American tribes treated arrows with snake venom, extracting it from live rattlesnakes' fangs, causing a snake to repeatedly strike a piece of deer liver, or burying snake heads with other poisons to putrefy. These practices of combining venom with toxins and allowing them to putrefy are remarkably similar to the Scythians' techniques: Jones 2007, 40–42, 47.

29. Plutarch, *Artaxerxes*. Punji sticks: Christopher et al. 1997, 412. In the New World, sharpened splinters dipped in rattlesnake and other venoms and stuck in the ground were used against enemy tribes and Europeans by Catawba, Kwakiutl, and Yaqui Indians: Jones 2007, 50–51.

30. Strabo 11.2.19 (first century BC). Excrement as weapon in prescientific era: in China (AD 800–1600) defenders of cities poured boiling urine and feces on attackers, Wheelis 1999, n. 4, and see Temple 1991, 223, for the use of poison arrows and 216 for excrement explosives in early

China. In 1422, two thousand cartloads of excrement were hurled at foes at in the Battle of Carolstein (Bohemia): Eitzen and Takafuji 1997. On stinking arrow poisons made by Native Americans: Jones 2007, 41.

31. Stench weapons ancient and modern: see also chapter 6; Wheelis 1999, 11 n. 10; Creveld 1991, 25; *New York Times Magazine*, December 15, 2002, 126; Harris and Paxman 2002, 206. By 2003, US military scientists were developing stench and colored smoke weapons that target racial groups: "When Killing Just Won't Do" 2003. For descriptions of modern stench, choking, and dye agents delivered by powerful water cannon and the resulting injuries: *Lethal in Disguise* 2016, 54–61.

32. Rolle 1989, 65. On tetanus in domestic animal dung and death from tetanus after arrow wounds, see Majno 1991, 199–200. Ancient descriptions of gangrene and tetanus: Salazar 2000, 30–34. Parts of this section on Scythian arrow poison appeared in different form in Mayor 1997a. Thanks to herpetologist Aaron Bauer, Villanova University, for information on poisonous snakes of Scythia and India and the feasibility of venom arrows.

33. Ovid, *Tristia* 3.10.55–64; *Letters from Pontus* 1.2.17; 4.7.11 and 10.31, cited in Reinach 1909, 55, n. 5. Poison, breakaway, barbed arrows in Armenia: Cassius Dio 36.5–8; Mayor 2010, 303. For the Romans' tribulations with biochemical weapons, see chapter 7.

34. Rolle 1989, 65. Barbed arrows in antiquity: Salazar 2000, 18–19, 49, 232–33. Superfluous injury: unlike the blade of a Greek hoplite's javelin or Roman soldier's sword, which passed cleanly through a body and could be easily pulled out, the use of long-distance projectiles and missiles with hooked shapes caused more tissue damage and loss of blood. Modern analogies to the misgivings evoked by such arms are evident in the 1899 Hague Convention's Declaration Concerning Expanding Bullets, prohibiting the newly developed "manstopping" dumdum bullets that expanded on impact and left gaping, ragged wounds instead of penetrating cleanly at high velocity like streamlined metal-jacketed bullets. The expanding bullets were invented at Dum Dum Arsenal in India in the 1890s to stop fanatical fighters in Afghanistan and India. Current US and NATO copper-jacket, lead-core bullets do fragment on impact, but still cause less damage than exploding bullets. One might compare the Greek hoplite's spear to

the metal-jacket bullet as ancient and modern icons of "clean" warfare "by the rules," whereas a hooked arrow coated with venom was the ancient equivalent of a dumdum bullet combined with a biotoxin. See 1907 Hague Convention IV, also 1977 additions to the 1949 Geneva Convention. As early as 1868, the Saint Petersburg Declaration prohibited exploding bullets on the rationale that such weapons are contrary to the laws of humanity because they "uselessly aggravate the sufferings of disabled men, or render their death inevitable." Howard, Andreopoulos, and Shulman 1994, 6–7, 120–21 (1899 Hague rules). Thanks to Mark Wheelis for helpful information on dumdum bullets.

35. Rudenko 1970, 217–18, and color plates 179–80. For patterns of poisonous snakes of Scythian territory, see Phelps 1981, 97–102, 162–64, figs. 26–30, color plates 16 and 17. A scene showing a Scythian horsewoman-archer painting her arrow shafts with these designs appears in Smithsonian Channel's *Epic Warrior Women* series, episode 1, "Amazons," 2018. https://www.smithsonianchannel.com/shows/epic-warriorwomen/amazons/1004515/3437447.

36. Mining gems with arrows: Pliny 37.110–12. Rolle 1989, 65–66; *Oxford Classical Dictionary*, s.v. "archers." Modern ethnological parallels suggest the rate of twenty arrows a minute, but the expert Scythians may have been faster.

37. Aelian, *On Animals* 4.36, describes death by ingestion of tiny amounts (the size of a sesame seed) of the Purple Snake poisons placed in wine, but the sticky residue would serve very well as arrow poisons. For an ancient account of men killed by drinking from a spring poisoned by snake venom, see Aelian, 17.37; and on similar fears in Libya, see Lucan, *Civil War*, 9.605–20. Kautilya 1951, 449. Thanks to Aaron Bauer and Robert Murphy, senior curator of herpetology, Royal Ontario Museum, Toronto, for help in identifying the Purple Snake.

38. Strabo 15.2.5–7. See Majno 1991, 283, citing the ancient historian Arrian, *Indica* 8.15. Aelian, *On Animals* 12.32, remarks that Indian doctors knew which herbs counteracted the "very violent and rapid spread" of snake venom. About fifteen thousand people die annually from snakebite in India today: Majno 1991, 283.

39. Alexander and contemporary historians referred to the "Brahmans" of Harmatelia as an ethnic group, unaware of the Hindu caste system.

This account is taken from Diodorus of Sicily 17.102–3 and Quintus Curtius Rufus 9.8.13–28. Other sources for Alexander's campaign in India are Justin and Diodorus of Sicily. See Polyaenus 4.3.22 for Alexander's strategies against Porus. Arrows, Strabo 15.2.7. Viper constipation: Angier 2002.

40. Symptomology of viper and cobra envenomation from discussions with Aaron Bauer and Scarborough 1977, 8–9.

41. According to Reinach 1909, 55–56, n. 9, the Rigveda epic of India contains references to poison arrows. *Laws of Manu* 7.90, see Buhler 1886, 230. Majno 1991, 264. The *Arthashastra*, attributed to Kautilya (also known as Chanakya), in its surviving form also contains material from the first to fifth centuries AD. The work was thought to be lost until 1905 when a Sanskrit copy on palm leaves was discovered. Kautilya 1951, 442–55, 449 (terror effects), and bk. 14.

42. Indian Defence Ministry experiments at University of Pune and National Institute of Virology: Rahman 2002. US military research into pharmaceutical and genome-based antisleep agents: Onion 2002; DARPA website: www.darpa.mil. History of DARPA, Weinberger 2017.

43. Pliny 34.152–54; 25.33, 42, 66–69, 99. The rust treatment is mentioned by Apollodorus and Ovid too: Gantz 2:579.

44. Majno 1991, 218, 370, 387–89, and fig. 9.25. Aelian, *On Animals* 1.54. Scarborough 1977, 11, 12–18. Salazar 2000, 29.

45. Immunity to venom and poisons: Aelian, *On Animals* 5.14; 9.29; 16.28. Pliny 7.13–14, 27; 8.229; 11.89–90. Strabo 13.1.14.

46. Mayor 2010, on Mithradates, snake venom, and antidotes; also Mayor 2019a.

47. Aelian, *On Animals* 9.62. Majno 1991, 381. Suetonius *Augustus* 17; the detail suggests that Augustus and others believed that a cobra bite was involved in Cleopatra's suicide. Celsus *De medicina* 5.27.

48. Strabo 13.1.14, on Psylli and other snakebite experts. Cato and the Psylli: Lucan, *Civil War* 9.600–949. Pliny 11.89–90.

49. On treating poison arrow wounds, see Salazar 2000, 28–30; black blood of poison wounds; 29; removing barbed projectiles; 48–50. Majno 1991 compares Greek and Indian arrow wound treatments in the fourth century BC. See 142–45 on treating arrow wounds in

Homer: of 147 wounds, the survival rate was 77.6 percent (quote, 143). See 171 (red vs. black blood); 193–95, 266, 271–72 (treating arrow wounds); 279–80 (sucking out venom); 359–61 (removing barbed arrows); 381 (Celsus on the Psylli). "Gloom and frustration": Scarborough 1977, 3.

CHAPTER 3. POISON WATERS, DEADLY VAPORS

1. Epigraph: Florus 1.35.5–7. Thucydides 7.84.
2. Strabo 15.2.6.
3. Poupard and Miller 1992, 10, on thirst and poisoning water. Wheelis 1999, 9 n. 3, agreed with military historian Milton Leitenberg that contaminating water in antiquity was intended to deny potable water rather than to spread disease. But the examples in this chapter and chapter 4 show that poisoning water was often deliberately intended to cause illness.
4. Aeschines, *Against Ctesiphon* 3.107–24, curse 109.
5. Frontinus, *Stratagems* 3.7.6. Polyaenus 6.13. Kirrha was also known as Krisa. Strabo 9.3.3–4 recounts the destruction of Kirrha and mentions the profusion of hellebore at Anticyra, but omits mention of the poison's role in the city's demise.
6. Pausanias 10.37.
7. Slaughter of children and old people, and rape during the sack of Troy: Quintus of Smyrna, *Fall of Troy* 13.78–324; Apollodorus, *Epitome* 5.21–23, and Frazer's nn. 1–2, pp. 238–39. On Greek atrocities during the sack of Troy in ancient literature and art, see Gantz 1993, 2:650–57.
8. Ulrichs: Peter Levi's n. 259 in vol. 1 of the Penguin edition of Pausanias (1979). See also Plutarch, *Solon* 11.
9. The account attributed to Thessalos implicating the doctor Nebros is included in the corpus of Hippocratic texts, as *Presbeulicos*; Grmek 1979, 146–48, citing *Oeuvres completes d'Hippocrate*, trans. E. Littre (Paris, 1861), Lettres, 9:412–13.
10. Churchill and Iraq: Simons 1994, 179–81. Gas was prohibited by the 1899 Hague Convention, Howard, Andreopoulos, and Shulman 1994, 7, 121, 123. Churchill's willingness to use gas against the Germans in World War II is discussed by Harris and Paxman 2002, chap. 5. The

British used mustard gas against rebels in Afghanistan in 1919, prais-
ing its effectiveness on ignorant and unprotected tribesmen (43–44).
Similar lethal effects of deploying a supposedly "nonlethal" gas indiscriminately during a hostage crisis in Moscow in 2002 resulted in more
than one hundred deaths of the innocent hostages: see chapter 5.

11. Grmek 1979, 146–48.
12. In the early 1700s, an English account states that an Indian shaman
    known as "the Indian River Doctor brewed a large quantity of poison"
    intended to infect the colonists' drinking water": Jones 2007, 50. Doc-
    tors were accused of propagating pestilence in the Middle Ages, and
    suspicions continued in early modern times: see Bercé 1993. Examples
    of Italian, American, French, and Japanese doctors involved in bio-
    logical warfare are discussed by Lesho, Dorsey, and Bunner 1998, 513;
    Robertson and Robertson 1995, 370 (Civil War). The army physician
    who rose to the rank of general in World War II, Dr. Shiro Ishii, is one of
    the most notorious medical war criminals of the modern era. As director
    of Japan's extensive biological war effort, the doctor was responsible
    for many thousands of deaths from a vast array of biochemical agents
    in China and has been accused of creating "the most gruesome series
    of biological weapons experiments in history." His staff included more
    than three thousand entomologists, botanists, and microbiologists, and
    fifty physicians. Harris and Paxman 2002; Robertson and Robertson
    1995, 371; Christopher et al. 1997, 413; Williams and Wallace 1989. South
    African "doctors of death": "The Science of Apartheid" 1998; Finnegan
    2001. Iraqi doctors: Colvin and Mahnaimi 1998.
13. The Geneva Convention resulted in the Geneva Protocol of 1925,
    prohibiting the use, but not the production, of biochemical agents.
    Harris and Paxman 2002, 47–52. Grmek 1979, 147, 141–42. Poupard
    and Miller 1992, 13, on 1925 Geneva Convention, "Protocol for the
    Prohibition of the Use in War of Asphyxiating, Poisonous or Other
    Gases, and of Bacteriological Methods of Warfare." Isocrates, *Plata-
    icus* 14.31. Whitehead 1990, commentary on Aeneas 8.4, p. 115, cites
    the Athenian orator Aeschines, *On the Embassy* 2.115, on the vow by
    Delphi's Amphictionic League never to totally destroy any league city
    or interfere with "flowing water." See also Ober 1994, 12.

14. "As old as the weapons themselves," Lesho, Dorsey, and Bunner 1998, 515; see also Lanni 2008. *Laws of Manu* 7.90, see Buhler 1886, 230, 247; Maskiell and Mayor 2001, 25.

15. Athenians fouling their own wells: Whitehead 1990, 115, commentary on Aeneas 8.4. Thucydides 2.47–55; 3.87.

16. Aeneas's shocked British commentators: see Whitehead's commentary, 1990, 115. Iroquois: Wheelis 1999, 27; other reports of Native Americans poisoning drinking waters, Jones 2007, 50. Historical and recent examples of poisoning wells: Christopher et al. 1997.

17. Frontinus, *Stratagems* 3.7.4–5 (Semiramis and Alexander). Philostratus, *Apollonius of Tyana* 1.25, credited Medea with the same engineering feat. Diverting the Euphrates was attributed to Cyrus by Xenophon, *Cyropaedia* 7.5, and Polyaenus 7.6.5, 8.26 (Semiramis inscription). Nitrocris: Herodotus 2.100.

18. Frontinus, *Stratagems* 3.7 (Caesar, Metellus, Servilius).

19. Polyaenus 1.3.5. Polyaenus begins his treatise with an "archaeology of stratagems" and presents mythic heroes like Heracles and Odysseus as master strategists who win victory through deception, to appeal to Stoic emperors who wish to avoid risks of direct combat. Krentz and Wheeler, introduction to Polyaenus 1994, 1:vi–xxiv.

20. Lesho, Dorsey, and Bunner 1998, 512. Diverting rivers was used by the Dutch in their flood-prone land against Spanish invaders in 1584–86, and against French armies in the seventeenth and eighteenth centuries, and by both sides in World War II. Causing massive flooding that indiscriminately killed noncombatants involved ethical issues for early Islamic scholars: Hashmi 2004, 329, cites "numerous records of flooding as a battlefield tactic by Muslim armies" and notes "the many instances in which it backfired against its perpetrator, sweeping away his own besieging troops along with his enemies."

21. Frontinus, *Stratagems* 4.1.36. Florus 1.35.5–7. Aristonicus and Aquillius: Mayor 2010, 59–61.

22. Tacitus, *Annals* 3.1.59–68; 5.2.84. Aulus Gellius, *Attic Nights* 3.8. Aelian, *Historical Miscellany* 12.33.

23. Virgil, *Aeneid* 9.770–74. For Amycus, adept in poisoning weapons, see chapter 1.

24. Penzer 1952, 3–5, citing Kautilya's *Arthashastra*. Kautilya 1951, 432–33, 435, 441–45, 455–57. On poisoned clothing in Mughal India, see Maskiell and Mayor 2001.

25. *Sushruta Samhita*, Majno 1991, 511 n. 26; Sushruta Samhita trans. 2018.

26. Xenophon *Cyropaedia* 1.6.16.

27. Styx river poison: Mayor 2019b.

28. On deadly, sulfurous exhalations from bodies of water or the earth: Pliny 2.207–8; 2.232 (deadly springs); 31.26 and 49; 35.174. See also Virgil, *Aeneid* 6.236–42, and Healy 1999, 246. Lucretius, *On the Nature of the Universe* 6.738–79, 6.817–38. Foul odors and disease or poison: Poupard and Miller 1992, 10. Strabo 8.3.19 (marsh poisoned by Hydra poison). Quintus of Smyrna, *Fall of Troy* 2.561–66 (poisonous stench in water where Memnon died). On the dangerous emanations from modern biochemical and nuclear waste, see the afterword.

29. Empedocles and draining malarial marshes: Diogenes Laertius, *Lives of the Philosophers* 8.70; Grmek 1979, 159; Faraone 1992, 64.

30. Virgil, *Georgics* 3.478–81. Varro's *De re rustica* 1.12.2. Lucretius, *On the Nature of the Universe* 6.1091–1286; Lucretius also described the Plague of Athens.

31. Livy 5.48.

32. Livy 25.26. Silius Italicus, *Punica* 14.580–626. Both historians give detailed accounts of the symptoms.

33. Diodorus of Sicily 12.45.2–4; 13.12; 14.70–71. Vegetius, *On Military Matters*.

34. Thucydides 6–7; Plutarch, *Nicias*; and Diodorus of Sicily 13–14, same camp, 14.70.

35. Grmek 1979, 151 ("particular measures"), citing Thucydides 6–7, esp. 7.47.1–2.

36. Military disasters due to malarial swamps and the "strategic uses of insalubrious terrain": Grmek 1979, 149–63.

37. Frontinus, *Stratagems* 2.7.12. Plutarch, *Moralia* 202.4. Bradford 2001, 201.

38. Tacitus, *Annals* 3.1.58–70. Pliny 25.20–21.

39. Grmek 1979, 149–50. Polyaenus 2.30. Robertson and Robertson 1995, 369.

40. Grmek 1979, 161–63, believes that the grim story of Clearchus is true, based on many historical accounts that were available to Polyaenus but are now lost. Saddam's attack on Kurds: Simons 1994; Hashmi 2004. As the George W. Bush administration prepared to attack Iraq to destroy its stores of biochemical arms in 2002, reports emerged that suppliers in the United States had provided many of the raw materials for Iraq's biological and chemical weapons program during the Ronald Reagan administration of the 1980s; those reports were confirmed in 2003. Some US troops who destroyed Iraq's biochemical munitions in the Gulf War of 1991 suffer a cluster of health problems that stem in part from the very agents created by the United States and sent to Iraq. Acknowledging the age-old rebound problems for those involved with biochemical armaments, one US senator critical of the attack on Iraq asked in 2002, "Are we now facing the possibility of reaping what we have sown?" Origins of Iraq's bioweaponry: CBS News, and *New York Times*, August 18, 2002; Kelley 2002; Shenon 2003. Controversial allegations of poisons used against political insurgencies in Ethiopia and Southeast Asia between 1975 and 1981 are discussed by Eitzen and Takafuji 1997, chaps. 18 and 34; Lesho, Dorsey, and Bunner 1998, 515; and Christopher et al. 1997, 415. South Africa: "The Science of Apartheid" 1998; Finnegan 2001. Iraq and South Africa: Koblentz 2011. Widely discussed examples of US government bioweapons and nuclear tests endangering American citizens during the Cold War have been documented. For example, the release of supposedly harmless pathogens in San Francisco Bay in 1950 caused an outbreak of infections with at least one fatality, and in 2002 the US government acknowledged secret releases of biotoxins and chemical agents (nerve agents and hallucinogens being developed as offensive weapons) aboard navy ships, and several US locations in 1949–71. Lesho, Dorsey, and Bunner 1998, 513–14; Christopher et al. 1997, 414; Aldinger 2002; "Sailors Sprayed with Nerve Gas in Test," 2002. Japanese dissemination of cholera among the Chinese in 1941 resulted in about seventeen hundred fatalities of unprotected Japanese troops, besides the targeted ten thousand Chinese victims: Christopher et al. 1997, 413. On recent accidents with weaponizable biological agents: Guterl et al. 2020.
41. Grmek 1979, 149–50.

CHAPTER 4. A CASKET OF PLAGUE IN
THE TEMPLE OF BABYLON

1. Epigraph: *Lives of the Later Caesars* (*Historia Augusta*), *Life of Lucius Verus* 7–8. Today the word "plague" usually connotes bubonic plague, or the Black Death, but in antiquity "plague" was used for all epidemics. Kaffa or Caffa is modern Fedosia or Theodosia. Mussi cited in Barker 2021, 97. For ancient and modern stench weapons, see chapter 5.

2. Evidence for the revised theory of the spread of the Black Death from Kaffa via rats on grain ships: Barker 2021, quote 126. For earlier assumptions of deliberate bioterrorism at Kaffa, see, e.g., Wheelis 2002; Derbes 1966; Robertson and Robertson 1995, 370; Christopher et al. 1997, 412; Lesho, Dorsey, and Bunner 1998, 512; Poupard and Miller 1992, 11. See also Zanders 2021.

3. Barker 2021, 101; Tatar trebuchets, 112–13; 122–23 on popular knowledge of human-to-human aerosol transmission of bubonic plague in the 1300s. Human ectoparasites responsible for spread of bubonic plague: Dean et al. 2018, but this study is disputed by recent findings that the bacterium is not well adapted to human parasites, making the classic rat model and pneumonic transmission the most likely. Kyle Harper, personal communication, February 16, 2021; Harper 2021, 207–14.

4. Hasdrubal: Livy 27.43–50. Hannibal catapulting vipers, see chapter 6.

5. Communicable disease mechanisms were established by Louis Pasteur, Robert Koch, and other scientists in the nineteenth century, but disease transmission was observed and remarked upon very early in human history. Livy 25.26. Neufeld 1980, 32–34, discusses evidence for ancient intuitions about contagion. Bubonic plague was spread to the English village of Eyam via a box of clothing, killing 80 percent of the villagers, in the Great Plague of 1665–66; smallpox was spread in the village of Chelwood in 1784 when the coffin of a victim was opened after thirty years; other reports gathered in *New Scientist*, July 25, 1985, 58–59.

6. Cyzicus: Mayor 2010, 272–74; Appian, "Mithridatic Wars" 12.76; see also "Punic Wars" 73 for a similar corpse-borne plague that struck the Carthaginian army in 150 BC.

7. Livy 25.26 ("contact with the sick spread the disease"); Diodorus of Sicily 12.45.2–4; 14.70.4–71.4 ("those who tended the sick were seized by the plague"). The plague seemed to originate in Egypt and spread to Persia and Libya: Thucydides 2.47–55; 3.87. See also Lucretius 6.1090–1286. Zinsser 1963, 119–27; McNeill 1976, 105–6.

8. Sophocles, *Trachinian Women* 555–1038 (lines 956, 1038, *anthos*, "pustulant efflorescence"). Cedrenus cited in Zinsser 1963, 138. Chinese awareness of fomites in clothing: Temple 1991, 215. Epidemics in ancient China: Hanson 2012.

9. Cuneiform tablets about contagion, found in the archives of Mari: Sasson 2000, 1911–24, and personal correspondence, November 2002; also Neufeld 1980, 33. On early understanding of smallpox contagion, inoculation, quarantine, and long-term virulence of desiccated smallpox matter, see Fenn 2000, 1561, 1563–64; McNeill 1976, 253. On political assassinations by gifts of smallpox-infected clothing in Mughal India: Maskiell and Mayor 2001. Smallpox-infected blankets and missiles in early colonial American military history: Fenn 2000, 1577–79; Poupard and Miller 1992, 11–13. See Mayor 1995b for a cross-cultural survey of disease-infected items as bioweapons, such as smallpox blankets given to Native Americans, from antiquity to the present. Articles of clothing laced with nerve poisons absorbed through the skin were created to kill antiapartheid activists, according to testimony before the Truth and Reconciliation Commission, reported in "The Science of Apartheid" 1998; and in Finnegan 2001, 62.

10. Hittite plague rituals: Faraone 1992, 99, 109 nn. 37–39; see also 41–42, 44, 47, 59–73. Hittite plague: Lorenzi 2007; Trevisanato 2007, 1371–74; there is no known cure for tularemia, sometimes called "rabbit fever." Modern use of tularemia as a weapon: Harris and Paxman 2002, 164–72.

11. On Hittite and Babylonian plague gods, Faraone 1992, 61, 120–21, 125–27, and see 128–32, esp. 130 on rodents bringing pestilence. On pestilence and warfare through history, Zinsser 1963, esp. 139, 141; 125–26 on the epidemic that struck the Carthaginians. See also McNeill 1976, 115–27.

12. Exodus 1 and 7–12, and *New Oxford Annotated Bible* 1973, commentary. Poisoning fish with chemicals: Pliny 25.98. See Jones 2007, 49, for Native Americans poisoning water to stupefy fish and game.

13. Homer, *Iliad* 1.50–70.

14. On intention to spread contagion, see Wheelis 1999, 9. Tetrahedron, a New Age–survivalist company based in Idaho, sells "Bible-recommended" essential oils to protect against biological warfare, including one called Exodus II supposedly concocted by Moses "to protect the Israelites from plague" (see chapter 5, on attempts to immunize against bioattack).

15. On genocide and rape in antiquity, see Van Wees 2010. Systematic rape as a "weapon of war" to crush ethnic rebellion in Burma, *New York Times*, December 27, 2002. As early as 1975, a US military manual alluded to the theoretical possibility of developing ethnic biochemical weapons to selectively incapacitate or kill specific population groups by taking advantage of genetic knowledge, and in the 1980s the Soviets repeatedly accused the United States, Israel, and South Africa of seeking to develop "ethnic weapons," allegations denied by US authorities as "preposterous [and] out of the question." Wick 1988, 14–21. South Africa's "Project Coast": Finnegan 2001, 58, 61–63. The possibility of ethnic "genetic bombs" was discussed by Harris and Paxman 2002, 173, 248, 253. "Genetic alteration" weapons would create long-term birth defects over generations among enemy populations: "When Killing Just Won't Do" 2003. Genetically engineered bioweapons to target certain ethnic groups: Knapton 2019, citing Centre for the Study of Existential Risk, University of Cambridge. Genome editing as biothreat: "Spore Wars" 2020, 20.

16. "Pharaoh's orders," see Exodus 1; Herod's orders, see Matthew 2. Rose 1959, 234–35.

17. *Oxford Classical Dictionary* s.v. "Sabini"; Polyaenus 8.3.1. *Arthashastra*: Bradford 2001, 127.

18. Man-made pestilence: Grmek 1979, 148–50. Seneca, *On Anger* 2.9.3; Livy 8.18; Orosius, *Histories against the Pagans* 3.10.

19. Cassius Dio, *Epitome* 67.11 and 73.14. Harper 2017, 89. On plagues in antiquity, see *Oxford Classical Dictionary*, s.v. "plague"; and Faraone 1992, 128–32. Notably, suspicions of deliberate poisoning causing mass deaths also occurred during in epidemics in Rome in 331 BC and in Italy in 227 BC. In the first instance, according to Livy 8.18 and Valerius Maximus 2.5.3, 190 women were executed, suspected of mass

poisoning. In 227 BC, 3,000 women were convicted and killed for similar crimes, Livy 40.37 and 43.

20. Panic induced by modern bioterror fears in the United States: Meckler 2002. Conspiracy theories arose in China, Iran, the United States, and elsewhere, claiming that the coronavirus COVID-19 originated as a bioweapon, see, e.g., *Forbes*, March 26, 2020; *Bulletin of the Atomic Scientists*, March 19, 2020; Teoh 2020. In August 2021, US intelligence agencies were divided in their report on the origins of COVID-19. As of this writing, it cannot be ruled out that the COVID-19 virus accidentally escaped from a virology lab in Wuhan, China, where dangerous "Gain of Function" (GOF) experiments with bat and other coronavirus transmittal ("spillover") to humans are carried out, with obvious biological weapon potentials. https://www.theatlantic.com /ideas/archive/2021/05/chinese-lab-leak-hypothesis-coronavirus /619000/. Until 2017, the Wuhan studies were funded in part by US contributions. Guterl et al. 2020; "Spore Wars" 2020; "Origin of Covid-19" 2020. In 2020, white nationalists in the United States plotted to weaponize the pandemic coronavirus COVID-19 to foment civil war: Walker and Winter 2020.

21. Kautilya 1951, 443–46.

22. Mousepox virus was discussed in Preston's novel *Demon in the Freezer* (2002). Synthetic virus discovery: "Do-It-Yourself Virus Recreated from Synthetic DNA," *Science News*, July 13, 2002, 22; see also *Newsweek* July 22, 8. Microbiologists point out that the poliovirus is a relatively simple virus.

23. Genetically engineered pathogens: Flora and Pachauri 2020; gene-editing CRISPR bioweapons could create synthetic diseases to wipe out agriculture and spread disease: Dolgin 2020. Gain of Function (GOF) experiments with animal virus capable of spillover to humans, Guterl et al. 2020.

24. On cross-cultural ancient and modern legends about "bottling up" plague and releasing it against enemies, see Mayor 1995b and Maskiell and Mayor 2001. The Ark of the Covenant: 1 Samuel 4–7; 2 Samuel 6.6–7; Lockwood 2009, 49–50. For further discussion of the Ark-related plague, see chapter 6 and Trevisanato 2007, 1144–46. In India, Mari/Maariamma/Shitala, Hindu goddess of medicine

and pox, carries a vessel representing epidemics; thanks to Roshni Rajadorai.

25. Plague demons kept in the temple at Jerusalem, Testament of Solomon manuscripts and *Testimony of Truth*, Nag Hammadi library. Dating and text analysis: Johnston 2002 and James Harding and Loveday Alexander, Biblical Studies, University of Sheffield, "Dating the Testament of Solomon," May 28, 1999. Conybeare 1898; and Bonner 1956 (Faraone 1992, 72 n. 84, cited Bonner, but mistook Solomon for Samuel and Babylonians for Assyrians).

26. Bashiruddin Mahmood was accused in 2001 of ties to Islamic terrorists, after plans for anthrax balloons were found in the offices of an organization he headed in Afghanistan: reported in the *New York Times*, November 28, 2001. Islamic scientists on the legend of Solomon: Aftergood 2001, citing a *Wall Street Journal* article, "Islamic Science," September 13, 1988, and *Islam and Science* (1991) by Pakistani physicist Pervez Hoodbhoy. Islamic science and djinn, see Ali 2016.

27. *Testimony of Truth*, Nag Hammadi library. The plague during Titus's reign (AD 79–81) occurred about nine years after he destroyed the temple, according to Suetonius, *Titus*.

28. Seven to ten million out of a population of about seventy million: Harper 2021, 101–23; Harper 2017, 24, 65–118.

29. Faraone 1992, 61–64. The two ancient sources for the great plague of AD 165–80, are the biography of Lucius Verus, by "Julius Capitolinus" in *Lives of the Later Caesars* (*Historia Augusta*) 7–8; and Ammianus Marcellinus, 23.6.24. Zinsser 1963, 135–37. McNeill 1976, 116–17. Harper 2017, 98–100, deems the story of the casket in the temple a "just-so story" with no credence. For suggestions that the plague may have originated in Central Asia or China, see de Crespigny 2007; McLaughlin 2010.

30. Diodorus of Sicily 14.70.4. Appian, "Illyrian Wars" 4. Faraone 1992, 61–62. Harper 2017, 98–101. Justinian Plague, 541–750: Little 2008, 119–20.

31. Hamaxitus: Strabo 13.1.48–49. Faraone 1992, 129–30.

32. Aelian, *On Animals* 12.5; 4.40; 9.15; 10.49; 12.20; 14.20. "Cures" for rabies are given by Pliny 29.98–102.

33. Kautilya 1951, 444. Rabies "bombs": Robertson and Robertson 1995, 370. Leonardo da Vinci's bomb: Temple 1991, 218. The Polish general

was Kasimir Siemienowicz, author of *The Grand Art d'Artillerie* (1650): see Lesho, Dorsey, and Bunner 1998, 512–13; Partington 1999, 168. On the long viability of smallpox matter and aerosols: Lesho, Dorsey, and Bunner 1998, 512. Smallpox transmission by scabs and smallpox material: Harper 2021, 108–10. On archaeologists' concerns that smallpox could be accidentally released during excavations of ancient sites, see Fenn 2000, 1558 n. 9.

34. Catapult bolts: Harris 1995; IG II2 1422, line 9: two boxes of catapult bolts. Chaeronea: Lycurgus, *Against Leocrates* 43. Aristophanes, *Knights* 843–59 (424 BC) describes 120 Spartan shields with handles still attached (and therefore usable) kept in the Painted Stoa and the Nike Temple in Athens. See also Thucydides 4.28–40; Pausanias 1.15.5. Heracles's weapons were taken from his temple during Thebes's war with Sparta, 371 BC, Xenophon, *Hellenica* 6.4.7. Cicero, *Pro sestio* 34 notes that weapons were stockpiled in the Temple of Castor, first century BC. The Oxus temple, in Bactria, held a vast collection of composite bows, arrows, spears, swords, daggers, armor, helmets, and shields (sixth through third centuries BC), and the Urartian temple of the god Khaldi at Musasir, Anatolia (ninth century BC), was stocked with weapons, including swords, spears, bows and arrows, and shields. Thanks to Scott Chesworth, Ancient World Podcast; John Ma; Matt Simonton; and David Rafferty for these references to weapons in temples.

35. Greek Fire stored in Byzantine churches: Partington 1999, 25 and n. 218. Myra: Forbes 1964, 19.

36. Quotes from Faraone 1992, 63, 65, 66 (Heracles can offer only defensive aid to armies). The temple at Chryse was dedicated to Apollo, the god of pestilential mice, notorious carriers of disease, and it was not far from the temple of Apollo at Hamaxitus, which actually kept hordes of mice. In a striking coincidence in the ancient history of biological warfare, Chryse was also the name of the desert island where Philoctetes suffered a poison arrow wound.

37. Partington 1999, 21 and n. 191. Louis XIV, Hitler, treaties: Robertson and Robertson 1995, 369, 371, 372. Christopher et al. 1997, 413–16. Lesho, Dorsey, and Bunner 1998, 513–15. Circular logic that biochemical weapons must first be invented so that countermeasures can be

prepared: Harris and Paxman 2002, chap. 3; see also Guterl et al. 2020. In 1956, the United States "changed its policy of 'defensive use only' to include possible deployment of biological weapons in situations other than retaliation": Poupard and Miller 1992, 14–15. On last-resort strategies and extremities of war, see Nardin 1996, 28–29, 86–88, 133.

38. Booby-trapped chests: Partington 1999, 170.

39. Faraone 1992, 66.

40. Modern examples: Robertson and Robertson 1995, 371; Christopher et al. 1997, 413–14; Lesho, Dorsey, and Bunner 1998, 513. Ishii's chronic illness: Harris and Paxman 2002, 77–80. In 1971, a smallpox outbreak in Aralsk, Kazakhstan, may have resulted from the release of a strain of weaponized smallpox in the Soviet Biopreparat program at Vozrozhdeniya Island in the Aral Sea: Miller 2002b; Williams 2006; and see the afterword.

41. Faraone 1992, 120–21.

42. Mithradates and his universal antidote: Mayor 2010 and 2019a. As noted at the beginning of this chapter, during the Black Death of the fourteenth century, people understood that the plague could be spread by coughing, speaking, and breathing; Barker 2021, 122–23.

43. On the lore of Poison Maidens: Penzer 1952, 3, 12–71. The Poison Sultan: Maskiell and Mayor 2001, 165. Fears of "smallpox martyrs," infected individuals who could be dispatched by terrorists to spread contagion, rose in 2002: *New York Times Magazine*, December 15, 2002, 122.

44. Penzer 1952, 12–71. Hittites weaponized victims of plague, as discussed at the beginning of the chapter.

45. Grafton 1992, 181.

CHAPTER 5. SWEET SABOTAGE

1. Epigraph: Aelian, *On Animals* 5.29; Homer, *Odyssey* 2.325. The following events are from Xenophon, *Anabasis* 4.8.20–22.

2. Diodorus of Sicily 14.26–30. Pliny 21.74–78 (on poison honey); see 25.37 on antidotes from poisons. Interview with T. C., February 1986. On toxic honey in antiquity and modern times, see Mayor 1995a; Mayor 2010, 70, 88–89, 240, 242, 315.

3. Ambrose 1974, 34.

4. Pliny 25.5–7. Mithradates's biography: Mayor 2010. Agari snake-venom doctors: Appian, "Mithridatic Wars" 12.88. Mithradates's animal bodyguard: Aelian, *On Animals* 7.46.

5. *Laws of Manu* 7.218, see Buhler 1886, 251. Knowledge of Indian medicine in the Roman era, see Majno 1991, 374–78.

6. *Mithridatium*, see Mayor 2010, chap. 11; Mayor 2019a. Celsus, a physician during the reign of Tiberius, listed thirty-six theriac ingredients. Majno 1991, 414–17. Julius Capitolinus, *Lives of the Later Caesars, Marcus Antoninus* 15.3.

7. Majno 1991, 414–19; Sushruta Samhita 2018.

8. Kautilya 1951, 443, 455–57. Saddam sought an antidote for nerve gas: Miller 2002a.

9. Indonesian special forces drink venomous snake blood; see, e.g., *New York Magazine*, UPI news, *Business Insider*, January 24, 2018. Tetrahedron sold an oil "used by Moses to protect the Israelites from plague," containing cinnamon, cassia, calamus, myrrh, hyssop, frankincense, spikenard, and galbanum in olive oil. http://www.tetrahedron.org.

10. Germans and typhus: Christopher et al. 1997, 413.

11. Gulf War syndrome, a cluster of physical and psychological symptoms, has been attributed in part to the military's medical antidotes against bioweapons and in part to poisoning that occurred when US troops destroyed chemical and biological munitions in Iraq during the Gulf War of 1991. Hodges 2009; Department of Veterans Affairs 2014.

12. Marcus Aurelius: Majno 1991, 414–15.

13. Pliny 25.5–7, 37, and 62–65; 29.24–26. Mithradates: Cassius Dio 36–37; Appian "Mithridatic Wars" 12; Strabo 12.3.30–31. The foregoing events are related in detail in Mayor 2010.

14. For these incidents involving toxic honey, see Strabo 12.3.18; Mayor 2010, 88–89; 315; and Mayor 1995a.

15. Aelian, *On Animals* 5.29. Aeneas 16.5–7. Kautilya 1951, 441.

16. Hannibalic wars: Bradford 2001, 178–89. Frontinus, *Stratagems* 2.5.13–14, and 23.

17. Cassius Dio, *Epitome* 67.5.6.

18. Polyaenus 1.1.1; 1.1 and 1.3; 1.preface.1–3; 8.25.1.

19. Polyaenus 8.28; 31.18.

20. Herodotus 1.199–216. Strabo 11.8.4–6.

21. Polyaenus 5.10.1. See *Oxford Classical Dictionary* s.v. "Himilco." Mandrake: Pliny 25.147–50. Frontinus, *Stratagems* 2.5.12.

22. Polyaenus 8.23.1.

23. A Theopompus fragment and Polyaenus 7.42 recounted the Celts' plan.

24. Leprosy wine: Grmek 1979, 147. Anthrax candy: Lesho, Dorsey, and Bunner 1998, 513; and on Ishii, see Harris and Paxman 2002, 77–80. "The Science of Apartheid" 1998, 19, 24; Finnegan 2001. See Poupard and Miller 1992, 13, and Eitzen and Takafuji 1997, on the Nazis allegedly distributing infected toys and candy in Romania.

25. "Magical" biological and chemical weaponry was devised by "harnessing natural forces" in ancient India: Kokatnur 1948, 270. Native American shamans prepared toxic weapons: Jones 2007. In modern times, the scientists who develop biological and chemical weapons usually work in secrecy, and their names are rarely publicized.

26. Polyaenus, *Stratagems* 8.43. See Faraone 1992, 99, 59–65, 73–75, on "aggressive use of pharmaka in war." Faraone and Burkert both relate the Chrysame story to the ancient Hittite practice of sending poisoned or contagious animals toward the enemy. On modern strategies of poisoning enemy livestock in World War I, see Christopher et al. 1997, 413; Robertson and Robertson 1995, 370.

27. Quotes from Susan Levine, Joint Non-Lethal Weapons Directorate (JNLWD) research director, in *Navy News and Undersea Technology*, May 10, 1999; Col. George Fenton, director of JNLWD, in *New Scientist*, December 16, 2000; *New York Times* editorial, October 30, 2002, respectively. The DARPA project: Weinberger 2017, 161; see also 223 on plans for LSD. Ancient Indian recipes for sedative and disorienting agents were delivered by hollow darts: Kokatnur 1948, 269. On modern calmatives: Moreno 2016; *Lethal in Disguise* 2016.

28. Hitler: Moon 2000, 95; Harris and Paxman 2002, 207, psychochemicals and mind control, 290–93, 207–13. Polyaenus 7.6.4 recounted an ancient tactic by the Persians to "feminize" their enemies, the Lydians; cf. Moreno 2016 on using the hormone oxytocin to evoke trust or a feeling of "bonding" in enemies. From 2000 to 2008, the NGO Sunshine Project monitored and exposed research on biochemical

weapons. Now see *Lethal in Disguise* 2016; and Federation of American Scientists position papers and links about biochemical and "nonlethal" weapons at www.fas.org. "When Killing Just Won't Do" 2003; Broad 2002; and the Department of Defense and the JNLWD websites: https://jnlwp.defense.gov and https://www.dvidshub.net/unit/JNLWD.

29. The gas used by the Russians in 2002 is believed to have been an aerosol version of the powerful opioid carfentanil (banned by the Chemical Weapons Convention), one hundred times stronger than fentanyl, the opioid responsible for thousands of overdose deaths in the United States. After the Russian event, a spokesman for the JNLWD "denied that it was conducting research on nonlethal chemical weapons," despite the JNLWD's publicized 2002 budget of $1.6 million to develop such weapons: *New York Times*, October 28–31, and Broad 2002.

30. Wheelis 1999. Health threats posed by allegedly nonlethal CCWs are summarized in *Lethal in Disguise* 2016. Eumenes quoted by Justin 14.1.12, cited in Penzer 1952, 6.

CHAPTER 6. ANIMAL ALLIES

1. Epigraph: Aelian, *On Animals* 1.38. Herodotus 2.141. The pharaoh's name is unknown.

2. Herodotus 2.141. Bad omens of mice eating leather military gear: Pliny 8.221–23. Faraone 1992, 42–43, 65–66, 128–31.

3. 2 Kings 19.35. Josephus, *Jewish Antiquities* 10.15–27. Bradford 2001, 44.

4. Kahn 2014 integrates the diverse ancient sources for this event. Zinsser 1963, 194, believes that the rodents that attacked the Assyrians were rats rather than field mice. The pestilence that struck the Assyrians was the subject of a famous poem by Lord Byron, "The Destruction of Sennacherib," 1815.

5. Apollo's cult of pestilential mice and the temple of Hamaxitus with white mice: Aelian, *On Animals* 12.5; Polemon of Troy (190 BC) fragment, cited in Faraone 1992, 128; Strabo 13.1.46–48.

6. When "mice" are mentioned in ancient texts, "rats" may be meant: Zinsser 1963, 190–91; and see his chap. 11 on rats and mice.

7. Faraone 1992, 41–42 ("faulty reasoning," Faraone's emphasis), 50 n. 39, 128–31. Strabo 3.4.18.

8. 1 Samuel 5–6. Commentary in the *Oxford Annotated Bible* identifies the Philistine pestilence as bubonic plague. Tularemia is also spread by rodents and rabbits and has symptoms similar to those of bubonic plague: Trevisanato 2007, 1144–46. Modern experiments with tularemia as a bioweapon: Harris and Paxman 2002, 78, 145, 158, 164–72. The plague appeared in each Philistine town visited by the Ark, raising the question of fomites or insect vectors associated with the sacred chest: see chapter 4. Rats in "countless hordes" were a periodic plague in northern Iran and Babylon: Aelian, *On Animals* 17.17.

9. Neufeld 1980, 30–31. Ambrose 1974, 33–34. Aelian, *On Animals* 17.35. Technically, bees make nests; a hive is a man-made structure for a nest.

10. "Some authorities state that 27 hornet stings will kill a human being," Pliny 11.73. Some modern medical authorities say 30 or 40 wasp or hornet stings can be fatal.

11. Maya: *Popul Vuh*, lines 6800ff. Mayor 1995a, 36.

12. Neufeld 1980, 30–39, 43–46, 55. Exodus 23.28, Deuteronomy 7.20, Joshua 24.12, Isaiah 7.18–20. On the many species of venomous insects in the Near East, see Neufeld 51–52. Bees, wasps, and hornets in warfare: Lockwood 2009, 17–18; 21–30; 34; 74; 324.

13. Ambrose 1974. Development of weapons based on marking enemies with pheromones to induce attack by bees: "When Killing Just Won't Do" 2003; and Lockwood 2009, 207–9. Green bottle fly: Weinberger 2017, 162.

14. Neufeld 1980, 54–56. Harris and Paxman 2002, 50–51. Mayor 1995a, 36.

15. Aeneas 37.4. Appian, "Mithridatic Wars" 12.78. Mayor 2010, 279.

16. Japanese flea bombs: Lesho, Dorsey, and Bunner 1998, 513; Christopher et al. 1997, 413; Robertson and Robertson 1995, 371; Lockwood 1987, 77. Kahn 2002.

17. The defense of Hatra: Herodian 3.9.3–8 and commentary by C. Whittaker. The Hatra debacle is also described by Cassius Dio 68.31–75.10.31.2, *Epitome* 75.10–13 and 76.1012. Ammianus Marcellinus 25.8.2–6 visited the abandoned city of Hatra in AD 363, and described the desert as a "wretched" wilderness with no water and few plants.

18. All the descriptions of scorpions in this section from Aelian and Pliny are found in Aelian *On Animals* 6.20, 6.23, 8.13, 9.4, 9.27, 10.23, 15.26, 17.40 (a plague of scorpions in the Mideast) and Pliny 11.30, 11.87–91; 27.6. See also Scarborough 1979, 9–18; on winged scorpions, 14–15 and nn. 146, 147, and 170. Strabo 15.1.37, on winged scorpions.

19. Herodian 3.9.3–8 and commentary by C. Whittaker. Leo, *Tactica* 19.53, cited in Partington 1999, 18 and n. 174.

20. Assassin bugs: Ambrose 1974, 36; Thanks to entomologist Robert Peterson for information about assassin bugs, and see Lockwood 2014, 21, 41, 287–88.

21. See Campbell 1986 for scholarly opinions on the puzzle of Severus's defeat. Herodian 3.9.3–8; Cassius Dio on Hatra, 68.31–75.10.31.2, *Epitome* 75.10–13 and 76.10–12.

22. Hatra was the setting for the beginning scenes of the 1973 horror film *The Exorcist*. Modern reports on scorpion bombs, Carmichael 2003; Newman 2005; Eveleth 2012; Grossman 2014. Hatra's fortress, temples, and sculptures were deliberately damaged in March 2015 by ISIS, as reported by multiple news accounts, e.g., BBC News, March 7, 2015.

23. Assassin or cone-nose bug in Vietnam: Ambrose 1974, 38; Lockwood 2009, 21, 41, 287–88.

24. On the history of US research and production of offensive insect weapons, see Lockwood 1987, 78–82; Lockwood 2009, 210–29; 287–97; scorpions used by Viet Cong against American soldiers, 206. "Controlled Biological Systems" project to create sophisticated weapon technologies based on entomology and zoology is overseen by the Defense Sciences Office (DSO) of the Defense Advanced Research Projects Agency (DARPA). Remote-controlled rats were created by SUNY scientists funded by the Defense Department, *New York Times Magazine*, December 15, 2002, 116; and Meek 2002, citing *Nature*, May 2, 2002. Revkin 2002. On the future of entomological warfare: Lockwood 2009, 233–313.

25. Hannibal's ruse with cattle and the use of snakes: Cornelius Nepos, *Hannibal* 23.1011; see also Justinius 32.4.6–8; Orosius, *Histories against the Pagans* 4.20; and Frontinus, *Stratagems* 4.7.10–11, who says the trick was played by Hannibal and again by Prusius, king of Bithynia.

26. Neufeld 1980, 54–55. Grossman 2014.

27. *Greek Alexander Romance*, Stoneman 1991, 101.
28. Pelusium: Polyaenus 15.6, 7.9.
29. Lisle 2020.
30. Aeneas 22.14, 22.20, 23.2, 38.2–3; and Whitehead's commentary, pp. 156–57.
31. Mayor 2014, 286–87. A war dog helping the Titans fight a Giant appears on the Altar of Pergamum, Berlin. Dogs as sentries: Polyaenus 2.25; Aeneas 22.20; Vegetius 4.26. Pliny 8.61.142–43; 8.40. Aelian, *On Animals* 7.38; *Historical Miscellany* 14.46. Caspian war dogs: Valerius Flaccus, *Argonautica* 6.106–8. History of war dogs: Karunanithy 2008. Military dogs in ancient Greece, Rice 2020. For rabies, see chapter 4.
32. Polyaenus 7.2.
33. Aelian, *On Animals* 7.38.
34. During World War II, "barking dogs, notably collies, shepherds, and elkhounds, were trained as sentries [while] setters and pointers were trained to attack, scout, and carry messages on the battlefield." Thousands of canines were trained to find wounded soldiers, bombs, and mines, and to carry equipment; and some dogs even parachuted with airborne units. Svanevik and Burgett 2006. Karunanithy 2008; Stock 2017.
35. Magawa and the Hero-RAT program: BBC news, September 25, 2020 and June 4, 2021, https://www.bbc.com/news/world-asia-57345703.
36. Ambrose 1974, 33. Dolphins: PBS Frontline Report 1997. Sea lions: Williams 2003. Naval Marine Mammal Project: Watkins 2007; Aratani 2019.
37. At Alexander's defeat of King Darius in 331 BC at Gaugamela, his men captured the fifteen war elephants in the Persian forces before they saw action. Arrian 3.8.6, 3.11.6, 3.15.4. Alexander versus Porus: Quintus Curtius 8.13–14; Arrian 5.9–30.
38. Zonarus 8.3 cited by Stoneman 1991, 129–30.
39. These and other incidents with elephants: Scullard 1974. Livy 27.46–49; Ammianus Marcellinus 25.1.4. War elephants, camels, horses, donkeys, mules, see Mayor 2014, 288–92. Elephants in Greco-Macedonian warfare: Rice 2020.
40. Lucretius, *On the Nature of the Universe* 5.1298–1349.

41. Aelian, *On Animals* 8.15; 8.17. Pliny 8.68. On dogs, camels, and elephants in ancient Greek warfare, see Rice 2020; on war camels, Bartosiewicz 2014.

42. These stories come from Herodotus 1.80–82; 4.130–36.

43. Caesar's elephant: Polyaenus 8.23.5.

44. Polyaenus 7.6.6; Frontinus, *Stratagems* 2.4.12. Aelian, *On Animals* 11.36 (he confused Lydians with Persians). Polyaenus 4.21. Zoological tricks help clarify the difference between acceptable biologically based ruses of war, like creating shields against enemy cavalry with ranks of evil-smelling camels, and more reprehensible deployments of biotoxins against human soldiers. The imaginative range of ancient low-tech animal strategies makes one wonder what sorts of counterploys will be developed to subvert the high-technology biodefenses using insects and animals being created today. Mayor 2014.

45. Aelian, *On Animals* 1.38; 16.14; 16.36. Alexander legend: Stoneman 1994, 11–12.

46. Pliny 8.27 notes that elephants are scared by pigs' squeals; he also says that when elephants are frightened or wounded, they always give ground. Seneca, *On Anger* 2.11.5 remarks that "the elephant fears the sound of pigs."

47. Cassius Dio and Florus on the noise of the war elephants, cited in Kistler 2007, 85. Hannibal's elephants at Zama: Polybius 15.12.2.

48. *Baritus*: Tacitus, *Germania* 3. *Karnyx*: Diodorus of Sicily 5.30; they are depicted on coins and on Trajan's Column, and examples have been found in archaeological sites.

49. Whistling arrows of the Xiongnu, nomadic steppe archers, were first described in Sima Qian's *Shiji* (Record of the Grand Historian; 109–91 BC), and examples of several types have been found in archaeological excavations. Dekker 2013.

50. Chinese use of noise to disorient and terrify foes, see Temple 1991, 37–38, 96, 202–3; on Chinese gongs, drums, and "Iron Fire" and "Thunderclap" bombs to shock and awe enemies, Andrade 2017, 17, 41.

51. Ancient Indian methods of producing disorienting aural and optical effects: Kokatnur 1948, 269. Modern odor, optical illusion, and sonic weapons: "When Killing Just Won't Do" 2003; Niiler 2018; Chen 2019. The weaponization of music and sound is surveyed by Ross 2016. For

a thoughtful essay on "sound and pain," see Berson 2016. Canadian diplomats also experienced "Havana Syndrome." Since 2016, the syndrome has been reported in Germany, Austria, Russia, China, and Vietnam; as of 2022, theories focus on Russian-devised high-powered microwave or sonic systems; see Mackinnon and Gramer 2020 and https://www.nytimes.com/2021/05/12/us/politics/biden-cia-brain-injury.html. For antecedents, see Weinberger 2017, 189–200. See chapter 7 for microwave heat weapons.

52. The pigs at Megara reported by Aelian, *On Animals* 16.36, and Polyaenus 4.6.3. On flammable pitch and resin from trees and tar from crude petroleum deposits in the ancient world, see references cited in Whitehead's commentary at Aeneas 11.3, p. 129; and Forbes 1964. Mayor 2014, 290–93, elephants and pigs in war. Scullard 1974, 113–16, on the plausibility of using pigs against war elephants. Liv Mariah Yarrow 2021 argues against the historicity of pigs used to deflect any war elephants in antiquity.

53. Kistler 2007, 90 and n. 19, incorrectly claims that the Romans used "pigs coated with grease and pitch which they turned into live torches" at the Battle of Malventum in 275 BC. Kistler cites Karl Groning and Michael Saller, *Elephants* (1999), 218, but this source is also wrong and cites no ancient author for this claim, obviously confusing the Megarian tactic with flaming pigs against Antigonus Gonatus in 270 BC. Procopius, *History of the Wars* 8.14.30–43.

54. Frontinus, *Stratagems* 2.4.17.

55. Partington 1999, 46, 210, 262. Kautilya 1951, 433–34.

56. Morgan 1990, chap. 2.

57. Andrade 2017, 16–18, 42, and fig. 1.1.

58. Monkey militia: Jennison 1971, 38. Sie Chung-Ghi, in *Wu-Tsah-Tsu* of 1610, Japanese edition 1661, ix, fol. 15. Note that the Indian epic *Ramayana* features Hanuman's monkey army. A painted relief in a tomb shows a policeman or guard holding a whip with two trained baboons on leashes. One of the baboons is capturing a thief. Relief, Mastaba of Tepemankh, Old Kingdom, Fifth Dynasty, ca. 2498–2345 BC, Saqqara Necropolis, Egyptian Museum, Cairo, JE 37101.

59. Folklore motifs for burning animals: J2101.1 and K2351.1 in the *Motif-Index of Folk-Literature*.

60. The Tamerlane (Timur) legend comes from the University of Calgary Applied History Research Group, "Islamic World to 1600," copyright 1998.

CHAPTER 7. INFERNAL FIRE

1. Medea's deadly gift to Glauke was described in Euripides's tragedy *Medea* (431 BC): the burning scene (1136ff.) takes place offstage but is vividly described by horrified eyewitnesses. The story of Medea's fire weapon was retold in numerous versions by Greek and Latin authors; see, for example. Diodorus of Sicily 4.54; Apollodorus, *Library* 1.9.28. The princess in the burning gown was a favorite subject in vase paintings and sculpture. The fountain where Glauke sought relief was a landmark in antiquity and is still pointed out to tourists in ancient Corinth. Mayor 1997b.

2. Crosby 2002, 87–88. Lucretius, *On the Nature of the Universe* 5.1243–46; and 5.1284–86.

3. Partington 1999, 1, and 211 (*Laws of Manu*). SIPRI, *Incendiary Weapons* 1975, 15. According to Kokatnur 1948, 268–70, "chemical warfare or something similar thereto is strongly suggested" in the oral Indian epics of 2000–650 BC, written down in about the first century AD. On Chinese incendiaries, see Sawyer 2007; Ling 1947; Temple 1991, 215–18. Sun Tzu's tactics, Bradford 2001, 134–36.

4. Herodotus 8.51–53.

5. Crosby 2002, 88.

6. Crosby 2002, 88. On early methods of distilling wood pitch, discussed by Pliny, Dioscorides, and Arabic sources, Forbes 1964, 33–36, 38–39; Partington 1999, 4; on the last uses of blazing arrows, 5.

7. Thucydides 2.75–78. Sulfur and pitch: Healy 1999, 248–49, 257; Pliny 35.174–77; 16.52. On sulfur fires in sieges in Roman times, see Healy, 249 nn. 228–29, citing Martial, *Epigrams* 1.41.4 and 42; 12.57.14. Modern gas and chemical irritant weapons, *Lethal in Disguise* 2016.

8. Aeneas 33.1–3; 35.1.

9. Rhodes: Diodorus of Sicily 20.48, 86–88, 96–97.

10. Tacitus, *Histories* 4.23. Silius Italicus, *Punica* 1.345–67 (Hannibal).

11. Herodian 8.4–5; 8.3.9; Pearson 2017, 164–69, and nn. 31–37.

12. Vegetius 4.1–8, 18.
13. Ammianus Marcellinus 23.4, 14–15. See Partington 1999, 2–3. On petroleum weapons in antiquity, see Forbes 1964, chap. 7.
14. On the experimental weapons leading to the development of gunpowder guns and bombs in China and India: Crosby 2002, 93–129; quotes on 98; Temple 1991, 217–18, 224–29, 232–37, 241–48, for Chinese discoveries and military uses of saltpeter and gunpowder; Andrade 2017 for Chinese fire lances and the history of gunpowder and guns, ca. AD 1000 to 1250. James Riddick Partington 1999 was an authority on the early discoveries and formulas for Greek Fire and gunpowder. His work, originally published in 1960, is updated in the introduction to the 1999 edition; see esp. xxi–xxiii. Poisons added to Chinese incendiaries: Partington 1999, 270–71; Temple 1991, 216–18; Andrade 2017, 16, 52, 63.
15. Andrade 2017, 16, 52, 63.
16. Various scholars give dates for the *Nitisara* ranging from the fourth century BC to the eleventh century AD. Indian fire projectiles: Kokatnur 1948, 269.
17. Lucan, *Civil War* 3.680–96; 10.486–505.
18. Thucydides 7.53. Frontinus, *Stratagems* 4.7.9. and 14.
19. Arrian, *Alexander* 2.19. Quintus Curtius 4.2.23–4.3.7.
20. Diodorus of Sicily 17.44–45. Quintus Curtius 4.3.25–26.
21. WP, also called tetraphosphorus, is a colorless, toxic, whitish, waxy solid with a garlic odor, manufactured from phosphate rocks. When WP ignites, it produces thick clouds of white smoke and is so hot it burns through metal. SIPRI, *Incendiary Weapons* 1975, 150–51. Gibbons-Neff 2016; Human Rights Watch 2009.
22. Polybius 8.5; 8.8.
23. Cassius Dio, fragments of bk. 15 preserved by John Zonaras, *Epitome* 9.4; and John Tzetzes, *Book of Histories* 2.109–28. Plutarch, *Marcellus*. Capture or immunity for enemy scientists: after World War II, German nuclear scientist Wernher von Braun was given asylum in the United States, and Dr. Ishii of Japan was granted immunity in exchange for his records of bioweapons experiments. Poupard and Miller 1992, 16 (on the US cover-up of Japan's bioweapons). In 2002, the US government suggested a plan to "identify key Iraqi weapons scientists and spirit

them out of the country" in exchange for information about Saddam Hussein's biochemical arsenals. *New York Times*, December 6, 2002.

24. Proklos: Partington 1999, 5 and n. 56. For an alternative theory that Archimedes used steam cannons and a chemical incendiary: Hsu 2010. Modern experiments with Archimedes's invention: see *Applied Optics,* special issue 1976. Archimedes's mirror weapon was reproduced successfully by Dr. David Wallace and his MIT students on October 22, 2005, broadcast on Discovery Channel's *MythBusters* on January 25, 2006. http://web.mit.edu/2.009/www/experiments/deathray /10_Mythbusters.html.

25. Laser guns were allegedly used during the US military's Operation Just Cause, according to *Panama Deception*, the Academy Award–winning documentary film directed by Barbara Trent, 1992.

26. "Pentagon Looks to Sci-Fi Weaponry," Agence France Presse, January 30, 2007. "Pentagon Denied U.S. Calls for Ray Gun Weapon in Iraq," Associated Press news story, August 30, 2007. Shachman 2010. *Lethal in Disguise* 2016, 80–82. For other microwave sonic weaponry, see chapter 6. The latest designs combine lasers and mirrors to be mounted on destroyers to ignite enemy ships, bringing to mind Archimedes's mirrors: "Rise of the Ray Gun" 2020. Microwave weapons history: Weinberger 2017, 189–200. During demonstrations against President Donald Trump in 2020, the BBC (September 17, 2020) reported that US Military Police planned to deploy heat-ray tanks against the protesters across from the White House, but none were available.

27. Colonel Fenton described the microwave gun on NPR, *Morning Edition*, March 2, 2001, "New Crowd-Control Weapon That the Pentagon Is Developing." On severe burns and fatalities from tear gas weapons, Samuel and Picot 2020.

28. Catapults: Crosby 2002, 81–87; *Oxford Classical Dictionary*, s.v. "artillery." Spartan flamethrower: Thucydides 4.100; Crosby 2002, 89. On Chinese flamethrowers, see Temple 1991, 229–31. On modern flamethrowers, SIPRI, *Incendiary Weapons* 1975, 106–11.

29. Apollodorus, *Poliorcetica*, cited by Partington 1999, 2, 5, and see 199 for later medieval recipes for burning stone castles combining vinegar, sulfur, naphtha, and the urine of children (urine contains combustible

phosphates). Juvenal 10.153. Cassius Dio 36.18 reported that vinegar poured repeatedly to saturate a large brick tower weakened it and made it brittle enough to shatter. Vitruvius 8.3.1 noted that fire and vinegar dissolved flint rock. Livy 21.37, see skeptical commentary by the translator B. O. Foster.

30. Pliny 23.57; 33.71 and 94. Livy 21.37. Modern vinegar experiments: Healy 1999, 131–33.

31. Aeneas 33–35, and Whitehead's commentary pp. 197–98.

32. Pliny 15.1. Alum for Delphi: Herodotus 2.180. Alum in the Mithradatic Wars: Aulus Gellius 15.1; Mayor 2010, 92, 198–99. Constantine: Ammianus Marcellinus 20.6.13. See Partington 1999, 5.

33. Aeneas 33–35. Ancient fire retardants: Partington 1999, 5, 201.

34. Aeneas 33–35. For fire-extinguishing methods in practice, see Diodorus of Sicily 13.85.5; 14.51.2–3; 14.108.4. Cyzicus: Appian, "Mithridatic Wars" 12.73–78; Mayor 2010, 271–72.

35. Polyaenus 6.3.3; excerpts 56.3.6. The "powers of vinegar": Pliny 23.54–57.

36. Dust: Echols 1952. Smoke screens: Polyaenus 2.3 (Epaminondas); 3.9.7 and 3.9.41 (Iphicrates); 5.10.4 (Himilco); 2.4.1 (Pelopidas). Aeneas 37.3. China: Temple 1991, 215–17 (fumigants and poison gases for military use).

37. Croddy 2002, 127, citing the encyclopedic *Science and Civilisation in China*, Needham 1965. Croddy claims that Thucydides reported arsenic smoke used by the Spartans, but there is no mention of arsenic by Thucydides. Neufeld 1980, 38 and n. 26. Chemical smoke from burning sulfur or arsenic was used as a pesticide in antiquity (against lice, mites, fleas, wasps, etc.) by the Egyptians, Sumerians, and Chinese (2500 to 1200 BC), and burning sulfur and tar were used to repel insects in ancient Greece and Rome, according to Homer and Cato. Ancient Chinese insect fumigation techniques led to military uses of poison gases: Temple 1991, 215. Chinese smoke generators were used in siege mine warfare: James 2011, 97 n. 114, citing Needham 1965, 4:137–38.

38. Kautilya 1951, 434, 441–45, 457. Rahman 2002. Partington 1999, 209–11 (*Arthashastra*); 263, 284–85 (poison smokes in China and the New World).

39. Thanks to Alexander Samuel, molecular biologist and tear gas historian, for information on uses of "enfoumade," early smoke and dust weapons, including Japanese *metsubushi*, personal correspondence January 2–5, 2021. Traditional samurai considered the unconventional tactics and weaponry of ninja ("spies, mercenaries") to be dishonorable. On severity of modern tear gas injuries, Samuel and Picot 2020.

40. Weasels and magnets: Partington 1999, 149.

41. Creveld 1991, 25, on smoke in tunnels. Polybius 21.28.11–17. Polyaenus 5.10.4–5; 6.17. Incineration of poultry feathers, which constitute thousands of tons of waste per year around the world today, causes air pollution.

42. Most of the features and reconstruction of the skirmish in the tunnel mentioned in James 2011 were revealed by major excavations at Dura-Europos in 1920–37 by teams from France and Yale University, and after 1986 by French-Syrian teams. The basic facts of the underground battle were reconstructed in 1935, by R. Du Mesnil du Buisson, in the Sixth Season Report by Yale University and French Academy of Inscriptions and Letters, *The Excavations at Dura-Europos*, ed. M. Rostovtzeff et al., 188–205 and plate XVIII. This report stated that, based on the evidence of the skeletons and extensive fire damage, the Persians fought off the Romans inside the tunnel and set fire to straw using pitch (combustible tar) and sulfur to burn the timbers supporting the Romans' countertunnel. James 2011 suggests that earlier researchers had not observed the remains of pitch and sulfur crystals near the bodies. But the 1935 report did describe the residue of pitch and yellow sulfur crystals in a jar lying near the bodies, without pursuing the toxic gas idea, and their findings and implications were noted by Partington 1999, 171 and n. 154. Some argue that sulfur and pitch were used in torches, Farrokh 2017, 257–59.

43. Plutarch, *Sertorius*. Gypsum is soft calcium sulfate dihydrate, used to make drywall and chalk. When chalk was used to write on school blackboards, the brick-sized felt erasers had to be cleaned by being clapped together vigorously. I was often assigned this duty as a girl: the chore took place in the school boiler room and created unpleasant clouds of chalk dust, a small replication of the weapon devised by Sertorius.

44. Chinese "tear gas" –type weapons, see Temple 1991, 217. Partington 1999, 18, on Byzantine quicklime dust.

45. Partington 1999, 209–11, Kautilya's toxic smokes, powders, and incendiaries; Kautilya 1951 and 1992. Taking winds into account in early Chinese gunpowder weapons, Andrade 2017, 63.

46. Islamic smoke weapons: Hashmi 2004. Mongols: Partington 1999, 250. *Lethal in Disguise* 2016, 38–53.

47. Pliny 36.54. Theophrastus *On Stones*, 64–68.

48. See Forbes 1964, 96 on *pyr automaton*. Livy 39.13.1. Kings 18.23–38. On ancient knowledge of these chemicals, Bailey 1929–32, 1.111, 199, 209–10, 244–45; 2.121, 251–56, 272–77. See Mayor 1997b on combustible formulas in myth and history.

49. Some date the recipe in the compilation attributed to Africanus to the sixth century AD. Partington 1999, 6–10. Fragments of Africanus's writings have been found in the Oxyrhynchus manuscript, at Oxford University.

50. Seneca, *Medea* 817–34. See also Rose 1959, 204. Pliny 2.235–36; 35.178–82; 36.174. Plutarch *Alexander* 35.5.

51. The Pulitzer Prize–winning photo of Phan Thi Kim Phúc by Associated Press photographer Nick Ut, was taken in 1972 at Trang Bang, Vietnam. The full story is told in Chong 2000; for the girl's fate, Cotton 2013. Napalm (naphthene thickened with palmitate) canisters were ignited by superhot white phosphorus. On napalm's invention and its various formulas and uses from World War II through the 1970s, see SIPRI, *Incendiary Weapons* 1975, 39–67, 91–97, 122–55 (effects of chemical burns); Perry 2001; Taylor 2001; Cotton 2013.

52. Petroleum deposits of the Caucasus region, Medea's mythic homeland, between the Black Sea and the Caspian Sea: Haldon 2006.

53. On geography of petroleum, see Partington 1999, 3–5. For classifications, definitions, and locations of bituminous petroleum surface deposits in the ancient world, see Forbes 1964, who also surveys ancient references to petroleum and archaeological evidence for its uses. Baba Gurgur: Bilkadi 1995, 25.

54. Nehemiah: 2 Maccabees 1.19–30. Partington 1999, 6.

55. Forbes 1964, see 91 for Assyrian criminals punished with hot petroleum, and 29, 40–41 for oil deposits in India.

56. Herodotus 6.119. Ctesias quoted by Aelian, *On Animals* 5.3.
57. Philostratus, *Apollonius of Tyana* 3.1. On ancient descriptions of naphtha in India: Partington 1999, 209–11. Crude petroleum deposits exist in northern India and Pakistan.
58. Strabo 16.1.15 described fountains of burning naphtha and other forms of petroleum in Babylon.
59. Alexander's experiment was described by Strabo 16.1.15 and by Plutarch, *Alexander* 35. Forbes 1964, 23–28; Classical scholar David Sansone 1980 sees Plutarch's narrative of the dangerous experiment with naphtha as an extended metaphorical commentary on Alexander's "fiery temperament."
60. Philostratus, *Apollonius of Tyana* 2.33.
61. Ali et al. 2006.
62. *Arthashastra*: Partington 1999, 209–11. Kautilya 1951, 434. Shukra's *Nitishastra* also describes incendiary balls flung at foes in ancient India: Kokatnur 1948, 269.
63. Ammianus Marcellinus 23.6.15.
64. Cassius Dio, *Epitome* 76.10–12. Naphtha's ability to combust air, burn in water, and pursue fleeing victims: Pliny 2.235–41.
65. On burn injuries and smoke inhalation from fire weapons, see SIPRI, *Incendiary Weapons* 1975, chap. 3, and 187–99.
66. Naphtha incendiaries in battles of AD 551 and 588: Farrokh 2017, 60–61, 249, 253, 269, 272. The Parthian Empire, 247 BC to AD 224, was succeeded by the equally long-lived Sasanian Empire, the last state of pre-Islamic Iran, AD 224 to AD 651.
67. Arab legends of Alexander's inventions of incendiaries: Partington 1999, 47, 58, 198, 200–201; on petroleum weapons in India, 209–11. Illustration of the "Naphtha wall," *Shahnama*, Iran, 1330s, Arthur Sackler Gallery, S1986, 104, Smithsonian, Washington DC.
68. Thaqif: Hashmi 2004.
69. Mangonels and *naffatun*: Bilkadi 1995, 23–27. Partington 1999, 189–227. Asbestos was known to Pliny 36.139: "Asbestos looks like alum and is completely fireproof." Ancient Persians imported from India a "stone wool," magic cloth cleansed by fire, used for magic tricks. Asbestos in war: Forbes 1964, 100; see also Partington 1999, 22, 201, 207 and fig. 11 (burning riders in Islamic armies). According

to Crosby 2002, 91, the Mongols used trebuchets to hurl naphtha bombs.

70. Partington 1999, 25; Bilkadi 1995.

71. Miller and Vieth 2003.

72. Archaeological discoveries of naphtha pots from destruction of Cairo in AD 1167–68: Bilkadi 1995.

73. Kautilya 1951, 434. Accidental explosions of Greek Fire mixtures: Forbes 1964, 96, citing Leo's military handbook of the ninth century AD. Crosby 2002, 89, 96–97. SIPRI, *Incendiary Weapons* 1975, 91, 106–7. Partington 1999, 24–25 (Acre); 28–32; 45.

74. Mecca: Bilkadi 1995, and see Nardin 1996, 164–65, on the Quran's ban on fighting near the Ka'aba, 2.191.

75. Chinese warnings and naval disaster: Temple 1991, 228, 230; and see Croddy 2002, 130, quoting historian Shi Xubai, cited by Needham. In the thirteenth century AD, the Chinese defended against specially trained "naphtha troops" of the Mongol Hulagu Khan, Kublai Khan's predecessor, by covering dwellings with roof mats of grass coated with clay.

76. Crosby 2002, 89–92, quote 92. Partington 1999.

77. Roland 1992 on the secret technology of Greek Fire and the defense of Byzantium. The ancient source for Kallinikos's invention of Greek Fire is Theophanes.

78. Haldon 2006 summarizes the scholarship and theories about Greek Fire's invention, recipe for the ammunition, storage under pressure, and complex deployment system, and describes his dangerous and successful experiment to reproduce the ancient apparatus and to demonstrate propelling Greek Fire to burn another ship at Malta, for the UK television show *Machines Time Forgot*, 2003. For another, more recent re-creation by chemical weapons expert Stephen Bull, see Smithsonian Channel episode "How Greek Fire Was Used to Target Enemy Ships," Smithsonian Channel, *World of Weapons: War at Sea* series, April 13, 2020. https://www.youtube.com/watch?v=lPUgvYZ5UDk.

79. Roland 1990, quotes 18; and see diagram on 19 for a reconstruction of the Greek Fire system. The famous medieval image of a Byzantine ship propelling Greek Fire in a naval battle of AD 821 is from the Greek illu-

minated manuscript by John Scylitzes, ca. AD 1181, National Library, Madrid.

80. Petroleum weapons: Forbes 1964, 33–41, 99–100; Byzantine hand-syringes for squirting Greek Fire, 96 and figs. See Partington 1999, 21 and 26; 10–41, 44; for modern chemists' reconstruction of Greek Fire, see Bert Hall's introduction, xxi–xxiii.; see also Roland 1992. See Haldon 2006 for the most recent knowledge of Greek Fire. For the development of Muslim oil weapons, see Bilkadi 1995. On early medieval Muslim-Asian exchange of naphtha weapon knowledge, Croddy 2002, 128–30. According to Healy 1999, 121, Pliny anticipated the basis for the process of modern fractional distillation, in *Natural History* 31.81. On the question of whether Pliny described saltpeter, see Healy 134, 198–99; and Partington 298–306. The first military use of gunpowder was linked (as the ignition source) to Greek Fire deployed by Chinese warships in about AD 900. Croddy 2002, 129, citing the Chinese *Gunpowder Epic*. The Byzantine historian Theophanes wrote that enemies "shivered in terror, recognizing how strong the liquid fire was." Crosby 2002, 90. Forbes 1964, 98, for capitulation to Greek Fire: a Russian fleet of a thousand ships retreated from fifteen Byzantine ships carrying Greek Fire in AD 941.

81. The Mithradatic Wars are fully described in Mayor 2010: see esp. chap. 1 (massacre); 265–314 (Lucullus).

82. Appian, "Mithridatic Wars" 12.18–23; Mayor 2010, 146–50.

83. Cassius Dio 36.4–6; and Xiphilinus 36.1b. Croddy 2002, 128.

84. Cassius Dio 36.5–8.

85. Mayor 2010, 302–3 (Samosata).

86. Cassius Dio 36.4–6. Pliny 2.235. The strategic open oil pits near Hatra, Samosata, and Tigranocerta were guarded by early Muslim "oil czars"; see Bilkadi 1995, 25. The ruins of Samosata (Samsat, Turkey), the ancient capital of Commagene, were inundated in the late twentieth century by the Ataturk Dam. These rich petroleum fields now produce tens of thousands of barrels of oil in northern Iraq and southeastern Turkey.

87. Muhammad: Partington 1999, 189.

88. Cassius Dio, Xiphilinus 36.1b. Appian, "Mithridatic Wars" 12.77. Pliny 2.235; 34.93; see also 35.178–82. Mayor 2010. The ancient statue of

Heracles in the tunic has not survived. Ironically, in the second century BC, before Roman armies had experienced attacks by fiery naphtha, Roman soldiers desecrated the famous painting of Heracles dying in the poison robe, painted in 360 BC by the Greek artist Aristeides. During their sack of Corinth, it was among the fine paintings that the soldiers pulled to the ground and used to throw dice on. Strabo 8.6.23.

89. Mayor 2010, 275–76.

90. Plutarch, *Lucullus*. Mayor 1997b, 58. Seneca, *Epistles* 14.4–6. Martial, *Epigrams* 4.86, 10.25. Juvenal 1.155, 8.235 and nn. Coleman 1990, 60–61.

AFTERWORD. THE MANY-HEADED HYDRA

1. Lucretius, *On the Nature of the Universe* 5.1295–1308. Appian, "Mithridatic Wars" 12.74.

2. Vozrozhdeniya Island in the Aral Sea: "Poisoned Island" 1999; Pala 2003. Biopreparat: Alibek 2000; Williams 2006. On worst-case scenarios posed by biochemical weapons, see Miller, Engelberg, and Broad 2001. Numerous incidents of bioweapon accidents between 1915 and 1946 are described in Harris and Paxman 2002. More recent US bioweapons accidents: Piller 2003; D'Arcangelis 2015; Teoh 2020; Guterl et al. 2020. See also Koblentz 2011 on the history of biological weapons in Europe, Russia, America, South Africa, and Iraq.

3. Chemical Weapons Convention: https://www.opcw.org/chemical -weapons-convention. The storage site at Pueblo Facility, Colorado, holds more than 3,000 tons of mustard agents in artillery shells and mortars, to be destroyed by biotreatment and detonation carried out by robots. Johnson 2019; Army Technology News 2020. The US Army Medical Research Institute of Chemical Defense still operates at Aberdeen Proving Ground, Maryland. For the history of chemical weapons storage sites and disposal, see CDC website: https://www.cdc.gov /nceh/demil/history.htm.

4. Incinerating and burying biochemical weapons: Leary 2002; Wald 2002. Vitrification of nuclear weapons material is carried out at Savannah River, South Carolina. Burial of transuranic (high-level radioactive) materials from nuclear weapons in the Waste Isolation Pilot Plant (WIPP) near Carlsbad began in 1999. Early boreholes in

the salt beds were rejected because of fears of potential leakage due to geologic deformations and pressurized brine, but the present site is said to have been "stable for more than 200 million years," so the weapon materials are deemed to be safely stored forever (by "forever" the government means ten thousand years). Waste began to be stored again at WIPP in 2017: Conca 2017. WIPP website: https://www.wipp .energy.gov/.

5. The Yucca Mountain plan is for storing radioactive material from nuclear reactors, not weapons. The US Geological Service determined that leakage of toxic fluids from chemical weapons buried in deep wells at Rocky Mountain Arsenal reduced friction and allowed slippage along fault planes, resulting in earthquakes. In May 2021, the Department of Energy announced that Yucca Mountain was not supported by President Joe Biden's administration. Thanks to Will Keener, Sandia National Laboratories, personal correspondence, February 10–14, 2003, for facts and helpful comments about Rocky Mountain Arsenal, Carlsbad WIPP, and Yucca Mountain. Yucca Mountain: Jaczko 2019, chap. 4; University of Nevada Yucca Mountain Research Collection: https://guides.library.unr.edu/yuccamountain/collectionhistory.

6. Gordon 2019. Information about various European geological repositories is available online at Wikipedia.

7. Pala 2003. "Nerve Gas" 2000. Baltic: Gordon 2019. Washington, DC, and other chemical munitions dump sites: Tucker 2001. Presidio: "Vile Finds" 2003.

8. The Human Interference Task Force, created in 1981 by the US Department of Energy (DOE), solicited suggestions beginning in 1993 for long-term warnings and nuclear semiotics to help Sandia National Laboratories plan the Carlsbad weapons burial site, but the concepts, updated with the latest technologies, are required for all such repositories. Pollon 2002; Hutchinson 2002; Pethokoukis 2002; Macfarlane and Ewing 2006; Gordon 2019. Detailed DOE information on proposals for warning succeeding generations ten thousand years into the future, based on Trauth, Hora, and Guzowski 1993, was provided by Steve Casey, WIPP Carlsbad Field Office, February 12, 2003. For further information: https://digital.library.unt.edu/ark: /67531/metadc1279277/.

9. Schwartz 2015; semiotician Thomas Seboek came up with atomic priests; sci-fi writer Stanislaw Lem proposed DNA in plants. The "radiation cats" idea was proposed by philosophers Françoise Bastide and Paolo Fabbri, 1984. These nuclear semiotics plans and others are summarized by Piesing 2020. On the Ray Cat Solution, see Bricobio's award-winning animated film and other information http://www .theraycatsolution.com/#10000.

10. Blanquer quoted by Gordon 2019. See WIPP information: https:// wipp.info/.

11. Anthropologist Ward Goodenough quoted in Forest 2002. "Remember to forget" from the 2010 Finnish documentary film *Into Eternity*, about Onkalo repository: Gordon 2019.

BIBLIOGRAPHY

ANCIENT GREEK AND LATIN SOURCES

Unless otherwise noted, the Greek and Latin texts are available in translation in the Loeb Classical Library, published by Harvard University Press, Cambridge, Massachusetts.

Aelian, *On Animals*; *Historical Miscellany*

[Aeneas] Aineias the Tactician, *How to Survive under Siege*. Trans. and comm. David Whitehead. Oxford: Clarendon Press, 1990.

Aeschines, *Against Ctesiphon*; *On the Embassy*

Ammianus Marcellinus, *Roman History*

Apollodorus, *Library*; *Epitome*

Appian, *Roman History*

Aristophanes, *Knights*

Arrian, *History of Alexander*

Aulus Gellius, *Attic Nights*

Cassius Dio, *Epitome*; *Roman History*

Celsus, *De medicina*

Cicero, *On Duties*; *Pro sestio*

Cornelius Nepos

Ctesias, *History of Persia, Tales of the Orient*. Trans. and comm. L. Llewellyn-Jones and J. Robson. London: Routledge, 2010.

Diodorus of Sicily, *Library of History*

Diogenes Laertius, *Lives of the Philosophers*

Euripides, *Medea*

Florus

Frontinus, *Stratagems*

Galen

Herodian

Herodotus, *Histories*

Historia Augusta. Lives of the Later Caesars. Trans. Anthony Birley. Harmondsworth: Penguin, 1976.

Homer, *Iliad*; *Odyssey*

Isocrates, *Plataicus*

Josephus, *Jewish Antiquities*

Justinius

Juvenal

Leo's *Tactica. The Taktika of Leo VI: Text, Translation and Commentary* (CFHB 49). Trans. and comm. D. T. Dennis, Dumbarton Oaks: Washington, DC, 2010.

Livy, *Roman History*

Lucan, *Civil War*

Lucian of Samosata. *Works*. Trans. H. W. and F. G. Fowler. Oxford: Clarendon Press, 1905.

Lucretius, *On the Nature of the Universe*

Lycurgus, *Against Leocrates*

Martial, *Epigrams*

Oppian, *Halieutica*

Orosius, *Histories against the Pagans*

Ovid, *Metamorphoses*; *Tristia*; *Letters from Pontus*

Pausanias, *Description of Greece*. Trans. Peter Levi. 2 vols. Harmondsworth: Penguin, 1984.

Philostratus, *Heroes*; *Apollonius of Tyana*

Pliny the Elder, *Natural History*

Plutarch, *Moralia*; *Lives of Alexander*; *Artaxerxes*; *Lucullus*; *Marcellus*; *Nicias*; *Sertorius*; *Solon*

Polyaenus, *Stratagems of War*. Ed. and trans. Peter Krentz and Everett Wheeler. 2 vols. Chicago: Ares, 1994.

Polybius, *Histories*

Procopius, *History of the Wars of Justinian*

Pseudo-Aristotle, *On Marvelous Things Heard*

Quintus Curtius Rufus, *History of Alexander*

Quintus of Smyrna, *Fall of Troy*

Sallust, *Jugurthine War*

Seneca, *On Anger*; *Epistles*; *Medea*

Silius Italicus, *Punica*

Sophocles, *Philoctetes*; *Trachinian Women*

Strabo, *Geography*

Suetonius, *The Twelve Caesars*. Trans. Robert Graves. Harmondsworth: Penguin, 1979.

Tacitus, *Annals*; *Germania*; *Histories*

Theophanes. *Corpus Scriptorum Historiae Byzantinae*. Ed. B. G. Niebuhr, 1:540–42. *Compendium Hist.* (ed. Bekker, Bonn, 1839), 765.

Theophrastrus, *On Stones*

Thucydides, *History of the Peloponnesian War*

Valerius Flaccus, *Argonautica*

Varro, *De re rustica*

Vegetius, *On Military Matters*

Virgil, *Aeneid*; *Georgics*

Vitruvius, *On Architecture*

Xenophon, *Anabasis*; *Cyropaedia*; *Hellenica*

Xiphilinus

MODERN WORKS

Aftergood, Steven. 2001. "Djinn Energy." *Federation of American Scientists Secrecy News*, October 30. https://fas.org/sgp/news/secrecy/2001/10/102901.html.

Ahmadi, Sorour Farrokh. 2020. "Bioethics in War, Biological Weapons and Genetic Means of Warfare." PhD diss., Faculty of Law. McGill University.

Aldinger, Charles. 2002. "Bioweapons Tested in US, Records Say." Reuters news story, Washington, DC, October.

Ali, Syed Hamad. 2016. "Pakistan's Pseudoscience Menace." *Gulf News*, November 10. https://gulfnews.com/lifestyle/pakistans-pseudoscience-menace-1.1927430.

Ali, Taj, et al. 2006. "Southern Asia's Oldest Incendiary Missile?" *Archaeometry* 48:641–55.

Alibek, Ken, with Stephen Handelman. 2000. *Biohazard: The Chilling True Story of the Largest Covert Biological Weapons Program in the World.* New York: Random House.

Ambrose, John. 1974. "Insects in Warfare." *Army*, December, 33–38.

Andrade, Tonio. 2017. *The Gunpowder Age: China, Military Innovation, and the Rise of the West in World History.* Princeton, NJ: Princeton University Press.

Angier, Natalie. 2002. "Venomous and Sublime: The Viper Tells Its Tale." Science Times, *New York Times*, December 10.

Aratani, Lauren. 2019. "Licence to Krill: Why the US Navy Trains Whales, Dolphins, and Sea Lions." *Guardian*, May 1.

Armbruster, Barbara. 2009. "Gold Technology of the Ancient Scythians— Gold from the Kurgan Arzhan 2, Tuva." *ArcheoSciences* 33:187–93.

Army Technology News. 2020. "US Extends Bechtel Contract for Chemical Weapons Destruction." April 2. https://www.army-technology .com/news/us-extends-bechtel-contract-for-chemical-weapons-destruction/.

Bailey, K. C. 1929–32. *The Elder Pliny's Chapters on Chemical Subjects.* London: Edward Arnold.

Balmer, Brian. 2016. *Secrecy and Science: A Historical Sociology of Biological and Chemical Warfare.* London: Routledge.

Barker, Hannah. 2021. "Laying the Corpses to Rest: Grain, Embargoes, and *Yersinia pestis* in the Black Sea, 1346–1348." *Speculum* 91, 1 (January): 97–126.

Bartosiewicz, László. 2014. "Camels in the Front Line." *Anthropozoologica* 49, 2:297–302.

Bastide, Françoise, and Paolo Fabbri. 1984. "Living Detectors." *Zeitschrift fur Semiotik* 6, 3:257–64.

Bercé, Yves-Marie. 1993. "Les semeurs de peste." In *La vie, la mort, le temps: Mélanges offerts à Pierre Chaunu*, ed. J. P. Bardet and R. M. Foisil, 85–94. Paris: PUF.

Berson, Josh. 2016. "Sound and Pain." *Technosphere Magazine*, November 15. https://technosphere-magazine.hkw.de/p/Sound-and-Pain -cNunTfEa1zYsN4UKa4scx2.

Bilkadi, Zayn. 1995. "The Oil Weapons—Ancient Oil Industries." *Aramco World*, January–February, 22–27.

Bonner, Campbell. 1956. "The Sibyl and Bottle Imps." In *Quantulacumque: Studies Presented to Kirsopp Lake*, ed. R. P. Casey et al., 1–8. London: n.p.

Borgia, Valentina. 2019. "The Prehistory of Poison Arrows." In Wexler 2019, 1–10.

Bradford, Alfred. 2001. *With Arrow, Sword, and Spear: A History of Warfare in the Ancient World*. Westport, CT: Praeger.

Broad, William J. 2002. "Oh, What a Lovely War. If No One Dies." *New York Times*, November 3.

Buhler, Georg, trans. 1886. *Laws of Manu*. Oxford: Oxford University Press.

Burns, Mike. 2005. "Review of Total War." *Archaeology*, March–April, 54.

Campbell, Duncan B. 1986. "What Happened at Hatra?" In *Defence of the Roman and Byzantine East*, ed. P.W.M. Freeman and D. L. Kennedy, 51–58. Oxford: Oxford University Press.

Carey, Daniel. 2003. "The Political Economy of Poison: The Kingdom of Makassar and the Early Royal Society." *Renaissance Studies* 17, 3 (October): 517–43.

Carmichael, Mary. 2003. "WMD: They're History." *Newsweek*, October 5. https://www.newsweek.com/wmd-theyre-history-138823.

Chen, Stephen. 2019. "Chinese Scientists Develop Hand-Held Sonic Weapon for Crowd Control." *South China Morning Post*, September 19. https://www.scmp.com/news/china/science/article/3028071/chinese-scientists-develop-handheld-sonic-weapon-crowd-control.

Chong, Denise. 2000. *The Girl in the Picture: The Story of Kim Phuc, the Photograph, and the Vietnam War*. New York: Viking Press.

Christopher, George, Theodore Cieslak, Julie Pavlin, and Edward Eitzen. 1997. "Biological Warfare: A Historical Perspective." *JAMA* 278:412–17.

Ciaraldi, Marina. 2000. "Drug Preparation in Evidence." *Vegetation History and Archaeobotany* 9 (July): 91–98.

———. 2007. *People and Plants in Ancient Pompeii*. London: Accordia.

Cole, Leonard. 1996. "The Specter of Biological Weapons." *Scientific American* 275, 6 (December): 60–65.

Coleman, Kathleen. 1990. "Fatal Charades: Roman Executions Staged as Mythological Enactments." *Journal of Roman Studies* 80:44–73.

Colvin, Marie, and Uzi Mahnaimi. 1998. "Saddam Tested Anthrax on Human Guinea Pigs." *London Sunday Times*, January 18.

Conca, James. 2017. "WIPP Nuclear Waste Repository Reopens for Business." *Forbes*, January 10. https://www.forbes.com/sites/jamesconca

/2017/01/10/wipp-nuclear-waste-repository-reopens-for-business
/#5a22708e2052.

Conybeare, F. C. 1898. "The Testament of Solomon." *Jewish Quarterly Review* 11 (October): 1–45.

Cotton, Simon. 2013. "Explainer: What Is Napalm?" *The Conversation*, September 5. https://theconversation.com/explainer-what-is-napalm -17795.

Cowley, Robert, and Geoffrey Parker, eds. 1996. *The Reader's Companion to Military History.* Boston: Houghton Mifflin.

Crespigny, Rafe de. 2007. *A Biographical Dictionary of Later Han to the Three Kingdoms (23–220 AD).* Leiden: Brill.

Creveld, Martin van. 1991. "The Gulf Crisis and the Rules of War." *MHQ: Quarterly Journal of Military History* 3, 4 (Summer): 23–27.

Croddy, Eric. 2002. *Chemical and Biological Warfare.* New York: Springer-Verlag.

Crosby, Alfred W. 2002. *Throwing Fire: Projectile Technology through History.* Cambridge: Cambridge University Press.

D'Archangelis, Gwen. 2015. "U.S. Bioweapons Research: Are Anthrax Lab Accidents All We Have to Fear?" *Biopolitical Times*, June 10. https:// www.geneticsandsociety.org/biopolitical-times/us-bioweapons -research-are-anthrax-lab-accidents-all-we-have-fear.

Dean, K. R., F. Krauer, L. Walloe, O. C. Lingjaerde, B. Bramanti, N. C. Stenseth, and B. V. Schmid. 2018. "Human Ecoparasites and the Spread of Plague in Europe in the Second Pandemic." *Proceedings of the National Academy of Sciences* 115, 6:1304–9.

Department of Veterans Affairs. 2014. *Gulf War Illness and the Health of Gulf War Veterans: Research Update and Recommendations, 2009–2013: Updated Scientific Findings.* May.

Dekker, Peter. 2013. "Whistling Arrows and Whistle Arrows." *Manchu Archery*, April 25. http://www.manchuarchery.org/content/whistling -arrows-and-whistle-arrows.

Derbes, V. J. 1966. "De Mussis and the Great Plague of 1348: A Forgotten Episode of Bacteriological War." *JAMA* 196:59–62.

Dirlmeier, Franz. 1966. *Die Giftpfeile des Odysseus (zu Odyssee 1, 252–266).* Heidelberg: Carl Winter.

Dolgin, Elie. 2020. "Kill Switch for CRISPR Could Make Gene Editing Safer." *Scientific American*, reprinted from *Nature*, January 17. https://www.scientificamerican.com/article/kill-switch-for-crispr-could-make-gene-editing-safer/.

Drummond, Andrew J. 1989. "Ammianus Marcellinus and the Roman Rules of War of the Fourth Century A.D." MA thesis, University of Kansas.

Echols, Edward. 1952. "Military Dust." *Classical Journal* 47:285–88.

Eitzen, E. M., Jr., and E. T. Takafuji. 1997. "Historical Overview of Biological Warfare." In *Textbook of Military Medicine: Medical Aspects of Chemical and Biological Warfare*, chap. 18. Washington, DC: US Department of the Army.

El Fadl, Khaled Abou. 2007. "The Rules of Killing at War: An Inquiry into Classical Sources." *Muslim World* 89, 2 (1999): 144–57 (pub. 2007).

Eveleth, Rose. 2012. "Here's How to Make a Scorpion Bomb." *Smithsonian*, December 6. https://www.smithsonianmag.com/smart-news/heres-how-to-make-a-scorpion-bomb-154013653/.

Faraone, Christopher. 1992. *Talismans and Trojan Horses*. New York: Oxford University Press.

Farrokh, Kaveh. 2017. *The Armies of Ancient Persia: The Sassanians*. Barnsley, UK: Pen & Sword.

Fenn, Elizabeth. 2000. "Biological Warfare in Eighteenth-Century North America: Beyond Jeffery Amherst." *Journal of American History* 86 (March): 1552–80.

Finnegan, William. 2001. "The Poison Keeper." *New Yorker*, January 15, 58–64.

Flora, S.J.S., and Vidhu Pachauri, eds. 2020. *Handbook on Biological Warfare Preparedness*. London: Elsevier.

Forbes, R. J. 1964. *Bitumen and Petroleum in Antiquity*. 2nd ed. Leiden: Brill.

Forest, David. 2002. "Burial Ground: Fear and Loathing at Yucca Mountain." *On Earth*, Summer, 20–21.

Frontline Report. 1997. PBS television transcript of "A Whale of a Business: The Story of Navy Dolphins." November 11.

Gantz, Timothy. 1993. *Early Greek Myth: A Guide to Literary and Artistic Sources*. 2 vols. Baltimore: Johns Hopkins University Press.

Gibbons-Neff, Thomas. 2016. "Saudi Arabia Using White Phosphorus Supplied by US in Yemen"; "US Forces Are Using White Phosphorus Munitions in Iraq." *Washington Post*, September 19, 23.

Goldstein, Laurie. 2001. "Islamic Scholars Call September 11 Attacks a Distortion of Islam." *New York Times*, September 30.

Gordon, Helen. 2019. "How Do You Leave a Warning That Lasts as Long as Nuclear Waste? *Mosaic* and *Phys Org News*, September 10. https://phys.org/news/2019-09-nuclear.html and https://mosaicscience.com/story/how-do-you-leave-warning-lasts-long-nuclear-waste/.

Grafton, Anthony. 1992. *New Worlds, Ancient Texts*. Cambridge, MA: Harvard University Press.

Grmek, Mirko. 1979. "Les ruses de guerre biologiques dans l'Antiquité." *Revue des Etudes Grecques* 92:139–63.

Grossman, Annabel. 2014. "ISIS Using Bombs Containing Live Scorpions in Effort to Spread Panic." *Daily Mail*, December 2014. https://www.dailymail.co.uk/news/article-2875968/ISIS-using-bombs-containing-live-SCORPIONS-effort-spread-panic-tactic-used-2–000-years-ago-against-Romans.html.

Guterl, Fred, et al. 2020. "The Controversial Experiments and Wuhan Virus Lab Suspected of Starting the Coronavirus Pandemic." "Dr. Fauci Backed Controversial Wuhan Lab [for] Risky Coronavirus Research." *Newsweek*, April 27 and 28. https://www.newsweek.com/controversial-wuhan-lab-experiments-that-may-have-started-coronavirus-pandemic-1500503; https://www.newsweek.com/dr-fauci-backed-controversial-wuhan-lab-millions-us-dollars-risky-coronavirus-research-1500741.

Haldon, John. 2006. "Greek Fire Revisited: Recent and Current Research." In *Byzantine Style, Religion and Civilization*, ed. E. Jeffreys, 291–325. Cambridge: Cambridge University Press.

Hanson, Marta. 2012. *Speaking of Epidemics in Chinese Medicine*. London: Routledge.

Harper, Kyle. 2017. *Fate of Rome: Climate, Disease, and the End of an Empire*. Princeton, NJ: Princeton University Press.

———. 2021. *Plagues upon the Earth: Disease and the Course of Human History*. Princeton, NJ: Princeton University Press.

Harris, Diane. 1995. *The Treasures of the Parthenon and Erechtheion.* Oxford: Clarendon.

Harris, Robert, and Jeremy Paxman. 2002 [1982]. *A Higher Form of Killing: The Secret Story of Chemical and Biological Warfare.* Rev. ed. Harmondsworth: Arrow.

Harrison, S. J. 1994. "Yew and Bow: Vergil *Georgics* 2.448." *Harvard Studies in Classical Philology* 96:201–2.

Hashmi, Sohail. 2004. "Islamic Ethics and Weapons of Mass Destruction: An Argument for Nonproliferation." In Hashmi and Lee 2004, 321–52.

Hashmi, Sohail, and Steven P. Lee, eds. 2004. *Ethics and Weapons of Mass Destruction Religious and Secular Perspectives.* Cambridge: Cambridge University Press.

Healy, John. 1999. *Pliny the Elder on Science and Technology.* Oxford: Oxford University Press.

Hodges, Kyle. 2009. "Researchers Narrow Gulf War Syndrome Causes." Army News Service, May 26. Washington, DC. https://www.army.mil/article/21654/researchers_narrow_gulf_war_syndrome_causes.

Howard, M., G. J. Andreopoulos, and M. R. Shulman, eds. 1994. *The Laws of War: Constraints on Warfare in the Western World.* New Haven, CT: Yale University Press.

Hsu, Jeremy. 2010. "Study: Archimedes Set Roman Ships Afire with Cannons." Live Science, June 28. https://www.livescience.com/8383-study-archimedes-set-roman-ships-afire-cannons.html.

Human Rights Watch. 2009. "Rain of Fire: Israel's Unlawful Use of White Phosphorus in Gaza." March 25. https://www.hrw.org/report/2009/03/25/rain-fire/israels-unlawful-use-white-phosphorus-gaza.

Hutchinson, Paul. 2002. "Warnings for the Year 11,997." www.ABCNEWS.com.

Jaczko, Gregory B. 2019. *Confessions of a Rogue Nuclear Regulator.* New York: Simon and Schuster.

James, Simon. 2011. "Stratagems, Combat, and 'Chemical Warfare' in the Siege Mines of Dura-Europos." *American Journal of Archaeology* 115: 69–101.

Jennison, George. 1971. *Noah's Cargo: Some Curious Chapters of Natural History.* New York: Blom.

Johnson, Stu. 2019. "Last U.S. Chemical Weapons Stockpile Set to Be Destroyed." NPR, Weekend Edition Saturday, March 23. https://www.npr.org/2019/03/23/706143989/last-u-s-chemical-weapons-stockpile-set-to-be-destroyed.

Johnston, Sarah Iles. 2002. "The *Testament of Solomon* from Late Antiquity to the Renaissance." In *The Metamorphosis of Magic*, ed. J. Bremmer and J. Veenstra, 35–49. Leuven: Peeters.

Jones, David E. 2007. *Poison Arrows: North American Indian Hunting and Warfare*. Austin: University of Texas Press.

Kahn, Dan'el. 2014. "The War of Sennacherib against Egypt as Described by Herodotus II 141." *Journal of Ancient Egyptian Interconnections* 6, 2:23–33.

Kahn, Joseph. 2002. "Shouting the Pain from Japan's Germ Attacks." *New York Times*, November 23.

Karunanithy, D. 2008. *Dogs of War: Canine Use in Warfare from Ancient Egypt to the Nineteenth Century*. London: Yarak.

Kautilya. 1951. *Arthashastra*. 4th ed. Trans. R. Shamasastry. Mysore: Sri Raghuveer Press.

———. 1992. *Arthashastra*. Trans. L. N. Rangarajan. Delhi: Penguin Classics.

Kelley, Matt. 2002. "Records Show U.S. Sent Germs to Iraq." *Newsday*, October 1, Associated Press.

Kistler, John. 2007. *War Elephants*. Lincoln: University of Nebraska Press.

Knapton, Sarah. 2019. "World Must Prepare for Biological Weapons That Target Ethnic Groups Based on Genetics." *Telegraph*, August 13.

Koblentz, Gregory D. 2011. *Living Weapons: Biological Warfare and International Security*. Ithaca, NY: Cornell University Press.

Kokatnur, Vaman R. 1948. "Chemical Warfare in Ancient India." *Journal of Chemical Education* 25:268–72.

Konijnendijk, Roel. 2018. *Classical Greek Tactics*. Leiden: Brill.

Krentz, Peter. 2002. "Fighting by the Rules: The Invention of the Hoplite Agon." *Hesperia* 71:23–39.

Lanni, Adriaan. 2008. "The Laws of War in Ancient Greece." *Law and History Review* 26, 3, "Law, War, and History" (Fall): 469–89.

Leary, Warren. 2002. "Scientific Panel Urges Incinerating Obsolete Chemical Arms." *New York Times*, December 4.

Lendon, J. E. 2006. *Soldiers and Ghosts: A History of Battle in Classical Antiquity*. New Haven, CT: Yale University Press.

Lesho, Emil, David Dorsey, and David Bunner. 1998. "Feces, Dead Horses, and Fleas: Evolution of the Hostile Use of Biological Agents." *Western Journal of Medicine* 168:512–16.

Lethal in Disguise: The Health Consequences of Crowd-Control Weapons. 2016. Physicians for Human Rights/International Network of Civil Liberties Organizations. https://www.aclu.org/sites/default/files/field_document/lethal_in_disguise_inclo_single_page.pdf.

Ling, Wang. 1947. "On the Invention and Use of Gunpowder and Firearms," *Isis* 37 (July): 160–78.

Lisle, John. 2020. "The Unsuccessful WWII Plot to Fight the Japanese with Radioactive Foxes." *Smithsonian*, September 29. https://www.smithsonianmag.com/history/unsuccessful-wwii-plot-fight-japanese-radioactive-foxes-180975932/.

Little, Lester K., ed. 2008. *The Plague and the End of Antiquity: The Pandemic of 541–750*. Cambridge: Cambridge University Press.

Lockwood, Jeffrey A. 1987. "Entomological Warfare: The History of the Use of Insects as Weapons of War." *Bulletin of the Entomological Society of America*, Summer, 76–82.

———. 2009. *Six-Legged Soldiers: Using Insects as Weapons of War*. Oxford: Oxford University Press.

———. 2014. "Scorpion Bombs: The Rest of the Story." Oxford University Press Blog, December 17. https://blog.oup.com/2014/12/scorpion-bombs-isis-insect-fear-terror/.

Lorenzi, Rossella. 2007. "Killer Donkeys Were First Bioweapons." Discovery News, December 3. https://www.abc.net.au/science/articles/2007/12/03/2108080.htm.

Macfarlane, Allison, and Rodney Ewing, eds. 2006. *Uncertainty Underground: Yucca Mountain and the Nation's High-Level Nuclear Waste*. Cambridge, MA: MIT Press.

Mackinnon, Amy, and Robbie Gramer. 2020. "What's Behind the Mysterious Illness of U.S. Diplomats and Spies?" *Foreign Policy,* October 21.

Majno, Guido. 1991 [1975]. *The Healing Hand: Man and Wound in the Ancient World*. Cambridge, MA: Harvard University Press.

Martin, Emmanuel. 2001. "Hadzabe: The Last Archers of Africa." *Primitive Archer* 10, 1:1–8

Maskiell, Michelle, and Adrienne Mayor. 2001. "Killer Khilats: Poisoned Robes of Honor in India., Parts 1 and 2." *Folklore* [London] 112:23–45, 163–82.

Mayor, Adrienne. 1995a. "Mad Honey." *Archaeology*, November–December, 32–40.

———. 1995b. "The Nessus Shirt in the New World: Smallpox Blankets in History and Legend." *Journal of American Folklore* 108:54–77.

———. 1997a. "Dirty Tricks in Ancient Warfare." *MHQ: Quarterly Journal of Military History* 10 (Autumn): 32–37.

———. 1997b. "Fiery Finery." *Archaeology*, March–April, 54–58.

———. 2010. *The Poison King: The Life and Legend of Mithradates, Rome's Deadliest Enemy.* Princeton, NJ: Princeton University Press.

———. 2013. "Greek Fire." In *The Encyclopedia of Ancient History*, ed. Roger Bagnall et al. London: Blackwell.

———. 2014. "Animals in Warfare." In *Oxford Handbook of Animals in Classical Thought and Life*, ed. Gordon L. Campbell, 282–93. Oxford: Oxford University Press.

———. 2015. "Biological and Chemical Warfare." In *Encyclopedia of the Roman Army*, ed. Yann Le Bohec. London: Wiley and Sons.

———. 2019a. "Mithridates of Pontus and His Universal Antidote." In Wexler 2019, 161–74.

———. 2019b. "Alexander the Great: A Questionable Death." In Wexler 2019, 151–59.

———. 2019c. "Chemical and Biological Warfare in Antiquity." In Wexler 2019, 243–54.

McLaughlin, Raoul. 2010. *Rome and the Distant East: Trade Routes to the Ancient Lands of Arabia, India, and China.* London: Continuum.

McNeill, William H. 1976. *Plagues and Peoples.* New York: Doubleday.

Meckler, Laura. 2002. "Mental Impact of Bioterror Studied." Associated Press report on the Biosecurity Conference, Las Vegas, NV, November 20.

Meek, James. 2002. "Live Rats Driven by Remote Control." *Guardian*, May 2.

Miller, Greg, and Warren Vieth. 2003. "Showdown with Iraq: U.S. Would Move to Safeguard Oil." *Los Angeles Times*, January 25, A9.

Miller, Judith. 1998. "Biological Weapons, Literally Older than Methuselah." *New York Times*, September 20.

———. 2002a. "Iraq Said to Try to Buy Antidote against Nerve Gas." *New York Times*, November 12.

———. 2002b. "C.I.A. Hunts Iraq Tie to Soviet Smallpox." *New York Times*, December 3.

Miller, Judith, Stephen Engelberg, and William Broad. 2001. *Germs: Biological Weapons and America's Secret War*. New York: Simon and Schuster.

Moon, Tom. 2000. *This Grim and Savage Game: OSS and the Beginning of U.S. Covert Operations in World War II*. New York: Da Capo Press.

Moreno, Jonathan D. 2016. "The Emerging Life Sciences and the National Security State." *Strategic Studies Quarterly*, Fall, 9–14.

Morgan, David. 1990. *The Mongols*. Oxford: Blackwell.

Murray, Oswyn, and Alfonso Moreno, eds. 2007. *A Commentary on Herodotus Books I–IV*. Oxford: Oxford University Press.

Nardin, Terry, ed. 1996. *The Ethics of War and Peace: Religious and Secular Perspectives*. Princeton, NJ: Princeton University Press.

Needham, Joseph. 1965. *Science and Civilisation in China*. Vol. 4, pt. 2. Cambridge: Cambridge University Press.

"Nerve Gas Discovered at Old Arsenal Near Denver." 2000. Associated Press story, *Chronicle* (Bozeman, MT), November 18.

Neufeld, Edward. 1980. "Insects as Warfare Agents in the Ancient Near East." *Orientalia* 49:30–57.

New Oxford Annotated Bible with the Apocrypha. 1973. Ed. H. G. May and B. M. Metzger. New York: Oxford University Press.

Newman, Cathy. 2005. "Twelve Toxic Tales." *National Geographic*, May.

Niiler, Eric. 2018. "Sonic Weapons' Long, Noisy History." History Channel, August 27. https://www.history.com/news/sonic-weapons-warfare-acoustic.

Ober, Josiah. 1994. "The Rules of War in Classical Greece." In Howard, Andreopoulos, and Shulman, 12–26, 227–30.

Onion, Amanda. 2002. "The No-Doze Soldier: Military Seeking Radical Ways of Stumping Need for Sleep." December 18, ABCNews.com.

"Origin of Covid-19." 2020. *Economist*, May 2, 67–65.

Oxford Classical Dictionary. 1996. 3rd ed. Ed. Simon Hornblower and Antony Spawforth. Oxford: Oxford University Press.

Pala, Christopher. 2003. "Anthrax Island." *New York Times Magazine*, January 12, 36–39.

Partington, J. R. 1999 [1960]. *A History of Greek Fire and Gunpowder.* Introduction by Bert S. Hall. Baltimore: Johns Hopkins University Press.

Pearson, Paul N. 2017. *Maximinus Thrax.* New York: Skyhorse.

Penzer, Norman. 1952. *Poison-Damsels and Other Essays in Folklore and Anthropology.* London: Sawyer.

Perry, Tony. 2001. "Relegating Napalm to Its Place in History." *Los Angeles Times*, April 1.

Pethokoukis, James M. 2002. "A Curse to Last 10,000 Years." *US News and World Report* 133, 5 (August 5): 51.

Phelps, Tony. 1981. *Poisonous Snakes.* Dorset: Blandford.

Piesing, Mark. 2020. "How to Build a Nuclear Warning for 10,000 Years' Time." BBC, August 3. https://www.bbc.com/future/article/20200731 -how-to-build-a-nuclear-warning-for-10000-years-time.

Piller, Charles. 2003. "Biodefense Lab on the Defensive." *New York Times*, February 12.

"Poisoned Island." 1999. *Economist,* July 10, 38.

Pollon, Christopher. 2002. "Danger! Do NOT Dig Here." *Archaeology*, May–June, 8.

Poupard, James, and Linda Miller. 1992. "History of Biological Warfare: Catapults to Capsomeres." *Annals of the New York Academy of Sciences* 666:9–20.

Rahman, Shaikh Azizur. 2002. "India Defence Looks to Ancient Text." BBC News, May 14.

Reinach, A. J. 1909. "La flèche en Gaule, ses poisons et ses contrepoisons." *Anthropologie* 20:51–80, 189–206.

Renic, Neil. 2020. *Asymmetric Killing: Risk Avoidance, Just War, and the Warrior Ethic.* Oxford: Oxford University Press.

Revkin, Andrew C. 2002. "Bees Learning Smell of Bombs with Backing from Pentagon." *New York Times*, May 13.

Rice, Jenna. 2020. "Animals in Ancient Greek Warfare: A Study of the Elephant, Camel, and Dog." PhD diss., University of Missouri.

"Rise of the Ray Gun." 2020. *Economist*, March 7, 71–72.

Robertson, Andres, and Laura Robertson. 1995. "From Asps to Allegations: Biological Warfare in History." *Military Medicine* 160:369–73.

Robertson, Hamish. 2002. "How San Hunters Use Beetles to Poison Their Arrows." Iziko Museums, Biodiversity Explorer website, Cape Town, South Africa, www.museums.org.za.

Robinson, Julian Perry. 2002. "Germs, Warfare, and the Human Impulse to Keep Them Apart." Paper presented at the Biotechnology, Weapons and Humanity Conference, sponsored by the International Committee of the Red Cross, Montreux, Switzerland, September 23–24.

Roland, Alex. 1990. "Greek Fire." *MHQ: The Quarterly Journal of Military History* 2 (Spring): 16–19.

———. 1992. "Secrecy, Technology and War: Greek Fire and the Defense of Byzantium." *Technology and Culture* 33, 4 (October): 655–79.

Rolle, Renate. 1989. *The World of the Scythians.* Trans. F. G. Walls. Berkeley: University of California Press.

Rose, H. J. 1959. *A Handbook of Greek Mythology.* New York: E. P. Dutton.

Ross, Alex. 2016. "The Sound of Hate: When Does Music Become Torture?" *New Yorker,* July 4, 65–69.

Rudenko, Sergei. 1970. *The Frozen Tombs of Siberia.* Berkeley: University of California Press.

"Sailors Sprayed with Nerve Gas in Test, Pentagon Says." 2002. *New York Times,* May 24.

Salazar, Christine F. 2000. *The Treatment of War Wounds in Graeco-Roman Antiquity.* Leiden: Brill.

Samuel, Alexander, and André Picot. 2020. "L'Utilisation du gaz lacrymogene CS: Ses effets toxiques" (An Assessment of CS Tear Gas: Public Health and Riot Control). Paris: Association Toxicologie-Chimie de Paris, June. https://www.gazlacrymo.fr/ANDREPICOT/CSgas.pdf

Sansone, David. 1980. "Plutarch, Alexander, and the Discovery of Naphtha." *Greek, Roman and Byzantine Studies* 21:63–74.

Sasson, Jack M., ed. 2000. *Civilizations of the Ancient Near East.* Peabody, MA: Hendrickson.

Sawyer, Ralph. 2007. *The Tao of Deception: Unorthodox Warfare in Historic and Modern China.* New York: Basic Books.

Scarborough, John. 1977. "Nicander's *Toxicology.* Snakes." *Pharmacy in History* 19, 1:3–23.

———. 1979. "Nicander's *Toxicology*: Spiders, Scorpions, Insects, and Myriapods, Parts I and II." *Pharmacy in History* 21, 1 and 2:3–35, 73–92.

Schultz, Harald. 1962. "Brazil's Big-Lipped Indians." *National Geographic* 1, 121 (January): 130–32.

Schwartz, Ariel. 2015. "Color-Changing Cats Were Once Part of a US Government Plan to Protect Humankind." *Tech Insider*, August 16. https://www.businessinsider.com/the-plan-to-protect-humans-from -radioactive-waste-with-cats-2015-8.

"The Science of Apartheid." 1998. *Harper's*, September, 19–25.

Scullard, H. H. 1974. *The Elephant in the Greek and Roman World*. Ithaca, NY: Cornell University Press.

Shachman, Noah. 2010. "U.S. Testing Pain Ray in Afganistan." "Pain Ray, Rejected by the Military, Ready to Blast L.A. Prisoners." *Wired*, June 19, August 24. https://www.wired.com/2010/06/u-s-testing-pain-ray -in-afghanistan/; https://www.wired.com/2010/08/pain-ray-rejected -by-the-military-ready-to-blast-l-a-prisoners/.

Sheldon, Rose Mary. 2007. *Intelligence Activities in Ancient Rome*. New York: Routledge.

———. 2012. *Ambush: Surprise Attack in Ancient Greek Warfare*. London: Frontline Books.

Shenon, Philip. 2003. "Iraq Links Germs for Weapons to U.S. and France." *New York Times*, March 16.

Simons, Geoff. 1994. *Iraq: From Sumer to Saddam*. London: St. Martin's Press.

"Spore Wars: The Havoc Wrought by Covid-19 Will Spark New Concern over Bio-weapons." 2020. *Economist*, April 25, 19–20.

Stock, Kyle. 2017. "The Dogs of War Are in High Demand." *Bloomberg News*, August 28. https://www.bloomberg.com/news/features /2017-08-28/military-dogs-are-becoming-an-increasingly-precious -weapon.

Stockholm International Peace Research Institute [SIPRI]. 1971. *The Rise of CB Weapons: The Problem of Chemical and Biological Warfare*. New York: Humanities Press.

———. 1975. *Incendiary Weapons*. Cambridge, MA: MIT Press.

Stoneman, Richard, trans. 1991. *Greek Alexander Romance*. Harmondsworth: Penguin.

———. 1994. *Legends of Alexander the Great*. London: J. M. Dent.

Sushruta Samhita. 2018. *An English Translation of the Sushruta Samhita, Based on Original Sanskrit Text.* Trans. K.K.L. Bhisthagratna. 3 vols. London: Forgotten Books.

Svanevik, Michael, and Shirley Bergett. 2006. "Tales of a Few Good Canines: Unique World War II Training Facility." San Mateo County *Daily News*, October 14.

Taylor, Michael. 2001. "Napalm No More: Pentagon Recycles Remaining Stock of Notorious Weapon." *San Francisco Chronicle*, April 4.

Temple, Robert. 1991. *The Genius of China: 3,000 Years of Science, Discovery, and Invention.* London: Prion.

Teoh, Flora, ed. 2020. "Did the COVID-19 Virus Originate from a Lab or Nature? Examining the Evidence for Different Hypotheses of the Novel Coronavirus' Origins." *Health Feedback*, April 24. https://healthfeedback.org/did-the-covid-19-virus-originate-from-a-lab-or-nature-examining-the-evidence-for-different-hypotheses-of-the-novel-coronavirus-origins/.

Trauth, Kathleen, Stephen Hora, and Robert Guzowski. 1993. "Expert Judgment on Markers to Deter Human Intrusion into the Waste Isolation Pilot Plant." Sandia National Laboratories report SAND92–1382/UC-721, November. https://digital.library.unt.edu/ark:/67531/metadc1279277/.

Trevisanato, Siro. 2007. "The Biblical Plague of the Philistines Now Has a Name, Tularemia"; "The Hittite Plague, and Epidemic of Tularemia and the First Record of Biological Warfare." *Medical Hypotheses* 69:1144–46, 1371–74.

Tucker, Jonathan. 2001. "Chemical Weapons: Buried in the Back Yard." *Bulletin of Atomic Scientists* 57 (September–October): 51–56.

Valente, Guy. 2019. "The History of Chemical Weapons: Uses and Efforts to Contain." Organisation for the Prohibition of Chemical Weapons, Oslo, Norway, April 24.

Van Wees, Hans. 2010. "Genocide in the Ancient World." In *Oxford Handbook of Genocide Studies*, ed. D. Bloxham and A. D. Moses, 240–65. Oxford: Oxford University Press.

Vaughan, Don. 2011. "Ancient Innovations." *Military Officer*, April, 56–61.

"Vile Finds." 2003. *Archaeology*, January–February.

Wald, Matthew. 2002. "Nevada States Case against Waste Dump in Mountain." *New York Times*, December 3.

Walker, Hunter, and Jana Winter. 2020. "Federal Law Enforcement Document Reveals White Supremacists Discussed Using Coronavirus as a Bioweapon." Yahoo News, March 21. https://news.yahoo.com/federal-law-enforcement-document-reveals-white-supremacists-discussed-using-coronavirus-as-a-bioweapon-212031308.html.

Watkins, Thomas. 2007. "Facing Redeployment: Navy Wants to Send Dolphins, Sea Lions to Patrol Puget Sound." Associated Press story, February 13.

Weinberger, Sharon. 2017. *The Imagineers of War: The Untold Story of DARPA, the Pentagon Agency That Changed the World*. New York: Knopf.

Wexler, Philip, ed. 2019. *Toxicology in Antiquity*. 2nd ed. London: Academic Press, Elsevier.

Wheelis, Mark. 1999. "Biological Warfare before 1914." In *Biological and Toxin Weapons: Research, Development, and Use from the Middle Ages to 1945*, ed. Erhard Geissler and John van Courtland Moon, 8–34. Oxford: Oxford University Press.

———. 2002. "Biological Warfare at the 1346 Siege of Caffa." *Emerging Infectious Diseases* 8, 9 (September): 971–75.

"When Killing Just Won't Do." 2003. *Harper's*, February, 17–19.

Wick, Charles Z. 1988. "Soviet Active Measures in the Era of Glasnost." Prepared by Todd Leventhal, for the US House of Representatives, by the US Information Agency, July, Washington, DC.

Williams, Carol. 2003. "Navy Adds Some Bark to Its Bite: San Diego–Trained Sea Lions Help Guard against Attacks." *Los Angeles Times*, February 12, A13.

Williams, Mark. 2006. "The Knowledge." *MIT Technology Review*, March, 1–18.

Williams, Peter, and David Wallace. 1989. *Unit 731: Japan's Secret Biological Warfare in World War II*. New York: Free Press.

Wrightson, Graham. 2019. *Combined Arms Warfare in Ancient Greece*. London: Routledge.

Yarrow, Liv Mariah. 2021. "#NotAllElephants (Are Pyrrhic): Finding a Plausible Context for RRC 9/1." *Ancient Numismatics* 2:9–42.

"The Yazidis: Divided, Oppressed, and Abandoned." 2020. *Economist*, December 12, 50–51.

Zanders, Jean Pascal. 2021. "De Mussi and the Siege of Caffa: Origins of a Biological Warfare Allegation." Working paper, Historical Notes, The Trench. https://www.the-trench.org/.

Zimeta, M. G. 2013. "Why Are We So Afraid of Chemical Weapons?" *New Internationalist*, January 19. https://newint.org/features/web -exclusive/2013/06/19/syria-chemical-weapons-existential-threat/.

Zinsser, Hans. 1963 [1934]. *Rats, Lice, and History.* Boston: Little, Brown.

INDEX

Note: Page numbers in italic type indicate illustrations; color plates are indicated by bold **C**.

ALSO BY ADRIENNE MAYOR

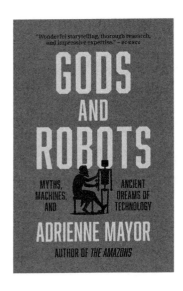

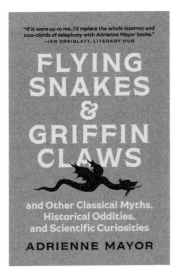

PRINCETON UNIVERSITY PRESS

Available wherever books are sold.
For more information visit us at press.princeton.edu